In this study Roland Fletcher argues that the built environment becomes a constraint on the long-term development of a settlement. It is costly to move settlements, or to demolish and rebuild from scratch, so the initial layout and buildings, and the associated forms of communication, may come to shackle further development and also to place constraints on social and political change. Using this theoretical framework, Dr Fletcher reviews world-wide settlement growth over the past 15,000 years, and concludes with a major discussion of the great transformations of human settlements – from mobile to sedentary, sedentary to urban, and agrarian urban to industrial. This book is an ambitious contribution to archaeological theory, and the questions it raises also have implications for the future of urban settlement.

NEW STUDIES IN ARCHAEOLOGY

The limits of settlement growth

NEW STUDIES IN ARCHAEOLOGY

Series editors
Clive Gamble, *University of Southampton*
Colin Renfrew, *University of Cambridge*
Jeremy Sabloff, *University of Pittsburgh*

Archaeology has made enormous advances recently, both in its volume of discoveries and in its character as an intellectual discipline; new techniques have helped to further the range and rigour of enquiry, and have encouraged interdisciplinary communication.

The aim of this series is to make available to a wider audience the results of these developments. The coverage is world-wide and extends from the earliest period to the present.

ROLAND FLETCHER
University of Sydney

The limits of settlement growth

A theoretical outline

CAMBRIDGE
UNIVERSITY PRESS

Published by the Press Syndicate of the University of Cambridge
The Pitt Building, Trumpington Street, Cambridge CB2 1RP
40 West 20th Street, New York, NY 10011–4211, USA
10 Stamford Road, Oakleigh, Melbourne 3166, Australia

First published 1995

Printed in Great Britain at the University Press, Cambridge

A catalogue record for this book is available from the British Library

Library of Congress cataloguing in publication data

Fletcher, Roland.
The limits of settlement growth: a theoretical outline /
Roland Fletcher.
        p.   cm. – (New studies in archaeology).
Includes bibliographical references and index.
ISBN 0 521 43085 2 (hardback).
1. Social archaeology. 2. Human settlements – History.
3. Cities and towns – Growth. I. Title. II. Series.
CC72.4.F54 1995
930.1–dc20   94–18290   CIP

ISBN 0 521 43085 2 hardback

WD

FOR DAVID AND ERIC, IN MEMORY

I have considered it necessary for archaeologists to investigate the archaeological record as a different order of reality, the patterned structure of which represents not a simple accumulation of little events but rather some of the basic organisational constraints and determinants operating on the events or episodes of daily living. The archaeological record is therefore not a poor or distorted manifestation of 'reality' but most likely a structured consequence of the operation of a level of organisation difficult, if not impossible, for an ethnographer to observe directly. This level of organisation is likely to be the unit upon which evolutionary selection operates, rather than at the level of specific events. (Binford 1981: 197–8)

Certainly we will not be answering the questions archaeologists have traditionally asked . . . One thing is clear: no one will want to know. We have strong ideological commitments which none of us would like demonstrated to be wrong. Archaeologists are not going to receive much encouragement if we actually approach our goal. (Dunnell 1982: 21)

CONTENTS

FIGURES

Note: North is at the top of page unless indicated by an orientation arrow, or the statement 'no orientation'. Metric values added to illustrations previously calibrated in imperial units. Illustrations 'after Fletcher' have been edited, re-lettered and re-positioned to fit the format of this publication. No scale given for mobiliary items.

TABLES

ACKNOWLEDGEMENTS

For more than a decade I have taught and talked about the topic of this book, sought advice from many people and questioned numerous helpful and often generous regional specialists. I am indebted to my colleagues and my students for their opinions and criticisms. The book began as three introductory chapters (the ancestors of Chapters 4, 5 and 6) in a study of the early stages of urbanism and expanded under insistent demands for more theoretical context and more discussion of the implications. Seeking an alternative way of studying human behaviour has been fascinating, frustrating and on occasions profoundly satisfying. This book can only be a brief moment in a dialogue which will gradually produce a form of archaeology none of us can now envisage. I do not claim to know the end point of this enquiry. So far the study has led me to an astonishing variety of regions and periods. I hope there are few errors of reporting, and none serious, though this may be a pious hope given the range of examples. Any such errors are my responsibility alone.

From among those who discussed this work with me my especial thanks go to Tim Murray for his conversation, cogent criticism and friendship. I am indebted to Geoff Bailey for offering substantial advice and intellectual companionship over long years and much separation. Perhaps he knows the beginnings of this study better than anyone. His paper on Quaternary timescales was an immense encouragement. Chris Chippindale offered reassuring advice at a bleak moment. Alison Wylie gave me gracious interest and encouragement when I most needed it to finish the task. To Robyn Williams, Phillip Adams and Leigh Dayton my thanks for their interest and the opportunities to present my case. Long ago Bob Adams gave graciously of his time and Bill Rathje told me to get on and do it! To Greg Wyncoll, Daniel Tangri, Ben Cullen and John Kelt, Tia Negerevitch, Helen Clemens, Diana Willingham, Jeannette Lerbscher, Pam Hourani, Julie Dinsmor, Douglas Sun, Fiona Hook, Lynn Meskell, Alison Nightingale, Robin Torrence, Ian Johnson and Richard Wright my thanks for their intellectual company, co-operation on projects and some vigorous criticism. Peter White provided gracious criticism of a draft. To Don Aitken I owe an especial thanks for his interest in an abstruse grant application and his eternally vexing question – 'Why do humans conform to the Napoleonic code?'

The case studies in this book result from fieldwork in a wide variety of regions. In all the places I worked I was received with kindness and goodwill, despite my curious habit of measuring other people's doorways. This activity confirmed my African hosts' view of the odd tendencies of Europeans, especially Englishmen, and I was treated with the consideration they accord to the harmlessly mad. To the Ghanaian people in whose settlements I worked I owe a great debt for much friendship, hospitality and the sharing of food and drink. In particular I thank Munyimba, the head of the Konkomba community near Kpandai which I studied in such detail. The men and women of the community willingly allowed me to carry out my surveys of anyone who moved and my measurements of anything that stayed still. Augustine Sampa Tiwambi was most helpful as my interpreter. An especial acknowledgement to Jebuni the Tindaana of Choriban for his kindness and understanding – a fine man. He died in 1971. I am saddened that such times of our lives can be so summarily reduced. In Egypt Reis Achmed and his family gave me hospitality. My thanks to Lannie Bell for his help and advice at Deir el Medina. Hanafi El Mulwani welcomed me and fed me numerous glasses of mint tea. For the Mug House study Art Rohn gave me vigorous encouragement. In Mesa Verde I was greatly assisted by the goodwill of Superintendent Heyder and Dr Jack Smith. Bringing ladders down the cliff into Mug House is no mean feat and I am very grateful for that and other assistance provided by the research staff and maintenance crews of the Park.

Sturt Manning, Anne Jones, Elizabeth Pinder, Julian Holland, Ben Cullen, Pam Watson, Adrienne Powell and Phil Edwards laboured to collect and organise the information for the Settlement Data Register. My thanks to them. Their efforts were funded by the University of Sydney and by the Australian Research Council. For the initial preparation of the manuscript I am indebted to Robyn Wood. Andrew Wilson generously gave his time to help me with the final form of the illustrations. My thanks also to Lynn Petrie and Kylie Seretis. I am especially grateful to Juliet Richters for her swift indexing. Tony Hodgson of *Asia Week* (Hong Kong) sought out Ian Lambot, who very kindly gave me the spectacular photograph which graces the cover. Their efforts, Robin Derricourt's encouragement and Jessica Kuper's advice and Margaret Deith's invaluable work have been much appreciated. The penultimate version of this book was completed in Cambridge while I was an affiliate of the Department of Archaeology and a Visiting Fellow at Clare Hall. My thanks to my colleagues for their hospitality.

To Ouma I am ever grateful for her love and aggressive concern. She did not put up with it so I need not add the usual! My son Eliot has interrupted much, absorbed hours of my time and delighted me.

INTRODUCTION

Thirty years after the rise of the New Archaeology the use of social theory in archaeology is spread across a vast and incommensurable spectrum of explanatory viewpoints. To the past decade of dichotomised archaeological debate between contextualism and processualism we have now added the complexities of dynamical systems theory and the several variants of cultural selectionism. It is even doubtful whether conceptual integration is either possible or sensible. Unless archaeology can develop some other logic of discourse, the future of the discipline is liable to reside either in a retreat from cogent theoretical debate or in endemic conflict, or else in the periodic dominance of one fashionable version of the current perspectives. But the discipline will lost its intellectual integrity if any one restricted viewpoint gains ascendancy. No matter what may have been claimed, environmental analysis cannot make the study of individual intent redundant. Nor can the contextually unique be useful or appropriately rendered down to universal generalisation. Conversely, action-oriented analysis and contextualism cannot properly ignore selective pressures and adaptation or reduce environment to mere background. Meanwhile, dynamical systems theory has yet to present its own model of human behaviour, and cultural selectionism still lacks a paradigm of cultural replication.

Instead of continuing futile dichotomised contests, or seeking the triumph of any one side in the various disputes, we might more usefully debate the nature and content of a hierarchy of explanation which could integrate aspects of these diverse positions. A single all-inclusive theoretical position need not be sought, nor could one be persuasively constructed at the present time. We already use a variety of different kinds of explanations. Our understanding of the relationship between the material and the active components of our behaviour requires attention to at least three different scales of analysis – the small-scale spatial and temporal patterning of social life; the longer-term behavioural parameters of human interaction; and the large-scale constraints of resource supply which affect the capacity of a community to replicate itself and its material context. Our partial hierarchy of differing viewpoints and epistemologies should now be integrated into a logically coherent hierarchy of explanations. Because this will require the inclusion of both biological and cultural perspectives, the conceptual chasm which persistently dichotomises the explanations and epistemologies applied to 'animal' and 'human' behaviour has to be removed. Neither a biological nor a cultural perspective should be allocated priority, otherwise we will be unable to produce an integrated hierarchy of different explanatory levels. What is required is an interpretative device which can stabilise the otherwise inherent slippage along a conceptual fault line between conventional social theory on the one hand and the differing scales of behavioural, ecological and environmental explanation on the other.

The logical chasm can be filled by recognising that the long-term, operational role of the material component of human behaviour should be inserted as a necessary and appropriate part of a hierarchy of explanation. At this scale of operation the material has a dual role: as a fundamental regulatory factor which assists the growth of human communities, and as a restrictive, potentially deleterious constraint on social life. The material component of human behaviour can be considered as a factor having long-term effects independent of the intentions of its makers. The effect on the viability and growth of human communities may be both advantageous and disadvantageous. Substantial growth may be made possible by effective material controls on interaction and the critical boost required for communication to function over much larger settlement areas. Alternatively, a material assemblage might restrict the possibilities of settlement growth because it does not provide sufficient screening for interaction and cannot facilitate communication, or it could produce a milieu too rigid and inertial to allow adequate adjustment to rapid social change. A complex relationship exists between the rate, nature and magnitude of settlement growth, the behavioural parameters of community life, and the effects of the material on interaction and communication. We should find that distinct, quantifiable rates and magnitudes of settlement growth are recognisable within the broad social categories of cultural change, such as the formation of sedentary communities and the rise of urbanism, which have already been identified by social theory.

This book is concerned with the role of the 'material as behaviour' in restricting and aiding settlement growth. My purpose is to produce a theoretical outline of an operational, uniformitarian model of the behavioural constraints which affect the way the people in a community can interact and communicate adequately; to identify large-scale cross-culturally consistent patterns of settlement growth; and to direct attention to critical cases, some of which may be potential refutations of aspects of the model. The interpretation of the 'material as behaviour' neither seeks to supersede other modes of explanation nor claims to encompass them. The material has variously been regarded as an epiphenomenal derivative, a functional adjunct or a recursive associate of human action and systems of verbal meaning. It can also be viewed as regulatory or restrictive. Questions about the reasons and motives behind the initial appearance and associations of particular material features properly reside in the domain of social theory concerned with human action and the structures of verbal meaning. That human action generates the material component of our social lives or that, in the short term, the material acts as a recursive aid to active social life, is not in dispute. The study of the 'material as behaviour', because it looks only at the consequences which derive from the presence or absence of particular material patterns, does not infringe the concerns of conventional social theory.

Although the search for high-level archaeological theories of cultural behaviour has so far been rather unsuccessful, the alternative emphasis on contextual, regional case studies leads to a lack of cross-cultural explanatory coherence and even to the feeling that such coherence is unnecessary and meaningless. If, however, our prior premises about the form of a high-level theory of human behaviour are erroneous, there may be a way out of the present impasse. Large-scale consistent patterns need not be present in those characteristics of daily life which are the prevalent concern of social theory, such as human action, power and social organisation. Instead they may reside in the overall behavioural characteristics of interaction and communication in community life. We need not suppose that 'social phenomena' (as conventionally recognised) and their material associations have simple cross-cultural correlations in order to provide explanations of the different, predictable cross-cultural outcomes which may arise from different, possible material – 'social' relationships. The material, active and verbal components of social life are not deterministically linked and we should envisage that they can become decoupled. For instance, a community might fail to produce the material shielding and behavioural controls necessary for its social organisation to persist. Conversely, a community might generate material patterns which will only serve to promote settlement growth when they combine with later changes in verbal meaning and human action. The associations differ but should be consistently and predictably linked to their respective outcomes.

For the purposes of current social theory the material fabric of a society recovered from the archaeological record has usually been treated as the basal data to which interpretations about higher levels of meaning are applied (Rapoport 1988: 326). We have sought to convert the material into an expression of actions. Using social analysis we try to comprehend those reconstituted actions according to the logic of verbal meaning. The material has been viewed as the bottom of the interpretative ladder (Figure I.1), unfortunately conflating its ontological position in the analytic sequence of the discipline and its role in human society. Statements about the nature of the material are regarded as basal descriptions without substantial meaning content. They are treated as merely the raw material of social interpretation. But the premiss that the material can play a large-scale, slow behavioural role which affects the viability of human communities opens up a new interpretative direction. Instead of moving from the material towards the meticulous, short-term detail of the 'social' we can expand enquiry in the opposite conceptual direction into a vast research field concerned with the coarse-grained analysis of the long-term 'behavioural' role of the material (Figure I.2). The long term is the distinct province of archaeology (Binford 1981; Hodder 1986: 89, 177–8; Isaac 1972; Jochim 1991; Renfrew 1982). Archaeology has access to a two-million-year record of the ways in which hominids have patterned space and time using material entities (Fletcher 1993a). We can ask about the non-verbal patterns of meaning which reside in material assemblages, study the operational effects of the material on human interaction over long periods of time, and seek to identify the material, behavioural parameters of everyday social life.

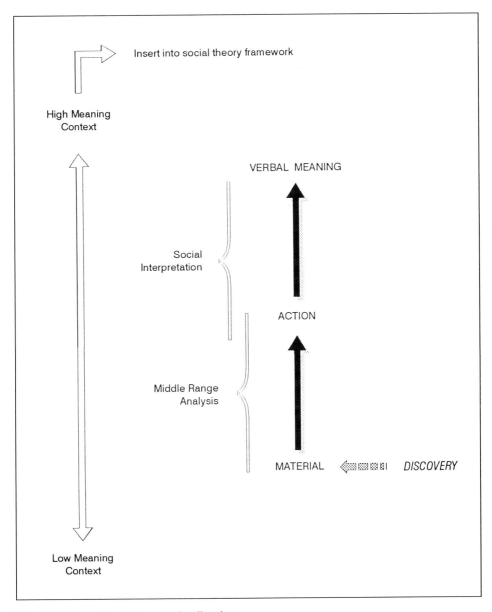

Figure I.1 Conventional interpretative direction

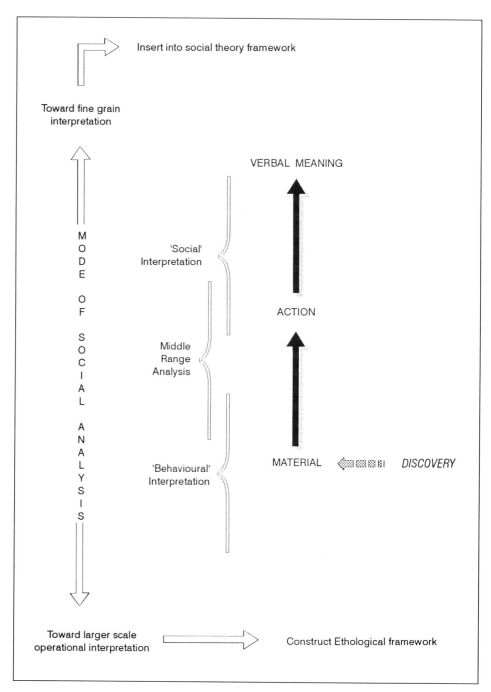

Figure I.2 Alternative interpretative direction

SUMMARY OF THE
INTERACTION–COMMUNICATION MODEL

The proposed theoretical model of interaction and communication outlines the basic operational constraints on community life and predicts distinct, large-scale patterns of settlement growth. The model specifies three major classes of behavioural constraint. In a long-term, large-scale perspective they constitute the operational parameters of social life in settlements. The first class of behavioural constraint is an upper limit on tolerable residential density, referred to as an Interaction limit (I-limit). The second class of constraint concerns the limits on the areal extent of a settlement set by the distances over which a communication system can operate adequately. Such a limit is referred to as a Communication limit (C-limit). However, at low residential densities the C-limit constraints do not apply. Communication systems do not delimit the areal extent of dispersed, low-density settlements. Below a threshold density, referred to as the Threshold limit (T-limit), settlement extent is almost unconstrained or else is undefinable. But having exceeded a C-limit by dropping below the Threshold limit, such settlements cannot then easily attain densities above the T-limit again. The three classes of behavioural limit form a matrix of the interaction and communication stresses which affect human communities. The stresses can be managed in various ways by material features such as walls, or script systems, which help to control or aid interaction and communication. On the matrix we can therefore plot different kinds of settlement growth trajectories whose outcome depends upon the relationship between residential density, settlement size and the material assemblage available to the occupants. Viable communities have to reside below their appropriate I-limit and the size of compact settlements is generally constrained by the C-limit for the means whereby they communicate. A community may therefore become trapped in a stasis settlement close behind a C-limit because it does not possess the communication systems which could allow a larger, compact settlement area to be sustained. However, if a community in a compact settlement already possesses a new communication assemblage and the potential to regulate interaction stress, it can follow a transition trajectory across a C-limit and will possess the potential to generate substantial, sustained settlement growth. The third possibility is a bypass trajectory below the T-limit along which a community drops to a low residential density without employing a new interaction and communication assemblage. Very extensive dispersed settlements may result which have only a restricted capacity for change.

Abbreviations

Interaction limit	I-limit
Communication limit	C-limit
Threshold limit	T-limit
Interaction and communication assemblage	I–C assemblage
Interaction and communication stress model	I–C model
Interaction and communication stress matrix	Stress matrix

PART I

Theoretical context: the role of the material as behaviour

1

Archaeology, settlement growth and the material component of human behaviour

The increasingly rapid growth in the size of human communities and the area of their settlements over the past 15,000 years has been accompanied by a substantial increase in the amount and diversity of the material component of community life. These parallel trends may be unconnected, coincidental or indirectly linked. On the other hand, they may be directly associated because material entities have a consequential effect on the degree to which the stresses of interaction and communication inherent in community life can be managed.

The impact of the material on social life
Verbal communication and familiar social action play an important day-to-day role in community life, but material entities also possess a substantial capacity to regulate interaction and communication. The walls of the buildings in which we live and work create a sensory milieu by restricting the transmission of sound and by delimiting our field of vision. The 'workmen's village' at Harappā in the second millennium BC (Figure 1.1) was a tightly packed occupation area, with buildings close together along narrow, restrictive access routes. A simple, spatial device served to minimise intervisibility. The entry corridor to each residence unit was at an angle to the street (Figure 1.2). Instead of looking directly into the inner room, even people who were intending to enter would have their view obscured by the wall angling across in front of them. Casual passers-by would have found it very difficult to see into the private interior space. The entry corridor, in itself, provided privacy without obstructing physical access, whether or not there was a door. The residence complex had apparently been provided with a deliberately repeated, systematic and parsimonious architectural device which, in Newman's (1973) terms, created a transitional zone between the street and the inner rooms of each residence unit. The gross perceptual effect was the same then as it would be now, restricting the frequency of contact whether the occupants wanted it or not. The patterning and ordering of residential space provides a means of managing interaction and communication. The effects are amenable to systematic analysis and should be of consequence for the long-term operation of social life.

The material context of a community can also have an adverse effect on social life. Once a durable material framework, such as the brick walls of a building, is established it can continue to have an effect for a long time. We are scarcely aware of this long-term, stable context, though we may well be aware of the fact that our material surroundings are not easily changed and can create social problems. A significant

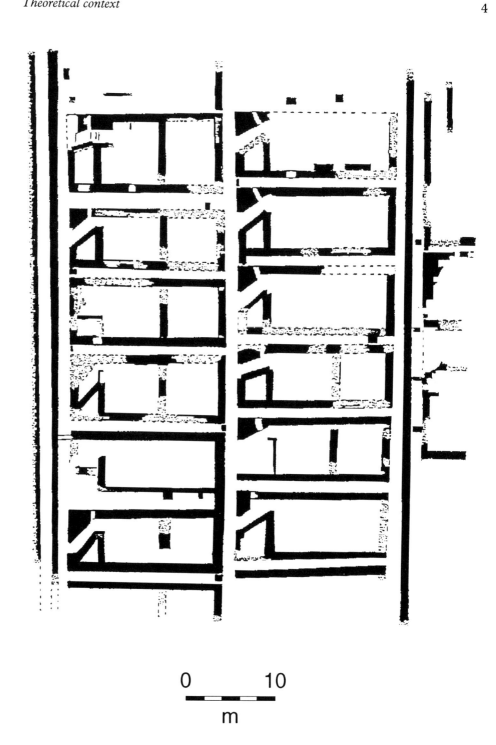

Figure 1.1 'Workmen's village' at Harappā, Pakistan, third–second millennium BC (after Vats 1940)

▰▰▰ extant walls   – – – – presumed wall line

Note: Later additions and alterations deleted

obstacle to social change in the large cities of the late twentieth century is presented by the substantial stock of old housing and utilities. These must either be removed or else renovated at considerable cost, if they are to serve the purposes of a community whose way of life is changing rapidly. Planning does not necessarily resolve the problem. Indeed, planned urban space in the latter part of the twentieth century has itself produced severe obstacles to viable social life. Some material contexts may exacerbate the stress of daily domestic tasks (Sommer 1974), adversely affecting, for instance, women's daily life and freedom of activity (Adams and Conway 1975; Matrix 1984). The difficulties imposed on women with children living in high-rise apartments are well known. Even worse, the overall spatial layout of a housing estate can be socially destructive. Newman's analysis of public housing in the USA emphasised that the absence of transitional zones between public and

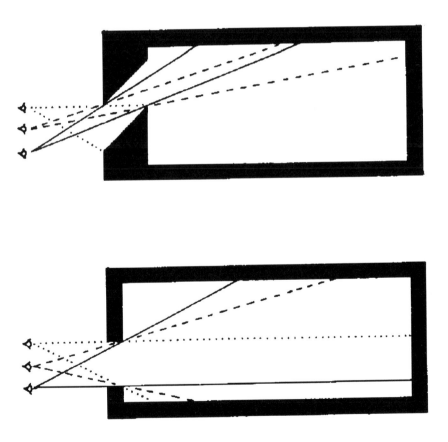

Figure 1.2 Schematic viw of constraints on intervisibility

◁ viewpoint

private space, and the presence of large corridors and spaces that were not under the direct observation of the residents, produced a dangerous and insecure social milieu. (Newman 1973). Such problems might perhaps be contextually unique to industrialised societies; alternatively they may represent the most overt expression of a more general feature of the relationship between human action and its material context.

The material and social action

The material is far from neutral in its effects on the exercising of human intent. Changes in social life may end up at odds with housing stock which, depending on the durability of the material (Donley 1982; Fletcher 1985; Rapoport 1990), constrains action to varying degrees. If such disharmony can exist between action and the material, then we can predict two kinds of outcome. The first and most obvious is that the material may obstruct us in the pursuit of our chosen options. In this case a change in social action may fail to produce the material forms which would sustain its development. It is not, therefore, valid to assume that particular material phenomena are necessarily the result of particular social phenomena, or that there is a consistent relationship between them. In the short term a myriad possible combinations might occur, some advantageous and some deleterious. The implication is that the relationship between the material and the social is not a universal, cross-culturally defined one but is, in the short term at least, particular and contextually defined.

The second kind of outcome resulting from the lack of correlation between the material and the social is a corollary of the first. Although particular kinds of material feature may be essential for some kinds of change in human action to be sustained, they are not necessarily brought into being simply because they are needed. For instance, devices for counting may greatly assist the growth of commerce. But we can neither expect that the beginnings of commerce cause counting devices to be developed, nor can we assume that such devices will not, and cannot, arise in other entirely different contexts, e.g. for divination. If they are absent from a community's cultural repertoire, commerce may start but then falter. However, a society with divination devices that can be used for counting may thereby be 'pre-adapted'[1] to commercial expansion. When the necessary social change occurs, the community would already possess the material means to support it.

The material facilities required for a sustained social change might, then, arise for a variety of reasons. But they can only have large-scale, long-term behavioural consequences in conjunction with a narrow range of specific social systems. The social changes might either precede or follow the development of the requisite material feature, or might not happen at all. The formation of 'advantageous' relationships is neither inevitable nor universal. Cumulatively more lasting material features, which initially play a useful role, may later impede the activities of a community. What ought to be cross-culturally consistent is the potential effect of such associations on the growth and persistence of a community. Therefore, we should not require an answer to the question about why the association came about in order to pursue the broader issue of whether or not the magnitude and nature of its outcome is cross-culturally consistent. We should look for connections between varying combinations of material assemblages and social change and economic patterns, and the degree to which the communities carrying them survive, persist or fail. Predicting the differing outcomes will require a model which explains the relationship between the varied possible material–'social' associations and the general behavioural parameters which define the limits within which communities are viable.

The behavioural limits to settlement growth

Humans are social animals. We habitually live in residential communities however small or transient. For communities to function individuals have to interact with each other. But interaction involves the strain of dealing with other people, the effort of coping with the products of group activity such as noise and trash, and the energy we must expend to make communication possible. In communities with high residential densities these costs increase markedly as a community size increases. As more people come together, their activity and communication become more and more densely interconnected and more of the derivatives and debris of interaction are generated. Interference between messages tends to occur. Unless more energy and more signal consistency is provided to transmit messages coherently over longer distances, increasing settlement sizes and high information traffic loads would eventually produce a residential pattern in which the community could not viably persist (Johnson 1982; Meier 1962; van der Leeuw 1981).

Personal experience tells us that there are limits to the amount of interaction we can tolerate. Community size and residential density consequently cannot increase infinitely without some critical changes in cultural behaviour. There is a need, for instance, for ways of ensuring that people can avoid meeting while being able to transmit messages more readily. Social life would otherwise become intolerable for the members of a community. The inanimate material component of human behaviour provides a means both of carrying information (Rapoport 1988) and of reducing the impact of the signals produced by community life (e.g. Sanders 1990: 65). Newspapers, for example, both carry information and reduce the interaction needed to obtain it. Walls block direct interaction between people and can cut out distracting noise and activity. The material component of human behaviour should therefore have a crucial role to play in the development of cumulatively larger, densely occupied communities. It is available to act as a regulator of interaction and an aid to communication. Without the assistance of the material, our sensory system could not cope with the inevitably increased demands resulting from increased group size.

The argument might then be made that major change in community size can only be sustained if a new assemblage of material aids to interaction and communication happens to be developed. The new material assemblage would enable change in the active component of social organisation, which could not, in itself, sustain growth. This argument goes further than the view of some social historians (Lloyd 1988), or the action-oriented social theorists (Giddens 1979) and their archaeologically trained counterparts such as Miller (1987) and Moore (1986), on the predominantly recursive relationship between the social and the material. According to that view the material serves to negotiate relationships within the social milieu. But the role of the material cannot be reduced to a derivative of social action, or a recursive complement of social meaning. The role of the material as a decisive behavioural factor in its own right must continually be taken into account because of its capacity to divert our intended social actions. It can operate both negatively and positively to frustrate or enable change in community life but the effects are not determined by what people say, want, strive for, or need to do. The problems and the possibilities produced by the relationship between the material and human action are inherent in our behaviour. We cannot detach the material from the condition of being human.

The implications are serious both for the future and for our views of the past. According to this view the future, like the past, will be characterised by the intervention of the material. Its serious effects are already manifest in worsening pollution, the increasingly onerous maintenance costs of roads and services, and the apparently intractable problems of garbage disposal. On average each of the 5 million inhabitants of New South Wales in Australia in the early 1990s produced 302 kg of domestic trash per annum. The population of New South Wales, in total, wasted 610,000 tonnes of paper and 249,000 tonnes of glass each year, even with recycling (*SMH* 1990). The impact of our material context raises a central issue in the explanation of human behaviour. A further approach is required, complementary to the more familiar ethnographic or historical scales of enquiry, which will enable us to comprehend the way in which the material component of human behaviour relates to the long-term prospects for viable community life. The purpose of this study is to outline an operational model of the material as an effectively independent form of behaviour which, over the long term, has a distinct regulatory and restrictive role as a manager of community life.

Social theory and the role of the material
An analysis of the long-term role of material assemblages requires an archaeological perspective. No other discipline has the orientation or domain of enquiry that it needs. However, to comprehend the processes of human community life archaeologists have, in general, sought explanations and categories from the shorter term perspectives of the social sciences and history (Chang 1967; Courbin 1988: 150–5; Gibbon 1989; Hodder 1986: 2–17; Kent 1990; Miller 1985, 1987: 11, 215; Orme 1981; Redman *et al.* 1978; Schiffer 1985; Trigger 1978, 1991) as has been noted (Fletcher 1989; Murray 1988, 1991; Smith 1992: 30–1; Wobst 1978). The problem is that anthropology has been narrowly construed in terms of a standard defined by the content and treatment of ethnographic experience. The adage that archaeology is anthropology or it is nothing (Binford 1962; Willey and Phillips 1958: 2) has usually been understood in those terms. This stance has since received vigorous criticism from Binford (1987: 395–8). A single inclusive category of 'culture' is

usual, subsuming the active and the material components of community life. The active, social aspect has been considered to predominate, as is apparent in two substantial overviews with very different perspectives in the mid-1980s (Hodder 1986; Ingold 1986), and in discussions of evolutionary theory and the social sciences (Schmid and Wuketits 1987). The familiar perception of daily life, in which buildings, small objects, speech and actions are a single, synchronic cultural assemblage, dominates our viewpoint. On a day-by-day perspective their differing patterns of endurance and inertia are not markedly apparent, nor do those differences appear to be very significant. What appears to matter in the short term is the role those entities play in the expression of our daily lives (Miller 1987), not their gradual, cumulative impact. The former necessarily requires a contextual, local perspective. The latter only become apparent as longer term general effects, when viewed cross-culturally.

For the past thirty years archaeological theory has been dominated by social reconstructionist approaches derived from the cultural definition of the discipline in the 1920s and 1930s (Childe 1946; Daniel 1981; Meltzer 1979; Murray 1987; Redman 1991; Willey and Sabloff 1980). Both the functional materialists and the historically oriented contextualists, no matter how far divided on epistemology, use social theory and have regarded it as both the beginning and the end of enquiry (Deetz 1970; Hodder 1982; Leone, Potter and Shackel 1987; Miller 1982; Redman 1978). But social theory is neither stable nor paradigmatic. Theorising in archaeology extends across a diverse range of analytic procedures and epistemological premises (Earle and Preucel 1987; Kobylinski, Lenata and Yacabaccio 1987; Washburn 1987). Meticulously segregated views of considerable similarity are mixed with carefully presented positions divided by major logical disagreements (Fletcher 1989; Kohl 1985; Wylie 1989). There is vigorous dispute about the various possible combinations of historical viewpoint and the theories of the social sciences which might be used (Bamforth and Spaulding 1982). Extreme divergence exists on fundamentals of ontology and epistemology (Binford 1987; Crawford 1982; Flannery 1973; Gould R. A. 1980; Hodder 1985, 1987; Miller 1982; South 1977; Spaulding 1988; Trigger 1991; Wylie 1985a, 1985b, 1986a; Wylie and Pinsky 1990). Yet, despite such disagreement, the protagonists, with a few notable exceptions, accept the use of current social theory, as do the philosophers who have contributed to the debate such as Salmon (1982) and Wylie (1982a, 1982b, 1985a), and the archaeologists who discuss philosophy (e.g. Bell 1982; Gibbon 1989; Renfrew 1982; Schiffer 1981; Watson, Redman and LeBlanc 1971, 1984).

Two different views about the relationship between contemporaneous material and social phenomena are prevalent. The still dominant processual, functionalist view regards material entities and patterns of entities as reflections of social phenomena. The material is seen as a by-product of the 'social'. Room size has persistently been regarded as a derivative of numbers of people (Hassan 1982; LeBlanc 1971; Naroll 1962; Sumner 1989), though the risks of doing so have been pointed out (Casselbury 1974; Casteel 1979; and see Fletcher in Kolb 1985). Patterns of residence have been ascribed to the effects of kinship systems (e.g.

Agorsah 1985; Hill 1968; Longacre 1970; O'Connell 1987: 100–2; Whitelaw 1983, 1989). The logical corollary is that social cause is reconstructed from the material product by combining local, contextual particularity with extrapolation from ethnographic and historical cross-cultural associations. Contemporary associations, repeatedly confirmed in different cultural contexts, are treated as sufficient evidence for the same kinds of paired association in the past. Such substantive extrapolations are validated by various logical devices such as specific historical continuity or general analogy from equivalent economic and environmental contexts (Crawford 1982; Gould and Watson 1982; Smith 1977; Stanislawski 1976; Wylie 1985b).

The alternative, social recursive view recognises an interaction between the material and social aspects of a community, as in the work of Bourdieu (1977, 1984), Berger (Berger and Luckmann 1967) and Giddens (1979). In this recursive relationship, things are not merely reflections of a social order. Instead the inanimate entities, such as material symbols and spatial form, play a meaningful role in society (Appadurai 1986; Miller and Tilley 1984; Moore 1986). Actions and material features may acquire contradictory verbal meanings and the relationship between them can serve to express contradictions within the community. Since the late 1970s Hodder has emphasised the complex relationship between people and things (1986: 8, 12) in a restricted, recursive model which retains the conventional predominant, prior status of verbal meaning and human action. The social recursive position logically rules out what it refers to as uniformitarian cross-cultural associations as a basis for reconstructing the past. The importance of an entity depends upon its meaning and that can only be derived from the history of its context in a particular community or society (Hodder 1986: 118–46). A hermeneutic relationship between the observer and the observed (Hodder 1984a, 1987) leads to proposed meanings which are properly to be understood in terms of verbal categories.

Though the social recursive view does not privilege social determinants as completely as is usual in processual, functionalist social reconstruction, the tyranny of the ethnographic and historical record persists in the form of a prior status allocated to social theory (Wobst 1978). This is conspicuously apparent in the views of Shanks and Tilley (1987a, 1987b). The prior status is taken for granted in the social, processualist approach, while it is forcefully articulated in the radical, contextualist view (Fletcher 1989: 66–7). Tilley, for example, has contended that 'Failure to tackle problems within sociology and philosophy can only lead to a blind, unsystematic groping towards an understanding of the past. It is sheer dogmatism to suggest otherwise, to suggest that problems within philosophy and social theory can be neatly circumvented in the actual business of carrying out research' (1982: 36). That the premises of social theory are appropriate for the study of human beings is not in question. They have demonstrated their value in archaeology and continue to do so (Flannery and Marcus 1983; Paynter 1982; Spriggs 1988; Stone 1987; Yoffee 1977). When the required texts, in the form of oral tradition and/or written comment, are available, the social approach transforms the interpretation of the archaeological record. However, the prevalent social and historical approaches are predicated on various combinations of verbal meaning, intentionality, premises of rationality, and the ethnographic scale of cultural life (Lloyd 1988: 7, 10). The problem with an archaeological ontology founded on these premises is that the material component of community life is logically reduced to an adjunct of human action. It is ascribed a secondary role as an epiphenomenon recruited into the meaning structures of action and verbal expression.

The current paradox of social theory

Archaeology does not, at present, have its own fully effected theories about the nature and role of the material component of human community life. Instead it works through connections to the established theories of other disciplines. But we are not obliged to follow this approach. There are indications that the current use of social and historical perspectives in archaeology is not entirely satisfactory. Members of the donor disciplines of history and social anthropology like Hobsbawm (1979: 249–50) and Leach (1973, 1979: 123–4) have long expressed doubt about the proposed articulation of such divergent ontologies. Outsiders to archaeology, such as Yengoyan, though they regard a social view as appropriate, are critical of the contextualist programme in archaeology and its use of social theory (1985: 329–34). Interdisciplinary discussions have persistently tended to produce a multi-disciplinary *mélange* rather than integration (Bintliff and Gaffney 1986; Burnham and Kingsbury 1979; Green, Haselgrove and Spriggs 1978; Renfrew 1979: 253; Spriggs 1977). Nor has social theory or archaeology produced a cross-culturally consistent model of the relationship between material and 'social' phenomena (Fletcher 1989: 72; Murray 1988). It is therefore unlikely that the current restricted classes of social explanation in archaeology and anthropology are sufficient for studying human behaviour. Nor does the continual change in social theory over the past 150 years suggest that the current position in archaeology is somehow final. As Rapoport has noted (1988: 326), archaeology has only just begun to consider what he calls the 'everyday' behavioural meanings of community life, rather than the higher level meanings of social rank and prestige or ideology and cosmology.

Though there are self-evident connections between archaeology, social processes and the time depth of history and ecological-environmental studies, these connections cannot logically lead to the conclusion that explanations of material items are to be sufficiently understood in terms of theories originally developed to make other classes of information comprehensible. Only a premise that the material is epiphenomenal can lead to such a conclusion. Although archaeology is anthropology in the sense of studying human beings, anthropology should be defined more widely. It need not be defined by the current practices of the social sciences or the current content or fashions of social theory. Archaeology needs instead to develop additional ways of doing anthropology, complementary to the existing approaches, by introducing a form of explanation specifically appropriate to the longer term, behavioural role of material entities.

A few archaeologists have, for some years, argued that our current theoretical structures are inadequate (Binford 1981; Dunnell 1982; Higgs and Jarman 1975). As had been repeatedly noted over the past thirty years, archaeology lacks an integrative high-level theoretical structure of its own (Binford 1977; Clarke 1968; Courbin 1988: 108–6; Dunnell 1978; Meltzer 1979; Price 1982; Raab and Goodyear 1984: 263; Renfrew 1982: 463). Two interconnected problems result from the current perspective. First, because the material component of behaviour is subjected to explanations developed to understand human action over short time spans, its longer term role is refracted and distorted through familiar social categories. Secondly, the potentially differing role of the material component of behaviour at different scales and magnitudes, over differing durations of time, is obscured. There has been a tendency to presume that the material has a single, specific kind of role. In his critical review of other opinions on the material–social relationship, Hodder has contended that it 'depends on the actions of individuals within particular culture-historical contexts' (1986: 12). But this merely restricts interpretation to a reductive derivative of the short-term time frame within which the material is initially produced, and then opts to continue observing it at such a timescale. But there is no *a priori* reason why the various material components of social life cannot have differing roles depending on their magnitude, the scale and duration of their effects, and the timespan over which we choose to observe them. They have to be viewed from the perspective of several different timescales (Bailey 1983, 1987; Fletcher 1981a, 1986; Gamble 1987). By arguing that the relationship between a community and the material component of its behaviour is conditional on the actions, verbal meanings and attitudes of individuals, the social recursive theorists hold a position which diminishes the potentially distinct role of material entities as a context for social life. Similarly, in historical studies whose concern is the elaborate texture of human activity and intention, the material assemblage is rarely allocated more than a modest recursive role. The prevalent viewpoints in social anthropology, archaeology and history do not as yet sufficiently emphasise the potential autonomy of the material aspect of human behaviour as a critical factor in the functioning of human groups. A rare but outstanding exception to this criticism is Keegan's *Face of Battle* (1976), which stunningly evokes the material conditions and constraints of military combat over the past five centuries of European warfare. Though the *Annales* historians have discussed the role of the material (Lucas 1985), they have not put into effect consistently their theoretical approach. Braudel (1981, 1985) is famous for proposing that there are differing scales of cultural process, one of which involves the material fabric of daily life. He has given to material factors 'an active and even dramatic presence nearly unparalleled in previous historiography' (Kinser 1981: 91). But, though he was interested in its properties and its role in social life, Braudel did not produce an Annaliste theory of the material as a variable operating on its own terms.

As yet, a more radical form of the recursive relationship tentatively suggested by Rathje (1978: 52; 1979) has not been comprehensively articulated. He provided the initiative for developing a model of the long-term behavioural impact of the material, emphasising the capacity of the material to act, in turn, on the community and to provide the basis for future social change. Giddens (1979: 210) follows Mumford in emphasising the profound impact of material systems, such as calendars and clocks, on the management of time. However, the debate has not been taken further into an integrated view of the material regulation of space and time in the social world. In 1979 Giddens remarked (p. 202) that neither space nor time has been centrally incorporated into social theory. Nor have they been since then, though environmental psychology has begun to articulate some of the issues (Rapoport 1988, 1990; Sanders 1990: 45–51). As I will discuss in the next chapter, the predominantly verbal meaning content of social theory is incommensurable with the inevitably non-verbal meaning content of space–time patterning. That incommensurable association is a critical feature of the dynamics of social change, not a sign of the failure of our explanatory efforts to make them conform with each other. We now need an integrated, workable theoretical perspective on the role of material entities as spatial and temporal contexts for action and as constraints on behavioural change.

The domain of social theory has to be extended beyond the partially reflexive role of the material and its significant recursive function in the practices of ordinary daily life, to incorporate the long-term regulatory and restrictive roles of the material. We might expect these differing roles to be played out in differing contexts and over differing spatial and temporal scales. They should not be considered to exclude or preclude each other. While they should be integrated in some fashion, my purpose is not so presumptuous as to define the exact nature of that integration. Instead, the concern of this study is the development of a theoretical basis for understanding the regulatory and restrictive roles of the material. While the study of reflexive and recursive relationships is prevalent in the detailed enquiries of social and historical analysis, and analyses of the contextually unique aspects of each community or society, the regulatory and restrictive roles are more likely to be consequential at larger spatial and temporal scales. They ought to show up in long-term cross-cultural comparisons. A gradation of effects is to be expected with numerous, varied, minor consequences at the smaller scale and distinct, substantial effects on the large scale. At the latter end of the scale the issue becomes entangled with the convoluted and acrimonious debate about the connection between cultural and biological explanations of behaviour. The theoretical implications ought therefore to be of consequence for an assessment of the logical relationship between concepts of cultural process and biological evolution.

The current chasm between social and biological explanations

Archaeology, because of the time spans and the diversity of issues with which it is concerned, has to use both social and biological theory in conjunction to understand human behaviour. But the prevalent tendency to privilege either the social or the biological tends to dichotomise our explanatory time perspectives. Theoretical preferences are polarised either towards short-term particularities or towards the long term and the large scale (Bailey 1983: 180–2), obstructing the development of an integrated view of human behaviour. At the same time social theories of human action and the large-scale component of biological evolutionary theory have been uneasily juxtaposed. The paradox of logical separation and operational proximity has been persistent and regrettable (Ingold 1986: xiii–xiv). The study of proxemics and kinesics, i.e. active non-verbal communication, was introduced, in part, to try and bridge the chasm (Sanders 1990: 44).

The divergent emphasis on our nature either as biological organisms in the long term or as actors in an intersubjective life in the short term produce a serious logical quandary. The problem is that explanations are offered in which disjunctions of scale break up a probable continuum of outcomes while simultaneously forcing together theoretical positions which we correctly perceive are applicable to inordinately different scales of operation. Even if we desire to integrate these two, perforce abutted views, we cannot readily do so because they also *appear* to use incommensurable logical procedures to connect propositions and observational statements. At its most extreme the social view excludes generalised regularities and emphasises contextual uniqueness, while the large-scale aspect of the biological view is mistakenly regarded as determinative and is detached from its short-term historical component.

This conceptual chasm, recognised by Bonner (1980: 5–9, 187) and Durham (1982), has been masked in several ways – either by rendering anthropology as the anthropology of the social sciences or alternatively by reference to its purported 'biological foundations'. The effect has been readily observable for more than a decade in the sociobiology dispute (Sahlins 1977; Samuel 1990). Various theoretical bridging and compression approaches have been employed. Either biology is conceived as explaining and subsuming culture (Alland 1967; Bhaskar 1981; Hinde 1974), specifically in sociobiology (Barlow and Silverberg 1980; Wilson 1971, 1978), or terms related to human behaviour such as 'culture' (Bonner 1980; Langer 1971; von Frisch 1974) are projected in an evolutionary model onto the imitative and learned behaviour of other animals, producing the logical disjunctions about which Langer has remarked (1971: 328). Even the rigorous description of animal 'cultures' as 'traditions' maintains a dichotomy between proto-culture and human culture yet infers that there is no basic difference (Czanyi 1989: 150). The alternative is varying degrees of complementarity between the 'nature' and 'culture' views, and the endemic problem of the relationship between biological fitness and the persistence of cultural attributes (Boyd and Richerson 1985; Cavalli-Sforza and Feldman 1981; Cullen 1990; Dunnell 1980; Leonard and Jones 1987; Lumsden and Wilson 1981; Shennan 1989).

Profound disagreement exists over whether or not cultural and biological evolution can be, should be, or are encompassed by the same paradigm. Is cultural evolution Lamarckian, as some biologists, notably Stephen J. Gould (1980: 71; 1991: 65–6), and many anthropologists apparently believe, or is it essentially Darwinian in some form (Blute 1979; Butzer 1982: 284–5; Cullen 1993; Durham 1990; Fletcher 1977: 139–46; Mithen 1989; Rindos 1989)? In the 'social sciences' the fundamental, directive role of human intent must be acknowledged (Hodder 1986: 6–9; Lloyd 1988: 81; Miller 1982). But one effect is to risk creating a Lamarckian connection between circumstances, intent and response. Conversely, if a 'natural selection' view is used erroneously (Rindos 1989: 9–10) and long-term selective outcome is mistakenly compressed into a consequence of short-term response, the role of individual intent in a cultural milieu is denied – one of Hodder's forceful criticisms of the adaptationalism of the New Archaeology (1984b). Profound differences about reductionism and holism (Bonner 1980: 8–9), determinism, free will and intent, affect the association of the two major theoretical stances. The divergence is so great that there is even a lack of consistency in the respective views about the fundamental nature of the uniformitarian basis of explanation. While biological theorists such as Gould and Simpson distinguish two or more logically distinct kinds of uniformitarianism,[2] no such distinctions are mentioned in overviews of social theory and philosophy (Lloyd 1988), or in general theoretical discussions of philosophy and archaeology (Kelley and Hanen 1988: 263–4; Salmon 1982: 79–82). Only a few papers consider the significant difference between substantive and methodological uniformitarianism (Bailey 1983: 174–80; Fletcher 1992; Gould and Watson 1982: 340).

At present the social sciences and history can avoid the contradictions because they deal in relatively short-term contexts. Bourdieu, Lloyd, Gellner and Giddens do not discuss them in any fundamental way. But archaeology requires an explanatory logic which can encompass the continuum of its concerns, from the biological evolution of the hominids to the actions of contemporary individuals. As yet none has been provided. Instead, several ways of dealing with this problem have been advocated which bypass the conundrum. The emphasis on social and historical approaches in archaeology has produced a predominance of explanatory approaches oriented towards the short timescale of human action and expressed in terms of the verbal meanings of social life. Either social theory about activity is extrapolated to the longer term, as in most social reconstructions, or explanatory priority is allocated to human action on the small scale (Hodder 1986). The extreme version proposed by Shanks and Tilley specifies a single causal scale of explanation, compressing cultural process and mapping it on to political action (1987b: 61–78). Nature is marginalised to emphasise the internalist processes of culture, dissociating them from an assessment of the issues of adaptation (1987b: 118–36, 137–85), a view vigorously criticised by Mithen (1989). Even the biologists interested in human ethology concentrate almost entirely on activity in the short-term context (Bonner, Wilson and Lumsden 1981; Eibl-Eibesfeld 1975, 1989; Esser 1971; Thorpe 1979), as do human ethologists from the social sciences (Kendon and Ferber 1973; Kudoh and Matsumoto 1985; Poyatos 1988; Reynolds 1972) and social anthropologists (Ardener 1981). The other polar option has been to concentrate on large-scale behavioural patterns over long time spans, such as resource procurement, which can be understood in biological terms. An extreme version of this strategy disregarded social process by treating it as a 'wobble in the biotope' (Higgs 1968; Higgs and Jarman 1975).

The disjunctions of scale and logic which the conventional dichotomy produces have generally been masked by bridging theories or denied by an emphasis on the ends of the continuum. The obstacle to an integrated view is the lack of a hierarchical perspective on cultural explanations which could emphasise that biological and cultural operations both occur across a wide range of spatial and temporal scales. Once cultural phenomena can be identified which have their effects over longer rather than shorter time spans, we should be able to devise new kinds of explanations which will neither reduce cultural perspectives to the biological nor marginalise the biological.

Filling the logical chasm: the role of the material
The terminology of current social theory in archaeology merges actions, speech and the material milieu of a community into a holistic, all-inclusive, simultaneous explanatory form. But the material frame of a community has a slower replication rate and possesses more inertia than activities such as vocal communication, gesturing and sequences of movement. As a consequence these various aspects of human behaviour should always tend to decouple, producing internal dissonance which must be a continual liability for predictable, viable social life. Instead of using the inclusive approach which homogenises different cultural signals, we ought instead to use an integrative approach which allows us to treat these three aspects of social life as interrelated but different modes of communication which replicate at different rates. Because the material component of human behaviour possesses inertia and can endure over longer periods of time without replication, its potential temporal span and its possible spatial magnitude fit between the long-term, large-scale component of evolutionary biology and the shorter term, smaller scale contexts for which current social and historical theories are appropriate. Instead of trying to bridge the perceived chasm in anthropological theory between social action and biology, we can provide a new explanatory level in a hierarchy of explanation which will also act as a buffer between them, to prevent overextrapolation from either extreme of the continuum.

The logical addition to the explanatory models, which ought to overcome the prevalent dichotomy, is an intermediate class of explanation dealing with phenomena like the inertial impact of material entities, which have behavioural effects over the longer term. Such an ethology of the material would not be committed to dense social detail or to social categories defined by the relationship between action and verbal meaning, but would extend the 'social' to incorporate fully the inertial role of the material in everyday life (Fletcher 1988). An alternative explanatory scale can be created, linking in one direction to the rapid functioning of social life and in the other to the larger scale biological constraints on behaviour, whether these are the physiology of the species or the ecological and environmental processes affecting human communities. In essence the approach is concerned with the form and consequences of actual patterns of behaviour and the signal systems by which they function, not with the structure and role of declared meaning.

An enquiry about the role of the material in managing social life allows the same terminologies and analyses to be applied to the study of all those animal species which incorporate material entities into their behavioural repertoire. This avoids the dichotomising that is otherwise inevitable when the perspective on human culture is oriented towards intent, action and verbal meaning. Without that option commensurable comparison of humans and other animal species becomes impossible except by references to acultural fundamentals of physical biology. This has the regrettable effect of creating a culture–nature polarity while deterministically locking the inclusive class of cultural behaviour on to biology. However, if we introduce the role of the material as a distinct class of behaviour through which action is mediated or restricted, we can decouple the deterministic link from biology to active behaviour. We can then distinguish the hominids as unique because of the particular way in which they came to interact with material, *and* we can retain the capacity to compare the behaviour of different species using inter-consistent behavioural criteria. The presupposed dichotomy inherent in the label 'culture' can be avoided, at least in the analysis of the relationship between action and the material component of behaviour. The material has to be envisaged as a class of operator possessing behavioural characteristics. An explanation of how this operator functions has to be inserted into a hierarchical explanatory structure which links together phenomena observable over varied temporal and spatial scales.

Conclusions

At present archaeology is searching through ontologies, epistemologies and explanations. The discipline is in a period of unstable experimentation and epis-temological anarchy. The opportunity is available to encourage a diversity of views. As part of the process, this book is about another way of dealing with the study of human behaviour. I am not arguing against other kinds of social theory which have different analytic purposes. My aim is to extend the spectrum of social theory to incorporate the long-term, large-scale role of the material as a regulatory and restrictive influence on the management of community life. To do this we need to construct a hierarchy of explanations of human social life and then provide a proper operational uniformitarian model of the role of the material.

2

The material as behaviour

The term 'behaviour' conventionally refers to the actions of individuals or the activities of a community. For research concerned with very short time spans, in which the role of words, actions and human intent is critical, the definition of behaviour is conventionally unambiguous. It refers to what people do. According to this usage constructing a building is behaviour. By contrast, the building itself is regarded as a product – a thing, not a kind of behaviour. This is rather different from an approach to the behaviour of other species. A termite nest is a product of termite activity, but it is also integral to the termites' behaviour because it is the conduit for the biochemical signals essential to the functioning of the community. It regulates the activity of the community (Krishna and Weesner 1970; Wilson 1972). Likewise the behaviour of badgers and wombats includes the kinds of burrows they make (Hansell 1984). For bower birds the colours and shapes of objects, such as blue plastic clothes pegs, are important signals in the birds' reproductive behaviour (Chaffer 1984). Tinbergen's classic study of seagulls (1951) illustrates the kind of activities that arise from the durable debris which the birds produce. When the seagull chicks hatch, the distinctive colour of the fragments of eggshell attracts predators and puts the offspring at risk. Those birds which fling the eggshells away from the nest remove this signal, reducing the threat to their young. The rubbish, in conjunction with the predators, has acted as a selective agent leading to the preponderance of a type of active behaviour with adaptive value. This should potentially apply to any material features such as constructions, markers, colour coding and even waste products. Hominid behaviour has evolved over the past 2 to 3 million years to include a substantial material component, which is now integral to the behaviour of *Homo sapiens sapiens*. Successive genera of hominids defined their living areas by durable materials, made and used durable tools, managed fire, allocated material markers to their dead, and most recently created images from shape and colour. Humans learn from their local community how to produce particular versions of this behaviour, as do some other animal species with their own forms of material patterning (Hansell 1984; Von Frisch 1974). When we are comparing humans and other animals, we cannot justifiably assume that the relationship between action and the material component of behaviour is quali-tatively different. The behaviour of humans and other animals may be different but this must be demonstrated by a consistent approach to both, not reified by a simple assumption that they are non-equivalent.

Defining behaviour

Only on a very short timescale does there appear to be an absolute distinction between material entities and active events. 'Things' are perceived as essentially static and as secondary to human intentions and actions. But on a larger timescale than is usual in ethnographic research neither of these perceptions can be sustained. The material entities are themselves slow events happening at varying rates, some so slow that they can scarcely be observed on our familiar daily timescale. For instance, all entities are degenerating, going through changes over time which thereby alter their relationship to the faster events around them. On the other hand, the relative inertia of the material acts as a constraint on people's actions and intentions. Durable entities change slowly. They persist and have an influence that goes far beyond the lives of the people whose intentions created them. Without denying the role or existence of intent, we can nevertheless consider how the material component of human behaviour operates independently of intentionality. We can look instead for patterning in what happens within communities and how the material places restrictions upon what happens. The area of enquiry is the material forms and signals a community produces, the degree to which these signals can be effectively transmitted or regulated and the consequences of that material milieu for the size, viability and duration of a community's existence. These questions require an ethological approach to social analysis in addition to the ethnographic, socio-logical and historical forms of enquiry with their emphasis on verbal meaning, action and human intent.

Ironically, biological ethology has not yet produced a comprehensive approach to the material component of behaviour. In the biological sciences the theoretical development of ethology has led to an equivalent of ethnographic participant observation (Thorpe 1979). The study of contemporary animal species has engaged primarily in the analysis of activity. Though the nature of the material component of the behaviour is discussed and its evolution has been recognised, at least for the immediate derivatives of activity such as the feeding tracks of marine worms (Eibl-Eibesfeld 1975: 232–3; Seilacher 1977), this topic is not as yet central to ethological debate. Some evidence does survive in the palaeontological record, e.g. termite nests (McBreaty 1990),[1] trilobite resting hollows (Hantzschel 1975: 22) and rodent nests (Voorhies 1975), but it is very partial compared to the vast array of active behaviour which can be studied in contemporary contexts. The emphasis on action and the restricted palaeontological data have, up to now, obviated the need in ethology for a new, longer time-depth perspective on the relationship between action and the material component of behaviour. This may perhaps be one of the hidden reasons why a workable cultural ethology has not developed. Cloak noted the problem in 1975 and Rapoport reiterated it in 1988. The initiative has to come from an archaeology which is concerned with the substantial evidence for the antecedents of the contemporary material component of human behaviour.

To emphasise what is distinctive in the way the material component of human behaviour operates we need a convenient label, to distinguish it from other ways of looking at the things which accumulate around human beings. 'Material culture', the prevailing label in anthropology, contains within it a dichotomy between non-cultural and pre-cultural/cultural behaviour. Within the study of animal behaviour this either creates a differentiation between the derivatives of fixed-action patterns and those features which result from learned behaviour, or else it tends to make a general distinction between 'animal' behaviour and human behaviour. The label is habitually enlisted by action-oriented viewpoints and clearly refers to entities as 'things', distinguishing them from a class of 'doings'. To expect the term 'culture' to include the reflective and recursive positions which retain an animal–human dichotomy, and also to incorporate the regulatory and restrictive role of the material component of human behaviour, which does not create such a prior dichotomy, requires too much of the label. Contradictions and ambiguity are likely to result. The former positions tend to treat the inertial effects of the material as incidental derivatives of the link between action and verbal meaning; they fail to take account in any coherent way of the regulatory and restrictive role of the material.

We should view 'things' as the class of slow behaviour that has effects over a wider range of timescales than active behaviour, as we now do when we study other species. This would avoid the confusions, ambiguities and false dichotomies which the label 'culture' produces. Under the alternative terminology we may study both active behaviour and the material component of human behaviour, distinguishing the study of the latter as the 'material behaviour' approach. Depending on our interests and the timescale relevant to our enquiry, the material component of community life might either be viewed as reflexive or recursive or alternatively as a behaviourally autonomous operator exerting its regulatory and restrictive function as an influence on social life. The former roles are properly analysed using current social and historical theory in a 'material culture' approach. The latter role is the concern of a 'material behaviour' approach. Together with economic and ecological analyses, these differing forms of analysis should form an integrated hierarchy of approaches to the study of human behaviour. What must be emphasised is that illustrating and advocating the use of any one approach does not condemn others as useless. However, it does presume that each will be inappropriate in some contexts and that none will suffice as an all-inclusive explanatory procedure applicable to all the differing scales of operation observable in ethnographic, historical and archaeo-logical contexts.

The behavioural role of the material
The material provides an integrative framework for daily life yet it can also obstruct otherwise viable, active behaviour. Its obstructive capacity derives from its inertia, whether this is due to its durability or its slow replication rates. Material entities act as barriers to signal transmission by their familiar capacity to restrict sight and sound. But the material also provides a frame of reference for active behaviour because it carries non-verbal signals about the patterning of space and time.

Both signal management and signal carrying can be effected by the same entity. Clay tablets with script written on them assist signal transmission: they carry information. By doing so they can also help to reduce the amount of interpersonal interaction required to obtain that information. Likewise, but not so obvious to us, a building carries a non-verbal message about the distances at which entities are habitually located from each other as an inherent part of the community's behaviour. At the same time, enclosed rooms and durable construction block sound transmission, serving to control the level of interaction. This is not to say that the material frame cannot also be a partial reflection of what people do, and may have a recursive relationship to their social activities. However, the functional interpretation of a building as a chief's residence or the mapping of kinship ties across settlement space (Whitelaw 1983, 1989) does not render invalid or unnecessary a formal or a metrical analysis of the assemblage of spatial signals which the buildings carry. Just as the social use of verbal language depends upon its periodicities and grammar, so likewise, in an extension of Kauffman's argument (1993: 369–76), we should expect the social use of space to be mapped onto an equivalent formal pattern of distances and spaces.

The material and the 'social'

Only if active behaviour and verbal meaning had absolute deterministic control over material form could consistency in the material be an epiphenomenal derivative, lacking an internal order of its own and given coherence only by the logic of the verbal meanings and actions with which it is associated. But such determinism would have to generate complete correspondence between material and 'social' conditions. A given social system could do nothing other than produce a particular form of material expression. The material would merely be a casing somehow moulded by the social categories of activity in a community. If complete correspondence does not exist, then the material aspect of social life would merely be a functional by-product of social action and environmental pressures and would lack a formal order of its own. If, however, it does possess formal order, then it must also have a particular behavioural function of its own and a code order which gives it a regular form. There need not then be high statistical correlations between social phenomena such as kinship distance and the patterns of residential space but there will still be significant ties between them. We might reasonably expect that, for communities to function, social action must at least mesh with the non-verbal message system which it uses. What is not required is the determinate reduction of one to the other. Given that we can repeatedly recognise groups of settlements as similar or different because they are consistent and repetitious in form, the claim for arbitrariness in material patterning is improbable. Nor do we derive our recognition of the order in material patterns from their associations with verbal and social actions, since we can see pattern without reference to those criteria. We can recognise regionally distinct settlement forms in the archaeological record because of their actual attributes of shape, size and form without reference to any of the verbal labels and social categories with which they were, presumably, once associated.

What we should expect to find is some correspondence between social activity and material space, both generally and contextually, but not universal predetermination.

Though it is possible to observe contextual correspondence between social organisation and material, spatial context, in practice there is also divergence and non-correspondence (Cameron 1992; Trigger 1967: 150–1; 1981), even differing use of the same amount of space in different communities (Casselbury 1974). The disjunction between the material and the 'social' can be illustrated by two alternative views of residential space and kinship ties. Fortes neatly expressed the notion of a link between the material and the 'social' in a comparison of Tallensi and Ashanti housing (Figure 2.1) (Fortes 1959). The Tallensi are described as patrilineal. The domestic family of a husband and wife or wives and their children live in a clearly defined residence unit centred around the household granary. The Ashanti are described as matrilineal. A household basically consists of brothers and sisters and the offspring of the women. The men's wives reside with their own brothers in another building elsewhere in the settlement. A woman prepares food for her husband and the food is carried across the settlement to the man's domicile. The two kinds of residence units look very different and their differences can be related to the differing social organisation of the two societies, but they also have one substantial material feature in common. Despite the completely different route activity and the different composition of the food-preparing and food-sharing units in the two societies, both occupy residence units with strongly delimited boundaries. Both present the outside world with a solid blank outer wall and a single entryway. The social permeability of the Ashanti residence unit does not simply correlate with open access to its material form.

There are no regular, simple, cross-cultural rules of material–social correspondence in this case. The relationship is contextual not universal. Verbal meaning and social construction are far more versatile than material expression because inversions of meaning are possible. An indigenous commentator or a skilful anthropologist might argue that the closed form of the Ashanti residence exists precisely to act as a counter to the permeability of its social life. Nor is there a logical inconsistency in the opposite case being made for the Tallensi settlement. In that case the claim might be that the boundary walls of a residence reinforce the

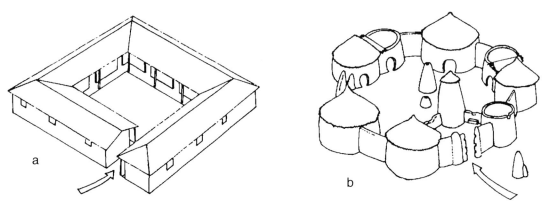

Figure 2.1 (a) Ashanti and (b) Tallensi houses in Ghana (after Fortes 1959)

separateness of the domestic units. My concern is not whether these declarations are true or false, since that could only be gauged contextually, with reference to the verbal expressions of each society. Instead we need to ask new kinds of questions about what the material does, as material, in each society, rather than concern ourselves primarily with the meanings given to it verbally.

In both cases the boundary walls do actually get in the way of route movement and to a similar gross degree, even though the broad nature of the domestic and food-sharing units is very different. The walls have a general cross-cultural function of dividing up space and restricting access. We might ask about the effects of the ordering of space and the barriers to interaction in such communities, even when their social systems are very different. The walls define what people cannot do, regardless of what is said about social meaning. They affect how often and in what ways people can interact. For instance, the continuous room blocks of an Ashanti residence more effectively limit interaction than the low curtain walls of the Tallensi houses. The material frame has a substantial behavioural role and should be amenable to analysis both as a contextual associate of the verbal meanings of social organisation and ideology and as an independent regulator and restrictor of behaviour.

The material as a signal regulator

The most familiar function of the material is its role as a regulator of signal transmission and as a means of restricting interaction within a settlement. A familiar example is provided by the control of noise. If you are trying to read in the middle of an open space full of noisy people you may perhaps finish the book but at the cost of being tired and probably very irritated, or you may well have given up trying to read at all. Active behaviour and personal determination do not sufficiently relieve interaction stress. But if you are inside a room built of brick or concrete you can read relatively undisturbed, however noisy it is outside. The cost has already been borne by the effort expended on building the room. It has been transferred to the economic capacity of the community, shifting the load off our finite capacity to ignore the noise onto a material which absorbs and blocks the sound.

We cannot always assume that a community will be able to afford the constructions which could block the amount of interaction its active behaviour is producing. A community's economic capacity or its spatial preferences might be unable to provide the necessary material controls on interactive intensity. The management of interaction stresses will therefore be beyond its control. This has serious implications for future urban planning and economics. Freedman points out that the costs of making some kinds of mass housing tolerable are considerable (1975: 126–7). For example, in Hong Kong the maintenance of high-density housing has been essential to the functioning of the colony since the 1960s (Goodstadt 1969; Pryor 1983). Conversely, the material may restrict interaction too much and make social life incoherent. A symbolic explanation is offered by the LoWilli for the fragmenting of large residential units: 'they were formerly "housepeople" (*yidem*) living in one vast homestead which became so large that some of the many inhabitants might be gaily dancing to the xylophones without realising that a funeral had taken place in another courtyard. So they split" (Goody 1956: 72). Cumulative numbers of kin living next to each other in limited social proximity were unaware of adjacent activity because of the labyrinthine durable spaces in which they lived (Figure 2.2). The distance across the mythical house, and the ever-increasing material frame which prevented people from knowing what was going on elsewhere in the building, neatly expresses a mundane, endemic social problem.

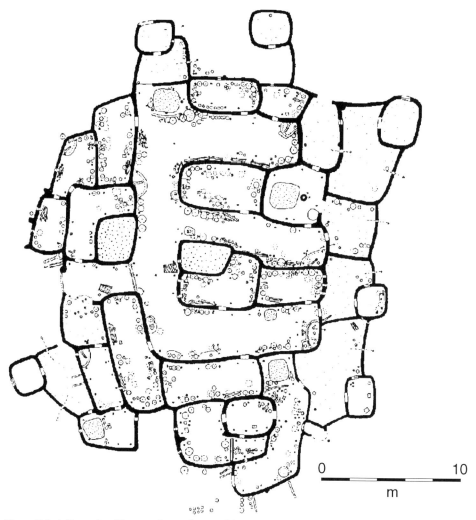

0   10
m

Figure 2.2 A Dagarti residence unit, north-west Ghana, 1970–1 (after field survey by author)

 granary   objects   drain

room fill   courtyard

Note: The Dagarti are closely related to the communities referred to as LoWilli by Goody and live in very similar houses.

Because the effects of material behaviour are a function of physical characteristics such as size, density or shape and their influence on frequencies of interaction or communication range, we need only be concerned with the material entities themselves. Whether or not the occupants of a settlement believe that durable walls block sound transmission, and regardless of whether or not they built them for that reason, the walls still have that effect. The effects on human perception derive from the topography of the space, the nature of the visual fields, and the materials of which the buildings were made. No necessary link exists between the thoughts, sentiments, intentions, declared attitudes or imagined opinions of the human actors whose material behaviour we are examining and the effects of the material. There need not even be a consensus among the members of a community about the social nature of their residential space (Parsons 1929) (Figure 2.3). Nor is there an absolute correspondence between what people say and what they do (Ardener 1976; Rathje 1974: 236–41). Their assumptions can be wrong but the effects of the material will still be there. Even if the members of a community imagine that their attitudes define those effects, we are not obliged to concur. Those attitudes are relevant if we need to know why a material feature was created in the first place and if we are concerned with declared attitudes or tacit intent towards it. But we do not have to pursue those particular concerns. For an analysis of the material constraints on community life we do not need such information. How these material constraints actually work, and the effects they have on community life, need to be viewed from a larger perspective than the verbal expression of the premises and assumptions in the minds of the actors who made and used a material assemblage. If they were indeed subject to such assumptions, then the mind would possess dominance over the nature of matter and would predetermine the degree to which the material can regulate signal load.

The material as a message carrier
Though the function of material behaviour in controlling signals is familiar, its role in carrying messages has not been readily recognised. That role has been obscured by the transformation of size, shape, colour and design into the verbal meanings of social theory, whether in conventional social reconstruction or by the contextualists, as can be seen in social and conceptual studies of 'traditional' architecture and residential space (Blier 1987; Kent 1990; Lawrence 1982; Moore 1986; Rapoport 1969; Robben 1989). The material attributes and spatial forms of the buildings are submerged in expressions of verbal meaning, as, for instance, in the claimed linkage of social status with position in a hut (Grøn 1988: 103), or they are connected to the verbal terminology of a community's cosmology and the ambiguities of changing social relations. The analysts discuss the role of the buildings in terms of the verbal meanings and significance ascribed to their form, while writing as if they are referring to shape, size and location. Hodder has argued that material expressions have their essential relevance for human communities primarily in terms of the 'verbal meaning constructs' associated with them (Hodder 1986: 39–54). This view is also predominant in structural analyses of material culture (Glassie 1975; Kobylinski 1986; Leone 1982a, 1982b; Small 1987), precisely because it has

dominated structuralism in the social sciences (Pettit 1975). Even though Shanks and Tilley, in their discussion of formal analysis, verge on defining the material as a distinct class of message transmitter (1986b: 95–6), they revert to its correspondence with verbal meaning in further discussion (e.g. 1987b: 97–117). When several levels of meaning are recognised, as in Rapoport's earlier work (1982), non-verbal meaning is still converted to verbal symbolic form. But we cannot logically limit meaning in human behaviour to verbal categories or commit structuralism exclusively to the conversion of formal, material patterns into the patterning of higher level verbal meaning. The effect of doing so has been to obscure the non-verbal message function of material patterns while at the same time claiming to describe the meaning of the material. To express the non-verbal meaning of the material requires numerical statements about visual fields, perceptual barriers and the sensory effects produced by the building materials.

What kinds of message structure might we find in collections of material signals, and what dynamics of change would such sets of meanings produce? The normative view and assumptions about 'ideals in the mind' are inadequate (see below pp. 36–7). An illustration of the nature and role of material messages is provided by the patterning of space. Material signalling can be viewed as part of the immense amount of spatial and temporal non-verbal signalling which sustains community life (Argyle 1975; Campbell 1989; Tringham 1973; Weitz 1984). People appear to learn how to perceive space from the material context of their lives (Böök 1991) and from observing action. A considerable portion of the communication which goes on within a community is non-verbal and is not consciously recognised by the people who use it (Berry 1971; Birdwhistell 1970; Hall 1966, 1968, 1974; Mehrabian 1976). It consists of gestures (kinesics), the frequency and intensity of activity (Campbell 1989: 229–46; Hall 1983), as well as spatial patterning (proxemics) (Hall 1966: Watson 1970), all of which are amenable to quantified formal analysis.[2]

The study of proxemics indicates that interpersonal distances tend to be different in different communities. In one community the average 'conversation zone', the distance between two interacting speakers, may be as small as 30 cm while in another community it may be as much as 70 cm. The biomechanical characteristics of an interpersonal encounter do not dictate the use of any particular, universal distance. Non-verbal messages cannot be reduced to biological universals or to general derivatives of social activity and intent.

What has become apparent since Hall's pioneering work is that his simple concept of zonation does not sufficiently describe the active, social use of space. Factors of personal psychology and social standing also intervene to produce variants on 'standard' interpersonal distances even within a single society or subculture (Altman 1975: Canter *et al.* 1975; Sanders 1990: 48). Yet even in the highly plastic milieu of active signalling, spatial behaviour is not incoherent. In a Vagala community in northern Ghana groups of men congregate to eat in the evening at distinct points on the roofs of the buildings (Figure 2.4). Though their members come from widely separated residence units, the eating groups persistently use the same location and are separated by quite similar distances.[3] The active patterning of space seems to occur even for distances in excess of 10 m. In any community some interpersonal distances are infrequently utilised. Interpersonal space is quantised – spacing distances do not form a continuum. Recognisable differentiated distances are used in different social contexts (Watson 1970), yet the actors are unaware of the actual distances which they use. Hence the title of E. T. Hall's book in 1966, *The Hidden Dimension*.

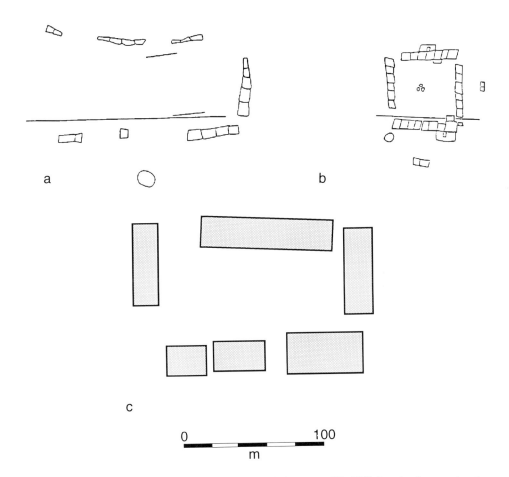

Figure 2.3 San Ildefonso, south-west USA, early twentieth century AD. Differing visual perceptions by members of the community (after Parsons 1929); (a) by a woman (b) by a man and (c) schematic plan from a survey of the pueblo in 1959 (after Scully 1975)

dance places ———— race track trees buildings

The study by Parsons was carried out in 1925. She asked a male and a female informant to draw their image of the plan of the pueblo. Two views of social distance are represented, each made from a different social stance. Neither contradicts the information content of the surveyed ground-plan, which merely illustrates space in terms of how far one would have to walk and the perceptual field in which the human eye would actually have to make distance estimates.

At a gross level of analysis Hall's insight is a valid guide to the study of general behavioural patterns (Sanders 1990: 48–9). Accurate estimation of distance and consistency in maintaining it are features of the active behaviour of human communities independent of any deliberate, overt intent. The obvious extension of this behaviour is that humans should also be capable of tacitly arranging their inert, material spatial context in an orderly fashion (Argyle 1975: 301–4; Fletcher 1977: 49). On the basis of the general aptitudes identified in proxemic analysis we should find that each community can produce a material context possessing a tacit order in which particular distances are more frequent than others. We might expect material space to display this characteristic more emphatically than active interpersonal space, whose use is clearly mediated by other, more immediate psychological factors. Preliminary analyses indicate that material space is ordered. When we look at spatial form (Alexander 1964) and route organisation the same applies. The ordered logic of space can be specified by complex algorithms (Hillier and Hanson 1984). For mobile communities, Gould and Yellen note that 'The distances at which household units physically space themselves within a larger social grouping are neither random nor invariate from society to society' (1987: 77). This also applies to the behaviour of other primates. Gorillas create defined material space by building overnight nests on the ground (Schaller 1963: 172–94). Because they usually sleep in groups they produce 'camp sites' containing several adjacent nests. The camp sites display spatial consistency and local residential traditions (Elliot 1976; Groves and Sabater Pi 1985: 24–6).[4]

The members of a community should be able to produce material spatial messages without being aware that they are doing so, and should not be aware of the exact metrical values of the material spatial message carried by their settlement. Characteristic products of the human ordering of space can be observed in the settlements of permanently sedentary, agrarian communities who erect their own buildings.[5] The 'grammars' of such messages should be expressed as a community-specific material arrangement of space independent of the immediate environmental context. When two culturally different communities occupy the same settlement location and arrange their own residential space, we should find that they produce distinct, gross metrical patterns. In the Hopi pueblo of Awatovi during the seventeenth century AD (Figure 2.5) (Montgomery *et al.* 1949), the distributions of spacing distances in the Hopi buildings and in the Spanish, Franciscan mission had very different shapes (Fletcher 1977) (Figure 2.6). Not only are the sizes of rooms and spaces different for the two communities, but even the degree to which particular distances are repeated differs. The available raw materials cannot therefore be regarded as the factor which defines the ordering of distances within a settlement (Fletcher 1977: 104–8). In the same environment, over the same period of time, different communities will use the available resources in different ways. This can be seen very clearly in the differing use of the same raw materials – timber, adobe and rock rubble. For instance, the Franciscans made far more use of large timber in the form of entire tree trunks (Fletcher 1977: 49). Climate and environment cannot sufficiently explain why settlements take particular forms or use particular sets of distance values at any one point in time. The Franciscans did not adopt Hopi architectural features in their own buildings and when the Hopi slaughtered the monks in AD 1670 and took over mission buildings they divided up the rooms to create their own kinds of space (Figure 2.5).

If communities which build for their own use each generate their own distinct material spatial messages, we should find consistency in the metrical nature of their residential space even when the form of the space changes. For instance, the introduction of rectilinear roofed buildings into the previously curvilinear spatial format of the Konkomba settlement of Munyimba in Ghana used the distances standard to the behaviour of the community.[6] The lengths of buildings and rooms correspond with the distances expressed elsewhere in the settlement as the distances between the centres of adjacent round huts and the distances across the smaller residence

Figure 2.4 Choriban, north Ghana, 1970–1. Sketch view of settlement with location of eating groups on the roof (after field survey by author). No orientation

paths   trees   ● eating groups   courtyard

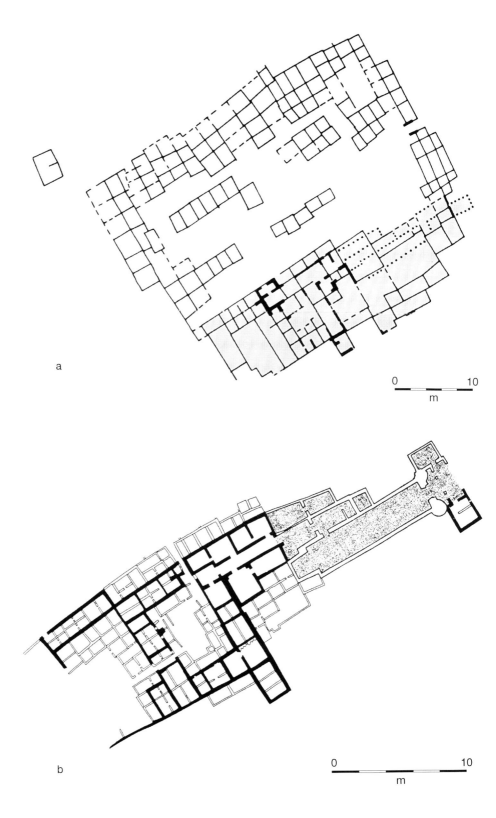

a

0   10
m

b

0   10
m

units (Fletcher 1977: 80–1). We should also find that, when a single community used and built two different settlements, both display components of the same metrical pattern. The workmen's residential complex (Figure 2.7) of the Ramesside period (sixteenth century BC) at Deir el Medina in Thebes (Egypt) provides an example.[7] Members of the community lived in two settlements. Their permanent homes were in the main village at Deir el Medina just off the edge of the Nile floodplain. During their duty period the workmen from the village lived in the Top site (Černý 1973), which is located on the ridge above the southern end of the Valley of Kings. Initial studies suggest that, even though the specific forms of the settlements differ, the linear distances used were drawn from the same suite of values (Fletcher 1981b: 100–3). In essence the Top site is an aggregate of the small-space component of the Main site arranged into a different form. According to a spatial message model, superficial shape and arrangement may change, but the linear dimensions and room sizes should be more stable because they represent the expression of a basal 'grammar'.

In principle a consistent spatial message ought to produce a relatively stable signal over time. This is essential if a community is to possess a reasonable predictable spatial milieu and if material space is to act as a coherent message carrier. That material spatial messages possess some consistency and stability is indicated by the tendency for the repeated use of a limited range of distances over time. The growth of the sectors of the Top site provides an illustration of the consistency of the distances within rooms as a repeatedly replicated signal (Figure 2.8).

Discussion

The non-verbal language of a particular community cannot be reduced to a subsidiary effect of the associated suite of verbal meanings. Mother-in-law avoidance might require a particular arrangement of seating distances in any one community, but there is no prior possibility that the actual distance could be predicted from the structure of the verbal declarations about the practice of avoidance. Verbal meaning and metrical distance are incommensurable. Verbal meaning is structured in binary oppositions such as 'near–far', 'front–back' (Giddens 1979: 207, after Goffman), or in a ranked hierarchy of several classes. The differences inherent in the classification cannot be precisely quantified. Neither the relationship between the components of the code of a metrical message nor its degree of inherent variability can therefore derive from a verbal meaning system.

Figure 2.5 Awatovi pueblo, south-west USA, seventeenth century AD
(a) plan of ruins: the Franciscan mission is the south-east side of the pueblo (shaded area)

╱ wall line   ◤ thick standing walls 1882–3

(b) the Franciscan mission at Awatovi and its Hopi occupation in the late seventeenth century AD
(after Fletcher 1977 – sources Mindeleff 1891 and Montgomery *et al.* 1949)

▓▒ mission area abandoned   ▬▬ reused mission walls

══ Hopi walls

Consequently, the distances in a spatial message must possess meaning because they have a consistent relationship which makes up the structure of the non-verbal, material message, not because of an association with verbal meaning. A structuralist analysis without reference to verbal meaning is feasible (Fletcher 1988: 35–7) and allows the production of assessable statements about the generative codes of material messages. Provided that the buildings and features which carry the material spatial message survive, we can study their signals, whether ethnographically or in the archaeological record. We should be able to recognise past spatial messages which have no contemporary equivalent. The form of the message derives from the sizes of the entities in the settlement, not from analogies to a contemporary equivalent. By extension from the hypothetical spatial model, we should expect

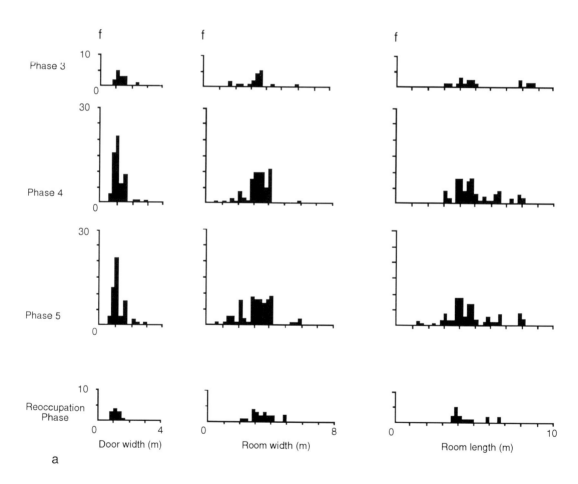

a

equivalent 'grammars' of shape, colour and the material ordering of time. A cultural assemblage should consist of several material grammars in some way related to each other and to the verbal grammar of the carrier community.

Non-verbal generative 'grammars' and the dynamics of the material

The effects of a material non-verbal 'grammar' can be illustrated by reference to spatial messages. A predictable behavioural space will reduce interaction stress by minimising the degree to which people have to pay conscious attention to their spatial milieu. If the sizes of entities and the distances between them are consistent and use a limited number of distance values, then response to that context will be facilitated because each individual could predict the probable size of an entity and

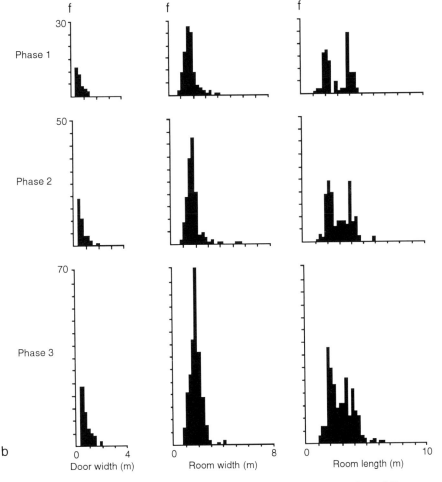

Figure 2.6 Awatovi pueblo, south-west USA, seventeenth century AD. Distributions of distances used in the two residence patterns at Awatovi (after Fletcher 1977)
(a) Franciscan (b) Hopi
f number of room lengths and widths (all walls measured) and all door widths
The development sequences provide an illustration of the way in which the spatial signals build up over time (see below for a more detailed example in Figure 2.8)

how far it will be separated from any other entity. Vernon remarks that 'the relation-ship of actual to perceived position is acquired and subject to modification, not built into the physiological structures of eyes and brains' (1962: 126). If the set of the most frequently used distances which make up the material space of a settlement has any coherence, i.e. the values relate to one another in some consistent fashion as a spatial message, then a simple mathematical model of the relationship between the distance values should suffice to give us a working model of a spatial message 'grammar'. A spatial message can be envisaged as a simple model of discrete distance values which are related to each other in a predictable manner. This would

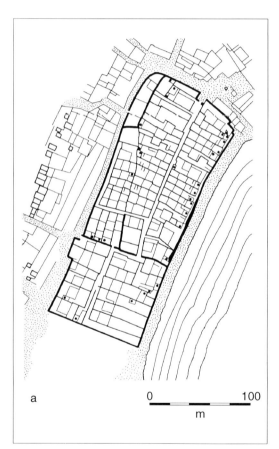

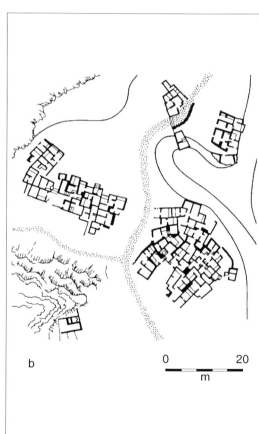

Figure 2.7 Deir el Medina, Egypt, sixteenth century BC (after Fletcher 1981b; sources Badawy 1965 and Bruyère 1939 and from field survey by author)
(a) the Main site

● ovens ◢ enclosure wall road

(b) the Top site

path cliff

Note: There is some housing outside the enclosure of the main site to the north and north-west on the tomb terraces.

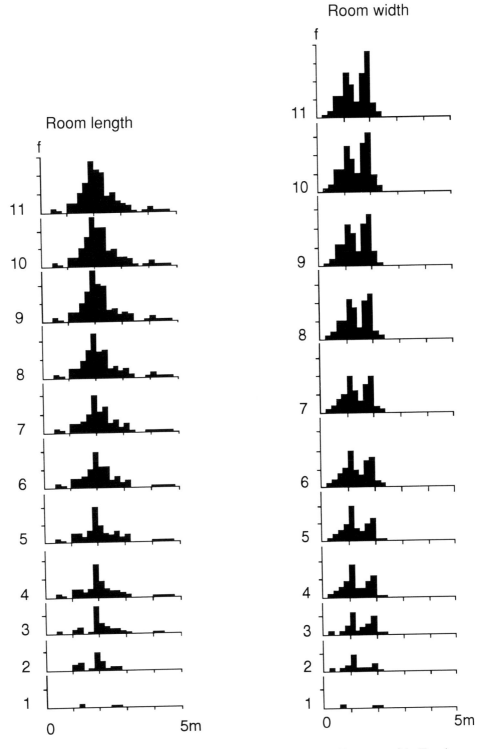

Figure 2.8 Spatial signals, replication and increasing sample size in the East sector of the Top site. Development sequence of eleven stages of building additions (from field survey by author and thesis 1976)

f number of room lengths and widths (all walls measured)

provide a community with a consistent and predictable frame of reference for its daily life. As with the ordering of time, intervals must be created in what is otherwise a continuum, if pattern and consistency are to be possible. The dynamics of a material message system can therefore be illustrated in terms of a simple mathematical series relationship between the distance values, as a preliminary, theoretical model.[8] A metrical series satisfies the basic requirements of a message system because it provides discrimination between the signals that make up the message (Leach 1976: 49) and defines a consistent rudimentary 'grammar' of the relationship between the kinds of signals that are permitted in the message (Kauffmann 1993: 382–4). A spatial message carried by the form of the settlement is generated by its builders and is transmitted to the occupants of the settlement. When we identify an ordered spatial pattern in an archaeological site, we are striving to read a slow message which has outlived the minds and memories of the people who made the buildings and features by which it is carried.

This hypothetical model allows us to escape the main logical problems of a normative approach. These problems are the assumption of closed logic, the dilemma of invariant 'ideals' and the ascription of change to the effects of external factors. Together they preclude explanations of internally generated dynamics of change. If the messages are closed systems of logic containing no anomalies, then endogamous change cannot happen. Only an exact duplicate of the existing form would be acceptable to the community. All change would have to be triggered by external pressures and distortions. An alternative is to claim that there are inherent dichotomies in logical structures which lead to change (Hodder 1984a). But the sequences of change that this is capable of generating are limited, consisting of inversion between successive states, e.g. from house form to grave form – still a closed logic, emphasising a restricted continuity of meaning through time. It does not logically entail or predict the possible failure of a community to maintain the code coherence of its messages.

The closed logic problem is obviated by Gödel's theorem. The theorem states that absolute closed consistency ceases to be possible for internally ordered sets as the content of the message becomes more complex (Chaitin 1990; Sangalli 1987). There ought to be some incoherence in the set of relationships between the ordered components of an information system. Change can go in many possible directions, each consistent with the structure of the existing code. Though restricted by the logic of that structure, the actual occurrence of a particular change is not predictable. Change is endemic to the system and can happen at any time because an arbitrary variant may generate a new coherent relationship with a previous inconsistency in the system. As a result, other previously coherent relationships in the message system might break down.

The variability problem is resolved by recognising that a finite amount of variability is integral to a definition of discrete classes of entities. If the actual material examples are a reflection of some Platonic ideal residing in the makers' minds, variability must be a distortion of the ideal, resulting from the impact of outside distorting effects and cannot be integral to the meaning of the message. No theory other than the pragmatic adoption of new forms is then available to explain why outside effects should cause the ideal to change. If pragmatics dominate community choices, then the normative rules have a trivial role. They would change as events demand, in a pure Lamarckian 'response' to needs or circumstances (Bateson 1972: 316–33). It is hard to envisage how they could produce ordered patterns or retain code consistency if this were the case. Conversely, if the 'rules' restrict the choices of the community, how can a change to new options ever occur if the logic of a normative system is closed and disallows disjunctive recombinations of meaning?

In a material message, by contrast to the normative view, variation is inherent in the meaning which is transmitted. The model of discrete distances specifies both the likely size of entities and the variation inherent in the relationship between the various possible values in the series (Fletcher 1977: 66–7, 94–9), unlike other proposals such as Preziosi's (1979). In a spatial message made up of values from a continuous variable, such as length, the relationship between variation and the discrete values of the message is easily described. The central tendencies for sizes of entities in a hypothetical settlement might be 2, 4, 6, 8 and 10 m, forming part of an arithmetic series, a rudimentary generative grammar from which other possible values in the series, such as 12, 14, 22, 30 m, can be predicted. This grammar will lose coherence if values of 3.7, 5, 5.5, 7.6, 10.4 m are included. If they are introduced, then the total collection of length values will no longer be able to function as a coherent message providing a predictable spatial milieu. By contrast, if the lengths differ only slightly from the values of the series, e.g. by 0.1 m either way, the coherence of the code is preserved. This brings us on to the other form of variability which can arise – change in the variation around a value in the hypothetical series. In a coherent message the amount of variation which can be tolerated for each value of the series is defined by the difference between the most similar values in the series. When we look at a different series, the relationship of variation to central tendency in a coherent code can be readily perceived. If the values form a Fibonacci series, e.g. 2, 3, 5, 8, 13 and 21, then less restriction on variability is tolerable around the larger values of the series. For example the nearest values to 8 are 5 and 13, not, as in the arithmetic series, 6 and 10. A Fibonacci series can carry much more fuzziness around the value 8 and still retain discreteness in its constituent serial values. The variability which a community can tolerate in its material messages ought therefore to be a function of the structure of the message codes (Fletcher 1977: 77–88). The loss of a tolerable, predictable material milieu would result when the variability that was being produced exceeded the amount that is consistent with the message structure. With the disappearance of order from the affected spatial messages, the spatial environment would lose its predictability. Such loss of behavioural coherence, because of cumulative error in the replication of material messages, should not therefore be unusual. According to this hypothesis the demise of settlements will be a normal function of their size and rate of growth and is inherent in the replication of their form, whether or not the community is economically viable. Spatial behaviour does not predetermine the existence of code coherence. Instead these material messages are a mode of tacit communication which can be successful or unsuccessful.

As the replication of a spatial message continues over time, variability in the signals is liable to increase. The active behaviour of the community continually tends to produce new variants which may or may not be consistent with the degree of variation internally coherent with the expressed grammar. With successive replication of buildings and features it is probable that dissimilar replications will tend to increase. A tendency for the gradual dispersal of values to increase over time should be observable even though the central tendencies may be fairly stable. Empirically we can observe that as settlement size increases the gradient of the variation values begins to rise (Figure 2.9).[9] The changes should not be referred to as 'error' since this implies that replication is somehow goal-directed to produce perfect copies but does not always succeed in doing so. No such assumption can be made.

The effect is to increase the variation associated with each central tendency and therefore to increase the fuzziness in the message. The variation cannot increase infinitely because it will lead to loss of signal coherence in the material message. Cumulative variability is a threat to the predictability of a community's material

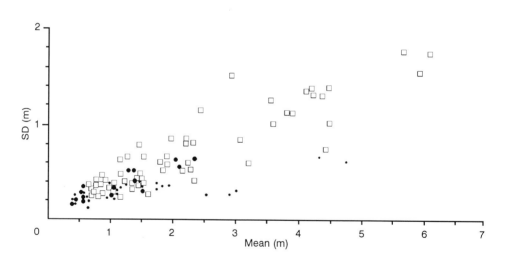

Figure 2.9 Increase in gradient of variation with increase in number of residence units per settlement. From a sample of Ghanaian settlements (after Fletcher 1977)

● 10–20   ● 20–40   □ 40–60 (number of residence units)

The number of residence units per settlement is used as a rough index of the size of the settlement and the number of replicative events that have been involved in the formation of its spatial message. Each variation value derives from a distribution of classes of distances e.g. door widths, room lengths, building widths in one settlement. The central tendency for each distribution is plotted against its variation value. As the number of residence units increases, the gradient of the variation increases with the increase in the central tendencies. The dispersion of the variation values for the different components of the message, e.g. room width, room length, etc., also increases as the number of residence units increases.

Note: Original caption is incorrect.

context. A message composed of discrete signal values cannot convey coherent meaning if the variation around the values comes to exceed the difference between them (Figure 2.10). If variation could increase without limit, there could be as much variety in the form and dimensions of the buildings used by a viable community as exists in the form of all the buildings used by human beings. Were this a general occurrence, no group-specific spatial forms could exist. However, as has been outlined earlier, the range of spatial expression used by one community is demonstrably not unlimited. The range of spatial expressions is bounded, as we would expect of any communication system.[10]

The critical constraint on the sustained adoption of a new spatial feature should be the degree to which it is code-coherent with both the existing metrical order and the level of variation tolerated in the community's spatial message. However, because the tolerated variability allows some latitude, new features can introduce spatial signals which cause the message structure to drift towards different values,

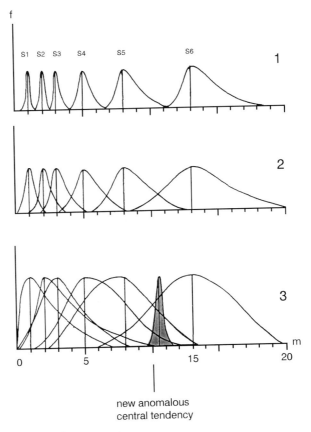

Figure 2.10 Variation and loss of message coherence
S1–S6 successive values of a metrical series
A schematic representation of change through three stages of additions to a spatial message, illustrating the swamping of a serial, metrical pattern by increasing variation and the loss of consistency order due to the appearance of a new central tendency value inconsistent with the series.

leading to a cascade effect of shifts in the values of the series. The new signals may be incidentally promoted by fashion and political–social activity. Once incorporated in the message, some of the size changes may have unintended, advantageous effects on community life and will thereby become more prevalent with the passage of time. But options which have an adverse effect on interaction levels might also get into the message structure in the same way.

From the analysis of spatial messages a mechanism can be formulated which converts random size changes into a directional change in a spatial message but may lead to the eventual loss of code coherence. At present the simple, hypothetical description of a spatial message provides a succinct paradigm for the relationship between variation and the pattern of central tendencies in a material message system. The hypothetical model allows simple predictions about the effects of continual replication on the degree of coherence in a community's space and allows initial predictions about the broad effects of spatial messages in settlements of differing magnitudes (see Chapter 6). If we find that the large-scale predictions are adequate statements about the material behaviour of past communities, then a time-consuming reformulation and upgrading of the modelling of material spatial messages will, in due course, be worth while.

Discussion

As I have already outlined, there are two primary classes of change in spatial messages. First, those changes which are consistent with the message will produce coherent transformational change, and secondly, change could result in increased levels of variability which are not coherent with the existing variability or the code order. We would usually expect the occupants of a settlement tacitly to prefer an overall message form that is coherent and predictable, not for rational or functional reasons but merely to retain adequate coherence in their message system. However, their replicative actions will tend to produce cumulative loss of message coherence because the members of a community are not consciously aware of the code and may lack the corporate capacity to prevent it from disintegrating.

This has implications for notions of cultural adaptation because of its equivalence to the biological processes of replication, selection and evolution. A material message 'system' behaves like the genetic 'system' in the sense that it is replicated by a procedure which possesses some tendency to produce change but has an internal ordering which may exclude variants that are not coherent with its grammar. Like the genetic system, the proposed spatial message structure provides stability through a code context within which the components of the message are integrated (Lewontin 1974: 318) – a fundamental requirement for any system to be capable of adaptive change and yet able to retain some degree of code coherence and operational stability. Similarly, the hypothetical model suggests that the internal structure of material messages be a significant factor in a community's capacity to adjust to circumstances, since the amount of variability which a message system carries will partially define the degree to which it can sustain coherent change. The message structure needs to be of a kind that allows a community the capacity to generate enough variants of its material behaviour to produce a pool of features, some of which may, by chance, be of adaptive value. The variability inherent in the material messages should have the same kind of role in cultural change as genetic variability has in processes of biological change. However, one critical difference between the cultural and the biological replicative mechanisms, according to the material behaviour approach, is that material messages can 'come apart', when non-coherent variation swamps the message, in a way not apparent in normal genetic replication. Cultural change is prone to produce abrupt and considerable disintegration and as a result relatively frequent reformulation of material code structures. The other difference from the biological mechanism is that a cultural assemblage contains different classes of code structure, in particular material messages, non-verbal communication and verbal grammars (Fletcher 1994). We cannot assume that all these classes of signal structure change in synchrony with each other. The case for material messages opens up the possibility of reinterpreting the nature of cultural change. Social action and verbal meanings may alter in parallel, along with changes in material message structures, but need not be the directive force behind a community's attempts to cope with behavioural stresses and external pressures. Indeed, the changes in a material assemblage may run according to their own replicative logic to produce a tacit meaning context and signal control milieu with which active behaviour has to interact and which verbal communication imbues with consciously articulated verbal meaning.

Conclusions
The analysis of behaviour can be divided into two broad approaches: the study of action and the analysis of the material as behaviour, both of which need to be integrated into an expanded definition of social theory. The concern of this study is the analysis of the effects of the material on human community life. To develop an integrated approach to the topic, an analysis of the impact of the material on interaction and communication within settlements will be used as a case study. The message-control functions of material entities produce a milieu which affects the degree of interaction experienced by the occupants of a settlement. The message-carrying function provides a predictable residential context and affects the capacity of a community to generate variant forms of its material framework. Because of inherent inertia the material fabric of the buildings, and the spatial message which they carry, also constitute a context with which the active behaviour of the community has to compete. Not only can the fabric of buildings obstruct a community's capacity for social change, but the material message grammars may also be unable to generate coherent variation fast enough to cope with the changing circumstances of the community. Archaeology offers the opportunity to pursue questions concerning the role of material barriers and material messages over long spans of time. We can enquire about the way in which such patterning is generated and analyse the consequences of a loss of behavioural coherence. Though material entities are produced by human intentions and actions, the overall effects of a community's material milieu ought to be apparent on a larger and slower scale than

the workings of declared intentions and social action. Given that the material may generate problems never envisaged by its makers, there should be some value in analysing its role in a hierarchical context concerned with differing magnitudes of effect over varying spans of time. This logical device should help to manage the analysis of the uneasy relationship between people, their active behaviour and the material context of community life.

3

A hierarchy of social explanation: locating the material

We seek to understand what human beings do by employing a spectrum of explanations ranging from the small-scale and short time spans of personal psychology to the immense time depths and vast regional extent of the large-scale component of biological evolution. None of these particular kinds of explanations is intrinsically better than any other and no single explanatory scale is exclusively necessary or proper, though each may be both appropriate and necessary for particular purposes.

The major theoretical constructs of the physical and biological sciences take the form of hierarchies of explanation. The hard sciences, biology and geology each use hierarchies of explanation about operations which are of different magnitudes and produce observable effects and outcomes over differing spans of time. Different scales of explanation are now linked by precise statements about indeterminacy (Davies 1987), not by reductionism or by deterministic causal links. Mechanistic and reductionist 'laws', typified by nineteenth-century physics (Glymour 1983), have not provided an adequate model for explanation since the rise of quantum theory in the first quarter of the twentieth century (Brush 1976). The Uncertainty Principle, which introduced indeterminacy to physics, was proposed in 1925 by Heisenberg (1959). Indeterminacy may or may not be a 'true' characteristic of the universe, life or human behaviour (Fetzer 1983; Higgs 1972; Koestler and Smythies 1969), but it is now the way in which the western scientific tradition strives to comprehend reality (Bronowski and Mazlich 1963; Wimsatt 1976). The specification that indeterminacy has a precise quality enables us to study large-scale phenomena without having to know the details of all the particular small-scale events that are or were involved. Carefully defined indeterminacy at the molecular or subatomic level is considered appropriate as a foundation for highly ordered patterns at successively larger scales of space and time (Gribbin 1989; Nash 1985). The indeterminacy is not due to our methodological inadequacies: it is inherent in the universe. Subatomic particles have to be considered in terms of precise statements of indeterminacy. No matter how detailed our observations, when we try to look at smaller and smaller physical phenomena, we still find fuzzy but precisely definable uncertainty (Bronowski 1973: 353–7). Large-scale physical transformations or states therefore cannot be reduced to predictable, determinate derivations of smaller scale phenomena. Instead, they possess their characteristics because of the scale at which they operate. Prigogine's work (1978, 1984) has shown that indeterminacy is a valuable conceptual tool both for macro-scale analyses and for subatomic phenomena, as is apparent in the discussion of 'self-organized criticality in dynamical systems' (Bak and Chen 1991; van der Leeuw 1990).

Trigger has emphasised (1984: 293) that biological evolution is conceptualised by means of a body of theory, not a single, big theory (Eldredge 1985; Gould 1982; Grene 1987; Jantsch 1979; Rindos 1988). What is used is a 'hierarchical theory of selection, independent at several levels . . . but with complex interactions across all levels' (Gould 1986: 60). Associated with each operational level of the hierarchy, e.g. ecology, are critical parameters such as viable predator–prey ratios that have a selective effect on the persistence of characteristics generated at a smaller scale and functioning over shorter time spans (Sober 1984; Vrba and Gould 1986: 219, 221–2). Because what will happen at each level, e.g. in genetic replication, is not predetermined by its large-scale context, a proposition about indeterminacy is needed to organise the relationship between successive levels in the biological hierarchy of explanation (Salthe 1985). At the small scale, genetic copying is understood in terms of the relationship between a defined code and the inherent uncertainty introduced by inevitable copying error.[1] At the large scale we do not need the genetic details of all the animals involved to understand the relationship between natural selection and plate tectonics. The segregation of levels of explanation can also be seen in the development of theories. The operational uniformitarian proposition (see pp. 230–1) of Natural Selection was envisaged by Darwin without a knowledge of the micro-scale level of genetics.

If our concern is the usefulness of research propositions, the hierarchical arrangement of indeterminately linked levels of explanation is an inordinately valuable logical strategy. A hierarchy of explanation divides enquiry into manageable parts. No single level of theory can be considered either necessary or sufficient in its current form for understanding all aspects of human behaviour.[2] If an explanatory hierarchy is recognised, we can opt to concentrate our enquiry at any given level, for instance at the scale of social processes as understood in the social sciences. However, indeterminacy also allows us to concentrate on larger scale operations and effects, if we wish to, without having to make reference to the details of all the included small-scale events (Higgs and Jarman 1975: 1–2). The use of indeterminate links between differing scales of operation or outcome merely regularises a well-established practice in archaeology. We study phenomena whose effects we can feasibly see in the available data. When some degree of detail is missing, indeterminacy allows us still to look for consistent patterns of human behaviour at whatever greater, appropriate scale may suit our analytic concerns.

Hierarchies of explanation for human behaviour

That human behaviour should be understood by means of hierarchies of explanation has been discussed in social theory (de Walt and Pelto 1985; Ingold 1986). The usual field of enquiry for social anthropology lies in the 'middle' of the hierarchy, between the micro-scale of molecular and subatomic processes and the macro-scale of environmental change, though the interpretations and rankings used vary a great deal in social anthropology (Ingold 1986: 128–72). Giddens' and Bourdieu's concepts of human action introduce a degree of scaling because they differentiate the timescale of the creative role of individuals from that of the duration of the milieu which they transform. Though archaeology, like biology and the time-structured aspects of the hard sciences such as cosmology, astrophysics (Hawking 1988), and geology-palaeontology (Eldredge and Gould 1972; Lewis 1980; Schumm and Lichty 1965), is similarly concerned with patterns of differing magnitude over differing time depths, it has only recently begun to direct serious attention to the nature of time and the scaling of explanations. The significance of differing scales of space and time has been pointed out over the past twenty years by several archaeologists (Binford 1981; Clarke 1968; Hoffman 1972; Isaac 1972). Hodder (1987) and Knapp (1992) have sought to use an *Annales* approach to study patterns in human activity over differing ranges of time. The issue of timescaling has been given a new focus by Bailey's discussion of its analytic significance (1983, 1987). His discussions serve as a foil to the view that the scale of appropriate explanation is defined by that of ethnographic and historical enquiry.

   An analysis of the material as behaviour is predicated on the different scaling of a variety of operations and effects and the temporal difference between initiating cause and indirectly consequent outcome. It must therefore be placed within a hierarchy of explanations in order to connect it to phenomena which operate at other magnitudes, such as the short-term functioning of active behaviour and the longer-term impact of resource supply and environmental change. Some of the levels in a hierarchy of explanations of human behaviour are familiar (Table 3.1). However, the interpretations of social theory tend to produce convoluted, inclusive statements about the synchronous interconnection between phenomena which operate at different temporal and spatial scales, as in the sophisticated conceptions of the 'social' and 'economic'. The problem with previous studies of explanatory hierarchies in anthropology and history is that they have attempted to work with familiar categories and do not express the various levels of explanation in logically equivalent terms. The categories cannot be properly inserted into a hierarchy.[3] Nor do they define the function of the material as a significant inertial factor operating over differing timescales from the actions to which it is also synchronically linked. A notable exception is the Annaliste historians who tried to break out of this conundrum by specifying several classes of timescale, such as conjuncture (Bintliff 1991: 7; Knapp 1992: 6), which partially overcome the inclusiveness of the conventional labels. But these categories are not consistently applied by different practitioners. There is no possibility of allocating standard proportionate magnitudes to the different levels (Kinser 1981: 93; Lucas 1985: 6); nor does *Annales* provide, or claim to provide, a common unified explanatory policy (Furet 1983: 390). The problem is that the hierarchy does not specify how the different levels are interrelated and consequently their use varies from study to study (Fletcher 1992). If they are to provide consistency, the levels of a hierarchy have to be delimited in such a way that they do not arbitrarily merge. This can be done by defining different magnitudes of constraint which have their operational effects at different levels of scale, and by specifying the impact of each kind of

Table 3.1 Familiar levels of a hierarchy of explanation for human behaviour

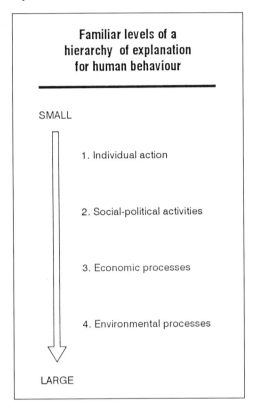

operational constraint as a selective factor affecting the products of smaller scales of operation.

Since differing scales of explanation can be interrelated without a deterministic, reductive premiss, we need not view the workings of society either as a derivative of individual action or as a predetermined consequence of economy, ecology or biology. The larger scale structure of the expressed or tacit attitudes of a community does not automatically determine the actions of individuals. Social pressures do not absolutely predetermine what individuals believe and try to do. The actions of specific individuals are indeterminate relative to the nature of within-group communication. Individuals can unpredictably exercise creativity and reformulate the expressions of their society. People can be at odds with their community. They can make serious, even personally disastrous, social mistakes.

In a very ordinary way individuals can create residential spaces which are regarded as anomalous by the other members of the community. In the Konkomba settlement of Munyimba (Figure 3.1a), the chief's brother, who had worked in southern Ghana, created an entirely rectilinear building (Figure 3.1b). Though he used the same suite of spatial distances as the other buildings of the village and people located themselves within it in similar ways, the house was regarded with some distaste by the man's wives and offspring. The building was not accretionary, as was usual for the other residence units. It could not be remodelled without substantial demolition, unlike the adjacent residence units, to which new courtyards could be added merely by removing the curtain wall between two adjacent huts, as in the chief's house (see Figure 3.1c). In consequence, the house lacked the flexibility needed to cope with the transformations of the domestic growth cycle (Goody 1956). It also constituted a serious barrier to interaction within the community. People could not call out messages between the interior courtyard and the outside space of the settlement. The usual, vocal clues, even vague auditory cues about what was going on in the courtyard, were not readily audible outside. The interior space, despite the considerable size of the courtyard, possessed few of the discrete peripheral niches where the curtain walls abutted the huts, which were used in the other residence units for specialised functions and temporary storage. Though created by a socially significant member of the community, who was both powerful in rank and relatively wealthy, the building was a behavioural anomaly which its occupants were gradually rejecting to live elsewhere.

At the much larger scale of ecology, environmental circumstances do not predefine that either individuals or communities will make the moves necessary for their survival. People can misjudge their situation. The consistencies in what people do or produce are therefore a function of factors internal to that behaviour. Circumstances have only a selective effect. They generate outcomes, of which we can make sense, by acting for or against whatever an individual or a group has tried to do on the basis of premises and expectations.

The hierarchical relationship between active and material behaviour
The material messages carried by the buildings and the contents of a settlement act as a perceptual template. Cree Indians who have been brought up in tents are more visually aware of diagonals than Indians or Whites who have grown up in rectilinear buildings (Annis and Frost 1973). The space of the settlement is a visual context in which the members of a community learn what their kind of space is like (Eco 1973), without being aware that they are doing so. In that sense a metrical message is a base code from which copies are taken by a messenger system in the brain, which then produces recombination and variant replication. During the procedure, new associations arise between the signals in the message structure, generating new forms never seen before, as in Chomsky's description of verbal language (1957). In addition, because the replicators do not usually observe all the parts of their settlement equally often, they will tend to have a partial view of the material message carried by its buildings. For several reasons therefore, the brain of each individual carries a partial electrochemical version of the material message. It is not the mental template for the assemblage even though it is essential to each replication of part of the assemblage. Rather, the electrochemical versions and the material message are slightly dissimilar partners in a replicative system. The material is the template. The signals in the brain are the messenger codes by which replication is effected.

What we are looking at in a settlement plan is the patterning actually expressed in the material message system and what it does in relation to interaction and communication within a community. We need not seek to locate some class of abstract 'rules' in supposed community consensus.[4] Our only concern is the consistencies in the actual practice of communication (Eco 1979: 125–7) and the relationship between a new feature and the existing expressions of the message system. As in the study of verbal communication, it is not the verbalised or even the tacit attitudes of the actors which are of concern (Eco 1979: 315). This resolves the dilemma raised by Leone (1982b) of how to link mind and material, though the answer is not quite what we might expect. We can carry out research on the patterning generated by the mind without concerning ourselves with what goes on inside people's heads. After all, anyone reading this book is interacting with a material entity, not with what is (or was) really going on in the author's mind. We often express ourselves as if we relate to the contents of other people's minds when we actually interact with the sounds and the signals which they send, not directly with their minds. The same

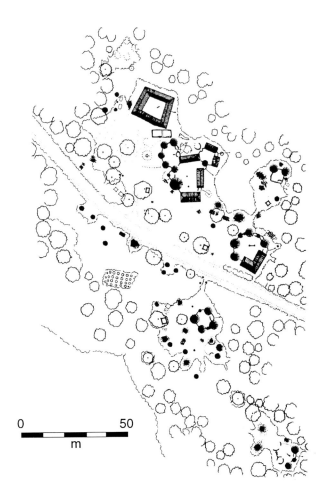

0   50
m

a

should apply to human communication using material signals. A mentalist palaeo-psychology is not necessary, as Binford has remarked (1965, 1967: 234), the views of Fritz notwithstanding (Fritz 1978). While we may one day be able to relate the internal and the external message versions to each other, we do not have to do so in order to study the workings of material behaviour. We can instead ask what the material does and how it relates to other modes of communication.

Social and political activity is overtly carried out through speech and action. But the grammatical structures of those 'languages' are not generated or regulated by the institutions of a community. They simply provide a message system which the institutions use. For instance, the structure of a verbal language does not alter even when a major endogamous political transformation occurs. How a language is used may change very considerably but its word structure, sentence periodicity and grammar alter at a much slower rate. Verbal languages possess a structure and grammar independent of their particular social milieu. So do non-verbal languages.

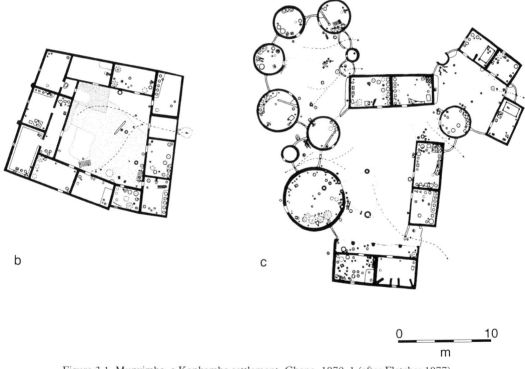

b

c

0   10

m

Figure 3.1 Munyimba, a Konkomba settlement, Ghana, 1970–1 (after Fletcher 1977)
(a) general plan

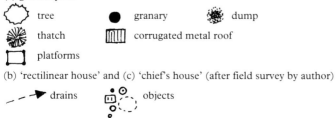

tree   granary   dump

thatch   corrugated metal roof

platforms

(b) 'rectilinear house' and (c) 'chief's house' (after field survey by author)

drains   objects

For example, in white middle-class, American society (Hall 1966) individuals who have ceased to be intimate will shift from a very close conversational distance to a visibly larger spacing in their public interaction. The distances were not created by the social situation; rather they are part of a non-verbal language used by the members of that community to express particular social states, serving the same kind of role as verbal language. This should also apply to the relationship between material spatial messages, the forms which they produce and the milieu in which those forms are used (see pp. 28–34).

There are at least three modes of human communication – the verbal, the non-verbal active and the non-verbal material. None of them can be reduced to either of the others. Each has its own generative hierarchy consisting of a comparatively stable grammar which changes very slowly; the messages, which are composed of several signals and possess some stability; and individual signals, which are repeated, replicated and replaced more rapidly. As well as having their own replicative hierarchies, each of the three modes of communication constitutes a level in an operational hierarchy of community behaviour. On a relative space–time scale each class of active behaviour communication generates and sustains its messages over differing time spans. The relationship can be seen in the nature of everyday life. The active, non-verbal languages of kinesics and proxemics are learned at a slower rate and transform more slowly than verbal language. They possess more inertia. Proxemic behaviour is learned in the first ten to twelve years of life and kinesics takes even longer, about fifteen to seventeen years (Aiello and Aiello 1974). A verbal language, by contrast, can be learned in the first five to seven years of a child's life (Wells 1985). Verbal languages allow rapid changes of expression. We can learn new verbal languages with some facility and are well able to learn specific professional verbal languages. Body language is not so tractable (Hall 1966). It is harder to deceive using body language unless you are deliberately aware of the nature of the body language which you wish to exploit. But such awareness is uncommon. Our body language also tends to lag behind the changes of attitude which can be expressed verbally, producing dissonance, sometimes with unfortunate consequences for the sincerity we wish to convey!

Material messages possess even more inertia than non-verbal active signals. For example, if the spatial message of a settlement is to be coherent, there need to be enough constructions to carry a sufficiently repetitious set of distances. With only a few buildings, a predictable pattern is unlikely because the sample size will be too small. This has implications for the stability of group behaviour in very small communities or recently established settlements with one or two residence units. A message develops only gradually but, once established, it could endure for many years if it is carried by durable materials. A gradual increase in sample size should at first produce better defined and more stable distributions of spatial distances, though further copying may lead to loss of message coherence (pp. 38–40). The functioning of material behaviour as a message system extends to a larger space–time scale than the declarations and actions which constitute social and political activity.[5]

If verbal and non-verbal active communication are potentially dissonant, then the lack of correspondence between verbal messages and material messages must be even more marked. Though there must be some correspondence between message systems if group behaviour is to function, continual, total, logical coherence between different systems which replicate and change at differing rates cannot exist. Lag and non-correspondence is inherent in the unstable relationship between them, because messages which can be replicated rapidly will be able to diverge from the content of the slower ones. Unlike the biological system, therefore, the cultural system has several different heritable codes, each of which transmits a different kind of message at a different rate.

The dilemma of trying to relate verbal meaning to the material component of community life has confronted archaeology for several decades but has not been adequately resolved because non-verbal active signalling has largely been ignored and the material has not been given sufficient autonomy as a distinct message system. Once the category of the 'social' has been deconstructed into its component message systems, and the inertial effect of the material on interaction has been incorporated into social theory, the conventional meaning of the 'social' can be reconstituted to include these slow effects. The explanatory priority ascribed to action and verbal meaning can then be obviated.

Material inertia and changes in social action

The larger and more durable the material milieu becomes, the greater is the inertia in the framework within which the relatively rapid operations of verbal and active signalling take place. That inertia, combined with the particular form of a settlement, may then produce complications in the active behaviour of the community. If the material frame of a settlement loses coherence, whether because of increasing internal variability, or because its signal-control function breaks down and interaction becomes increasingly stressful, the residential context will have lost its predictability. Restricted social options and a perceptually confusing milieu could be expected to have adverse effects on the coherence of social life. With such a material context the community could not persist just by making changes to its short-term adaptive mechanisms of verbal expression and action. In the long term, if the material does not sufficiently control interaction and sustain communication, then the community ought to experience behavioural stress and fail to sustain itself as a viable entity. The material milieu may adversely affect interaction and become at odds with the social cohesion of a community. Without adequate interaction the community may be unable to cope with externally imposed pressures.

Dissonance between social needs and the material form of residential space may provide part of the explanation for the abandonment of the Mesa Verde region of Colorado in the late fourteenth century AD (Cordell 1984: 324–5; Rohn 1971). The larger Anasazi communities in the region had built themselves into masonry constructions each of which entirely filled a rock-shelter (Figure 3.2). An analysis of one such site, Mug House,[6] indicates that the settlement had locked its residents into a web of complex, stressful interaction (Fletcher 1985). Construction out to the drip-line placed the new buildings, around Kiva A, across the access ways of the older core units B and C (Figure 3.3). The effect was to make route movement very inconvenient for the occupants of the older residence units (Figure 3.4). They had to go up and down several floors and over the roofs of neighbouring residence units in order to get in or out. The core units were the first sector of the settlement to be abandoned. Their kivas were stripped of the fittings, burnt out and in ruins before the upper terrace rooms were abandoned (Fletcher 1985: 674–7; Rohn 1971: 27, 37). When the roof of Kiva C collapsed it removed the support for the ladder that led to an access door on the rear upper terrace. After the door was sealed up, occupation debris continued to pile up in the rear corridor of the upper terrace. Perceptual space had also become much more varied and restrictive in the late stages of occupation. For instance, in the earlier phases the residents could expect a clear space, several metres across, immediately in front of their doorways, both inside and outside the rooms (Figure 3.5). The amount of assuredly clear space can be identified by plotting all the walls which are on either side of, and opposite, the doors and then superimposing all the door positions on one diagram. In the late phase the clear space was very restricted and the relative positions of walls and doors were much more varied.

According to this scenario the space had become much more inconvenient and behavioural stress had begun to fragment the resident community, removing or dislocating co-operative social associations within it. But those associations would have been necessary to keep the agricultural economy viable in a marginal environment. The system of crop management on the plateau presumably disintegrated (Fletcher 1985: 677–9) because the communities could not then cope with the effects of the usual environmental stress produced by endemic droughts. They would no longer possess the economic co-operation needed to sustain the number of communities that had developed over the preceding centuries. The rock-shelter settlements were gradually abandoned. But the departure of the occupants was neither abrupt nor necessarily a biological disaster for the communities. In Mug House sealed-up rooms and stacks of domestic utensils and equipment (Rohn – field notes, Mesa Verde National Park) suggest that the owners intended to return. If so, the abandonment of the settlements was a continuation of an already existing seasonal or episodic movement between Mesa Verde and other localities. Seasonal movement became permanent departure, though that might not have been the original intention. The entire process could have occurred without significant loss of life. Abnormally high mortality rates are not immediately apparent in the late fourteenth century (Cordell 1984: 308–9). What certainly happened is that the emphasis on an aspect of the active behaviour of the community changed.

The proposed model is that social action could not prevent the development of a material framework which began to generate severe interaction stress. Nor could the community appropriately edit its material behaviour. According to this model, the community's material framework was unable to sustain tolerable interaction between the intra-settlement residential groups which had to co-operate in a marginal environment in order to manage food production. Coping with drought was not in itself the critical factor. The occupants had centuries of economic experience with endemic drought. The problem, rather, was that the community could not exert enough action to alter the material framework of the cliff dwellings. An *in situ* change was too difficult in the larger communities while the people's active behaviour possessed enough flexibility to allow an alternative survival strategy for each part of the community, using seasonal movement and relocation. The larger scale, slower material mechanisms selected against the social structure of the former community.

We cannot presume that the behaviour of communities is in equilibrium until disturbed by outside factors. Because behavioural variants are generated at random relative to circumstances, larger scale conditions external to the community might even remain stable while the smaller scale internal workings of the community continue to produce change. Whether the material milieu of a community is subject to some degree of internal change or whether it remains static depends upon internal

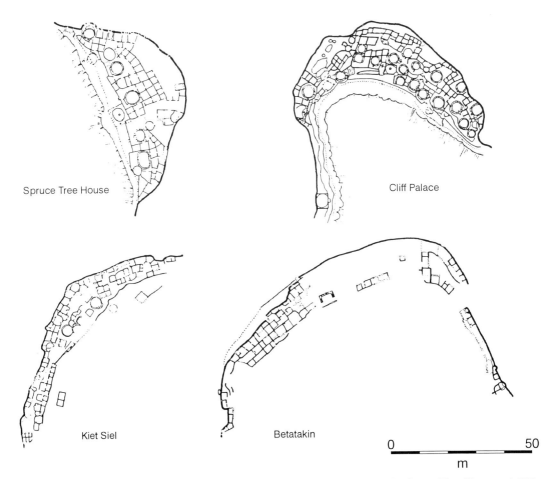

Figure 3.2 Large Anasazi sites, south-west USA, fourteenth century AD. Spruce Tree House and Cliff Palace are at Mesa Verde, Kiet Siel and Betatakin at Navaho National Park (after Marquina 1964)

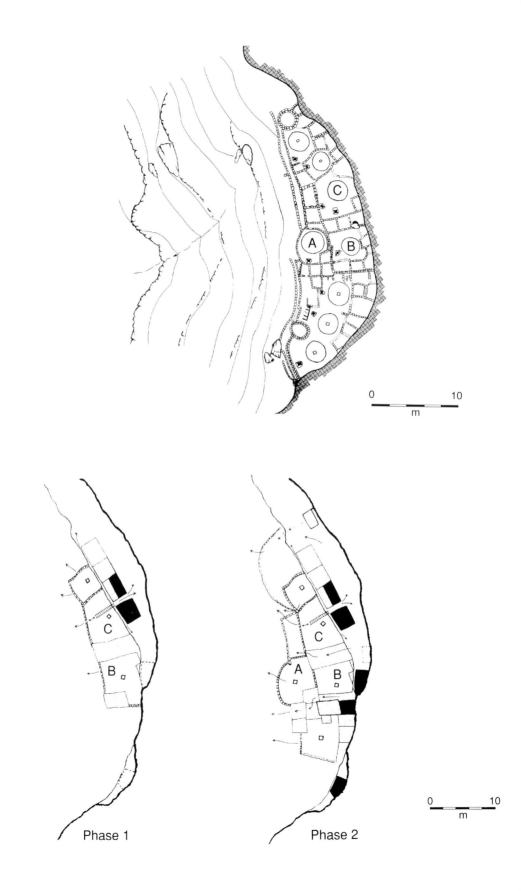

Phase 1   Phase 2

characteristics of its message structure not on directive influences from larger scale external factors.

A redefined explanatory hierarchy: the scaling of constraints and selection in human behaviour (Table 3.2)

Locating the material in the hierarchy
While material behaviour can constrain active behaviour, the effectiveness of a community's entire behavioural repertoire is, in turn, constrained at an even higher level by its supply of resources. The supply of resources and energy defines the working limits of a community's capacity to reproduce itself and its cultural assemblage. In principle, a community could have a viable, coherent system of interaction and communication and still fail to maintain itself because of a failure in its resource system. The community would have lost the input–output balance between its energy needs and its capacity to obtain energy. The appropriate operational level for the material lies below the scale of resource supply (which sets the limits on the overall viability of a community), while the large-scale component of the material lies above the level of active behaviour whose viability it delimits. Therefore the material as behaviour should be inserted into a redefined form of the familiar hierarchy at a level above the active non-verbal message systems and below the space–time scale of resource supply constraints.

The familiar hierarchy can now be converted into a hierarchy of behavioural operational levels with their corresponding message systems. The internal constraints on coherence within each level can be designated and the way in which each operational level exerts selective pressure on the functional viability of the levels below it can be specified. The behavioural hierarchy fits into a greater hierarchy of the external constraints arising from resource supply and environmental dynamics.

Internal sorting due to the constraint of code consistency
Biological replication has an internal hierarchy through which heritable characteristics are generated and made available for selection by environmental factors external to the phenotype (Vrba and Gould 1986: 220–1). In its most recent expression Kauffman has argued for self-organising within the genetic system as well as the role of external selection in the creation of biological forms (1993: vii, xiv–vi).

Figure 3.3 Mug House, Mesa Verde, south-west USA, fourteenth century AD (after Rohn 1971)
(a) general plan

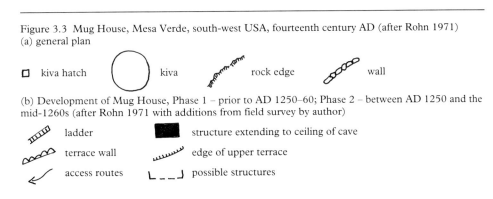

☐ kiva hatch   kiva   rock edge   wall

(b) Development of Mug House, Phase 1 – prior to AD 1250–60; Phase 2 – between AD 1250 and the mid-1260s (after Rohn 1971 with additions from field survey by author)

ladder   structure extending to ceiling of cave

terrace wall   edge of upper terrace

access routes   ⌐ _ _ ⌐ possible structures

Table 3.2 Locating the material component of human behaviour in a hierarchy of explanation for human community life

The parameters of resource supply which specify the limits within which communities can sustain themselves fit into the familiar biological and geological hierarchies which define the boundary conditions within which the stable transformation of ecosystems occurs. Above the level of resource supply is the even larger scale of major environmental change. Very long-term trajectories and periodicities of geomorphic and climatic changes such as plate tectonics and the glacial cycle set the parameters within which a community's resource supply system can operate adequately. They exert selective pressure upon ecological balance and thence on resource supply.

Rate of Signal Operation	Message Form	Internal Sorting	Operational Entity	Parameter Conditions	Scale
FAST	Electro-chemical	Logical code coherence	Individual	Social tolerance limit	SMALL
	Verbal and Active	Grammatical code coherence			
	Non-verbal active	Gestural - positional code coherence	Community		
SLOW	Material	Metrical code coherence	Material Behaviour assemblage	Interaction - Communication limits	
			Resource Supply	Energy Input/output balance	
			Natural Environment	Ecological balance	LARGE

COMMUNITY

ENVIRONMENT

Selection effect

Likewise each of the human message systems also has its own replicative hierarchy. Within a replicative hierarchy a process of internal sorting in terms of formal or meaning correspondence regulates the relationship between an existing message structure and a new signal. Each message system produces a surplus of signals. Because all communication involves some redundancy, there is, for instance, sorting pressure on material spatial signals, in terms of the degree to which a signal is adequately consistent with the internal structure of the existing material message system (see pp. 40–1). Similarly, for a community to have coherent social inter-action, or for cogent thought to exist within a human brain, new signals have to mesh adequately with the existing message codes and their elaborate associated verbal meanings and electrochemical format. In the process the details of the code formats are themselves partially altered. They do not possess closed logic and are vulnerable to change due to replicative variance arbitrarily inserting an anomalous signal, whether into a spatial message or into the coding of the human brain.

For either verbal or active non-verbal communication the likelihood of losing internal message coherence is low because continual, rapid replication can quickly provide a range of potentially coherent adjustments. For material behaviour, however, as the inertia of the material increases, so the loss of message coherence becomes more likely, because signals of disparate age can remain in the material assemblage. The range of variation is liable to increase and swamp the internal code order of the message. Similarly for the message-control function of the material a community continually creates new material features, both trivial and relatively substantial, which block active signalling. These material frames may also be cumulatively more difficult to remove. If they fail to assist signal transmission or actually create a milieu inconsistent with the active behaviour of the community, eventually the inhabitants will seek in some fashion to escape from it.

Boundary conditions and the role of selection between levels
External boundary conditions or parameters, such as the net balance between energy input and output in resource supply, delimit the degree to which the characteristics of substantial material features on the next step down in the hierarchy can persist. A community might attempt to construct buildings which use up more resources than the economic system can continue to obtain. Nothing prevents the community from causing enormous economic and ecological damage, but it will not be able to persist in doing so. In the most extreme case, either the construction policy will be abandoned or, in combination with other problems, the community will collapse. A community can alter and destroy specific features of its natural environment but that in no way changes the operational boundary conditions which define whether or not an ecological system will persist or will break down to a new stable level of lower energy and order. It is the parameters of the larger scale operational level which apply selective pressure, not the particulars of the economy or the environment. The latter, in conjunction with the contextually unique social character of a community, just produce distinct local effects. Similarly, human action can alter particulars of material behaviour, such as room sizes and their

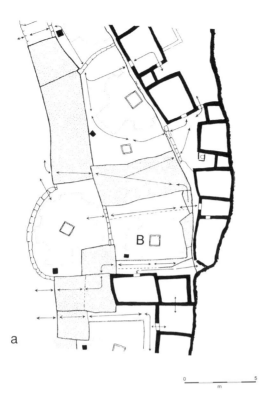

a

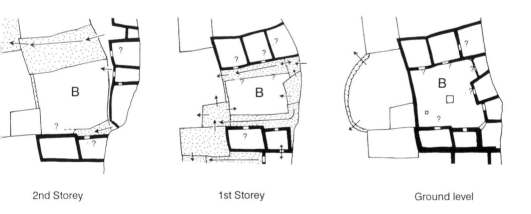

2nd Storey   1st Storey   Ground level

Figure 3.4 Route access problems in the core area of Mug House (after Fletcher 1985)
(a) kiva courtyards at level of upper terrace
(b) three levels of access around kiva courtyard B

☐   kiva hatch   ■   vent shaft   edge of balcony

     terrace wall   ladder grooves   routes

     roof and balcony surface   ? door uncertain

The plan represents a route pattern extending over a vertical height of three to four storeys. Occupants from the rear of the settlement had to climb over the roofs of other residence units up and down several storeys in order to get in and out of their residence units.

arrangement. But that does not change the limits of viable interaction and communication set by the requirements of predictability, i.e. tolerable information load and manageable interaction frequency. If the residential milieu lacks spatial consistency, creates severe inconvenience or does not adequately control noise, then the community will be adversely affected.

The failure of communities may therefore be due to factors operating at three different levels in the hierarchy. They may fail as a result of problems which accumulate over differing spans of time. At the level of verbal and active signalling, socio-political disintegration may result when there is a failure to manage short-term disputes and contradictions within the community. On a longer timescale, communities will fail when the general frequency of interaction cannot be kept under control by material phenomena or the communication system cannot cope with the

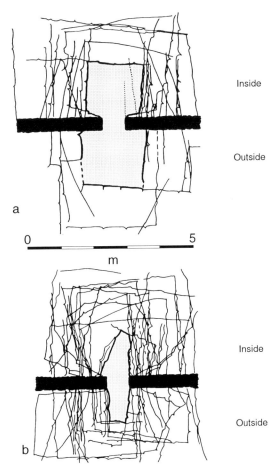

Figure 3.5 Plan view of the reduction in the spatial field around doorways in Mug House from (a) the early phase to (b) the late phase shortly before abandonment (from field survey by author)
The figure is produced by superimposing every doorway on the schematic door in the centre and then plotting in the nearest walls both outside and inside every room on the one diagram. The shaded area is the minimum, assured, open space on either side of the set of all doorways for each phase.

size of the community through which the messages must be transmitted. The source of the stresses will be ordinary daily activity, not overt, well-defined social or political oppositions, though presumably the breakdown of the community will, in due course, be expressed in that form in a contextually unique fashion. The third possibility is the demise of communities which are socially and behaviourally coherent but cannot survive as a biological group because of economic or environmental disasters.

Implications of the hierarchy and indeterminacy

When the notion of the material as behaviour is incorporated into the hierarchy, it introduces another class of player, the material framework of a community, into the ecological game. Varied combinations of internal and external change will be possible. The indeterminacy between levels means that the outcome will depend upon how they are associated, not on the content of one level determining the occurrence of the other. What can be specified, however, is that for particular circumstances there should be a potentially definable class of outcome, whether the expansion, persistence or failure of the community, depending on the material features which individuals introduce and the community adopts.

By breaking the inclusive category of the 'social' into its active and material components, social analysis can retain its distinctiveness from biological theory while both are simultaneously linked into a hierarchy of explanations. In archaeological contexts where long-term outcomes are to be explained, the freedom of conventional 'social' views from arguments in favour of biological determinacy can be secured without a rejection of the significance of behavioural and biological analyses of human communities. The risk inherent in asserting the dominance of verbal declaration and action in the interpretation of culture while marginalising material culture as epiphenomenal, is that a direct link is created from culture to biology via action. This juxtaposition is potent because it has permitted the specious assumption of a direct link between demography, the impact of resource supply and the nature of human social life which has been taken up to such effect in sociobiology. Though this view is vigorously opposed by social theorists, such as Sahlins (1977), the use of social theory in long-term contexts is continually vulnerable to this tempting segue from the action component of the 'social' directly to the biological, sometimes via 'economic' factors. The interposition of the material in a hierarchical approach to the explanation of human behaviour provides a shield to protect theories of human action from this liability.

A hierarchical reconciliation of viewpoints

The behaviour of a human community consists of a hierarchy of message systems with different rates of change and differing magnitudes of effect over different spans of time (Fletcher 1988: 37–8; 1992: 45–7). This hierarchy is the behavioural equivalent of the general hierarchy of physiological rates of change which is crucial to biological adaptation (Bateson 1972: 316–33; Bonner 1980: 62–3). It is of considerable adaptive value because rapid initial changes to the 'phenotype' (message form) can occur, to cope with abrupt changes of circumstance, followed eventually by longer term, enduring changes to the 'genotype' (message code). If all adjustments could only be abrupt and permanent, the changing entity would lose replicative coherence because each entity would produce sudden irreversible variants of itself in response to idiosyncratic circumstances. This is a fundamental criticism of the Lamarckian model of evolution (Bateson 1972: 324–5) and applies equally to physiology and behaviour. Alternatively, if all change could only be gradual, then coping with abrupt changes of circumstance would be difficult. The advantage of having several rates of adjustment is that rapid superficial change can occur in the message systems with a fast replication rate, continually producing changes which may be of adaptive value without requiring substantial and irreversible alterations of behaviour. More gradual, sustained change derives from the more slowly replicating material forms to provide a coherent, general framework for community life which does not tightly restrict active behaviour. A hierarchy of message systems with differing rates of coherent change serves our adaptive capacity.

In general, verbal messages provide a continual restatement of the possible meanings which can be applied to the daily concerns of the community. Individuals using this message system are deliberately seeking to create meaning. One particular role of verbal language is to try and make sense of the extensive unstated, tacit component of human non-verbal behaviour by offering explanations of the patterned behaviour which we unwittingly produce. People are generally not aware of the patterns in their non-verbal active behaviour and do not live long enough to make sense of the large-scale patterns or effects of their material behaviour. Verbal meaning is therefore applied to bring that uneasy ignorance under some conscious control. The actors themselves can do it. So can an observer, such as an archaeologist, striving to comprehend what the material is and actually does.

Introducing the behavioural role of the material as a distinct scale of analysis extends the content of social analysis and separates it out into components with differing operational scales, which have to be analysed differently. The active, verbal level of behaviour possesses the capacity for the proliferation of meaning which is its particular glory. The active expressions of culture are the means by which we remake our views of the world and ourselves. The material also carries meaning but in a far more rudimentary form than active message systems. Unlike the active forms of signalling, the material offers us less latitude to play games. Its inertia constitutes a distinct problem with which active behaviour has to cope but this inertia can also contribute to the coherence of community life.

The model predicts that if the coherence of the material message is lost and this cannot be rectified, or the material controls on interaction are inadequate, insufficiently maintained or unduly restrictive, then the effects of the material features will extend down the operational hierarchy and have a deleterious impact on the capacity of active behaviour to keep the community together. At the most extreme, the material frame would select against a community being able to continue in its settlement. But the converse will also be possible. Major changes in a material assemblage might act as a shield for the formation of a new mode of active behaviour. The material would preferentially select for particular variants of the verbal and active components of a community's behaviour. This may seem rather odd but the operational hierarchy implies no particular temporal order in the sequence of changes at different levels. The active correlate of a material feature can develop relatively rapidly and therefore should be able to come into being some time after the initial development of the material feature with which it eventually becomes associated. Somewhat paradoxically, therefore, a form of active behaviour which, in due course, coexists with a material assemblage need not have been the initial cause of the development of that assemblage.

The relationship between material and 'social' phenomena can now be further clarified in terms of the respective duration of the differing kinds of events. Within the class of material behaviour there are faster and slower events of varying magnitudes. For permanently sedentary groups some aspects of material behaviour, such as settlement form, transform comparatively slowly and are replicated relatively infrequently. This kind of material can endure for a long time and may be very extensive. Change in the smaller components of an assemblage, such as pottery form, is much more rapid and small scale. While the levels of the operational hierarchy can be arranged in terms of the magnitude of the larger scale phenomena which each produces, there is obviously a closer equivalence of replicative rate between the small behavioural features of one level and the larger scale component of the level below it. Close correspondence between material and active social phenomena should therefore depend upon near-equivalence in scale and rate of change. The more rapid the replication rates and the closer the correspondence of rate, the better the match between them should be. Changes in small decorative items and pottery should relate comparatively well to rates of active social change. But as the magnitude of the entities increases and the replication rates slow down, as is the case with durable buildings, more intervening inertia and differential replication arises, preventing sustained, stable, close correspondence between the material and the 'social'. The relationship between material and active behaviour will therefore vary across the scale of their respective operations. While the larger-scale aspects of the material act as a selective milieu for active behaviour, the small-scale features should be the appropriate field for the pursuit of social reconstructions based on material–'social' correlates (Deetz 1977; Miller 1987; Shanks and Tilley 1987a; Spector 1993).

Just as an analysis of material behaviour cannot provide deterministic statements about smaller-scale cultural phenomena, so likewise historical and social analyses of the activities and declarations of human beings cannot be a precondition for the study of the material as behaviour. An independent understanding of the long-term role of the material in controlling interaction and aiding communication is necessary. Without it, a contextual analysis of the relationship between social and material meaning structures will be incomplete and a functionalist search for large-scale 'processes' and explanations appropriate to the archaeological record will be partial and problematic. These various analyses are complementary and different, but are currently incomplete (Preucel 1991; Yoffee and Sherratt 1993). They are not in conflict, and artificial disputes in which one claims superiority over another are futile and self-serving. Versions of the contextual, formal and adaptational explanatory positions should be reconcilable since they properly apply to analyses of differing scales of cultural patterning.

Material assemblages, interaction and changes in resource supply
The material carries the largest-scale, slowest cultural message system. Not only must it be internally coherent if it is to assist the functioning of a community, but it is also constrained by the available energy supply. Only those material assemblages which are within the economic capacity of a community and are ecologically viable will persist in the long term. Disputes between internalist 'social' explanations of material assemblages and externalist 'adaptational' interpretations are unnecessary because there is no dichotomy between them once the differing operational levels to which they apply are appreciated. According to this model behavioural coherence needs to be satisfied within a comparatively short time if interaction is to be viable. Communities can cope with, or ignore, the slower impact of resource failure and ecological damage for far longer. Only in the long term can some aspect of the material be understood as having either an adaptive or a maladaptive effect on a community. The entity did not originate in order to have whatever outcome it has produced, nor need it have been of adaptive value to the community to form a coherent part of an assemblage.

The logic of the hierarchy removes the necessity for a direct connection between changes in the material behaviour which manages interaction and communication and changes in resource supply. Neither can have a directive effect on the other because the parameters of resource supply do not direct the production of material behaviour; they only delimit the consequences which follow from whatever is produced at that operational level. Therefore we should not expect direct and inevitable correlations between economic change and changes in material behaviour and settlement size. We should look instead at the varying outcomes of different combinations of change in actions, the material and resource supply.

Our view of the relationship is somewhat coloured by the recent juxtaposition of such changes during the 'Industrial Revolution' of the eighteenth to nineteenth century AD in Europe (Deane 1979; Langton and Morris 1986). This classic case of the coupling of social change, alterations in material interaction–communication assemblages and major changes in the supply and management of resources has given the impression that they normally go together, operate together and should be understood together. The problem with generalising from the Industrial Revolution is that there has been only one example of an initial industrial transformation of that magnitude. We have no independent comparative case. The Industrial Revolution extended the political dominance of European society and technology across almost the entire planet, in an expansion so rapid that it has precluded any other initial, indigenous development of industrial communities. As a result, the Industrial

Revolution is a single, potentially atypical case, as is suggested by the evidence that there was only a partial association of changes in resource supply and social change during the earlier great transformations – the development of sedentism and the growth of the early urban settlements of the first civilisations (Chapters 7 and 8). As Adams emphasises, in the complex linkage between resource management and social change the former cannot properly be regarded as the directive agent (1981: 243–7). According to the selectionist premiss of the explanatory hierarchy, we should take the decoupling of the different kinds of change even further. Instead of asking 'what causes what', we should instead consider what happens to settlement size and the persistence of the community when the various kinds of social, material and resource change do or do not coincide. There will be consistencies of outcome but not of deterministic association. Just because a community possesses the material behaviour which would allow it to grow, we cannot predict that a change in resource supply which would serve that purpose will inevitably take place. Nor, conversely, can we presume that human action will necessarily create the material means required to manage the behaviour of a population which is increasing due to changes in resource supply. If such linkage were predictable we would be living in a Panglossian world where opportunity is always seized and problems create their solutions. The association or lack of it in a particular region therefore becomes an issue of local cultural factors rather than a consequence of general causal processes. But, at a larger scale of enquiry, the consequences of an association between material behaviour and economics or of a change in one without change in the other should be predictable regardless of the unique initial cause. By decoupling the effects of behaviour and resource supply we can see what each contributes to settlement growth. We may then be able to predict what happens when they coincide, instead of concentrating on the search for universal explanations of why they are sometimes found together.

Conclusions

The proposed explanatory hierarchy integrates differing explanatory modes without reductionism or determinism. It uses selectionist logic and indeterminacy to relate different operational levels of behaviour. The hierarchy depends upon parameters which specify the outcome of a behavioural event but do not predefine the circumstances in which the event initially occurs. The operational limits of the capacity of material behaviour to manage interaction and communication will have a selective impact on community life, perhaps even against the continuing existence of a community.

Assessing the role of the material requires attention to its internal dynamics, the boundary conditions it sets on the functioning of the level below and the larger-scale factors which, in turn, act as selective agents upon it. The regulative and restrictive role of the material can therefore be analysed in its own terms without reference to the specific details of a community's verbal meanings and social actions. We can avoid falling into the dual trap of either rejecting adaptation or being obliged to produce a deterministic form of explanation. What must be taken into account, however, is the selective effect of resource supply, ecology and the physical environment. Within this analytic frame of reference the behavioural parameters of interaction and communication stress now have to be defined so that we may identify the contexts in which the material might significantly aid or obstruct settlement growth.

PART II

The limits of settlement growth: behavioural stress and the material management of community life

4

The behavioural parameters of interaction and communication

The degree to which material entities can effectively control or aid social life is defined by the finite capacity of the human sensory system. Because only a finite amount of information can be handled by the human brain in a limited period of time (Driscoll and Corpolango 1980: 207; Halford, Maybury and Bain 1988; Miller 1956; Pasher 1993; Van Dorn, Van de Grind and Koenderink 1984), the aggregate amount of interaction which we can manage is also limited. After a while continued input leads to incoherence of response, whatever the specific capacity of the sensory system. This is a very obvious, unremarkable and inevitable operational characteristic of the brain and its sensors. The system is finite and is subject to internal transmission delays and errors, along with random and false signals (Ashby 1960; Dixon 1981; Zechmeister and Nyberg 1982). These constraints are inherent to any biological mechanism for perceiving and processing information about reality. They are as applicable to the past as they are to the present.

Humans can think about almost anything but they cannot deal with everything at once. Overt decision-making is significantly affected by the limits on what we can take in. Some of the problems associated with rationalist models of economic behaviour are due to the assumption that people take into account all the relevant factors when they make decisions (Herrnstein and Mazur 1987; Pottinger 1983). The limitations on what we can assimilate have even more effect on tacit behaviour. As is apparent in proxemic behaviour, people have no conscious awareness of the selectivity they are practising. It creates a predictable context which keeps down the degree of stimulus produced by the social environment and allows individuals to function competently. Predictable contexts and material devices which control the signal load in a settlement are therefore of profound importance because they can create tolerable conditions for social life within the operable bounds of our finite ability to cope with stimuli. The corollary, of course, is that an inadequate material context would be one which does not create such a setting and allows active stress to affect a community adversely.

Interaction–communication stress model: an operational uniformitarian proposition

The finite analytic and data storage capacity of the human sensory system provides the basis for a further proposition, which falls into the class of operational uniformitarianism (see pp. 230–1), about the elementary behavioural parameters of social life. What is now required is to specify the behavioural parameters of interaction and communication and then to identify them empirically. From those parameters and the connection between them, it should be possible to specify the circumstances in which communities will be unable to interact and communicate adequately. The general characteristics of the different kinds of cultural assemblages which serve to manage communities of differing size and residential density can also be outlined. The relationship between them and the behavioural parameters of community life should be of some relevance for our understanding of the long-term consequences of settlement growth and the nature of large-scale transformations of residential organisation.

Interaction frequency

The term 'interaction' is used in its broadest sense to cover all media and channels of interaction. The actors need not intend to interact and affect each other. Their intentions do not concern this enquiry. Visual and auditory signals have an impact whether or not we want to notice them. They extract a behavioural cost: some effort is needed to ignore extraneous signals. Newspapers which blow away and wrap around your legs affect you.

The occupants of a settlement interact with each other not merely in face-to-face contact with a small number of people whom they know well but also in aggregate. We are affected by other people's actions whether or not we acknowledge the fact. Rush-hour traffic speeds, queuing for cinemas, the effects of pollution, roads blocked by the re-laying of gas pipes or by garbage trucks removing other people's rubbish are irritants produced by the aggregate interaction between all the people who live in a city. Similarly, telephone systems which allow you to speak across the world may be locally overloaded by more signal traffic than the mechanical system, the operators or the recipients of the messages can handle. Individual intentions to interact can be thwarted by the aggregate load which the communication system is obliged to carry. People you have never met or spoken to can, without deliberate intent on their part, prevent you from contacting a friend.

The effects of the aggregate interaction of a group of people who live near one another in a settlement influence the degree to which viable interaction and communication can be sustained. What, then, are the overall conditions which allow a resident community to be viable? The parameters can be given a material quantitative form because they are a function of rates of activity, numbers of people, amounts of space and degrees of material inertia. We should not imagine that social, active behaviour will suffice to control interaction stress. All such active behaviour is itself part of the interaction generated by a community. Practising a social rule which restricts particular interactions, e.g. mother-in-law avoidance, may make life easier for some people but requires the exercise of self-control by the avoider. The likelihood of the presence of the person who must be avoided demands information-processing and decision-making, however tacit. Social devices for controlling interaction events do not therefore absorb or reduce the aggregate degree of inter-action; they merely reallocate the stress to someone else.

In contrast, materials do cut down the absolute amount of signal transmission impinging on the occupants of a settlement. Brick walls block sound transmission. However, while some arrangement of walling will serve to cut down this kind of interaction without inconvenience, the relief provided by the material barrier may be gained at the expense of accessibility. Material barriers obstruct some of the freedom of movement across residential space. Particular journeys will be relatively inefficient because straight-line access is obstructed. These material barriers and facilities also extract a price in terms of the energy needed to produce them. Baffles and barriers, such as durable walling and double glazing, serve to reduce the signal load with which we must cope but themselves involve costs of production and maintenance. If insufficient investment is made in material screening, the costs of interaction stress should show up in problems of active behaviour (Fletcher 1981a: 98). The social effects might include varying degrees of social pathology (Calhoun 1971; Galle, Grove and McPherson 1972), social reallocation of stress (Anderson 1972; Kaye 1960; Mitchell 1971), or patterns of stress and group or individual mobility (Draper 1973; Krupat 1985: 95–127). If, however, the community attempts to invest in material controls, the stresses it is trying to combat may be so severe that it will be unable to sustain the economic cost of the required material context. The ability of human communities to control behavioural stress, produce material barriers to interaction and manage the consequences, is finite.

If human groups can therefore tolerate only finite amounts of interaction, because neither the social nor the material has unlimited regulatory capacity, there will be an upper limit on the residential densities which can be carried by a community. As more people are packed into a finite space, so the incidence of the interaction events between them will increase until it reaches an uncontrollable intensity. An expression of the limit should therefore show up as a constraint on the maximum operable residential densities (Fletcher 1981a: 98) beyond which human communities have difficulty in persisting. Such an interaction limit should be relatively intractable and quite conspicuous.

Interaction limits (I-limits)
The nature of such an upper limit on residential densities should allow us to assess whether or not the tolerance of interaction remains relatively constant for communities of differing size (Fletcher 1981a). If the constraint remains constant, then we should find that the density ceiling decreases with an increase in community size. As people aggregate in larger numbers they will need, on average, more space per person because they are increasingly subject to more interaction effects which increase exponentially (Johnson 1982: 392) (Figure 4.1). If there is an absolute limit to the amount of interaction that people can tolerate, then the maximum operable residential densities should generally be lower for increasingly large communities (Figure 4.2).

The problem in obtaining empirical evidence of residential densities for contemporary and recent communities lies in the uncertainty inherent in the definitions of both the size of the population and the settlement area. We therefore have to accept some degree of uncertainty and inconsistency if cross-cultural comparison is to be feasible.[1] Since we want to find out whether the comparative approach is informative or not, the most appropriate strategy is to examine large-scale patterns which do not require precise description. Once these have been identified and their significance has been evaluated, we can then decide whether a commitment to precise, exactly repeatable measurement is worth while or necessary. We may find that tolerance of some error and uncertainty makes little difference to the results. At present the search for exactitude is probably a forlorn enterprise. Exact, cross-culturally consistent definitions of settlement area cannot be specified. Estimates of settlement area are therefore inherently imprecise. Likewise, estimates of community size for many settlements will also remain inherently vague and unreliable, until we devise new ways, in the absence of detailed census records, to estimate precisely the numbers of people in a settlement. We have to accept that an inter-action density limit will not be recognisable as a rigorously defined exact line. Rather it will constitute a zone beyond which examples are improbable. To take account of the coarse quality of the data which we can expect from interregional comparisons, and to allow for cross-comparison between disparate classes of settlement, I have adopted the policy of using overall settlement area estimates which encompass 'built' space and an extensive definition of the adjacent occupation space (Fletcher 1981a, 1986), i.e. a broad characterisation of settlement area.[2] Similarly, community size is taken to be a general estimate of the number of residents at a given

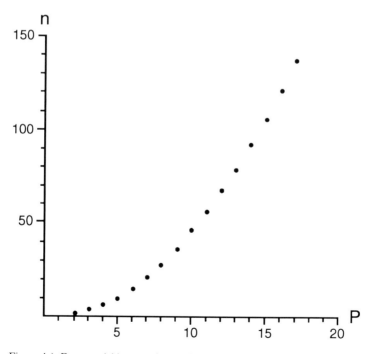

Figure 4.1 Exponential increase in potential interaction frequency as group size increases

$$n = \frac{P \times (P - 1)}{2}$$ where n is the number of potential interactions and P is community size

time. Direct estimates by observers of the settlement or reports from government agencies are used. Overall descriptions are used because they are the only kind of community size estimates which are readily available and whose interregionally comparative status is apparent.

On this basis overall residential densities can be obtained for settlements from all over the world with different economies and differing modes of social and political organisation. This grab sample from the past two millennia suggests that an approximate upper density limit, which declines as community size increases, can be recognised (Figure 4.3).[3] A further indication of the upper limit zone for the familiar category of permanent sedentary communities living in agrarian villages and in towns or cities can be provided by looking at some regional samples (Figure 4.4).[4] The three lines represent the band within which most of the cases of highest density lie. The top line merely includes possible high values, e.g. for the pueblo sample and from the Indian census of towns and cities in 1961. In any one region residential densities can lie well below the world-wide interaction limit (Figure 4.5). The limit is not a deterministic boundary to which all settlements will rise.

In broad terms there appears to be an upper limit but we should not attempt to define it too narrowly. The uncertainties in population estimates and in defining the edges of settlement area are acceptable provided we do not look for too much exactitude in the results. Though the overall interaction limit cannot therefore be precisely described, we can nevertheless bracket its position on the diagram. The likely band is discernible by looking at contrasting ways of describing settlement area in relation to the size of the resident community. If we use a narrow definition of the space within a settlement, such as central area density, we should expect the maximum densities to be at or to exceed the upper limit for the overall densities.

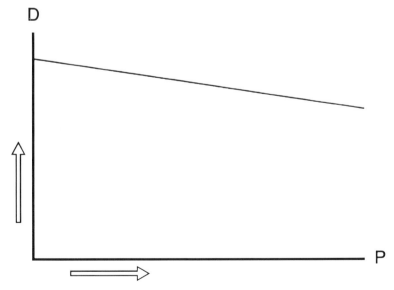

Figure 4.2 Hypothetical interaction limit (schematic)
D = density   P = community size

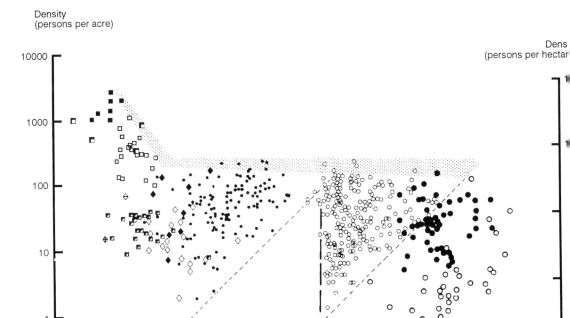

Figure 4.3 Interaction limits – a residential density index derived from densities in a sample of huma communities from 700 BC to the 1970s AD (after Fletcher 1981 – note original in imperial units)

⊕ ◇ ▫ ■ ▫ ◪ various hunter-gatherer communities

◆ Northwest Coast Indians

• small-scale agricultural communities

○ agrarian-based urban communities

● ○ industrial urban communities

│ minimum community size recorded for Indian census 1881

░░░ overall density limit (see later as an I-limit)

╱ major area front (see later as C-limits)

╲ proposed density ceiling for 'mobile' communities (see later as an I-limit)

Note: Original figure included data for the Tasaday, who must now be removed from the listing of mobile communities (see discussions on the 'invention' of the Tasaday). Tentative 'mobile' I-limit is marked by the solid line sloping down from the top left of the figure (see Figure 4.7 below for furthe: detail).

Conversely, if we use area estimates that include substantial portions of open agricultural land, then the maximum estimates should lie below the limit for the overall densities. The difference between the two sets of figures will indicate the approximate position of the interaction limit. For industrial cities this comparison can be made from two different sets of census reports, one referring to central area densities in the 1980s and the other from the 1960s, referring to extensive regional descriptions which include rural land (Figure 4.6a).[5] For preindustrial cities the same kind of contrast can be seen between an officially defined sample from India in 1881 and a world-wide grab sample of cases with varying degrees of reliability (Figure 4.6b). The 1881 census of India figures derives from the more inclusive administrative boundaries of the settlements which contain some

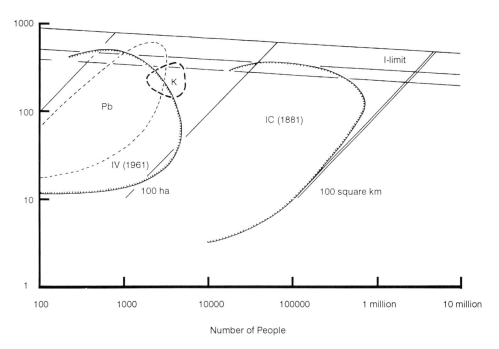

Figure 4.4 Residential densities by region

edge of zone of occurrence of density values for each region

Overall I-limit is a schematic representation and derives from the data in Figure 4.6 combined with the urban and village census data for India in 1961. The three lines of the I-limit do not have a precise mathematical status. They merely provide an impression of the upper and lower edges of the band within which the I-limit is likely to be located.
Pb = Pueblos (1940s) (see Stubbs 1950 and Figure 7.4)
K = Khatmandu (1960s) (see Khatmandu valley report)
IV = India – villages (see 1961 census)
IC = India – towns and cities (see 1881 census)

rural land. By contrast, the sample of towns and cities from all over the world during the past 1,000–1,500 years yields a higher upper density limit since it is based primarily on reports of observed settlement area or on the fortified perimeter of a settlement.

As well as a general decrease in maximum overall residential densities there also appears to be a more restricted range of residential densities for 'mobile' communities (Fletcher 1990, 1991a: 398–400) (Figure 4.3). A larger sample of residential density data of varying reliability for 'mobile' communities of widely differing sizes from the eighteenth to the twentieth century AD (Figure 4.7)[6] suggests that the upper edge of this range might therefore constitute another interaction limit. The issue is the kind of communities to which it might apply, since there appears to be a continuum of mobility between nomadism and sedentism (Kent 1989: 2–3). If, as currently seems to be the case, there is an interaction limit which constrains both the seasonally sedentary communities, of the kind seen on the north-west coast of America and in Amazonia, and also sets a ceiling on the average densities within nomadic camps, then it may be of some consequence for the way we understand the formation of permanent sedentary communities at high densities beyond that limit (see p. 171). Explaining how sedentism, as broadly defined,

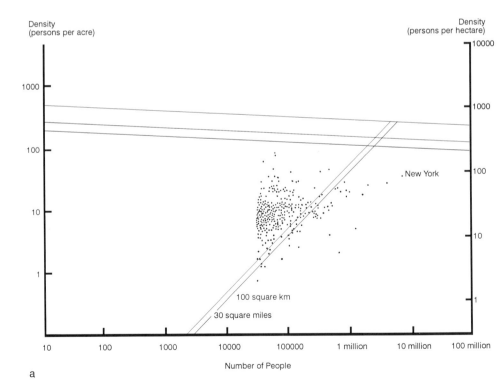

Figure 4.5 Local density limits for specific regions (after Fletcher 1981a – note original in imperial units)
(a) USA (*1940 Metropolitan Year Book*)

develops and is sustained has vexed anthropology and archaeology. We may find that too many different modes of behaviour have become subsumed under the label 'sedentism'. It is not that there is only one correct use of the term 'sedentary' but that different kinds of sedentism may be possible, depending upon residential density, community size and settlement size. Not only must we consider varied patterns of aggregation and dispersal in discussions of sedentism (Kent 1989: 135), but we must also consider residential packing in relation to the magnitude of the aggregate residential group.

If two different density-limit gradients exist, then mobile communities (including seasonal sedentaries) are less tolerant of increasing interaction stress as community size increases than are communities of the same size which we habitually regard as sedentary. Varying combinations of short residence periods, changing membership of resident groups and the seasonal formation of new occupation sites should militate against cumulative interactive predictability. Locational stress would therefore be more likely because the context of activity is less predictable. The details of the social relationships which manage interaction in the spectrum of 'mobile' communities at different residential densities have been analysed by Whitelaw (1983, 1989). Social complexity, for example, has been recognised as a

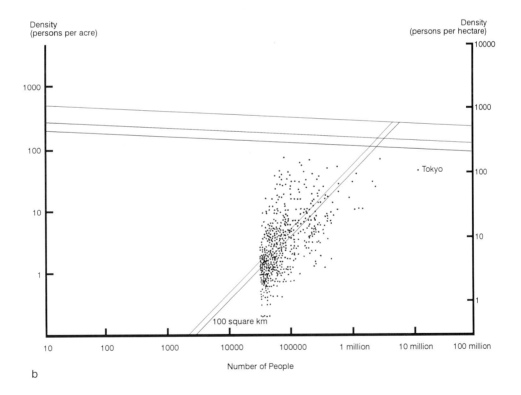

Figure 4.5
(b) Japan (1971 census)

concomitant of seasonal sedentism (Kent 1989: 5–6, 130; Price and Brown 1985). But, because active behaviour cannot absorb stress, active social strategies would not in themselves suffice to move communities beyond the density barrier. What the claim for a 'mobile' interaction limit predicts is that seasonal sedentism, whether or not associated with social complexity, cannot be regarded with assurance as an antecedent or incipient form of permanent sedentism in larger, compact settlements.

The 'sedentary' I-limit appears as a special extension beyond the combinations of density and community size found in nomadic and seasonally sedentary communities. The spectacular growth of human communities in the past 10,000 years might therefore be the product of a break-out beyond whatever constraints are represented by the proposed 'mobile' interaction limit. If, to achieve such a breakthrough, substantial problems of interaction and communication stress have to be overcome, then sustained permanent residence in one place should require material features which offer predictable patterning, signal control and spatial differentiation. These could initially help a community to manage interaction among people who

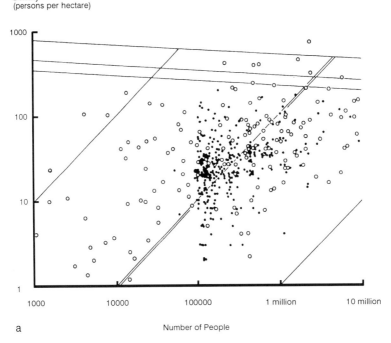

Figure 4.6 Bracketing the position of the sedentary I-limit
(a) different descriptions of residential density for industrial cities

o   central urban area densities of capital cities
    (from *Britannica Book of the Year* 1985: 832)

•   urban region densities
    (from *Annuaire de Statistique Internationale des Grandes Villes* 2, 1963)

are in habitual, unavoidably close proximity to one another and to the debris they produce. Combinations of stress, dietary problems and disease ought otherwise to be a severe obstacle to a viable, permanent, sedentary lifestyle (Cohen and Armelagos 1984; Kent 1986, 1989: 2). In mobile groups by contrast, individuals can resolve their interpersonal problems with little difficulty by leaving the resident community (Draper 1973) and, at the same time, escape the disease vectors and discomfort caused by domestic rubbish. If material features are required to enable an initial shift to permanent sedentism to occur, they must therefore first appear in communities which are not permanently sedentary.

However, it is not absolutely clear whether the proposed 'mobile' interaction limit is an otherwise immutable limit or whether there is a gradation of density constraints which might be attained as communities become more and more sedentary. If the former, it is an intensely restrictive limit which places tight bounds on the possible development of permanent sedentism. This would suggest a profound difference between the behavioural effects of brief, episodic, partial mobility in permanently sedentary communities and the mobility of seasonally sedentary communities which

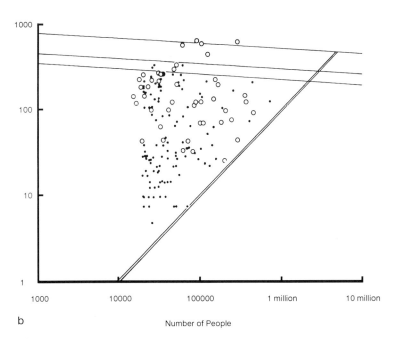

b   Number of People

Figure 4.6
(b) density estimates from two samples of agrarian-based urban settlements

• Indian urban centres (from Imperial census 1881)

o general sample of agrarian-based urban settlements prior to AD 1850
(from Chandler and Fox 1974)

Note: I have excluded Chandler and Fox's own estimates. An updated version of the 1974 volume has now been published by Chandler (1989).

retain a settlement of perennially reusable habitations. If, however, there is a gradation of density conditions, the maximum densities known for nomadic and seasonally sedentary groups could be readily and gradually exceeded by communities that are becoming progressively less mobile. Communities which gradually become less and less mobile would be able to shift towards the maximum densities of the 'sedentary' interaction limit. The two alternative models lead to divergent implications about the initial development of permanent sedentism. Neither option can be preferred on *a priori* grounds. This issue is discussed further in Chapter 7 when the implications of the alternatives for our understanding of the development of permanent sedentism are reviewed.

The interaction limit that has been identified for permanent sedentary communities is not a definitive or final assessment. It is a potentially useful conceptual tool, enabling us to place the settlement areas, community size and densities of particular settlements in a broad cross-cultural, theoretical context. The exact

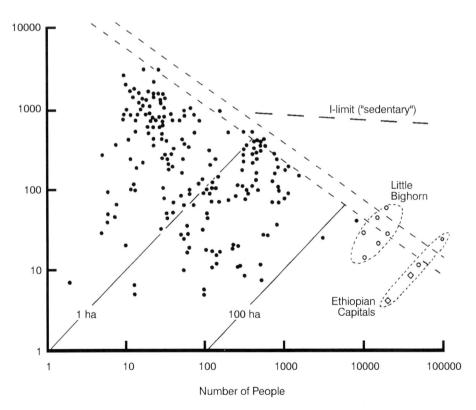

Figure 4.7 'Mobile' interaction limit – detail (after Fletcher 1990, 1991a)
Note: Alternative density values for Plains Indians encampment, Little Bighorn June 1876. Various density estimates for Ethiopian medieval and nineteenth-century AD mobile capitals.

definition of an interaction-limit zone will demand larger samples, precise inter-regional consistency in area definition and detailed analyses of particular critical settlements which lie on the upper edge of the zone. Before carrying out such time-consuming work we need to find out whether the additional effort in precise definition would serve a useful purpose. This can only be done by assessing the implications of the 'sedentary' interaction limit and provisional 'mobile' interaction limit for an understanding of settlement growth.

Issues

The logic of methodological uniformitarianism specifies that operational uniformities, such as finite sensory capacity, will produce universally constant parameter conditions. The existence of the class of I-limit can therefore be considered as a given for analysis and explanation throughout the entirety of hominid evolution. Specific theories of settlement growth can be predicated on the former existence of some kind or kinds of I-limits. Note, however, that the uniformitarian status of sensory finiteness does not inevitably lead to a conclusion that the limits have always had exactly the same magnitude or gradient. According to the logic of methodological uniformitarianism, a uniformly occurring process can generate different particular products over time (see p. 231). The positions of I-limits identified in the present cannot validly be extrapolated into the past just on the basis of substantive assumptions about their constancy. An additional case has to be made, if we are credibly to claim that the known positions are inherent characteristics of human behaviour.

An *a priori* case can be made that the I-limits have indeed been stable. In essence stability is the least improbable condition. Otherwise we have to envisage a mechanism which has kept the changes in each region of the world consistent with each other over long spans of time. The I-limits are known to be interregionally consistent and therefore cannot have varied arbitrarily over time in different places. If the I-limits had changed, they must have shifted by a constant amount in the same direction in all regions. But it is hard to envisage a mechanism which could have kept the Old and New World cultures behaviourally synchronised with each other or fixed into constant directional change in their maximum residential densities. What is far more parsimonious is to ascribe the I-limits to the effect of some basal behavioural characteristics of *Homo sapiens sapiens* which has been invariant over space and time.[7] Not only can we securely expect I-limits to have existed in the past but we can also even work on the basis that the current positions of the limits are stable. What may have varied over time is the substantive social detail of the specific events which happened at the limits, not the general outcome of colliding with such a limit. The significance of the expectation is that large-scale theoretical propositions about settlement growth over the past 15,000 years can be made. We can even be confident enough to consider what the past would have been like if the limits were not where we now see them (see pp. 179–81).

Residential density provides a rough index of the effects of interaction stress. However, we do not as yet understand why the I-limits are actually where they are.

We cannot explain why a density of approximately 300–600 p/ha marks a critical upper limit for sedentary communities of a million or more people. It is important to emphasise that residential density does not in itself cause the constraint but is simply a convenient index for frequency of interaction. The density index is just a handy and familiar way of illustrating the phenomenon of interaction limits because its significance for the condition of people's lives can be readily envisaged. But it is not the only appropriate index; it should also be possible to relate the amount of interaction in a community to other indices of activity, some of which may eventually be more useful in archaeology. A cross-cultural standard for describing intensity of site usage would be necessary. More rigorous definition of the I-limits and their identification in the archaeological record will be a substantial task, requiring either a way of quantifying usage which subsumes community size or a biomechanical basis for estimating the number of people who once lived in a settlement.

At present, claims about the position of the I-limits are open to direct refutation in contemporary and recent contexts but not in the archaeological record. The latter must await a new index of interaction which can be calculated directly from attributes available in the archaeological record. However, sufficient potential refutations should be available in the historical and ethnographic record to gauge whether or not the class of I-limit exists. If the model does not suffice as a description of the constraints on residential interaction it must be equally inappropriate at any time. Therefore, if the model does provide an adequate description of communities that are observable now or in the recent past, the expected anomalies could not just happen to be restricted to a particular temporal phase in the more distant past where they are currently immune from observation. Potential refutations would be cases which lie well above the relevant limit and persist for long periods of time without the application of external force to keep them at that level. Ordinary communities might exceed an I-limit for short periods of time, such as brief periods of a few years, e.g. during sieges, but should promptly fall back to lower densities once the crisis is over. However, even though the anomalous duration of a settlement at a density above the ceiling cannot as yet be directly quantified, excessive densities for periods of several hundred years would be a serious problem for the general I-limit model.

Communication range
Communication includes all the varied signal systems which human communities use. We use verbal communication in many forms, a wide range of non-verbal messages systems such as interpersonal body language and material messages, various material information carriers, and the means to move personnel and resources. Because of our finite sensory capacity, cumulative errors during message transmission, inertia in traffic movement, inherent delay time in signal transmission and a finite energy supply, communication systems can only be effective over a finite range. Natural speech, for example, will suffice for communication over a small range while the greater energy invested in telecommunications enables us to talk around the planet. As the amount of energy committed to the system increases, so

its capacity to transmit over greater distances also increases. The increased energy input helps to overcome signal and message degeneration (Cherry 1966). Redundancy also achieves this by reiterating the same signal many times.

The limits of communication effectiveness can therefore be envisaged in terms of settlement area. The effective limit for a given assemblage of transmission mechanisms is the maximum settlement area over which coherent messages are carried clearly and promptly enough to operate adequately as a communication network. Rather than consider speech as a set of signals which become inaudible over distance, we should seek to identify the size of the settlement area across which verbal messages can spread out and overlap without losing their communication efficacy. Since we will be dealing with the overall effect of a community's assemblage of communication systems, the size limit actually relates to the joint operations of the assemblage as a whole. The nature of the network regulates the degree to which the members of the community can adequately transmit and receive coherent messages or shift themselves and other items. The workable settlement size limit represents a size beyond which a significant number of the messages carried by the communication system will be lost, delayed or garbled during transmission, and the movement of people and items suffer from inordinate time lag.

As the energy content of the whole network goes up, with more power needed to make it work, so we should expect the maximum settlement area over which it can operate to increase. A community whose means of communication include writing should be able to function in a much larger settlement than is possible using unaided 'word of mouth'. With electronic communications and the production of digital signals settlements are able to grow even larger. Again we are looking at an aggregate effect. For instance, a non-industrialised urban community may be using word of mouth, a material information storage device such as the *quipu* or writing, and runners to carry information. Conversely, a society with a given communication assemblage might then expand the size of its largest settlement up to some maximum area constrained by the adequacy of the overall communication system. Growth beyond that maximum size could not be sustained for long because the occupants would be unable to maintain the transmission capacity and efficacy needed to remain workable. Loss of communication effectiveness would prevent the organisation of the activity which could expand the settlement area. We should therefore expect this to be a constraint on the growth of settlements. It will be most conspicuous in compact settlements where people are close together, generating and experiencing stress from the overloading interaction effects of their proximity. Transmission capacity is most likely to fail in circumstances which involve high signal loads and a high incidence of obstacles to transmission, e.g. numerous other communicators getting in the way. In conjunction with the I-limits we should find areal limits on communication.

Communication limits (C-limits)

The major constraint on the growth of settlements should be the maximum extent of the compact settlement area across which a given assemblage of communication systems can function adequately. What we ought to find is that communities using a particular suite of transmission devices will be able to sustain a maximum settlement area which is relatively constant regardless of local environment, economy and the details of social and political organisation. Rather than a maximum community size defined by the supply of resources, we should find a maximum settlement area which is a function of communication range and traffic capacity (Figure 4.8).[8] This can be assessed from the size distributions for cities prior to the appearance of the suite of mechanised communication systems in Europe in the early nineteenth century AD.

First we have to identify the ranges of settlement size for communities with non-mechanised modes of communication. Before the use of mechanised printing, newspapers, and trains to move people the distributions of settlement size suggest that few compact cities exceeded areas of 50 to 80 sq km and most were much smaller (Figure 4.9). Even allowing for different definitions of settlement area, the sizes of Indian towns and cities in 1881 were not markedly different from European settlement sizes in the eighteenth and the early nineteenth century. Most settlements were less than 20–30 sq km in extent; very few covered more than 50 sq km. Only in the mid-nineteenth century did London begin to exceed 100 sq km. This implies that the largest compact cities prior to that date should have maximum areas in the range between 50 and 100 sq km.

An assessment of the size of pre-AD 1850 compact, agrarian-based urban settlements indicates that there was apparently an area limit restricting their growth. Compact settlements did not exceed areas of 90–100 sq km (30–40 sq miles) (Fletcher 1981a: 112–13) (Figure 4.10).[9] Ch'ang-an in China, the capital of

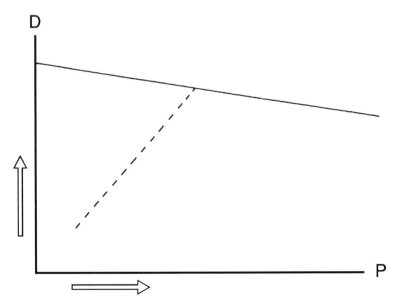

Figure 4.8 Hypothetical communication limit (schematic)
D = density   P = community size

the T'ang dynasty in the eighth to the tenth century AD, and Edo in Japan, the Tokugawa capital from the seventeenth to the nineteenth century, were the largest pre-industrial cities in the world, covering areas of 80–90 sq km. Baghdad, the Abbasid capital in the tenth century AD, and Peking, the capital of China from the fifteenth century to nineteenth century, reached sizes of 50–70 sq km. The areal constraint is independent of community size, as is apparent in the Indian and the world-wide samples (Figures 4.4 and 4.5). If economic factors such as food supply have a predominant effect by determining the number of people in a community, the population figures would show the constraint. Community size rather than settlement size would be the limiting factor and a single maximum community size should be found in a wide range of settlement sizes. But in practice what we find is a limit on settlement area which applies to communities with diverse numbers of people. Resource supply cannot be the controlling factor because it would directly affect the number of people who can be sustained rather than the area of the settlement they occupy.

If successive interaction–communication assemblages can each sustain a finite, maximum, compact settlement area, then the history of settlement growth should include distinct maxima of settlement size for each successive major communication transformation. The difference between two hypothetical successive C-limits therefore represents the settlement size range for which a given assemblage provides an adequate communication system. The actual magnitude of the change in settlement size is a topic for empirical enquiry. Communities have a variety of interaction and communication requirements, ranging in scale from domestic life to transmissions, of whatever form, across the entire settlement. A major new transmission assemblage which met all of these needs should lead to a marked increase in the size

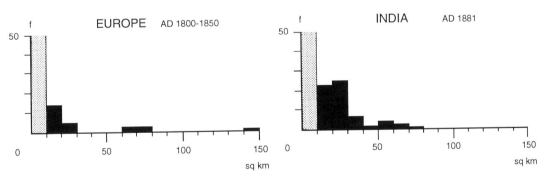

Figure 4.9 European and Indian urban size distributions in the nineteenth century AD (after Fletcher 1986, see for n-values and sources)
The areas of the Indians towns and cities in AD 1881 derive from the designation of municipal districts by the British Imperial administration. The districts included the civil station for the administration and the military cantonment. These were located a short distance away from the indigenous settlement, e.g. at Delhi the cantonment lay beyond the civil lines on Delhi ridge (0.5 km to the north-west of the city wall of Shahjahanabad) (Frykenberg 1986). These area reports therefore tend to be rather more inclusive of rural land near the settlements than area estimates for the early part of the century and for the eighteenth century AD.
Note: By convention the first class interval is filled (see Fletcher 1986: 61); f represents frequency of occurrence, i.e. number of settlements in a given class interval of areal extent.

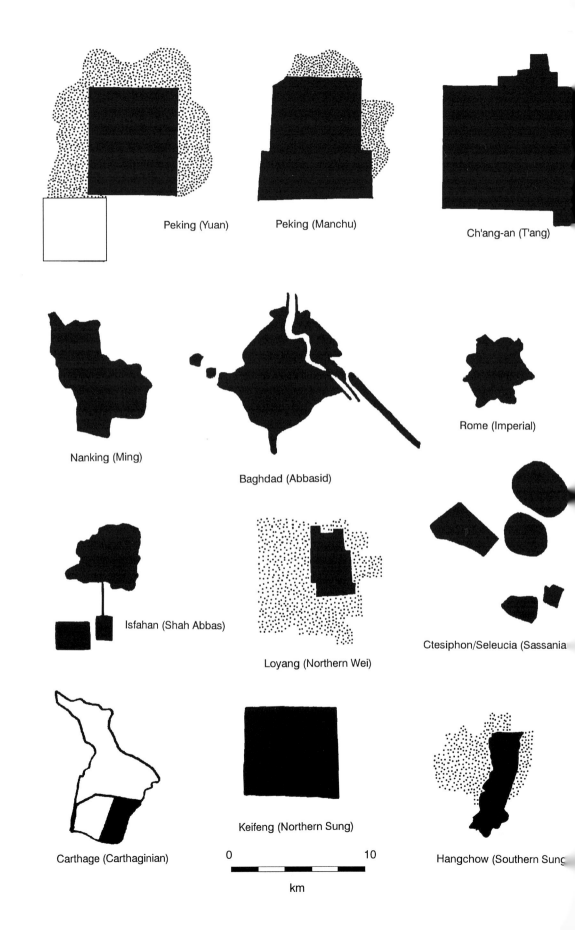

Peking (Yuan)

Peking (Manchu)

Ch'ang-an (T'ang)

Nanking (Ming)

Baghdad (Abbasid)

Rome (Imperial)

Isfahan (Shah Abbas)

Loyang (Northern Wei)

Ctesiphon/Seleucia (Sassania

Carthage (Carthaginian)

Keifeng (Northern Sung)

0   10

km

Hangchow (Southern Sung

Edo (Tokugawa)

Kyoto (Imperial)

Nara (8th C AD)

Delhi (Various dates)

Vijayanagar (16th C AD)

Cairo/Fustat (Mameluke)

Samarra (Abbasid)

Cordova (Umaiyid)

Constantinople (Byzantine)

Figure 4.10 Pre-industrial capital cities; maximum size of compact agrarian-based urban settlements (a comparative sample to indicate their relative size: see in comparison to London and Paris in the early nineteenth century AD (Figure 6.1)).

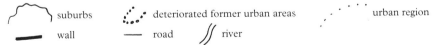

suburbs   deteriorated former urban areas   urban region

wall   road   river

Sources: Baghdad, Iraq – after Le Strange 1924. Cairo/Fustat, Egypt – after Lapidus 1966. Carthage, Tunisia – after Tlatli and Reyniers 1978. Ch'ang-an, China – after Skinner 1977. Constantinople, Turkey – after *Encyclopaedia of Islam* 1972 and Toynbee 1967. Cordova, Spain – after Pidal 1957. Ctesiphon/Seleucia, Iraq – after Fiey 1967. Delhi, India – after Sharma 1974. Edo, Japan – after Yazaki 1968; Mogi 1966. Hangchow, China – after Moule 1957. Isfahan, Iran – after Gaube 1979. Kaifeng, China – after Skinner 1977. Kyoto, Japan – after Ponsonby-Fane 1956. Loyang, China – after Wheatley 1970. Nanking, China – after Herrmann 1935 and Hsieh 1973. Nara, Japan – after Yazaki 1968. Peking, China – after Jellicoe 1975; Yong Yap and Cotterell 1977. Rome, Italy – after Frutaz 1962. Samarra, Iraq – after Herzfeld 1948. Vijayanagar, India – after Sewell 1977.

of the sustainable compact settlements. This increase will happen after the transition has occurred across the C-limit set by an older communication assemblage. There should be a succession of C-limits (Figure 4.12). The impact of the successive, more effective communication assemblages which enable communities to grow beyond each of those C-limits should be observable as a succession of abrupt size increases as communities make the transitions.

A preliminary assessment can be made from the overall trend of settlement growth over the past 15,000 years (Fletcher 1986). It has been punctuated by three major familiar changes in settlement size: first the formation of permanent sedentary communities, secondly the growth of agrarian urban communities and thirdly the formation of industrial cities. Figure 4.11 indicates that these broad transformations contained particular, abrupt, consistently scaled punctuated changes in settlement growth. The general social changes are not reducible to those punctuated events. Not all settlements experienced such marked increases in settlement size (Fletcher 1986: 72). What we appear to be observing are the effects of a powerful specific behavioural constraint and release mechanism which affects particular classes of settlement within those broad social trends.

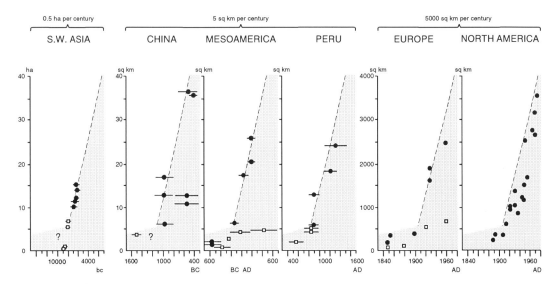

Figure 4.11 Maximum growth rates for settlements 15,000 bc to twentieth century AD (after Fletcher 1986: see for n-values and sources)

░░░ possible growth field for compact settlements

SW Asia	? = Karaneh 4	□ = PPNA	● = PPNB
China	□ = Shang	● = Chou	
Mesoamerica	□ = Monte Albán	● = Teotihuacan	
Peru	□ = Mochica	● = Huari and Chan Chan	
Europe	□ = Paris	● = London	
North America	● data for Chicago, Detroit, Los Angeles, New York		

Note: North America added to original diagram.

Each major increase in settlement growth should be associated with a transition across a C-limit. The increase represents the release of growth once a community has a mode of interaction and communication which can overrule the old C-limit. In the case of the 'Industrial Revolution' the old limit was the maximum size of about 90–100 sq km which constrained compact, agrarian-based cities. The massive growth of industrial cities in the nineteenth century AD is associated both with a combination of new modes of communication, such as mechanised printing, newspapers and passenger trains, capable of aiding communication for more people in much larger settlements, and with a change in resource supply which was able to support more people.

If the third, and most recent, of the major settlement size increases was a transition across a C-limit, it is parsimonious to suppose that the same applies to the other two great increases in maximum settlement size. We can identify their approximate magnitude by comparing the settlement size increases associated with each of these settlement transformations. Those initial urban settlements which grew rapidly were approximately 100 times smaller than the first great industrial cities, and the rapidly growing settlements which we conventionally associate with the development of sedentism in south-west Asia were about 100 times smaller than the early urban examples. If, therefore, we label the C-limit, which was crossed during the Industrial Revolution by means of industrial modes of interaction and communication, the 100 sq km limit, the limit which was crossed by the largest initial agrarian urban settlements can conveniently be referred to as the 100 ha C-limit and the shift to permanent sedentism should have involved a move across a designated 1–2 ha C-limit.[10] The associated initial maximum rates of growth for

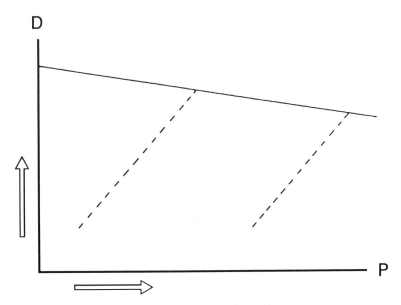

Figure 4.12 Hypothetical successive C-limits (schematic)
D = density   P= community size

compact settlements went up from up to 0.5 ha per century beyond 1–2 ha, to about 500 ha (5 sq km) per century beyond the 100 ha limit, to somewhere around 5,000 sq km per century for settlements of over 100 sq km, i.e. the growth rate increased by a multiple of approximately 1,000 after each size transition.

The 1–2 ha and 100 ha values are only conventions and need to be clarified by more detailed analysis.[11] There are two main potential sources of data: first, the size distributions of settlements immediately prior to the earlier periods of maximum size growth and secondly the maximum sizes of settlements in regions where a major size increase did not take place because no new mode of interaction and communication was developed. The proposed C-limits mark the size at which settlements become very rare. By extension they should also be settlement sizes which are not exceeded for long periods of time. The sizes of the great pre-industrial, compact capital cities such as T'ang Ch'ang-an are therefore the key clue to the magnitude of the C-limit which was crossed by the industrial cities of Europe in the nineteenth century AD. Likewise, the predicted C-limit which was crossed by the initial urban settlements such as Uruk in Mesopotamia and Monte Albán in Mesoamerica will be indicated by the maximum settlement sizes in regions with permanently sedentary communities and agrarian economies but where the size of the few, largest settlements was stable for long periods of time.

What may happen at the limits should be predictable from general principles but the interaction–communication stress model is not mechanistic in the sense of the nineteenth-century physical sciences. It specifies strict conditions only at the limits of the viability of human communities, but these do not exercise a determinate effect on the initial occurrence of cultural phenomena. The conditions set by the model are selectionist. The presence of severe stress does not predetermine that a community will devise effective solutions to the problem. What the model does rule is that the proposed parameters severely restrict the behaviour of a comparatively minuscule, though crucial, category of settlements whose trajectories approach the I- and C-limits. By contrast, the outcome of cultural change in communities well away from the behavioural limits should be subject to relatively little generalisable, predictive restriction. The lower stress levels will not have consistent selective effects on the varied, contextually generated cultural patterns of each different community – the settlements which lie in the general zone behind a given C-limit will possess a diverse range of characteristics. However, cross-cultural behavioural consistency will be a feature of each transition across a particular C-limit. It is the transitions that will display a consistent patterning of behaviour, not the general classes of settlements which either precede or postdate the change. This may help to explain why much cultural activity appears to be so varied and idiosyncratic, yet also displays distinct behavioural consistency when viewed on a larger temporal scale. The disputes about whether or not there are cross-cultural social regularities may therefore be at cross-purposes. The answers will differ depending upon the size and density of the community, and will also vary depending upon the degree to which the material is seen as incorporated in the social or as an epiphenomenal adjunct.

Issues

There is no specific explanation, as yet, for the particular sizes of the C-limits that are indicated by the data. The aggregate capacity of the suite of pre-industrial communication systems has not yet been calculated and we therefore do not know why it could not enable compact settlement sizes larger than approximately 100 sq km. Despite this, we can study the consequences of these limits and what communities do when they reach them. We do not need to know the exact reason for the magnitudes allocated to the effect of a uniform operational constraint in a methodological uniformitarian proposition in order to do worthwhile research. The theory of Plate Tectonics, for instance, even in the late 1980s, more than a decade after its initial development, had not furnished an explanation of the forces which move the plates nor had it then explained the rates of observed movement (Frankel 1988: 130; Hallam 1973, 1983; Oreskes 1988: 312, 346; van Andel 1985: 140). None the less, it had and has considerable predictive power. Explaining the size values of the C-limits would be a highly desirable increase in the scope of the model and would be a major insight, but research on the effects of the limits need not halt until it is known.

The standard difference between the proposed C-limits is a convention which provides a well-defined format whose degree of correspondence with observation can be readily assessed. Though I doubt that the differences between the C-limits are quite so straightforward, a simple explanation can be offered for the proportionately consistent relationship between the successive C-limits. A new material assemblage, which allows a transition across a C-limit, must be able to provide relief from the high stress which should exist close to both a C-limit and an I-limit. The assemblage will therefore possess a potential capacity to aid communication and interaction that is proportional to the stress which it mitigates. That enormous capacity is then available to be converted into the management of increased numbers of people on larger settlement areas but at much lower residential densities where the behavioural stresses are relatively low. The magnitude of the increase which the new assemblage can sustain should therefore be proportionate to the stresses associated with the preceding C-limit. The C-limits will be consistently scale-related because each new interaction–communication assemblage overcomes the stresses of one C-limit and simultaneously defines the magnitude of the next one.

The incremental change between the three marked increases in settlement size is so abrupt and the rates of growth associated with them are so large that empirical evidence for different values would have to be very considerable to affect the proposed model at all seriously. The case for the C-limits can be assessed throughout the entire archaeological record because they are potentially recognisable from settlement and site area. The pattern is extremely coarse and robust, yet the criteria of the interaction–communication model also lay it open to potential refutation. The obvious cases would be very large, compact settlements whose communication capacity has not increased to allow a transition across a particular C-limit, but which nevertheless exceed its size and manage to endure for long periods of time.

The interaction–communication limit threshold (T-limit)

At very low residential densities the communication constraint should not have an effect. When there are few people per unit area, interaction friction becomes minimal. As rapid interconnections are reduced by the amount of open space between residence units, aggregate communication adequacy is no longer consequential. We should find that communication loses its powerful role as a regulator of settlement size. A density threshold (the T-limit) should therefore exist, below which the communication system used by a community will cease to constrain settlement size (Figure 4.13). At very low residential densities communication range as such obviously does not define the size of rural regions occupied by interrelated people. Rural regional population densities are a function of a variety of other factors, in particular the economics of land use (Chisholm 1979; Clark 1989). Factors like soil fertility, agricultural practices and crop distribution will be the dominant variables affecting the distribution of population at these lower, regional densities. Settlements whose occupation densities drop to the level of regional densities should not be subject to the C-limit effects, and will be able to cover areas far in excess of the specified maximum size of compact settlement for a given communication assemblage.

The density below which the communication constraint ceases to apply ought, therefore, to correspond to the maximum population densities of extensive rural regions. The obvious cases are provided by some of the Chinese provinces, the

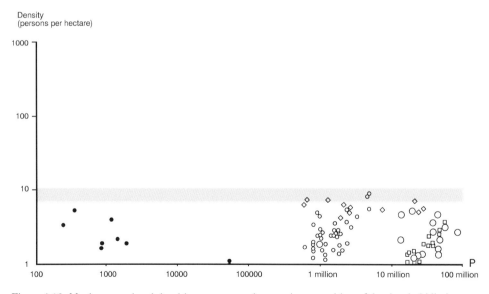

Figure 4.13 Maximum regional densities – a proposed approximate position of the threshold limit

● West Africa   □ China   ○ India   ○ Japan

◇ Indonesia (Java)

Sources: Africa – Netting 1968; Prothero 1972. China – *World Atlas of Agriculture* 1973. India – Baines 1893; Chaudhuri 1976. Indonesia – *Statistical Yearbook 1977–78*; Bryant 1973. Japan – Teikoku's *Complete Atlas of Japan* 1982.

prefectures of Japan and the districts of Java in Indonesia (Figure 4.13), which are among the most heavily populated regions on the planet. The Gangetic plain and the Basin of Mexico also carry very high regional densities (Clark 1989: 25). Although the density figures are approximations, due to error factors introduced by ignoring topography and by including some urban populations, they serve to indicate that maximum regional rural densities can possibly be as high at 7–10 p/ha. A low-density settlement functioning at a density below 10 p/ha should not be subject to the communication parameter.

Several dispersed, low-density, non-industrialised settlements have exceeded the size of the expected C-limit at 100 sq km without possessing industrialised means of communication. Tikal grew to approximately 120–160 sq km by AD 900 (Figure 4.14a). Angkor in the fifteenth century AD covered more than 500 sq km, with a dense core, an extensive low-density periphery and an almost indefinable edge (Figure 4.14b) (Higham 1989: 321–55, esp. 350–2). On a smaller scale, settlement patterns such as the Gallinazo occupation of the Viru valley (Figure 4.15a) and Great Zimbabwe (Figure 4.15b) are larger than the 100 ha C-limit, as are many contemporary rural dispersed settlements in West Africa (e.g. Archer 1971; Netting

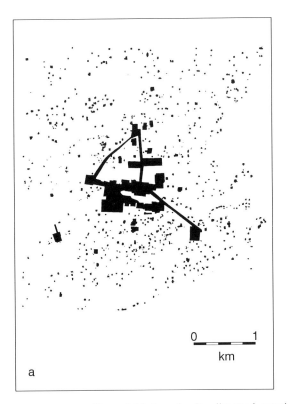
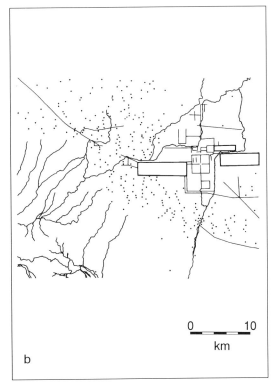

a

b

Figure 4.14 Low-density, dispersed, agrarian-based cities
(a) Tikal (central area) Yucatan, Mexico, first millennium AD (Haviland 1970 and Puleston 1973)
(b) Angkor, Cambodia, fifteenth century AD (after Martel 1975)
On the Martel illustration, the dots mark villages in the twentieth century AD, identifying the area of land available for residence around the core of Angkor.

1965). Ethnographic examples of such dispersed settlements in northern Ghana and Nigeria cover many square kilometres (Denyer 1978: 74) (Figure 4.15c). Low-density occupation sites may therefore have distinctly different growth trajectories from those of compact settlements. The communication constraint applies only to settlements with a restricted range of residential densities below the I-limits and above the T-limit.

Issues

I have assumed that the T-limit is horizontal but it need not be. It may decline like the 'sedentary' I-limit. The gradient ought, in due course, to be predictable from a further elaboration of the interaction–communication model. The particular form of the T-limit will have to be identified empirically from numerous recent regional case studies. Since the maximum operable regional densities are the result of economic and ecological factors, it should be possible to devise a methodological uniformitarian form of explanation for the T-limit which can be securely extended to the past. On first assessment it seems unlikely that in the past some regions reached viable densities higher than modern ones since we do not suppose that the

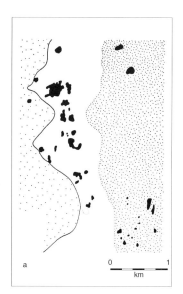

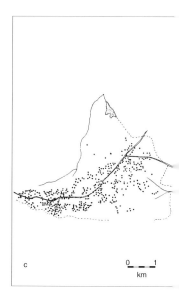

Figure 4.15 Dispersed occupation
(a) Gallinazo site, Peru, late first millennium BC (after Bennett 1950)

occupation mounds   desert   crop land

(b) Great Zimbabwe site, Zimbabwe, fifteenth century AD (after Sinclair 1993)

wall   scatters of huts

(c) Ibo settlement, Nigeria, twentieth century AD (after Denyer 1978)

• residence compounds   .... boundary of 'village'

operational constraints on carrying capacity and economic viability have varied over past millennia.

To make the propositions about the relationship between the C-limits and the T-limit assessable using archaeological evidence, a coarse distinction between compact and dispersed settlements has to be applied. To be consistent with the model, compact settlements must conform to the predictions about communities which have high interaction frequencies, while dispersed settlements with low occupation densities need not. However, those which appear to be so constrained will be relevant to predictions about the nature of the C-limits because they will eventually provide an independent index of the lowest interaction frequencies at which the communication constraint takes effect.

The interaction–communication stress matrix

In the interaction–communication model the constraints which derive from people's finite tolerance of interaction and the finite efficacy of communication are inter-linked parameters. When a transmission system is overloaded, i.e. it is generating too much 'noise' for coherent signal transmission, or there are severe delays in the arrival of information, people or items, the community is suffering from serious or even intolerable problems of interaction. Too many signals and entities are competing for the available channels (Shannon and Weaver 1949). The specific problems and potential of different communities might therefore be mapped onto a stress field which presents the various possible combinations of interaction and communication difficulties encountered by different communities.[12]

The model is converted into an interaction–communication stress matrix (Figure 4.16) by adding the magnitude or position of the proposed limits to the schematic format. The stress matrix summarises the proposed behavioural constraints on the growth of human communities and the current indications of the position of the various limits. They are represented as zones because they are not rigid, deter-ministic, instantaneous halt lines. Rather, the zones are indicators of an uncertain range of likelihood within which the behavioural limitations become severe. The nearest iconic equivalent would be a wide, sticky strip which is increasingly viscous towards its furthest edge. A precise statement of the indeterminacy of the boundary zones will eventually be required. They possess this characteristic not because we lack data or knowledge but because the 'choices' which communities make as they approach a limit are not deterministically predictable. Depending on the material characteristics of the community, people's decisions may have results ranging from failure to survival. The degree to which a settlement can move into a boundary zone and persist will therefore vary. Some settlements will be heading for severely maladaptive behaviour and will halt at varying sizes that depend upon purely contextual, cultural factors, while others will be moving towards attempts to cross the limit. When we sample the size of the settlements or their densities at a given moment of time, the exact future of their growth cannot be known. Nor can we exclude the effect of external variables such as abrupt environmental change in the form of volcanic eruptions or dune movement (see p. 238) which could terminate the existence of a settlement at an arbitrary size or density. Only by looking cross-culturally at trajectories through time can we identify which settlements have or have not sustained a transition across a C-limit. But we can never then know exactly where the 'edge' of the boundary zone is because there is inherent uncertainty in the measurement of settlement area and community size. Nor can we ever gauge exactly where the limit should be set between the largest cases which stop growing and the cases which continue to expand. The I- and C-limits possess indeterminacy. If we know exactly where a community is located on the matrix, we cannot know simultaneously where it will go. Conversely, if we know what its trajectory was, we cannot then know from that trajectory the exact position of a limit which it may have crossed or approached.

  The particular usefulness of the matrix is that it facilitates comparisons between settlements at equivalent loci, such as in close proximity to an I-limit or at the junction of an I- and a C-limit. The matrix allows the advantages of field analysis and the comparison of different systems at equivalent critical states, as has become usual in modern field theory (De Greene 1981: 103, 105). As well as the positions of equivalence that can reasonably be expected, such as the location of the largest settlements jammed up against the behavioural limits, the matrix also has the potential to suggest other, more surprising forms of equivalence. For instance, an intriguing and counter-intuitive feature of the residential stress matrix is that the

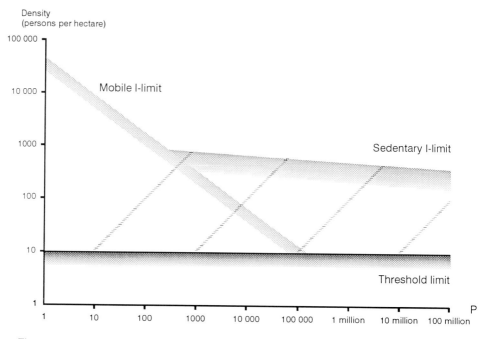

Figure 4.16 Interaction–communication matrix (derived from Figures 4.4, 4.6, 4.7, 4.13)

P = community size   communication limit

same C-limits should apply to mobile groups below the proposed 'mobile' I-limit as apply to permanent sedentary communities. The most parsimonious form of the matrix requires that this be the case. The C-limit condition applies whether the 'mobile' I-limit is a rigorous constraint or represents a gradation in possible maximum densities as communities approach the condition of permanent residence. Permanent sedentary communities, for example in India (Fletcher 1981a: 100) (Figure 7.7), exist at the same low residential densities as mobile communities of equivalent size and therefore the C-limits must be present at those densities. Since the limits are a function of the range and capacity of communication systems they should be present whether or not a community is mobile.

This feature of the matrix provides strict, unexpected, testable claims applicable to communities and social systems which are otherwise very different. It specifies that predictable behavioural outcomes should be found at the limits while culturally contextual diversity prevails in the broad zones between the limits. Outcomes will be tightly constrained near the I- and C-limits but they will be characteristics of the vicinity of a limit, not generally applicable to all the settlements which lie between any two C-limits. The cross-comparability of the trajectories and the various classes of settlement also allows comparison between the rates of change affecting settlements of different sizes, and allows us to check whether the relative magnitude of change alters as settlement size increases. For instance, we can begin to ask whether the duration of the settlements behind each successive C-limit has increased or decreased with the increase in the areal magnitude of the C-limits. The implications of being able to ask this kind of question are considerable, since we might begin to predict the duration and maximum size of future settlements in similar situations.

Conclusions

The interaction–communication stress model predicts the existence of limits on aggregate interaction, and a succession of communication limits. The two kinds of limit are universal, operational parameters of community life and provide an explanatory framework for the study of settlement dynamics. The existence of I-limits, though not necessarily the exact magnitudes proposed for them, can be considered as a given for analysis and explanation. The overall effects of the I- and C-limits can be linked together and assessed in terms of the different resulting outcomes for compact and dispersed settlements. Compact settlements must conform to the restrictive effect of the C-limits unless they develop a new communication assemblage. Dispersed settlements need not be affected by them.

The stress matrix derived from the interaction–communication model provides a framework within which we can cross-compare myriad possible trajectories for settlements of different sizes. The framework allows multilinear tracks of settlement development but also provides a way of cross-comparing them. There can be varied outcomes, each of which is explicable in terms of differing aspects of the model and differing combinations of conditions. The outcome of a trajectory will depend on the material assemblage of a community, the supply of energy available to it and the position of the settlement in relation to the I- and C-limits. This study is specifically concerned with the role of the material in those high stress, punctuated events of settlement growth during the past 10,000–15,000 years.

The material behaviour approach places the successive size transitions in perspective and consistently relates them to the processes which delimit community life. The various major classes of trajectory which settlements might take in relation to the I- and C-limits now have to be outlined. The relative roles of resource supply and material assemblages also have to be clarified. We then need to gain some impression of the kind of material assemblage associated with the transition across a given C-limit, in order to assess its general character and significance.

5

Settlement growth trajectories

As settlements grow and move towards the I- and C-limits, the amount of stress with which they have to cope increases. These high levels of stress near the limits should reduce the likelihood of settlements becoming large and densely occupied. Those which happen to do so will tend to become static and be vulnerable both to internal stresses and to changes in their external circumstances. However, the severe stress near the limits should also act as a selective milieu which might promote new modes of interaction and communication that the community has generated by chance or has derived from elsewhere. The dynamics of the matrix ought to allow us to predict what behavioural contexts are critical and where the material behaviour of a community may be a significant factor in the trajectory of its settlement growth.

Identifying the interaction–communication stress field
The specific way in which aggregate stress cumulates behind the various limits should be indicated by the relative numbers of settlements which approach the limits: the higher the level of stress, the smaller the number of settlements should be. The distribution of settlement sizes behind a C-limit and the distribution of residential density below an I-limit should therefore provide a probability map of the stress field of the matrix.

Settlement size distributions
According to the I–C model, the frequency with which different sizes of settlement occur behind a C-limit ought to be governed by how difficult it is to sustain viable community life in increasingly large settlements with a specific material I–C assemblage. In a hypothetical population (Figure 5.1) the number of potential interactive events increases as community size increases. The cost of communicating goes up exponentially as group size increases because of the increasing likelihood of interference due to the ever-increasing number of other possible interactions. The settlement or site size distributions should therefore be the inverse of the interaction stress curve (Figure 5.1). This is consistent with the occurrence of 'hollow curve' distributions[1] for the sizes of the settlements in a region (Figure 5.2). Such distributions are what we would expect from the effects of random growth in a selective milieu (Hastings, Warner and Wu 1989: 164, 167). The stress matrix maps the behavioural parameters which constrain the persistence and growth of specific attributes of settlements, such as size. The archaeological distributions display the likelihood of settlements of particular sizes being able to come into being and persist

over time. They are 'through-put' samples spread over a span of time (Fletcher 1986: 65).[2] We are looking at a general behavioural effect, not the more specific effects of the short-term relationships in a hierarchy of contemporaneous communities. The behavioural stress parameters specify the general probability form of a distribution behind a C-limit over time. Local factors of resource supply and active behaviour will be required then to explain the degree to which the particular distribution in each region, over time, approaches that form.

To define the settlement size referent of the stress field we need a wide variety of examples of size distributions from all over the world. These can be compared using broad, equivalent class intervals to produce a standard frame of reference for distributions of disparate sizes.[3] 'Hollow curve' distributions are increasingly more likely as the sample size increases (Figure 5.3). The actual size ranges of these distributions provide a means of assessing the claim for the existence of C-limits. A sample of site area distributions for European small-scale, sedentary agricultural communities from the fifth millennium BC down into the first millennium BC, which occupied either relatively compact or well-defined settlement areas (Figure 5.4), illustrates the form of the distributions in the range up to 100–200 ha.[4] There is a steep decrease in the frequency of areas between 15 and 40 ha and there are usually a few rare examples with sizes up to 100 to 150 ha.[5] The likelihood of the

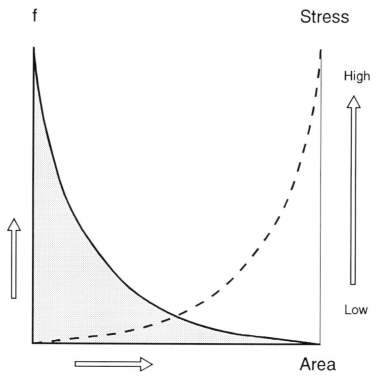

Figure 5.1 Hypothetical settlement size distribution
Stress levels in relation to frequency of occurrence of number of settlements (f)

occurrence of a large or very large site is extremely small and even medium-sized cases are uncommon. The gross impression of the distributions is that for several millennia there was an upper size limit on such settlements in Europe in the range of 50–100 ha, though we cannot identify the exact maximum settlement sizes from the site sizes. That this has some consistent connection to settlement area and the proposed C-limits is indicated by the distributions behind the 100 sq km limit. Prior to the early nineteenth century AD in Europe and also prior to industrialisation in India (Figure 4.9) most settlements were also confined to the lower third of the size range. For the provisional 1–2 ha C-limit the 'hollow curve' distribution is not so strongly displayed, but the sample sizes are rather small (Figures 5.3a, 5.5). There is, however, a marked tendency for the majority of the sites to lie at the smaller end of the range. The scarcity of larger sites is consistent with the distribution shape

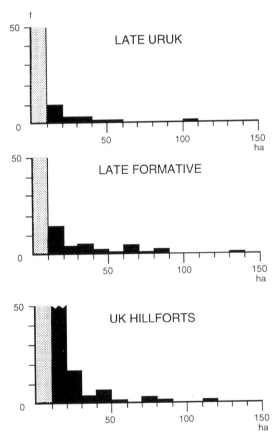

Figure 5.2 World-wide site size distributions for agrarian small-scale communities – Late Uruk, Mesopotamian valley, Iraq, fourth millennium BC, immediately prior to the expansion of urban settlements (after Fletcher 1986, see for n-values and sources); Late Formative, Basin of Mexico, Mexico, late first millennium BC, immediately prior to the expansion of urban settlements; Late Iron Age hillforts, UK, first millennium BC (oppida excluded – see pp. 200–3).
Note (for Figures 5.2–5): By convention the first class interval is filled (see Fletcher 1986: 61); f represents frequency of occurrence, i.e. number of sites/settlements in a given class interval of areal extent.

outlined above. Few sites in south-west Asia were larger than 0.5 ha until the marked size increases began in the tenth and ninth millennia BP, and most were smaller than 0.2 ha. The same distribution is found in the Upper Palaeolithic of the Perigord and in Epi-palaeolithic size distributions (Figure 5.5). The completely excavated Upper Palaeolithic sites of the Ukrainian plains are also predominantly less than 5,000 sq m (0.5 ha) (Soffer 1985: 116–17, 406). Sites over 10,000 sq m are either of uncertain extent and affected by redeposition, represent multiple sites, or have successive occupations merged into single cultural layers.

Further detail can now be added to the stress matrix. In terms of the model, I–C difficulties increase markedly in settlements whose sizes are greater than 30 per cent of a proposed C-limit. The dominant impression of the distributions is that they form bands of frequent occurrence, e.g. up to sizes of about 30 ha, with a peripheral band of rarer examples, e.g. up to 100 ha. A major size increase should eventually lead to the formation of a new standard size range, e.g. up to 30 sq km with a periphery up to 100 sq km. A potential 'hollow curve' distribution of settlement size lies behind each C-limit. In schematic terms there is a declining probability of continuing growth as settlements approach a C-limit (Figure 5.6). A transition

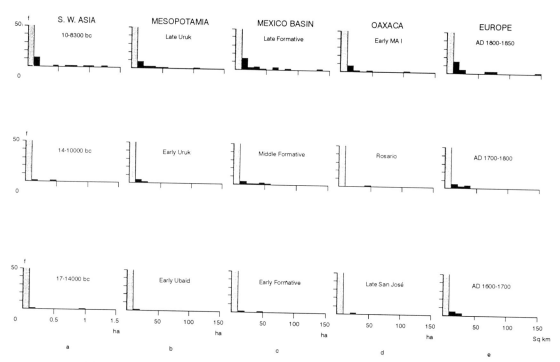

Figure 5.3 World-wide examples of the growth of site and settlement size distributions over time (after Fletcher 1986, see for n-values and sources)
(a) south-west Asia, 17,000–8,300 bc
(b) Mesopotamia, fifth to mid-fourth millennium BC
(c) Mexico Basin, second to late first millennium BC
(d) Oaxaca valley, late second to late first millennium BC
(e) Europe, AD 1600 to 1850.

across a C-limit initiates the growth of a new potential size range distribution. This should at first lead to partial probability forms lacking some part of the potential distribution shape, before all the size possibilities are fully represented. Eventually an actual distribution might approach that potential distribution shape. A distribution need not therefore always have that form. But the sustained frequency of occurrence of the settlement sizes in a region over time should not exceed the potential probability envelope set by the stress levels behind a C-limit,[6] as represented by a 'hollow curve' distribution.

Residential density distribution
Just as there is a gradient to the occurrence of settlement size behind each successive C-limit, there should also be a frequency gradient of communities below the I-limits. As with the case of communication stress and settlement size, an exponential increase in the stress levels with increasing proximity to the I-limit

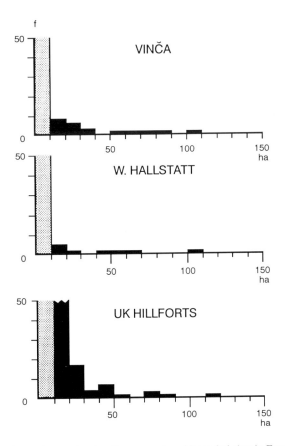

Figure 5.4 Stability in maximum site sizes for compact and bounded sites in Europe, fifth to first millennium BC – Vinča, Balkans fifth–fourth millennium BC; western Hallstatt, central Europe late second millennium BC; hillforts, UK first millennium BC (as in Figure 5.2 the oppida are excluded) (after Fletcher 1986, see for n-values and sources)

should produce a predominance of lower residential density cases and relatively few examples of settlements near the I-limit (Figure 5.7). The frequency of occurrence of communities decreases markedly at a density which is less than half of the maximum reported for each region (Figure 5.8). A crude 'hollow curve' occurs, with most settlements having relatively low overall residential densities.[7] The portion of the stress matrix below the sedentary I-limit can be envisaged in terms of the declining probability of continuing density increase as settlements approach the I-limit (Figure 5.9). The distribution of the residential densities for the communities within a given size range represents a section across the stress field. Whether the same frequency distribution also occurs below the 'mobile' I-limit has yet to be demonstrated. Substantial samples of settlements for which residential density figures can be obtained in any one region are rather scarce for mobile and seasonally sedentary communities. *A priori* the same pattern should occur.

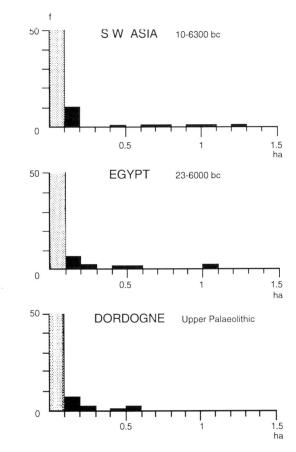

Figure 5.5 Site size distributions for 'mobile' communities – south-west Asia in the Upper and Epi-palaeolithic (after Fletcher 1986, see for n-values and sources), Egypt compared to period equivalent from the Dordogne in western Europe (after White 1985)
Note: For White (1985) sample n = 42.

Settlement trajectories and behavioural stress

As either settlement area or residential density increases, the probability that a settlement will be able to continue its growth decreases. Fewer and fewer settlements will be able to reach the maximum sizes or the highest residential densities. While each community may cease to grow at any size or density, due to a variety of local, specific factors, the aggregate outcome will lie within the probability limits set by the degree of communication and interaction difficulty behind each C-limit and below each I-limit. Many different trajectories are possible but some, which impinge on the various limits, should have distinct and predictable outcomes.

The stress field behind a C-limit varies from extreme difficulty at high density and large size to least difficulty at low density and small size (Figure 5.10). Intermediate levels of stress should affect cases nearer to one of the two limits but well away from the other. The most stressful condition for a community is a combination of high residential density (high interaction frequency) and large settlement area (high communication stress). Such a condition is located at the peak of the stress surface in the wedge between an I-limit and C-limit. The wedge graphically represents severely restricted freedom. These intensely stressful conditions will produce the

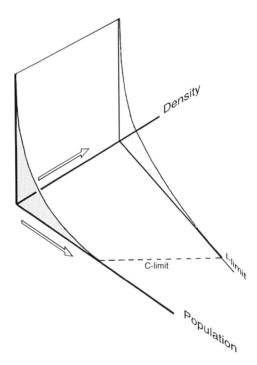

Figure 5.6 Hypothetical probability of continuing settlement area increase in the interaction–communication matrix (the exact nature of the probability decrease towards a C-limit is not known)
Note: Schematic block diagram – the vertical dimension refers to probability *not* to numbers of settlements of given area.

most severe selective pressure. Some communities will not be able to adjust to the stress and may either cease to grow or else collapse. Alternatively, such high, combined interaction and communication stress will have a massive selective impact. This will favour the use of a new I–C assemblage which has already been partially integrated into the social life of a community in or near the wedge, thereby enabling a transition.

The nature of interaction and communication limits
The limitations imposed by the two kinds of limits differ in the degree to which they can be overcome. In principle a C-limit can be crossed with the help of a new material assemblage and increased energy input. But an I-limit is much more intractable, as can be seen in the trajectories of London and Paris from the seventeenth to the mid-nineteenth century AD (Figure 5.11). In the three centuries prior to their transformation by industrialised forms of communication and inter-action control (Fletcher 1981a) both cities approached or entered the zone of the sedentary I-limit and then ricocheted out of it. The sedentary I-limit seems to be almost impenetrable despite the growth momentum of the large communities which approach it. This intractability is to be expected because, as has already been discussed (pp. 71–3), the maximum workable residential density of a community decreases as its size increases. A larger community cannot sustain the same maximum residential density as a smaller one. To keep going with the same level of interaction stress (below the I-limit) it has to drop to a lower density. The additional effort required to produce extra settlement expansion must be expended just to end up at a lower maximum density. Crossing an I-limit to the same or higher

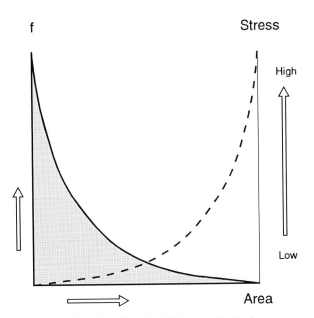

Figure 5.7 Hypothetical residential density distribution
Stress levels in relation to frequency of occurrence of number of settlements (f)

densities must therefore involve substantial costs and a profound behavioural transformation. For instance, because of the presence of the 'mobile' I-limit, this requirement is fundamental to explanations of the formation of permanently sedentary communities (p. 172). It also has implications for the long-term future of settlement growth (pp. 215–18).

Trajectories towards the limits

We know that some settlements approach a C-limit and cease to grow, as Baghdad did in the tenth century AD and Ch'ang-an in the eighth century AD (Figure 4.10). Other settlements have trajectories which rebound off the I-limit (Figure 5.11). Obviously the limits place constraints on the functioning of communities which are close to them. The consequences of different approaches to the limits can now be reviewed. Settlements may follow several different trajectories (Figure 5.12):

(1) A community which continues to grow after hitting the I-limit cannot continue to operate at the same residential density because its absolute interaction frequency would be continually increasing. A community which remains workable

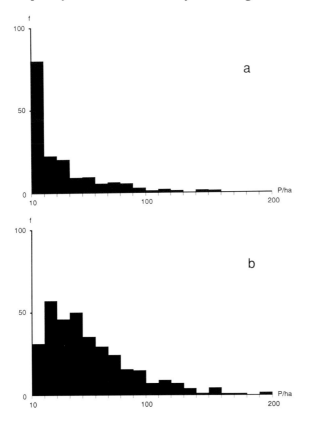

Figure 5.8 Residential density distributions for densities above 10 p/ha
(a) Japan 1971 – urban communities of over 30,000 (Census 1971) (n = 169)
(b) India 1961 – urban communities of over 30,000 (Indian Census 1961) (n = 339)
Note: A small number of settlements reached densities over 200 p/ha. See Figure 4.4 and Fletcher 1981a.

and still continues to grow will be one which would have begun to use devices that bring down residential density and thereby control interaction. Examples might include wider streets, more unoccupied barrier areas between parts of the settlement and more zones with few people in them (e.g. parks or 'official' buildings). Such a community cannot move through the I-limit. Instead it will rebound off it. The settlement area will have to increase since the residential density must decrease as the community continues to grow. Eventually the community will run into a C-limit. During the early phase of decreasing density the selective pressure in favour of new communication options will increase without having an adverse effect on interaction levels.

(2) To see what will happen along a C-limit we need to look at the second case. A community which runs into the C-limit but at interaction frequencies well below those of the I-limit will already be affected by communication stress. As the community continues to grow, its settlement area cannot increase in the absence of a new I–C assemblage. With continued population growth the community will increase its residential density and become more and more affected by interaction stress. Until it reaches the I-limit, the community could continue to function and grow without altering its mode of communication. There is no sense in which the community must necessarily create a new communication system. However, the management of the community will become more difficult as the aggregate inter-

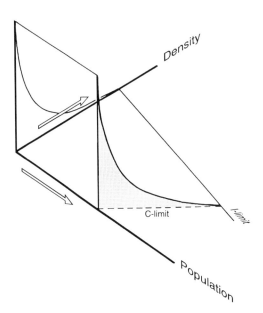

Figure 5.9 Hypothetical probability of continuing density increase in the interaction–communication matrix (the exact nature of the probability decrease towards an I-limit is not known)
Note: Schematic block diagram – the vertical dimension refers to probability *not* to numbers of settlements of given density.

action frequency goes up. Paradoxically, if a community does begin to use new communication devices, this would be likely to result in increased interaction and hence more interaction stress. People would be able to transmit messages across a greatly extended area, introducing a heavier signal load to a context that is already suffering from information overload. Behavioural breakdown, or reversion to smaller community sizes, ought to follow from this trajectory.

(3) A community which approaches the interaction and communication limits equidistant from both is a curious and an unlikely case. Both the interaction frequency within the community and its communication system will come under rapidly increasing stress so we might expect few communities to persist with such a trajectory. In order to remain operable the community will have to develop solutions to both sets of problems simultaneously. The urgent problem which confronts the community is population growth. Unless it can control this growth, it has only one opportunity to solve the problem of the I–C stresses. If such a community had no

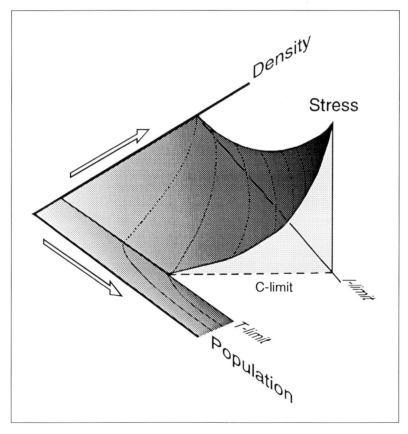

Figure 5.10 Hypothetical form of stress field in the interaction–communication matrix (schematic block diagram)
Note: The stress isolines are schematic only (see Figures 5.6, 5.9). As yet the precise topography of the comparative stress levels across the matrix cannot be ascertained. That will depend upon the calibration of the index of stress in a log-log graph of the I–C matrix.

controls on population growth it would swiftly be faced by behavioural crises. These problems would be likely to select against the variability that is essential for generating or adopting new I–C assemblage alternatives. High levels of behavioural variation are themselves a source of differences, uncertainties and unpredictability which contribute to stress.

(4) Some communities will move to low residential densities. This trajectory escapes the communication constraint altogether by going below the T-limit and bypassing the C-limits. These settlements will function quite differently from the compact examples. As the distance between residence units increases, so the interaction stress levels should drop markedly. When interaction stresses are extremely low and spread over substantial distances, the capacity and range of a communication system should cease to matter. Under the T-limit the stress gradient ought to flatten out (Figure 5.10). Signal transmission must shift to a different mode in which the timing and the form of the signals resembles interregional rather than within-settlement communication. In non-industrial communities, for example, the pragmatic limits on communication and interaction will be a function of walking time and the kinds of effort and distance factors which regulate rural economics.

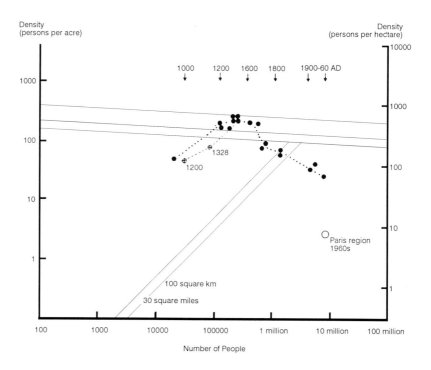

Figure 5.11 Density trajectories of the industrial urban transition in Europe (after Fletcher 1981a – note original in imperial units; also see for sources)
(a) Paris, France, tenth to twentieth century AD (Russell 1969 estimates for AD 1200 and 1328 marked)
Note: I- and C-limits from Figure 4.16 (cf. as estimated in 1981).

In principle there is no obvious limit to the growth of a dispersed settlement which has bypassed a C-limit, other than the supply of essential resources. Such a settlement could grow to enormous size, far in excess of the C-limit for its I–C assemblage. The model does not suggest whether there will be any limit to its area or its population growth. Other factors such as market economics and crop production may be more significant. Settlements which drop to a low enough residential density and escape the communication constraint will lack the selective pressures that might promote the increased use of the elements of a new assemblage. They will not be suffering from interaction stress and their communication problems will be of a different nature from those affecting communities which have higher overall densities. There is therefore a critical constraint on their endogamous growth. They will not be able to effect a gradual increase towards higher residential densities at settlement sizes in excess of the bypassed C-limit. If a community then commenced a move back up over the T-limit it would experience extreme communication stress because it would be operating at an area far in excess of the appropriate C-limit for its available communication capacity. Selective pressure would favour a reduction of residential density or the

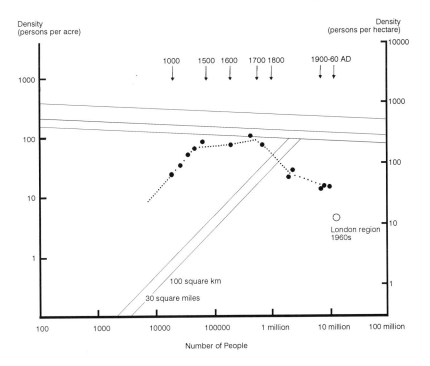

Figure 5.11
(b) London, UK, tenth to twentieth century AD
These are examples of Trajectory 5 (see Figure 5.12). See Figure 6.1b for maps of areal growth pattern.
Note: I- and C-limits from Figure 4.16 (cf. as estimated in 1981).

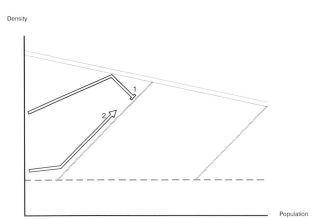

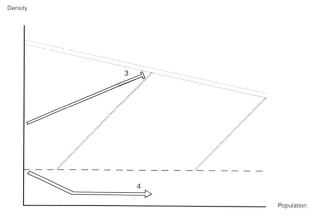

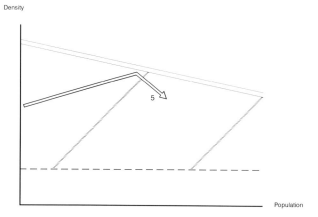

Figure 5.12 Hypothetical growth trajectories
Trajectory 1 – stasis
Trajectory 2 – stasis
Trajectory 3 – stasis
Trajectory 4 – bypass
Trajectory 5 – transition

fragmentation of the community into new compact settlements far smaller than the dispersed form.

(5) Communities which do not have controls on population growth but do possess a new mode of communication and new ways of managing interaction will have the potential to make a transition across a C-limit. These should be more likely along a top trajectory than on the lower (Case 2) or the equidistant (Case 3) trajectory. In Case 5, as community size continues to grow, successional development of changes in interaction control and communication range first favours changes that affect the former and only later those that aid communication. Interaction controls aid the approach to a C-limit because the effects of a new communication facility can be managed by the new interaction controls which are readily available. By contrast, in Case 2 new communication aids do not favour a viable approach to the I-limit because they merely increase the possible amount of communication and the liable 'noise' level. The problems of Case 3 have already been discussed.

On the transition trajectory, the new material aids will be preferentially selected in the high stress conditions of the larger settlements but should have begun to develop in the smaller settlements in which higher levels of variability would be more tolerable. A community may 'try out' numerous different options, only a few of which actually work as critical behavioural aids. In the wedge of high stress between the junction of the I- and C-limits the material features which transform the efficacy of interaction and communication will tend to persist and will be increasingly replicated.

Classes of settlement and trajectory
Transition settlements

Those settlements which approach the I-limits then move towards a C-limit and also possess the necessary new mode of interaction and communication, but do not have controls on community size, will be able to commence a settlement size transition across the C-limit. The degree to which growth is sustained depends on the magnitude of any associated changes in resource supply (p. 152). All transit settlements should display similar characteristics, with an abrupt growth from sizes of approximately one-third of the C-limit to sizes clearly in excess of that limit. The actual size they attain in each region will depend upon local factors. A rapid increase in settlement size should be followed by a decrease in compactness as the community shifts to less stressful levels of interaction. Possible candidates for this class in relation to the 100 ha C-limit are the initial urban settlements in Mesopotamia, China, Mesoamerica and Peru (Figure 5.13).[8] Since the C-limit which has been crossed will not restrict the growth of transition settlements, it will not deflect their trajectories or slow their growth, as can be seen when London and Paris crossed the 100 sq km C-limit (Figure 5.11).

Other settlements which are in the same cultural region should then also be able to cross the C-limit, at any density, by adopting the new material facilities. There should be a marked secondary increase in the number of relatively large settlements but they could be anywhere in the density spectrum. After each transition the largest

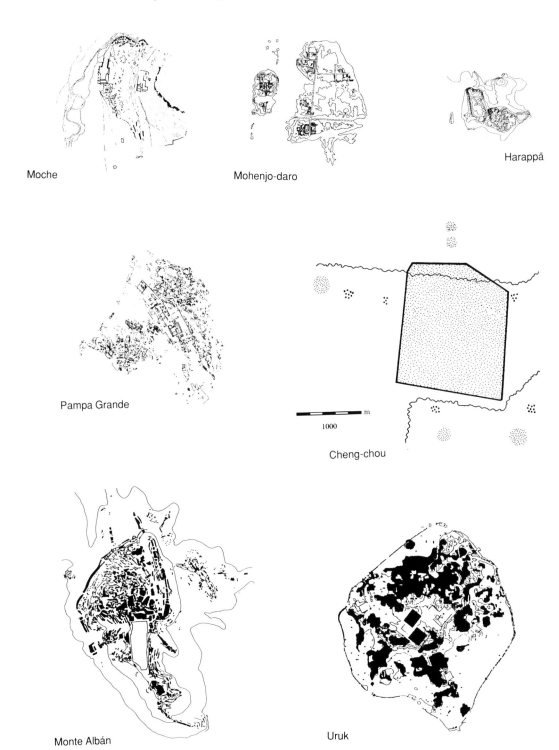

Moche

Mohenjo-daro

Harappā

Pampa Grande

Cheng-chou

1000 m

Monte Albán

Uruk

settlements either grow at the potential maximum rate, as illustrated by Teotihuacan and London (Figure 4.12), or at the much slower rates represented by the development of Monte Albán and Paris. The Mesopotamian regional sequence corresponds to the slower rate. Even though Uruk had reached an area of 4–5 sq km in the early third millennium BC (Boehmer 1991), the maximum settlement size in Mesopotamia 2,000 years later in the mid-first millennium BC was the 10 sq km of Babylon (Wetzel 1969: Fig. 1). While a probability statement may eventually account for the occurrence of these differing growth rates, it will not obviate the need for historical and social analysis to find an explanation for the particular constraints on growth in Mesopotamia. My concern here, however, is to point out the overall process and the comparisons it entails, not to claim specific explanations of directive cause for each regional case. Local explanations require specialist regional knowledge and a contextual perspective.

Stasis settlements
Settlements which have not substantially changed their ways of interacting and communicating before they reach a C-limit will not be able to make a transition across it (e.g. trajectory Cases 1 and 2). According to the I–C model this should apply whether or not substantial economic change has taken place. The stasis settlements near a C-limit should be identifiable by a restricted range of maximum sizes. They will be rare, very large settlements for their region. Some will be the largest that have occurred over a very long period of time, though the individual settlements may have been 'brittle' and of short duration. We should find that settlements can move along a variety of trajectories to reach stasis. When some communities meet a C-limit, they will probably stop growing rather than shift to a different residential density. Such communities might simply cease to function under the stress of hitting the limit or they might manage to stabilise. But they would be unable to develop any other options because all their energy would be absorbed in dealing with communication problems. High-density stasis communities, because they are under extreme stress, might even display supercriticality as small changes in social life could produce a cascade of instability (Bak and Chen 1991: 26–8). Those communities which are able to practise some form of population control ought to be more stable than those whose growth continually pushes them against the I- and C-limits.

The model specifies that we should find cases of settlements which have stabilised along a C-limit at different residential densities. They are valuable targets for

Figure 5.13 Largest initial urban settlements in Mesopotamia, the Indus valley, north China, Mesoamerica and the South American montane littoral
Cheng-chou, China – second millennium BC (after Honan Provincial Museum 1977; Chang 1980); Harappā, Pakistan – third–second millennium BC (after Kenoyer 1992); Moche, Peru – first millennium AD (after Donnan and Mackay 1979; Topic 1982; and courtesy Ian Farrington); Mohenjo-daro, Pakistan – third–second millennium BC (Casal 1969 and Jansen 1979); Monte Albán, Mexico – first millennium BC and AD (after Blanton *et al.* 1978); Pampa Grande, Peru – first millennium AD (after Shimada 1978); Uruk, Iraq – third millennium BC (after Boehmer 1991)
Note: For Old Kingdom Memphis see chapter notes (p. 238) and pp. 190–1.

archaeological research into the factors which constrain settlement growth. These settlements offer the main clues to the position of a C-limit. If we find that maximum settlement sizes have been roughly similar for very long periods in several disparate regions, then the proposed constraints on community behaviour should be considered significant. If settlements remain behind a C-limit even when they lack only a small part of the assemblage required to make a transition, that will be strong evidence that the importance of the various components of the assemblage is roughly equivalent. There are, however, complications in interpreting the evidence. The significant characteristics may well be very mundane features of residence patterns which would not necessarily be ascribed much significance in social theory and may be underreported.

What will have to be demonstrated is that, just as there was a maximum areal extent for literate, compact, agrarian urban settlements of about 70–100 sq km regardless of local political and economic regional differences, so also there has been a maximum operational settlement size of around 100 ha for long periods of time in different regions. Potential candidates for the class of stasis settlements behind the 100 ha limit (Figure 5.14a) are Nan Matol, Poverty Point, Passo di Corvo and the great Vinča sites such as Potporanj and Turdas (Chapman 1981: 44). The latter sites are controversial because of the issue of how much of the occupation area was in use at any one time,[9] and the occupation density (Chapman 1990: 38) (see also p. 240). They are particularly interesting because they possess a material information storage system which might be called writing or pre-writing (Todorova 1978; Winn 1981) depending on one's view on cultural ranking (see further discussion pp. 157, 159). The Vinča culture has been viewed by Chernikh as 'a civilisation which never came into its own' (Todorova 1978: 55). Despite their probable scarcity, further examples of stasis settlements should be identifiable. There are numerous regions where this type of settlement might have existed, well beyond the immediate influence of other urban developments. More problematic are large, compact settlements which were on the periphery of urbanised states but not directly managed by them, such as the Wanka II site of Hatun Marca in the Mantaro, Peru (Earle *et al.* 1987, Hastorf 1993: 65–7, 71).

Other possible candidates for 100 ha stasis settlements are Urmitz and Schierstein, Hambledon Hill and the Alamito sites of Argentina (Figure 5.14b), though they may have had relatively low occupation densities. At this stage of analysis we can only differentiate between the two gross categories of compact and dispersed settlements in the predictions of the model. Because settlement area and community size are not closely correlated cross-culturally (Fletcher 1981a: 99–100, 113), we cannot make a more precise differentiation between degrees of occupation density on the basis of settlement plans alone. We cannot assume that all settlements with dispersed residence necessarily operated at such low residential densities that the communication constraint did not apply. An example of a possible problematic case is Snaketown in the south-west of North America (Figure 5.15). It is considered to be among the largest recorded Preclassic Hohokam sites of the tenth and early twelfth century AD (Wilcox *et al.* 1981: 202). Its maximum size was relatively stable for 500–600 years, ranging around 100–160 ha (Wilcox *et al.* 1981: 11, 144), which suggests that the occupation density was perhaps just high enough to be constrained by the 100 ha C-limit. The growth of the community in the eleventh century AD is associated with a marked expansion of irrigation in the Gila river basin (Cordell 1984: 207–11; Wilcox *et al.* 1981: 203–11), making it an ideal test case for the assessment of the role of internal behavioural factors in restricting the impact of economic change. The dynamics of that site, and possibly also the Alamito sites, should be a useful guide to the nature of the 100 ha C-limit, the role of changes in resource supply and the position of the threshold T-limit.

What the trajectories across the matrix suggest is that the inclusive labels of the current social approaches, such as 'urbanism', may tend selectively to subsume several, distinctly different settlement growth trajectories. The stasis settlements behind the 100 ha C-limit are as different from the early stages of Uruk and Monte Albán as Abbasid Baghdad was from early nineteenth-century London. Baghdad had no growth potential but London was about to begin its spectacular expansion. The significantly different material assemblage used in London from the eighteenth century onwards would alone serve to differentiate it from other pre-industrial settlements, such as Baghdad and Peking, which were of greater magnitude and political centrality. The implication is that the material features of such settlements should be comprehensible as interaction and communication devices whatever other social role they possessed and should serve to classify them in terms of their potential trajectories.

The status of the usual class of 'urban' settlement should be protected from the inclusion of the stasis cases, but not on the grounds that large stasis settlements were really palimpsests of numerous smaller sites. Although some sites may be offset palimpsests, we should not be over-ready to assume that this applies to all large sites. It is hardly tenable for Poverty Point and Nan Matol because of their distinct spatial pattern. Nor does this tactic remove Urmitz, because the extent of the site is defined by a distinct boundary. Contriving to edit out the large stasis settlements promotes a unilinear view of cultural change which does a disservice to the diversity of possible settlement growth.

Bypass settlements
In the previous discussion I have mentioned settlements in which the demands of communication are so slight that there is no constraint on settlement growth. Such settlements can reach an enormous size, well in excess of the size limit of their communication assemblage, but they attain these sizes only by following a trajectory to very low residential densities below the T-limit (Case 4). Possible examples which bypassed the 100 ha limit are Cahokia in the Mississippi Bottoms, during the fourteenth to sixteenth centuries AD, and Chaco Canyon in the twelfth and thirteenth centuries AD (Figure 5.16a and b). They are the smaller-scale equivalents, relative to the 100 ha C-limit, of Tikal and Angkor (Figure 4.14) relative to the 100 sq km limit.

Other possible bypass candidates which have exceeded the size of the 100 ha

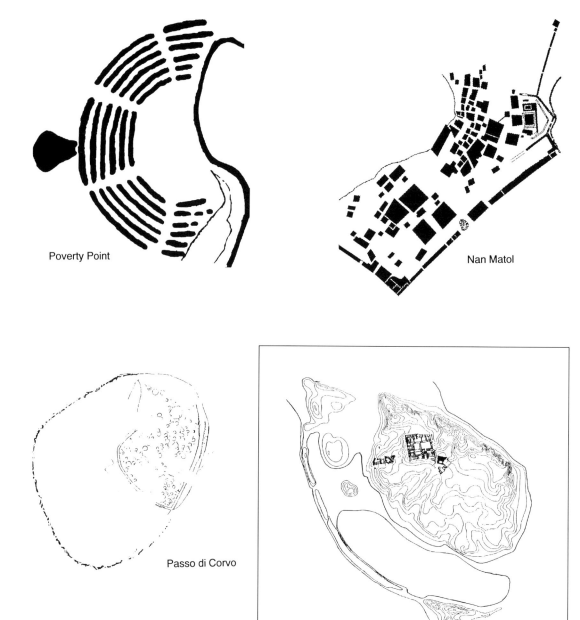

Figure 5.14 Proposed examples of stasis settlements < 100 ha cf. Mari
(a) Nan Matol, Ponape, Micronesia – fifteenth century AD (after Athens 1980; Hambruch 1936);
Passo di Corvo, Italy – fifth millennium BC (after Bradford and Williams Hunt 1946; Tinè 1983);
Poverty Point, USA – second and first millennium BC (after Webb 1977)
Note: Mari, Syria, third millennium BC (after Parrott 1949) included as an instance of a
Mesopotamian town to show the size of the proposed < 100 ha stasis settlements relative to the size of
a conventionally defined urban settlement

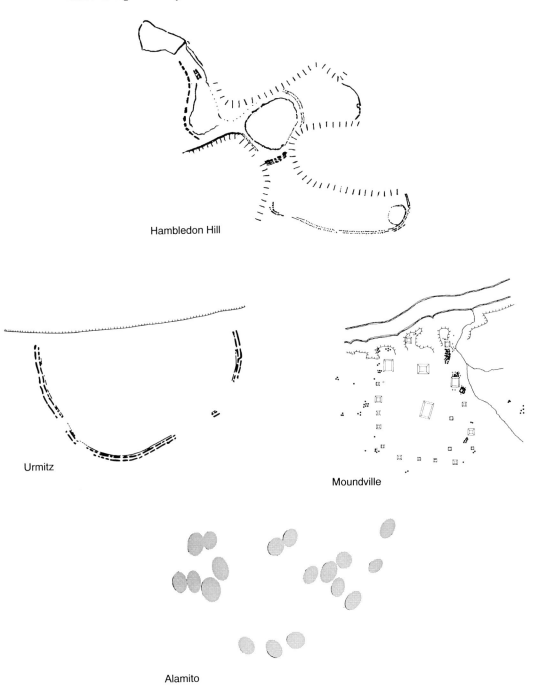

Hambledon Hill

Urmitz

Moundville

Alamito

Figure 5.14
(b) Alamito, Argentina – first millennium AD (after Reguerio 1970 and Willey 1971: 219–21);
Hambledon Hill, UK – fourth millennium BC (after Mercer 1985); Moundville, USA – fifteenth–
sixteenth century AD (after Steponaitis 1983), Urmitz, Germany – fourth millennium BC (after
Boelicke 1978)

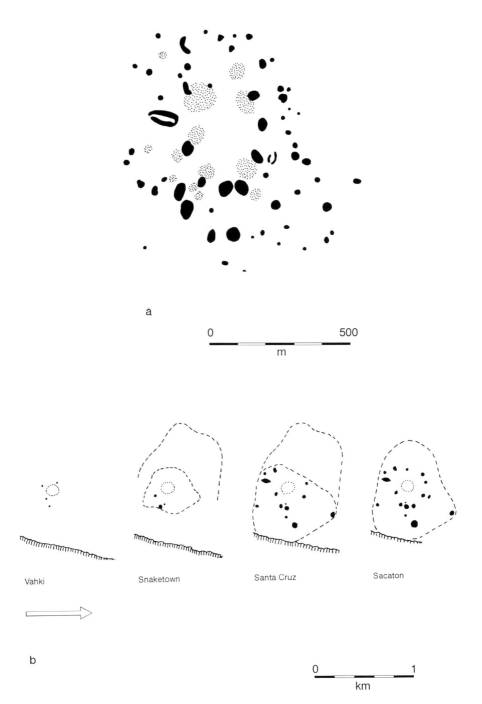

a

0   500

m

Vahki   Snaketown   Santa Cruz   Sacaton

b

0   1

km

Figure 5.15 Snaketown, south-west USA, *c.* 1000–1100 AD (after Wilcox *et al.* 1981)
(a) general plan

 mounds   trash heaps

(b) development sequence for Snaketown from early first millennium AD (the Vahki period) to early
second millennium AD (the end of the Sacaton period)

C-limit are the Hawaiian valley settlements prior to the late eighteenth century AD and the great Danubian (LBM) settlement complexes of Europe such as Merzbach on the Aldenhoven plateau in the fifth and fourth millennia BC (Figure 5.16c). The difficulty with the archaeological examples is ascertaining whether truly contemporaneous occupation was spread across the entire complex. In a dispersed settlement only a few of the buildings may have been contemporaneous. Estimates for two Danubian (LBK) sites, Elsloo and Bylany, range from seven to seventeen buildings in use in any one period. For each of the smaller clusters within the Merzbach complex, estimates suggest contemporaneous groups of only four long-houses (Whittle 1985: 82–7).[10]

Another special class of low-density settlement, which will probably be very rare but spectacular, comprises those which might increase abruptly to considerable size because their trajectory lies along the T-limit. The growth of such settlements would be subject to the usual short-term fluctuations that continually affect community size. Because population changes are relatively rapid but settlement area changes more slowly, a community's overall residential density could fluctuate slightly in and out of the density field in which the communication constraint begins to operate. Sometimes the community would be functioning under that constraint and sometimes not. Occasionally the brake on the extension of settlement area would be removed, and the highly structured spatial arrangement of a more compact settlement might therefore be rapidly translated outwards into a settlement of relatively vast extent. Such a community would then be extremely unstable. If its density continued to drop, the community would be confined within a highly ordered frame more appropriate for a densely settled community and without a suitable framework for its new, lower density, daily social life. If the density then increased again and the community lacked the I–C assemblage needed to function at such a large areal extent, it would face insuperable communication problems. The implications are that such settlements should be readily apparent, though rare. It is unlikely that the narrow density band would be hit upon for sufficiently long to produce such a settlement. Nor would it last very long because the conditions under which the community could operate are so restrictive. Very slight changes in residential density would lead to dispersal at lower densities or collapse under communication stress at higher densities. Such settlements should have a highly ordered spatial layout like that in the smaller settlements of the region and an anomalous spatial pattern in the later phases of settlement growth. Furthermore, we should expect them to be occupied for only brief periods compared to the smaller settlements which predate them. They ought to have low building densities but might look like compact settlements. If discovered, any such settlement will be of some importance to our understanding of the threshold (T-limit) value (pp. 92, 198–200).

The logical problem with low-density settlements
The class of dispersed settlement produces a disturbing epistemological problem. The class is logically valid given the premises of the model, but it unfortunately allows a convenient *ad hoc* solution to the problem posed by an archaeological site

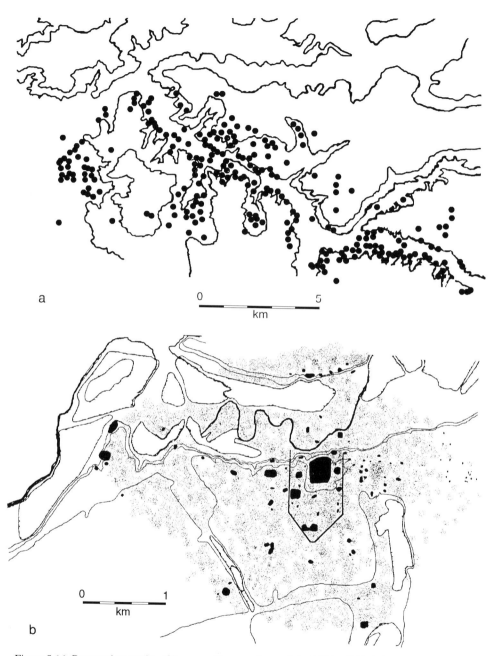

Figure 5.16 Proposed examples of bypass settlements beyond the 100 ha C-limit (contours schematic)
(a) Chaco Canyon, south-west USA, twelfth–fourteenth century AD (after Cordell 1984; Hayes, Bruyges and Judge 1981)

- buildings

(b) Cahokia, USA, thirteenth–sixteenth century AD (after Fowler 1975)

mounds   swamp   occupation (schematic)

Figure 5.16

(c) Merzbach, Germany, fifth millennium BC (after Kuper *et al.* 1977)

   ━━   buildings and findspots   enclosures

(d) Lapakahi, north Kohala, Hawaii, eighteenth century AD (after Kirch 1985)

       terraces   ■ □   buildings

which exceeds the area of a C-limit but does not have the material requirements for a transition across it. Possible instances are large sites with extensive monumental centres but with insufficient evidence of occupation density, for instance the great early first-millennium BC sites in Peru. The structure of Sechin Alto (Fung Pineda 1988) alone has an area of 300–400 ha and is part of a much larger site complex covering 10.5 sq km (Pozorski and Pozorski 1992: 860–1). If such a case can be identified as a low-density bypass case it does not threaten the model. The option is tempting because in some cases the claim may be valid and could lead to an interesting new insight into the settlement history of a region. The issue is further complicated because some apparently low-density occupation sites may have had sufficiently high interaction frequencies to fall just within the influence of the communication constraint. They will be non-decisive cases, because whether or not the sites conform to the model, they can be contained by it. Either way they do not provide a secure basis for a refutation. Our defence against possible self-deception is to recognise that this risk is present. The difficulty with low-density cases could be removed by devising a standard, cross-cultural, material index of interaction density which can precisely differentiate between those settlements which will or will not be subject to the communication constraint.

Conclusions

The stress matrix provides a way of making assessable propositions about the mechanics of settlement and community growth, and serves to organise a large amount of data into regionally cross-comparable, well-defined taxa. Among numerous possibilities three major classes of predictable settlement-growth trajectory have distinct, different implications for the future growth of a settlement. Many other trajectories can occur but if they do not approach the I- and C-limits there will not be predictable constraints on their outcome.

The first major class of predictable trajectory allows a transition across a C-limit. This requires a trajectory towards compact residence followed by an approach to the C-limit. Time and selective opportunity for the development of the necessary material facilities are required. Whatever the precise trajectory, only compact settlements, with the necessary material characteristics, should be able to make a sustainable transition across a C-limit and then begin to get away from the I-limit.

The second major class consists of trajectories which lead to settlements being in stasis close behind a C-limit. They do not possess all the requirements for a transition and cease to grow in areal extent. Communities on varied trajectories and with different material behaviour assemblages will stabilise as they come up against a C-limit. Their settlements will be the main guide to the actual areal value of the relevant C-limit. Because the degree of residential density is not a simple correlate of the degree of residential packing within a settlement, there will be some settlements which do not appear to be compact but are constrained by the C-limits. They may have had a higher residential density than the material evidence initially indicates. Such cases would also be very informative about the position of the T-limit.

The third major settlement-growth trajectory leads to settlements which operate at low residential densities and can bypass a C-limit to attain an area far in excess of the size limit for their I–C assemblage. These settlements should be able to cover very considerable areas but may be hard to delimit on the ground because their residential densities will grade into the average regional population densities.

We now need to consider the relationship between the trajectories and the development of the new material assemblages which manage interaction and communication and allow transitions across C-limits. What is required is an assessment of the residential contexts in which new material features have to develop, the different kinds of material changes needed for transitions across different C-limits and the role of changes in resource supply in maintaining settlement growth.

6

Settlement growth transitions and the role of the material

In the conditions of extreme stress that affect a compact community as it approaches a C-limit, substantial material aids will be required to act as behavioural buffers if the community is to make a successful transition across it. The nature of these aids depends on the tasks to be carried out by such a new mode of interaction and communication. People have to relate to their residential context and to each other. They must try to cope with visual and auditory signals and create predictable patterns of space and time – the four basic sets of signals on which community life depends. The material means that enable a transition should therefore involve changes in the ways in which all of these kinds of signals are controlled or reinforced. A single new feature will not be sufficient and cannot, in itself, be decisive.

The stress matrix illustrates why transition trajectories can only develop when they are accompanied by complementary changes in both communication efficacy and the control of interaction stress. At high residential densities in large settlements a marked increase in communication capacity would exacerbate behavioural stress, unless there was also a means of controlling the increase in the intensity of inter-action that resulted from it (see pp. 106–13). It is therefore essential, if a transition is to occur, that interaction controls and communication aids should develop concurrently. However, the model is not determinative: in similar circumstances communities might or might not innovate or adopt the prerequisites for a transition. Furthermore, though the components of the assemblage are necessary to initiate a transition, they are not, in themselves, sufficient to cause a major, sustained increase in settlement size across a C-limit. A capacity for sustained growth depends upon massive changes in the economic system. However, such change need not necessarily happen.

The implications for social theory of this decoupling of the material, the social and the 'economic' will be reviewed after a discussion of the different kinds of material assemblage associated with each of two transitions – the one across the 100 ha C-limit and the other across the 100 sq km C-limits. This may give us a better understanding of the implications of the I–C model, and the kinds of issues associated with the material behaviour approach. The analysis is concerned with the nature of transition assemblages. The behavioural consequences which should follow from possessing or not possessing the prerequisite components of the transition assemblage are reviewed along with the interpretative problems which derive from the variety of possible combinations of material features.

The nature and occurrence of transition assemblages

If several new material features must combine to produce a new I–C assemblage, then the chances of achieving a transition are small. The likelihood that a community will, by chance alone, develop all of the features of the required assemblage just when it needs them is exceedingly low. Nor is the community likely to produce the necessary controls to cope with its problems of behavioural stress when it has reached the crisis situation in which it is trapped between the I- and the C-limits. We cannot assume that communities understand the problems with which they are confronted. Time to allow for chance and serendipitous development to effect solutions will also be involved.

If a new assemblage is to develop, it should therefore be in place well before the C-limit for the older assemblage is reached. Only then would a community be able to adjust to the new communication and interaction patterns without the change itself exacerbating the overwhelming stress produced by continued growth. The matrix and the possible trajectories across it provide a specification of the range of settlement sizes in which the changes should begin to be apparent. For a transition to take place cumulative changes should start to appear in settlements with relatively low stress levels, i.e. in the lower third of the size range behind a C-limit. For example, the components of the 100 sq km transition assemblage should have begun to develop in settlements of 30 sq km or less. Later on the prerequisites for the transition will appear in a larger settlement, either because, at an earlier stage they have been borrowed from the repertoire of other communities or because the smaller settlements in which the prerequisites developed have expanded.

By the time a settlement is making the transition, it must already possess the basic form of the new assemblage. Within the terms of the model a community cannot cross a C-limit and then produce the assemblage needed to allow its interaction and communication to function at the new stress levels. The prerequisite assemblage is a preadaptation, i.e. it is taken up prior to the extreme stress conditions in the I–C wedge and then preferentially selected by the extreme demands on a community's behaviour. A 'Lamarckian' explanation in which circumstances define response is not appropriate. A logical equivalent of the neo-Darwinian biological explanation, in which variants are generated by processes whose internal functioning is independent of the context in which those variants may come to be of adaptive value, is more appropriate.

The transition assemblage of the 100 sq km C-limit

Some of the material associations of the great settlement size changes are not, in themselves, especially problematic. In the transition across the 100 sq km C-limit, associated with the 'Industrial Revolution', the means of providing effective communication in the expanding cities, such as trains to move people (Price-Williams 1885: 382–3) and printed newspapers to supply information promptly and cheaply, are well known. Their ancestry is also well documented. But we should not assume that the entire assemblage will be self-evident even for a case as well known as the 100 sq km transition. Other less obvious features, such as the increasingly prevalent use of brick and tile as building materials in the seventeenth and eighteenth century (Spate 1963: 530; Woodforde 1976: 62–73, 86–98), can also be seen as features that reduced the intensity of interaction by blocking signal transmission.

European towns were small in the eighteenth and early nineteenth century (Figures 4.9, 5.3). Most were less than 10 sq km in extent. Even London and Paris were no larger than the great pre-industrial imperial capitals (Figure 6.1a).[1] Their massive expansion began after the early 1800s AD (Figure 6.1b). The components of the I–C assemblage used in the industrial urban transition had antecedents that were spread over most of western and central Europe in the four centuries prior to the mid-nineteenth century. Their initial role was not necessarily the same as their eventual use. Industrialised modular architecture had its immediate ancestry in Georgian middle-class housing (Ramsey and Harvey 1972) and the elite archi-tecture of the eighteenth century. The elegant terraces of Bath and London (Cruickshank 1985) (Figure 6.2) established modular design in the architectural repertoire. This rigour and consistency was then re-expressed in the monotonous, back-to-back housing which dominates our perception of early industrial settle-ments, such as the great commercial ports of the western seaboard of the United Kingdom and the mining villages of Wales, the Midlands and Scotland (Chapman 1971). Whatever the aesthetic reasons for its initial development and the entrepreneurial reasons for its later use in producing the mass housing of the nine-teenth century, it also created a more predictable, interchangeable, standard space for residence than had previously existed. As well as being a commentary on class relations, it divided the social space of millions of human beings into repetitiously ordered, predictable units. We need to consider its behavioural role as well as the more familiar social role it played in the definition of social class in industrialising communities.

Newspapers are descended partly from the newsbooks of the seventeenth century which described political events in Europe. Through them the events of the Thirty Years War, for example, were reported in England (Westmancoat 1985: 19). In the eighteenth century printed newspapers were produced in London and in the major provincial towns. *The Times* (begun as the *Daily Universal Register*) was first published in 1785 (Westmancoat 1985: 24–6). By 1856 newspapers had prolifer-ated throughout Britain.

From the sixteenth century onwards in Europe there was a critical change in the human relationship to time, effected by the use of clocks. Carlo Cipolla (1967) and Landes (1983) provide summaries of the development and introduction of the clock in Europe, while Needham (1965; and Needham, Wang Ling and De Solla Price 1960) has offered a review of the contentions about the differing cultural expressions of time in China and Europe from the fifteenth to the nineteenth century. The role of material change is well expressed in a petition to the city fathers of Lyons in 1481 proposing, 'the need for a great clock whose strokes could be heard by all citizens in all parts of the town. If such a clock were to be made, more merchants would come to fairs, the citizens would be very consoled, cheerful and happy and would live more orderly lives' (Cipolla 1967: 42). Substantial production of clocks began in Geneva in the sixteenth and seventeenth century when the city was less than 1 sq km in extent and contained only 10,000–20,000 people (Monter 1975: 2, 6, 116). Time-pieces were then exported in large quantities to London and other European capitals (Cipolla 1967).

Railway trains were initially developed to transport coal in the North of England and the Midlands (Cromar 1979). They were primarily used in small towns which were less than 10 sq km in extent. After several decades the technology was introduced in an elaborated form into London and Paris, during the first half of the nineteenth century, to move people. This development occurred in parallel with attempts to extend the use of horse-drawn vehicles – the ancestors of the omnibus in the early nineteenth century (Barker and Robbins 1975: 1–33). Those communities which had substantial communication and interaction controls in place and already developing, however, rudimentary, made an immediate transition across the 100 sq km C-limit (Fletcher 1981a: 113, 116).

Studying the transition assemblage for the 100 ha C-limit

The obvious target for an extension of the analysis is an assessment of the earlier 100 ha C-limit which was involved in the initial formation of large urban settlements, as, for instance, in Mesopotamia, Egypt, the Indus valley, north China, Mesoamerica and western South America. The value of using the 100 ha transition as a case study is that, while the relevant regional data have been extensively studied and are potentially accessible for a test of any hypothetical model, there is obviously still much to learn and the model may help to suggest future research strategies.[2]

The chances of identifying each feature of a transition assemblage in the archaeo-logical record are relatively favourable. Since a community may borrow features from its neighbours and the relevant features should be part of a regional cultural assemblage, we ought to find the ancestry of the various prerequisites spread across the entire region in which a transition has occurred, not restricted to the basal layers of the few settlements which first achieved a vast increase in size. Assessing the claim for prerequisite assemblages is therefore archaeologically practicable.

Predictions about the transition assemblages for each of the proposed C-limits should be possible. Since each successively larger C-limit must involve cumulatively greater I–C stress, the features of each successive assemblage should be distinctly more efficacious as ways of controlling interaction and aiding communication, and probably also more substantial or elaborate to do that. Conversely, working back from the prerequisites for the 100 sq km transition, with which we are at least partially familiar, we should be able to predict some of the likely components of the 100 ha and 1–2 ha transition requirements. We need to envisage simpler material features that could manage the stimuli of sight and sound and help to order the dimensions of space and time. Suggestions about the kinds of material behaviour which may have served to control interaction and aid communication during the 100 ha transition can be derived in two ways: by envisaging an I–C assemblage which is less complex and less energy-demanding than the familiar industrial

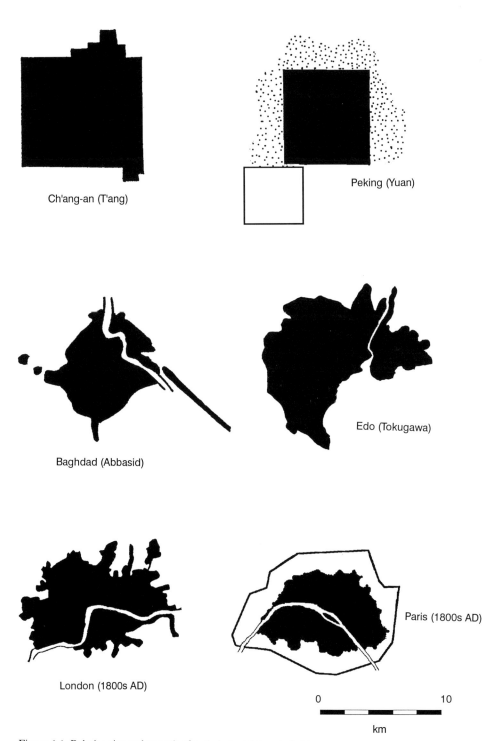

Ch'ang-an (T'ang)

Peking (Yuan)

Baghdad (Abbasid)

Edo (Tokugawa)

London (1800s AD)

Paris (1800s AD)

0   10

km

Figure 6.1 Relative size and growth of early industrial capital cities
(a) size of pre-industrial capital cities in comparison to London (after Clayton 1964) and Paris (after *Imperial Gazette* 1885) in the early nineteenth century AD. For sources on the other cities see Figure 4.10.

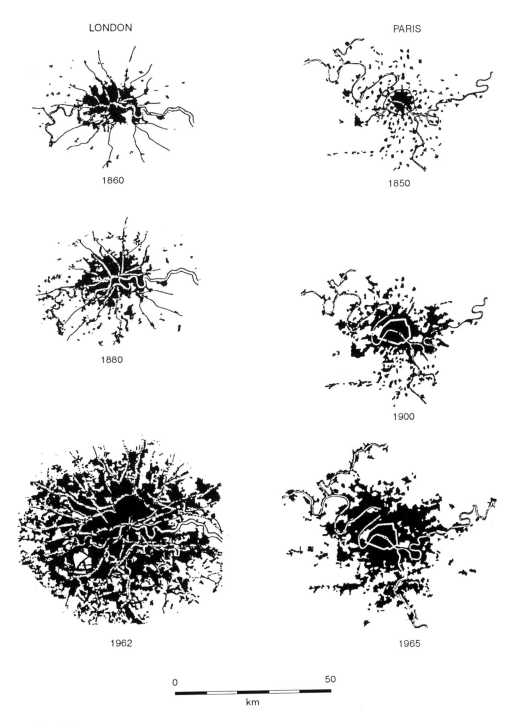

Figure 6.1
(b) growth and size of London (after Sutcliffe 1964) and Paris (after Doxiades 1968) in the nineteenth and twentieth centuries AD.

Figure 6.2 Georgian terrace housing in the UK, eighteenth century AD: the Royal Crescent, Bath, designed in 1767 by John Wood the Younger

equivalents and by looking at the variety of material attributes in those initial urban, compact settlements larger than 100 ha in extent.

Some of the specific features which were able to control interaction and assist communication are obvious enough, such as spatial segregation and writing. We need to see what additional aspects of early urban assemblages regulated interaction and communication, whatever other functions and social correlates they may also have possessed. Further empirical research will be needed to identify whether or not the proposed features are where and when the model predicts they ought to be found. Their presence in some urban settlements does not determine the answer to predictions about when the features first appeared nor their appearance before the expansion across the 100 ha C-limit. The archaeological record may refute the predictions about the prerequisites and the timing of their occurrence, or we may find that further specific enquiry is needed before the data can provide a decisive test of the argument.

My eventual concern is to outline the likely kinds of material behaviour required in compact urban settlements as they approached the 100 ha boundary. It is not my intention to produce a general definition of agrarian-based urban communities. As will become apparent, the model predicts that later urban settlements need not have retained all their initial behavioural characteristics. Later settlements may also have accumulated other varied, regionally specific material features. The proposed 100 ha C-limit and the features required to get across it do not constitute a definition of urbanism and are not intended as one. Current social definitions of urbanism recognise it in settlements much smaller than the proposed 100 ha C-limit. The C-limit is a convention for a specific critical transition within the general class of agrarian urban growth. The proposed transition assemblage is the means whereby that C-limit was crossed.

The predicted characteristics must be directly recognisable, not intangible or assumed from other evidence. In an archaeological context the existence of a missing prerequisite component cannot be assumed from the presence of the other prerequisites. Such an assumption would infringe the logic of the analysis by overruling potential refutation cases in which a predicted characteristic is absent. While a case can be made that the absence of a predicted feature is to be expected, because of taphonomic factors, the aim of enquiry must be to find a suitable test context. In due course an independent test will be available in the assemblages of the stasis settlements. If the behavioural constraint on growth is a significant factor, those settlements should lack some of the features of the transition assemblage.

The dual exercise of controlling interaction and aiding communication is more easily discussed in terms of the signals to be regulated than in terms of interaction and communication as separate categories. I will therefore specify the material phenomena and the classes of signals which they manage and then outline their effects on both communication and interaction. The required material entities for the more familiar management of sight and sound signals will be considered first, then the less familiar ordering of time, followed by a discussion of the problematic issue of spatial ordering.

Components of the 100 ha C-limit transition assemblage
Visual and auditory signals

Visual and auditory signals can be controlled in two ways: the transmission of signals can be blocked, or information storage devices can reduce the load on memory, and restrict disputes about contracts. The transmission of signals can be controlled in many different ways. Walls act as baffles to intervisibility even if they are very flimsy. The degree to which the locations in a settlement are intervisible depends upon its layout (Figure 6.3). Interaudibility is controlled by durable materials which absorb the sound or by walls that are high enough to block it. The arrangement of structures also defines our perceptions of the private and public spatial domains in houses and residential districts (Newman 1973; Rapoport 1969, 1982). Different kinds of spatial messages, in association with differing materials, will have different consequences for interaction. Prior to the high stress milieu of a transition we should find an intensified use of barriers to interaction.

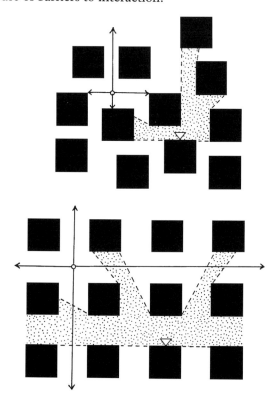

Figure 6.3 Settlement topography and intervisibility.

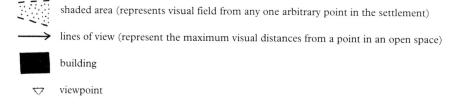

shaded area (represents visual field from any one arbitrary point in the settlement)

⟶   lines of view (represent the maximum visual distances from a point in an open space)

▮   building

▽   viewpoint

Durable materials   Within residence units there are several ways of blocking signals from outside, such as durable materials for walling, and the segregation of industrial districts. We should not expect to find a predominance of buildings made of reeds, light timber or flimsy screening materials during a transition. The proposition needs further empirical refinement, for instance on whether and to what degree wattle and daub walls of varying thickness would be adequate in these circumstances. The form of the buildings also requires attention. Presumably those with thick thatch roofs that descend to near ground level, as in the fourth and third millennium BC Yang Shao sites of China (Yang 1975), would suffice as signal controllers.

Baffles and barriers (Figure 6.4)   The removal of domestic activity from public view cuts down the amount of interaction between domestic groups and the public world. Withdrawal from public interaction can be obtained in several ways. The private rooms of a residence can be screened from main thoroughfares by the use of interior courtyards shielded by continuous blocks of rooms or within high enclosure walls. Direct intervisibility can be avoided by locating residence on the upper floors of a multi-storey building. Even placing baffle walls or offset doorways at the entrance to a residence unit will help to cut down interaction frequencies (Figure 1.1).

On a larger scale, offset streets and curved roadways or the use of irregular building frontages block intervisibility. The terracing of residence units also serves to reduce inter-association and break intervisibility: residence units face out over the top of the lower adjacent buildings and are offset from neighbouring buildings. Large open areas, surrounded by non-residential buildings, should also tend to restrict the noise and disturbance of big public gatherings. An additional location

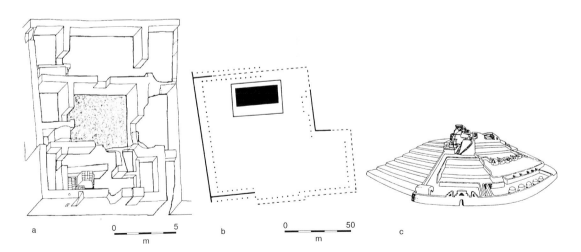

Figure 6.4 Baffles and barriers (no orientation)
Examples from (a) Indus valley – from Mohenjo-daro, later third millennium BC (after Jensen 1985); (b) China – from Erh-li-t'ou, early second millennium BC (after Chang 1977); (c) South American montane littoral – a Mochica example of the late first millennium BC, reconstructed from a pottery model (after Kubler 1962)

and one which should be carefully looked for is the use of areas outside the built area or outside the boundary walls of a settlement. In early Abbasid Baghdad a market was established at Kalkh on the outskirts of the urban area (Lassner 1970).

Stored data (Figure 6.5) – sign sets, referential sets and numbers A system which can hold data independent of human memory provides the means to aid communication and can help to regulate interaction frequencies. A concrete means of managing data assists the transmission of messages through time – by storage and conspicuous display – or through space by moving them from source to recipient without placing demands on memory or on speed of movement. Any material device, whether written or in the form of a referential mnemonic, such as the *quipu* (Ascher and Ascher 1981), can achieve these effects.

The obvious value of a system of hard information is that it helps to control selective recollection of agreements. Negotiations can be simplified over a wide range of exchange agreements because the contract can be made concrete. In a marriage exchange the three cows which were agreed to a year ago cannot turn, by convenient recall, into three goats when the day of exchange arrives. Long disputes to settle such incompatible recollections would be minimised, at least in the initial stages of the use of documented contracts. Trading can be expedited and transactions are more reliable because reporting is independent of human recollection. Most of these features need be managed by only a small number of people in the community for their effect on communal interaction and communication to be apparent. They allow large numbers of people to deal with each other by proxy instead of face to face. Even honorifics and names alone serve to regularise interaction and delimit access by emphasising the differences enforced by social practice. The significance of signs used in public display, as on the Danzantes wall at Monte Albán and at San José Mogote (Figures 6.6a, b), needs further assessment. If they are the only form that is visible, can we regard them as a sufficient prerequisite?

The use of numbers also serves to reduce ambiguity in enumeration and measurement. Their role in transactions is obvious enough. A finer correspondence between the relative values of items can be achieved. As a result there is less wastage or effort to achieve correspondence in exchanges. The use of numbers allows predictive procedures. The relationship between numbers can be observed over time and acted upon. New consistencies are available that are not apparent when memory has to act as the data carrier. Numbering is, of course, fundamental to calendric systems. Numbers also profoundly affect the possibility of linking the activities of large groups of people. Records of taxation rates and preceding payments help to order the resource yields of entire communities. While this may allow a small elite to aggrandise itself, it also creates further wealth in the form of redistribution and the need for new services. Whether or not this serves the individual well, it does allow greater integration of activities than is possible without a number and sign system. Much higher rates of resource supply and movement of personnel can exist when they are buffered by the use of sign and number sets.

a

b

HUA-T'ING

c

SHANG

Figure 6.5 Stored data
Examples from (a) Mesopotamia – tablets of Uruk IVb, mid-fourth millennium BC (after Falkenstein 1936); (b) Egypt – Nubian pre-dynastic signs, early third millennium BC (after Williams 1980); (c) China – (i) Hua-t'ing signs (potmarks) of the fifth millennium BC (after Chang 1977) and (ii) Shang dynasty inscribed tortoise shell, late second millennium BC (after Chou 1979)
Note: See also Figure 8.3 for South American montane littoral – Moche, brick marks Figure 8.2 (after Hastings and Moseley 1975) and Mochica decorated beans Figure 8.4 (after Larco Hoyle 1939).

Discussion

A behavioural analysis regards material barriers to interaction, together with material devices of communication, as complementary controls on signal load. The viewpoint is rather different from the usual approach, which would deal with sign and number sets either as interrelated components of language and science or as minor tools of political and economic power. While devices such as writing undoubtedly have a political role, the behavioural analysis is concerned with the general effects of such communication systems on the interaction within a community and not with the more specific social role of those systems in particular communities. The purpose of the approach is not to explain how writing was used in Mesopotamia or why it was developed in a particular way. Nor does it assume the same particular use of sign sets in China and Mesoamerica. Specialist knowledge of the background and institutions of each particular community is needed to deal with such questions (Cheung 1983; Schmandt-Besserat 1986, 1992). This enquiry is directed at the overall effects of concrete information systems and their consequences for community life and settlement growth. At this broad level of assessment, even systems as diverse as writing and the *quipu* can be considered in the same terms.

What a material behaviour approach emphasises is that the use of characteristics such as more durable walling, enclosed courtyard houses and sign systems ought to accumulate well prior to the marked expansion of the settlements beyond the 100 ha C-limit. They were not derivatives of the great cities but made them possible and were in turn elaborated by them.

Temporal referents

People pattern time, devoting much of their active behaviour to it (Betzig and Turke 1985; Carlstein, Parkes and Thrift 1978; Lenntorp 1976; Parkes and Thrift 1980; Siegman and Feldstein 1979). Gross (1984) and Munn (1992) have provided useful overviews of the topic. Carlstein has been developing a methodology for presenting time patterning (1982).[3] The active regulation of time, however, is not sufficient for the requirements of the model. The material ordering of time is also a mundane feature of our daily lives. For instance, the positioning of storage facilities and the locations of garbage dumps pattern the timing and frequency of movement within a settlement. The topography of route space acts in this way as a regulator of the timing of interaction frequency. Several of the material components of behaviour could have a profound impact on time management by controlling rates of activity and providing a material definition of time.

Route differentiation (Figure 6.7)   Time is patterned by the material framework which regulates route activity. If all the residence units and activity areas in a settlement are equally spaced, all route activity has to cover the same distances on average and competes equally with all other kinds of activity. By contrast, if major through routes are differentiated from minor access routes between residence units, then the rapid transit moves do not overlap so markedly with the shorter, less energy demanding journeys which connect adjacent domestic units. On the other hand, some movements between residence units can be made by going out on to a major route and then back into the limited access routes within and around the residence units. Time and distance relationships are specified and delimited by the differing degrees of access to points within a settlement. Extreme differentiation of routes into main roads, minor streets and alleyways creates a hierarchy of access time. Time, as experienced, has been divided into magnitudes of rate.

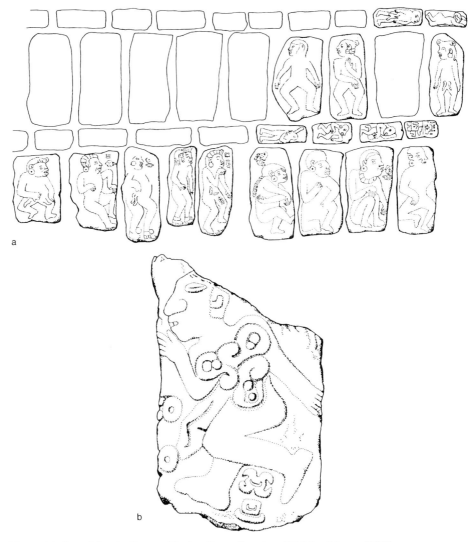

Figure 6.6 Stored data in Oaxaca, Mexico, first millennium BC (after Marcus 1980)
(a) 'Danzantes' wall from Monte Albán, later first millennium BC
(b) 'Danzantes' slab from San José Mogote, mid-first millennium BC
Note: In Fig. 6.6b the signs in front of the person's knee are considered to be early examples of a calendric notation (Marcus 1980)

Because route differentiation affects the time allocated to differing scales of route activity, and the scheduling of movement, it will tend to reduce interaction frequencies and also help to speed the transmission of information and resources. A specialised instance – the military requirement that garrisons must be rapidly directed to threat points on the periphery of a fortified settlement – is an obvious example of the role of route differentiation. What the material behaviour analysis suggests is that route differentiation rather than a change in transportation technology is the essential requirement. The instance of nineteenth-century European urban growth has given the impression that a new means of transport (e.g. the mechanised train) is necessary to achieve a marked settlement size increase by moving resources more rapidly. But the great initial urban developments do not support this generalisation for all C-limit transitions. In two cases, the Indus valley and Peru, changes in the transport system of the cities were well established before the large urban centres began to grow. The use of carts is claimed in the Early Harappan, half a millennium or more before the growth of Mohenjo-daro and Harappā (Mughal 1972; Possehl 1990), yet the Indus towns were among the smallest of the initial urban cases. In Peru domestication of the llama as a beast of burden is apparent in the second millennium BC (Strong and Evans 1952: 32; Wing 1980: 163–4), well before the Mochica settlements began their growth at the turn of the millennium (Moseley 1992: 161–84). On the other hand, Mesoamerica never developed new modes of moving resources, and used only human porterage and boats, yet the region produced settlements up to 25 sq km in extent (for Teotihuacan see Millon *et al.* 1973). The use of porters and boats was expanded but their movement rates are inelastic. In China the use of carts as transporters of bulk resources is not known from the Shang dynasty. It is apparent only in the Chou dynasty, long after the rise of Cheng-chou, the first extensive Shang urban settlement (Chang 1980: 263–88). Shih Shih refers to a merchant of Chou Loyang who had carts by the hundred (Trewartha 1952: 71). By contrast, the earliest use of wheeled vehicles, in the form of chariots which were used by the elite, only appeared around 1100 BC near the end of the Shang dynasty (Dewall 1964: Fig. 5; Littauer 1977). These cases suggest that the role of changes in route differentiation, as an aid to the movement of people and resources within larger settlements, is therefore essential, rather than the development of new transport technologies for regional resource movement.[4]

Calendrics (e.g. Figure 6.6b)   A material pattern of repeated periodicities is of consequence for group behaviour as a referent for many aspects of the periodicities of the natural world. Plainly the use of such periodicity marking would have some effect on the interactions of human beings with their context. More than anything else it reduces random searching through time and space for appropriate moments and localities where events are to occur. Elaborate expressions in the form of calendars or time markers which divide up the sidereal year provide consistent units against which other less regular events can be monitored. A material referent that marks constant units of time will assist the interaction frequency of a community by

Figure 6.7 Differential access
Examples from (a) Mesopotamia – Tel al-Raqa'i, fourth millennium BC (after Curvers and Schwartz
1990); (b) Indus – Mohenjo-daro, later third millennium BC (after Marshall 1931); Mesoamerica –
Teotihuacan (northern part), early to mid-first millennium AD (Millon et al. 1973)

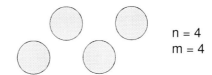

n = 4
m = 4

mi

mii

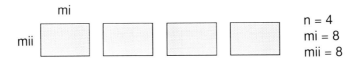

n = 4
mi = 8
mii = 8

n = 4
m = 16

a

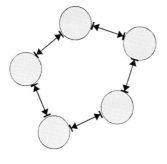

b

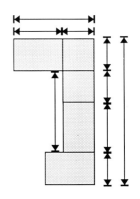

providing the possibility of a more precise coincidence of meetings and activities on varying scales of magnitude and precision than seasonal indicators such as equinoctial markers. This function needs more consideration, especially from the records of early urban communities (Aveni 1983).

Spatial referents

Spatial patterning requires specific attention because it visibly dominates community life and tends to be well represented in the archaeological record. However, it has not been extensively analysed in behavioural terms, as a non-verbal message system. A behavioural analysis is concerned with the particular critical perceptual effects which were part of the aggregate social impact of these spatial features. The analysis suggests that a complex suite of spatial patterning was necessary for the 100 ha transition, including not only two socially predictable features – segregation and great monuments – but also rectilinearity, for which a rigorous conventional 'social' explanation is lacking.

A simple hypothetical model of the structure of material spatial messages (see p. 37) in the settlements of small sedentary agrarian communities leads to some tentative suggestions about the particular behavioural role of these three major forms of spatial organisation. As well as having socio-political roles, they may also produce specific perceptual effects which serve to control variability in spatial signals. According to the spatial message model, persistent replication tends to result in loss of internal coherence (see pp. 39–40). In particular, the amount of variation in the sizes of entities in a settlement will begin to increase, swamping the discreteness of the signals on which the message structure depends (Figure 2.10). Empirical evidence suggests that variability increases, even in small-scale communities, as replication continues and the settlement grows (Figure 2.9). In time, as the spatial message becomes less predictable, larger communities in much bigger compact settlements should experience stress problems. The increasing variability has to be controlled otherwise the resident community will lose its coherent spatial framework. The three ways of ordering space constitute a behavioural suite which serves to control spatial variability as a settlement becomes larger.

Redundancy   The repeated use of similar signals helps to counter the effects of divergent replication. The more signals of a given kind are present, the smaller the impact of a rogue value. In a distribution with a population of 5 a single additional aberrant value can have a substantial impact on the central tendency and the degree of variation but in a population of 20 its impact is relatively small. For this scaling

Figure 6.8 Spatial signal redundancy
(a) rectilinear and curvilinear message repetition
n = number of buildings   m = number of similar measurements produced
(b) different spatial pattern replication for rectilinear and curvilinear buildings and features
The gaps between adjacent round rooms are a different class of distance from the radii. The gaps are also not regulated by the radii and can therefore each be unique. By contrast in a rectilinear building, rooms can be abutted, thereby repeating earlier distances and also making a combined distance (i.e. two distances added together, making a longer one) from the contiguous walls of two adjacent rooms.

effect to work, the incidence of aberrants per replicative event also needs to be kept down. In the absence of a means of measuring other than the human eye, consistency is subject to errors of observation and recollection. What will restrain increasing aggregate variance over time is the production of several discrete but very similar signals in one building event (m on Figure 6.8a, e.g. the construction of one building or one room), and the capacity for one built feature to be a direct template for the next. Neither of these conditions is provided by curvilinear spaces. The most effective ground-plan shape for doing this with a serial message is a rectilinear form. Four building events only produce 4 distance values (n) from the radii of circular buildings (Figure 6.8a). Each building event is separate and the addition of more circular structures does not lead to an additional occurrence of more radii. Instead, different kinds of distances are produced (Figure 6.8b). By contrast, a square building provides 4 closely similar lengths. Therefore only 4 building events are needed to produce 16 values. However, the message does not denote more than one value in a series. A rectangular building, on the other hand, provides two closely similar length values (mi) and two closely similar width values (mii) and only 4 building events are needed to produce 8 of each. Furthermore, as rectangular buildings are aggregated, more linear dimensions are produced. When a rectilinear structure is tacked on to the end of an existing building, the width value of the established building is available as a template. There is no equivalent constraint or direct referential aid for circular or curvilinear structures.

The rectilinear form is a more complex mathematical message than the circle: a circle can be described by fewer mathematical terms than a square or a rectangle. A rectilinear form has an additional quality as far as the serial patterning of space is concerned. It can provide at least two values in a pattern (e.g. in a series) rather than one and therefore provides a milieu with more spatial, predictive potential. This should lead to preferential tacit selection in favour of rectangular rather than square buildings or features. A square does have a higher redundancy level, with further repeats of the same distance, but does not express a relationship within a series. As has been noted on several occasions, there often appear to be ratio rules in the sizes of structures within a single settlement. The pattern is consistent with a serial order though a series does not in itself inevitably define a ratio regularity.[5] Curvilinear structures do not provide these additional signal associations. The analysis specifies the role of rectilinearity and even more particularly the perceptual function of approximately rectangular buildings, or of buildings carrying several different linear distances. The importance for studies of interaction is that the analysis shows how a class of building shape operates strongly to signal a message relationship. The message analysis predicts that the first settlements to make an internally generated transition across the 100 ha limit should do so with rectilinear buildings.

Mechanical, functional, common-sense explanations of the role of rectilinearity lead to different predictions from those of the message model. A mechanical functional explanation claims, for example, that rectilinearity aids rapid settlement growth because erecting a rectilinear building is quicker, especially with modular building units such as bricks. The argument, however, can only revolve around the use of such modular building components. With pisé or with stone rubble there would be no specific advantage in building either round or rectangular buildings. In practice the mechanical advantage probably lies with circular buildings because they are more structurally stable. Curvilinear forms do not suffer from corner collapse, a structural failure to which rectilinear buildings are very vulnerable. Furthermore, there is no mechanical reason why very large aggregates of round buildings cannot be constructed. A spectacular example is the nineteenth-century AD palace of the Kabaka in Kampala (Figure 6.9). A functional thesis that extensive settlements and major monuments could not be built from curvilinear structures is untenable. If they are rare or absent during the high-density trajectory across a C-limit, then an explanation other than technological pragmatics is required.

The argument about the functional value of rectilinear structures comes down to the role of modular building units such as bricks. The use of brick would make a difference in construction rates and convenience in building between rectilinear and curvilinear structures. This allows us to decide which of the mechanical-functional or signal function models is a more satisfactory explanation of the role of rectilinear buildings in the initial formation of the great urban settlements. If we find cases where pisé mud continued along with rectilinearity (as in China 2000–1600 BC) (Institute of Archaeology 1962) or examples where rubble masonry rather than brick was used (as in Mesoamerica 1000 BC to AD 500) (Grove 1985), then the mechanical-functional model, while it may appear to have local relevance in regions where mud-brick was used, is not generally applicable. Conversely, while the

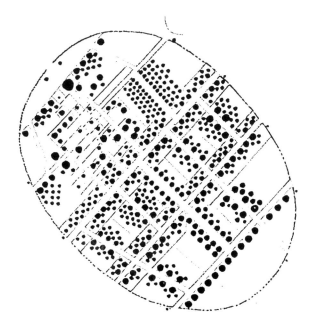

Figure 6.9 Kabaka's palace at Kampala, Uganda, nineteenth century AD. Plan drawn by senior member of the Kabaka's cabinet (after Gutkind 1963) (no scale)

mechanical-functional model cannot explain why the initial growth of large settlements will not take place with curvilinear structures, the I–C model would explain this situation. According to the model, the curvilinear forms are less effective as carriers of redundancy and spatial messages as outlined above. In circumstances of high communication stress they should therefore fail to allow the growth of compact settlements to the same potential size as rectilinear buildings will permit.

Segregation (Figure 6.10)   A large settlement which operates as if it were several small settlements fitted together would serve to contain the problem of increasing spatial variability. The rise, within each discrete part of the large settlement, in the variation in its spatial message, would be relatively small. To be effective, the major segregators must obstruct or restrict direct access across the settlement. Discrete barrios, substantial barriers dividing the settlement into sectors, and very large buildings or enclosures which restrict route access across the centre of a settlement, would achieve this effect. The latter serve to cut down interaction across the settlements by blocking the shortest access routes.

   Only substantial material segregators or large open zones between residence sectors can be accepted as definite barriers. Class formation or the growth of distinct service sectors could assist this segregation but would not be sufficient without the aid of material segregation by barriers or space. What is required is that the habitual movement of the occupants into different perceptual fields should be minimised, without the additional social stress of enforcing segregation by moral or active sanctions. From the perspective of a material behaviour approach, the spatial divisions must play the key role in segregating groups of people, rather than social distinctions alone. Sectors where people of similar social status live should therefore be divided from each other as well as from those where different social classes live. Spatial segregation, for instance, can be achieved by canals and other physical barriers around which the settlement gradually expands. Whether they lie within or between sectors of different social class, the restrictions on access still apply. Social values might be ascribed to the role of such internal features, but these values are epiphenomena in the terms of an analysis of material behaviour. Furthermore, to recognise that interaction in a community is being affected by internal barriers such as the barrier walls and the constrained traffic flow between households in Monte Albán (Blanton 1978: 99), or the large enclosure walls of the Harappan settlements (Allchin and Allchin 1982), does not require a specific explanation of why they were created in the first place. The human actors might have various explanations depending on their social position. The intentions of the power elite may have had little to do with trying to improve the quality of community life or managing interaction stress. People's perceptions are a legitimate topic of research in their own right but an investigation of intentions is not required here. What is predicted is that segregation by class or function, without a substantial material component, will not suffice for the initial transition across a C-limit.

   As is apparent, not only will spatial segregation help to control the message coherence of spatial signalling but it will also serve to control interaction frequencies

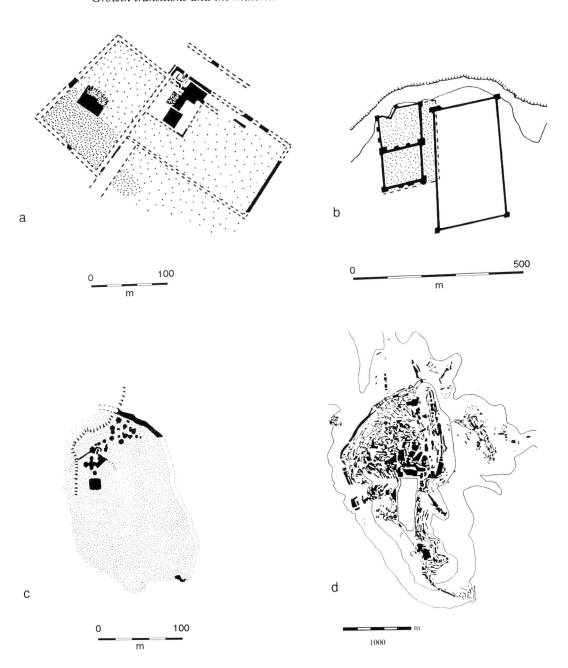

Figure 6.10 Spatial segregation of settlement space
Examples from (a) Egypt – Abydos, third millennium BC (after Kemp 1977); (b) Indus – Kalibangan II, later third millennium BC (after Thapar 1975); (c) China – Pan-po-ts'un, fifth millennium BC (after Institute of Archaeology 1962), (d) Mesoamerica – Monte Albán, first millennium AD (after Blanton *et al.* 1978).
Abydos is divided into two main enclosures bounded by thick walls with an additional smaller, central enclosure. Kalibangan II is divided into two residential sectors surrounded by large walls. Note that the shaded area is the location of Kalibangan I (see Figure 6.11). In Monte Albán the core area north of the great plaza is segregated by steep terraces and closed-off roads. The large circuit walls also segregate intra- from extramural residence, especially along the ridge to the east.

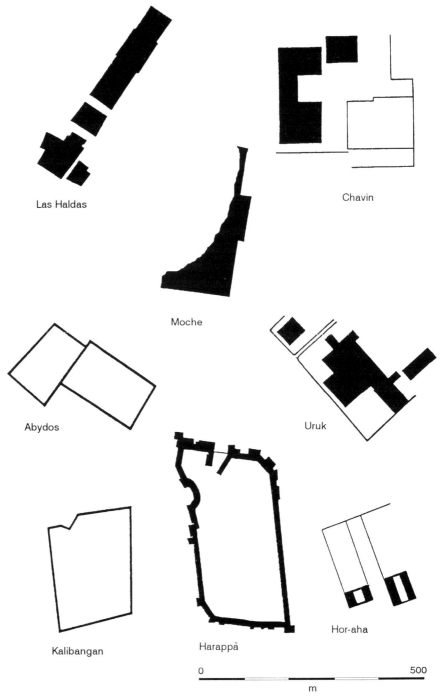

Las Haldas

Chavin

Moche

Abydos

Uruk

Hor-aha

Kalibangan

Harappā

0   500

m

Figure 6.11 Large linear monuments – scaled comparison
Examples from: Mesopotamia – Uruk temple complex, third millennium BC (after Mellaart 1979);
Egypt – Hor-aha estate, third millennium BC (after Emery 1949), and Abydos, third millennium BC
(see Kemp 1977); Indus – Kalibangan I, early third millennium BC (after Thapar 1975); Harappā,
third millennium BC (after Wheeler 1947); South American montane littoral – Las Haldas, early
second millennium BC (after Moseley 1975); Chavin, early first millennium BC (after Lumbreras
1974); Moche, Huaca del Sol, early first millennium AD (after Donnan and Mackay 1979)
Note: The plan of the Hor-aha 'estate' is a scaled reconstruction from the detailed model constructed
in the First Dynasty beside the tomb of Hor-aha at Saqqara.

within a community. This behavioural segregation, however, creates a new problem. If a large settlement is operating as a group of discrete residential entities, what coherent perceptual milieu is integrating its social behaviour? We have to find an explanation for the aggregate coherence of community behaviour, not only in social terms (e.g. the role of political control), but also in terms of non-verbal material behaviour. Just as a small sedentary community apparently has to have a coherent spatial message format in its settlement, so likewise we should expect that the community in a large settlement should also have some kind of spatial message integration but at a larger scale than the pattern of domestic space.

Large linear dimensions (Figure 6.11)   Very large built features can provide an aid to visual integration for populations which have different local spatial patterns within a single settlement. The effect of their spatial signals depends upon the increasing inaccuracy of the eye and the brain as a perceptual and analytic system when it is dealing with larger and larger entities. As the perceived distances increase, so the perceptual accuracy of the eye decreases (Gregory 1966: 53; Watt 1988). If, therefore, a community contains several residentially discrete groups, each with its own spatial message, a large building can provide an image which may be acceptable to all the groups within it. The serial model provides a conventionalised way of visualising how this works. If we have two spatial messages represented by the two sets of length values (Figure 6.12), then, if the uncertainty level for visual perception of a distance of 50 m were about 5 m, the value at 50 m would be perceivable as any value between 45 and 55 m, and 48 m would be perceivable as 43 to 53 m. Buildings around 48 m in length will therefore be visually acceptable to people familiar with either spatial message. The uncertainty in human perceptual precision rises very rapidly for lengths of 6 m or more (Gregory 1966: 53). For distances of over 30 m estimation is not assisted by visual disparity or convergence (Vernon 1962: 128), so we should find that, at the least, the critical structures have minimum wall lengths greater than the latter distance value.

   An additional explanation is available for the behavioural role of great structures independent of their specific social function or the verbal explanations offered for them and regardless of the social 'reasons' why they were built or who built them.

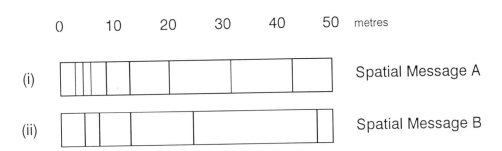

Figure 6.12 Relationship between different spatial messages
I = a value in a series

The structures do not inevitably need to have a function directly associated with large aggregations of people. Nor need they be of a consistent type or their antecedents of a consistent magnitude (Webb 1988). They can be anything from large circuit walls to official and administrative structures, or elite residences without a substantial public use (Figure 6.11). This empirical evidence suggests that building lengths of 50–70 m precede major urban expansion to sizes in excess of 100 ha and that boundary-wall lengths may be 250 m or longer, as in the development of the E-Anna in Uruk (Lenzen 1968). If these are the minimum sizes required, then the prerequisite size is much larger than the physiological limit of accurate distance perception. The magnitude of the value may therefore depend not on the loss of physiological accuracy alone but on the degree of divergence between the spatial patterns within the community.

The message model suggests an additional condition. The constructions should be at least rectilinear and probably rectangular, especially in a situation where distinct visual signals are required as integrators of the community. According to the visual redundancy requirement, the effectiveness of the large structures as part of a message system would depend upon repetition of the distances and the integration of those distances with the varied spatial patterns generated by the community. Rectilinear forms would provide this but curvilinear forms could not. In the transition settlements we should therefore find that the early, relatively scarce, visually conspicuous structures will tend to be rectangular. As the number of large structures in a settlement increases, so the larger ones could take on the powerful visual role of emphasising single, very large values over and over again through the use of a square form. The tendency should become more prevalent as the linking serial values become standard in other, slightly smaller rectilinear structures. This thesis can be assessed in the archaeological record. The change will not be inevitable but is a formal possibility when numerous conspicuous great monuments are in use.

This proposition about the perceptual impact of buildings does not require an understanding of why the actors thought they were doing what they did. Human intent may be interesting but it is not a precondition for studying the operational impact of the material – as is well illustrated by the case for rectilinearity. It is not enough to argue that the political correlates of the large buildings will suffice as an explanation of their integrative role. First, considerable structures can be built without large centralised authority systems (Erasmus 1965; Kaplan 1963; Oliveira 1986; White 1979; Webb 1988: 162–3). There is not a tight correlation between monumental scale and political organisation. Secondly, there is no political or social specification, as such, that rectilinear rather than curvilinear great structures will be more effective as integrators of communities in large compact settlements. The implication of the material behaviour approach is that the initial expansion of such settlements will be critically dependent upon the presence of a primarily rectilinear perceptual field, of which rectangular large buildings are merely a component. The need for a massive rectilinear frame of reference is the tip of a perceptual 'iceberg' of immense complexity.

Summary
The case for the prerequisites of the 100 ha transition is testable. From the predictions about when they must begin to be elaborated in the cultural sequence of each region and the sizes of the settlements in which they must be found, a condition of strong inference can be established. The claims are assessable directly in the archaeological record, though problems of taphonomy and sampling must be borne in mind.

The prerequisites should begin to develop in settlements in the lower third of size range behind the C-limit – i.e. in settlements of 30–40 ha or less in the case of the 100 ha limit. Individual components of the assemblage should be scattered throughout any region where a 100 ha transition occurred and should substantially predate that transition. As in the 100 sq km example, the 100 ha C-limit transition assemblage is apparently made up of several classes of material entity. The suggested components are rectilinearity (probably rectangular buildings), spatial segregation of areas within settlements, large linear dimensions (rectilinear), differential access, calendrics, durable building materials, substantial baffles and barriers, and material information systems. They are the non-industrial equivalents of the communication and interaction changes which preceded the growth of the industrial megalopolis beyond the 100 sq km C-limit. All the components of the assemblage required to cross a C-limit must be considered essential for the move across that limit, since each component deals with different but interrelated problems of interaction and communication. Verbal and non-verbal communication is covered, as is interaction within residence units, within the subdivisions of a settlement and within the settlement as a whole. There is no indication that some prerequisites are more important than others or that some can be substituted for others. The overview also helps to explain why transitions will be rare. A substantial number of features is required for a transition to be possible but the likelihood of such a coincidence happening at random will be low.

Further, rigorous work is needed to identify the material assemblages for the various C-limit transitions and to quantify the effects of the prerequisites. The techniques for assessing how much they minimise interaction or aid communication are already available from research on building standards, noise pollution and signal transmission (Glass and Singer 1972; Pearce 1976; Tempest 1985). A wide field of experimental archaeology can be opened up concerning the intervisibility and interaudibility characteristics of past residential patterns. The mechanical principles are well understood and the computer software to produce simulations is available. These analyses will then have to be integrated with an expanded sociology and psychology of residential space of the kind developed in environmental psychology (Altman *et al.* 1980; Ankerl 1981; Lym 1980; Gifford 1987; Rapoport 1990; Sanders 1985, 1990: 59–63).

The behavioural implications of transition assemblages

Material prerequisites and changes in resource supply (Figure 6.13)
Long-term constraints on settlement growth during a transition should derive from the relationship between the material assemblage and whatever degree of change

occurs in the resource supply (see p. 63). For compact settlements three possible classes of settlement growth outcome can be predicted, depending upon whether or not changes in resource supply (E) and material behaviour (M) occur together. First, a new material prerequisite assemblage might occur without an increase in resource supply. In this case a slight increase in compact settlement area in excess of the relevant C-limit should be feasible but growth will not continue (Figure 6.13) because there will not be sufficient energy to sustain both the largest settlement and the spectrum of smaller settlements which make up a viable settlement hierarchy. The second possibility is the development of a new economic system without a new prerequisite assemblage. No amount of change in resource supply can increase the maximum size of a compact settlement beyond a C-limit if the prerequisite I–C assemblage is absent (Figure 6.13). Alterations in the material context of community life will be needed to manage growth and allow the increased communication flow that will let more people associate in the first place. According to a timescaled perspective, behavioural stresses will intervene more rapidly to prevent growth than the more slowly operating economic factors can act to promote it. Thirdly, the combination of the two types of change will allow a transition to begin and will also sustain the growth of the largest settlements to whatever size the magnitude of the economic change will permit (Figure 6.13).

For compact settlements near the C-limit the model predicts that despite local cultural difference in substantive detail the outcome, in terms of overall growth, will be consistently related to the nature of the material assemblages and the degree of economic change. By contrast, for settlements with an area much smaller than the C-limit size, the effects of economic change should be much more varied and could differ markedly from region to region. Economic change should affect settlements differently depending on their size and degree of compactness, not according to the broad classes of settlement to which we usually refer, such as 'urban'. A substantial increase in the amount of food or resources in a region may support more people and increase the number of communities but it will not in itself change the maximum possible size of compact settlements. However, considerable increases in both community size and settlement area could occur in a region where the maximum size has previously been rather small and growth is simply moving towards the next C-limit value. The complication is that such growth could happen without substantial economic change other than the movement of a greater share of the existing resources to serve the growth of fewer settlements. The range of settlement sizes behind a C-limit should be sustainable by variants of whatever economy initially permitted growth after the previous transition. Because of these varying possibilities, urban settlements much smaller than 100 ha could increase in size with or without apparent major economic transformation.

The other set of possible trajectories leads towards low-density settlement growth. Because a new prerequisite assemblage is not needed for a bypass trajectory (Figure 5.12), the only consequential factor affecting settlement size should be the pattern of economic activity. For instance, if there is no economic change then a region could support the same maximum number of people, either in a high-density settlement or in a much more extensive dispersed settlement. Alternatively, if a major economic transformation has taken place, such as the development of irrigation, as in the south-west of North America in the Hohokam and the Postclassic, then far larger settlements might occur with no apparent limit on their extent.

Variability and the development of the prerequisites
The degree to which communities can tolerate variability in their material assemblages should be one of the critical factors in enabling a transition. Because the prerequisites have to come together at random, the likelihood of this happening must be linked to the rate at which they are produced or adopted. Numerous particular social and historical factors may combine to create or incorporate new classes of behaviour, but the critical constraint on which options are coherently adopted will be the degree of variation which the communities in a region are able to tolerate. In consequence, the probability of the assemblage coming together must derive from the internal patterning of the behaviour of the communities, in particular from the nature of their material behaviour. High tolerance of variability should lead to more variant material patterns and more acceptance of alternatives from outside the community. This suggests that the degree of variation which is

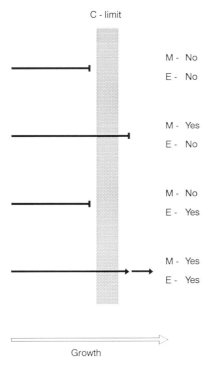

Figure 6.13 Hypothetical model of the constraints on growth
M = material behaviour   E = economy
N = no change   Yes = change

consistent with the ordering of a community's behaviour will be an important factor in its capacity to deal with circumstances. The tolerance of variability is not intangible. The spatial message model suggests that it can be readily visible in the material form of a community's behaviour. If particular aspects of cultural patterning, such as the ordering of space, possess a code-consistent degree of variability, then we might expect the same of other patterns, such as time-ordering or shape preference. Message structures may be of consequence for the degree to which a community can create 'preadaptations' and incorporate them into its behavioural repertoire. We should not assume, however, that there is some absolute standard of tolerable variability inherent in all aspects of a community's behaviour. More likely we will find differing ranges of variability, because the differing replicative rate of each aspect of material behaviour will produce differing degrees of variability at any one time.

Material prerequisites and 'social' change
In principle a new kind of material entity or feature, which produces a substantial improvement in communication efficiency and in the control of interaction stress, might develop without initially being accompanied by an obvious 'social' change in active behaviour. But randomly occurring 'social' alternatives, which then begin to develop and happen to work better with this increased interaction and greater communication range than other contemporaneous forms of social action, will become more common and will, in turn, serve to promote and replicate the new material features. The material therefore cannot be considered a secure predictor of the presence of a specific social action or value structure because it can antedate its 'social' correlate.

The material behaviour approach requires that the ranking of communities by their degree of social complexity be decoupled from the occurrence of material features, such as roads, writing systems and the sophisticated ordering of time. These can be isolated features. They need not be accompanied either by the remainder of the proposed prerequisites or by any other correlates of complexity. Though their effects on the rise of the state may be significant, we should not thereby presume that they are unable to exist without it. Instead an 'outcome' perspective is required – that if social complexity and particular material features happen to coincide, their engagement may have profound consequences for the societies which carry them. But they need not occur together and we should therefore expect the same kinds of material features in association with previously unanticipated 'social' contexts.

More generally, it can be argued that the combination of a given I–C assemblage with a broad class of social action will tend to have similar consequences under the same kinds of selective pressure, because the material will be having such a substantial impact on interaction and communication stresses. A transition assemblage is likely to end up with a suite of social action and verbal meaning which promotes settlement growth. But the 'social' change might have preceded or run parallel to the increase in settlement size or, as a result of selective pressure by the material, might even follow it. We therefore cannot make an assumption that action and verbal content are decisive in bringing about a transition. In the crisis conditions up against the I- and C-limits, 'social' action is unlikely to suffice as a decisive influence on viability because it can only reallocate stress, not absorb and diffuse it (p. 70). A social phenomenon, such as the state, might appear with or without the transition assemblage but will not, in itself, be able to initiate growth or push a large compact settlement beyond a C-limit. All we can specify is that a new material assemblage must antedate this growth, though in each region it might initially be associated with different transforming 'social' patterns. But because the material will readily select in favour of change in the rapidly varying social expressions of a community, in the long term the end result in different communities should be quite similar. In effect, there are many different routes by which the material might come to be associated with very similar forms of social organisation in different regions, starting from a variety of different initial conditions.

I–C assemblages after a transit across a C-limit
Although the transition assemblage is necessary as a means of getting through the stressful zone near the junction of the I- and C-limits, the old system will still be active and perhaps even predominant for much of the community. For instance, the majority of a population may remain illiterate despite the presence of a script system. The components of the new assemblage will be in a largely untried form. We can expect many changes in the details of the new assemblage under the stresses of interaction and communication as the settlement grows rapidly after the transition. In Mesopotamia, for example, considerable change occurred in the arrangement of the script system and its tabulation procedures in the third millennium BC (Green 1981). Rapid change and a complex association of old and new behavioural patterns are to be expected.

Once a shift across a C-limit has been made, however, the entire assemblage need not persist. Though some of its components are essential for communication over much larger settlement areas, others may become unnecessary. The assemblage of prerequisites can be envisaged in terms of a satellite launch vehicle, a means of carrying a community through a high stress situation and into a new stable state, after which parts of it are superfluous and may then even be an encumbrance. The material also acts as a carrier for the community during the transition and shields it from stress. Shielded by the material assemblage, therefore, new forms of active behaviour could develop which would eventually suffice, on their own, to manage the new magnitudes of interaction and communication. Different communities may partially ameliorate different aspects of behavioural stress after a transition. This requires a contextual analysis of the unique connections between material and active behaviour after a transition in each region.

At present we need to find out which characteristics are essential and endure after a shift across a C-limit and which can change into new, predictable, active behaviour strategies. We may find, for instance, that construction can shift back from rectilinear to curvilinear forms and that even such features as durable walling may be reduced. In Kyoto, Japan, during the ninth century AD, houses for the elite with walls of bamboo covered by plaster and daub were built within large enclosures surrounded by substantial walls (Beg 1986: 147–57; Frédéric 1972: 104–7). Commoners' houses were in rows along the streets, with enclosed garden yards behind (Frédéric 1972: 92). Though the walls were made of rushes and bamboo laths, sometimes covered with daub, they were reputedly quite thick. Additional segregation was provided by gates, along the roads running east to west, which separated the blocks (*bo*) of the city (Ponsonby-Fane 1956: 23). A strict social code regulated interaction (Wheatley and See 1978; Yazaki 1968). The houses of most later Japanese towns prior to the Meiji restoration were, in the main, constructed from timber without substantial masonry or brick barrier walls. The persisting, intensely active control of public interaction in Japan (Hall 1977: 66–7, 160–1; Rapoport 1975) might therefore be a behavioural correlate of reduced material screening. The degree to which reversion to ephemeral structures can occur long after a transition, or in secondary urban development derived from external examples or influence, deserves further examination. Some features, however, cannot undergo complete reversion. Large urban settlements do not have predominantly open-walled structures, of the kind observable in Fijian rural settlements (Duly 1979: 80), presumably because this arrangement cannot provide sufficient auditory shielding to make life tolerable in a dense urban area. We should note, however, that much of the housing in Chan Chan in the fourteenth century AD was quite ephemeral (J. R. Topic 1982), and vast squatter suburbs of flimsy shacks have developed around the capital cities of the Third World in the late twentieth century.

The implications for the use of ethnographic association analogies are somewhat ominous. While the model predicts close correlations in extreme stress contexts between the triad of material phenomena, 'active' social phenomena and the magnitude of possible settlement growth (i.e. the outcome), it specifically excludes any inevitable operational correlates for the majority of the communities which lie well behind a given C-limit. As I have argued above, the transition assemblages are not diagnostic of all post-transition communities. Some of the larger communities will offload aspects of the transition assemblage. Smaller communities behind the antecedent C-limit may adopt features of the transition assemblage which previously were only found in the largest settlements. The settlements which develop after a transition will have varied material–social associations which will be historically particular not anthropologically universal. We cannot securely retrodict material–social correlates from the present into the past, because the substantive relationship may vary with settlement size, and may have changed over time. Such change must itself be significant from the perspective of current social theory.

Stasis settlements and the lack of the material prerequisites
The testable corollary of the transition requirements is that the stasis settlements close to the 100 ha C-limit ought to lack some of the components of the prerequisite assemblage. The complete absence of a component, rather than the possession of a nascent form, is essential because we cannot, as yet, gauge the degree of elaboration

required for a prerequisite to have its effect. The model specifies that the absence of some of the prerequisites would, in itself, suffice to explain stasis without further appeal to factors such as a lack of economic change. In a hierarchy of explanation, larger-scale economic factors cannot be ascribed a predominant restrictive role if limitations of the material assemblage would in any case have acted as a restrictive factor. *A priori* we cannot ascribe a superior standing to resource supply explanations because cases may exist where substantial economic change was not accompanied by a behavioural change and maximum settlement sizes did not extend beyond the C-limit. The absence of one or more of the prerequisites should prevent the continued expansion of the settlement because some aspect of communication devices are lacking. For example, the spatial predictability provided by rectilinear spatial patterning was lacking in the Poverty Point assemblage (Figure 6.14). The perceptual milieu of the Poverty Point settlement is entirely curvilinear, including the large mound and the long arcs of the midden ridges along which the residence units were arranged. The huts from Poverty Point site at Jaketown are also curvilinear. Whatever portions of the site were used at any one time, the alignment of the buildings also created a conspicuously exposed visual field. Similarly, in Nan Matol the flimsy residential structures set on great stone platforms (Figure 6.15) could not have restricted the transmission of noise. The sides of the buildings were either open or were screened only by mats and flimsy walls. Only a few of the platforms have continuous high boundary walls (Ayres *et al.* 1963). Despite the presence of substantial rectilinear constructions carrying long linear dimensions and a wide range of spatial distances, the light fabric of the domestic housing presumably lacked the necessary degree of screening. Urmitz, an interrupted ditch enclosure of the fifth–fourth millennium BC in Europe (Figure 5.14b), lacked segregation of its internal space by major structural barriers and there is no evidence, as yet, of differential access routes within the other large Michelsberg sites. Analysis of settlements as sensory environments may help to clarify why they were or were not able to expand beyond a particular size.

The size limitations on the 100 ha stasis sites cannot simply or universally be ascribed to the absence of one primary feature – a material information storage system. The Vinča sites, which have been said to possess a form of writing or near-writing, were just as constrained as the other proposed stasis cases. They ought, therefore, to have lacked one or more of the other prerequisites. As yet there is little trace of large-scale spatial segregation, nor is there secure evidence of large linear constructions. The trench and posthole features in Selevac (Tringham and Krstić 1990: e.g. 78, 87–8, 97, 105, 108–9, 130–1, 142–3) appear to be walls of standard-sized houses. There is, however, an alternative which has to be considered. If the boundary walls of small settlements of the period, like Polyanitsa (Todorova 1978), have equivalents of greater extent in the bigger sites, such walls would provide the required behavioural milieu. The only other missing feature is calendrics, which taphonomic processes could make hard to recognise (see p. 197). If it were present, the Vinča sites might even have possessed versions of all the prerequisites.[6] If so, then the issue of what constrained the growth of the settlements has to be transposed

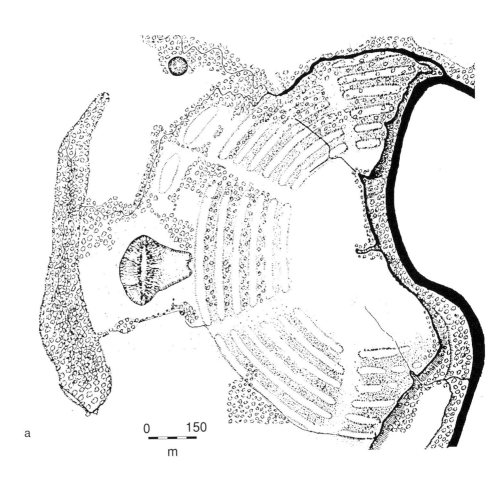

a

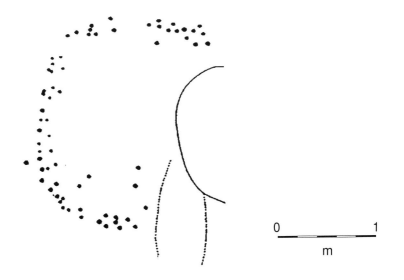

b

up the hierarchy to the operational level of resource supply. Attention would then turn to the question of whether or not the social and material changes in Vinča communities in the fourth and fifth millennia BC were accompanied by a substantial economic change capable of sustaining larger settlements.

The prediction about stasis settlements also produces a divergence between conventional social interpretations and those resulting from an extended 'social' theory that incorporates the role of the material as behaviour. Social theories that presume that particular material and 'social' features are consistently correlated must ultimately depend on the assumption that the assemblage might be traced back in time to a minimal form or to just one of its key attributes. On this view settlements would be identified as incipient forms of a future level of social complexity. In this kind of explanation emphasis is placed on a continuum of explanation and processes. But a 100 ha stasis settlement can possess most of the characteristics which we would be inclined to regard as the 'incipient' form of a major urban settlement. It may well look 'almost urban' and may even exceed the size of some sites which we usually refer to as towns. But stasis cases are an interesting phenomenon precisely because they had no growth potential and were not incipient to any future growth. Instead of identifying different settlements with varying numbers of the prerequisites as representative of successive hypothetical steps towards a general class of urbanism (Figure 6.16), the material behaviour approach treats each of them as a different, alternative, random possible approach to the C-limit. It does not seek to assess how near they were to being 'urban' but looks at each of them as an illustration of the different kinds of outcome which can result from varying combinations of material characteristics, settlement size and resource supply.

Conclusions

For a community to cross a C-limit and make a major increase in the size of its settlement, a transition assemblage composed of several different kinds of material features has to be developed or incorporated into the assemblage of the community's material behaviour. The example of the proposed transition assemblage for the growth of compact settlements over 100 ha in extent indicates that several different categories of material entity are required. Each of the features takes some time to develop and the likelihood of their occurring together, very rapidly, after a community reaches the zone adjacent to both an I-limit and a C-limit is very small. Probability and the behavioural stresses involved specify that the new assemblage must aggregate before the settlement size approaches the C-limit. A transition

Figure 6.14 Poverty Point site features, southern USA, first millennium BC
(a) detail of spatial arrangements of Poverty Point (after Webb 1977)

midden   vegetation

(b) curvilinear structure in the Jaketown site (after Ford *et al.* 1955)

postholes   pits

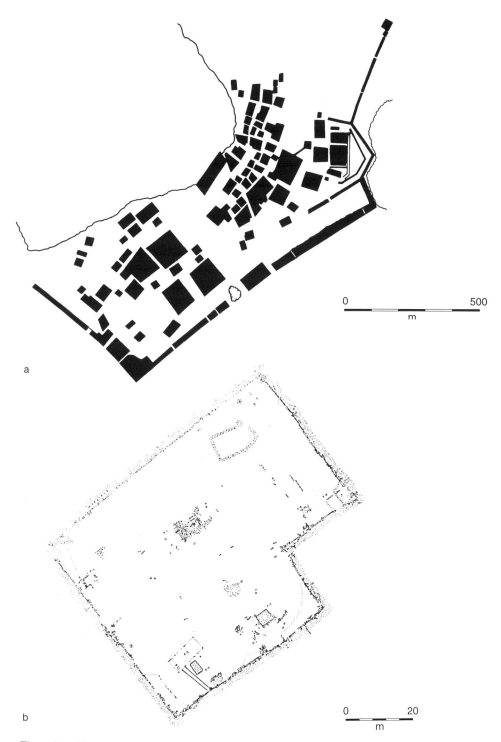

Figure 6.15 Nan Matol, Micronesia, early to mid-second millennium AD
(a) settlement plan (after Hambruch 1939)
Note: A recent plan of Nan Matol by Morgan (1988) has far less of a central gap.
(b) detail of a residence platform (after Athens 1980)

▱ basalt slabs   ·····•······• postholes

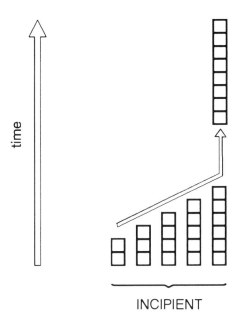

INCIPIENT

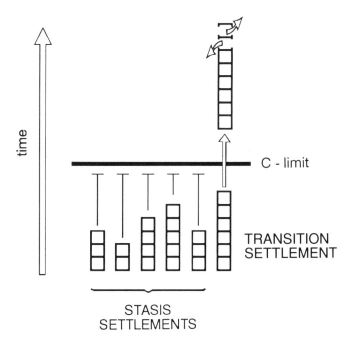

C - limit

TRANSITION
SETTLEMENT

STASIS
SETTLEMENTS

Figure 6.16 Cultural 'incipience' in contrast to transition

☐ prerequisites   ⤢ lost prerequisites

⇗ cumulative growth between successive assemblages

⇑ transition growth

assemblage should begin to develop in settlements which are in the lowest third of the size range behind the C-limit area value. However, though the absence of some of the prerequisites suffices to explain why a compact settlement cannot grow beyond a C-limit, the model is not deterministic. The prerequisites allow settlement growth but they do not predetermine that it will happen. For growth to be sustained, the system of resource supply must also channel increased yields into the settlement. The conjunction of a new material assemblage and a transformation in resource supply is a requirement for sustained growth across a C-limit. The I–C model also predicts, however, that either class of change can happen without the other and that neither, on its own, will enable a shift to larger compact settlements in excess of the C-limit size.

PART III

Implications: transformations and constraints of community life

7

The development of sedentism

The structure of the I–C model and the stress matrix offers a new perspective on several major issues of human behaviour. This chapter considers two alternative ways of looking at the development of 'sedentism' which follow from different readings of the I–C model. My concern is residential mobility. To refer to the kind of sedentism which we habitually and clearly distinguish from mobile and transient residential behaviour I have adopted the label 'permanent sedentism' from Kent (1989). The archetypal image of permanent sedentism is of a community which stays in one place all year in the same buildings for several or many years. Households generally retain the same primary, domiciliary residence unit in the settlement regardless of season. Even though households may travel away from their settlement at various times, for instance on vacation, some people (especially single males) may relocate their residence within the settlement or in another one (Berry and Silverman 1980), and households may occupy their residence units for only ten to twenty years, there is a sustained perennial continuity of occupation by a resident population.[1]

The growth of mobile communities

There are two possible, divergent views of the 'mobile' I-limit which follow from the premises of the I–C stress model. The first view presumes that the limit is fixed by the aggregate unpredictability of interaction in groups which practise some form of annual, seasonal relocation which effectively empties a settlement for part of the year. The corollary is that an initial shift to permanent sedentism involves a profound alteration in community life which could occur only in association with a particular suite of material behavioural changes. Since this 'restrictive' model leads to several radical implications, I shall discuss it in some detail. However, the alternative scenario, in which the 'mobile' I-limit is merely one in a succession of possible maximum density levels that can be attained as a community becomes more sedentary, will probably be more fashionable, as it accords with a prevailing gradualist attitude to mobility and sedentism (as reviewed by Kelly 1992). According to this alternative view, successively higher residential densities can be attained gradually by larger communities precisely because, as a result of other factors, whether economic or 'social', more and more members of a community happen to stay in one settlement for longer and longer periods of time. These two opposing views lead to substantially different explanations of the development of permanently sedentary communities. I will first discuss the implications of the 'restrictive' version for the development of both seasonally sedentary and permanently sedentary communities and then, in brief, the implications of the 'gradualist' version.

The definition of mobility and sedentism

Some of the larger communities of hunter-gatherers have been variously described as semi-sedentary or semi-mobile. The term 'semi-sedentary' should be avoided because it carries the tacit implication of a 'direction' towards permanent sedentism and assumes a gradualistic unilinear cultural evolution towards sustained sedentism. That has to be assessed not predefined. The hint of incipience is inappropriate and misleading. If it is applied to communities which may be significant precisely because they did not practise permanent sedentary residence, the semi-sedentary label may obscure a crucial disjunction in residential behaviour.

The term 'seasonal sedentism' advocated by Kent (1989) is a more appropriate label for communities which make episodic seasonal movements and repeatedly occupy the same base settlements. Though placed in the general class of sedentism, the term does not in itself predicate that it is in a continuum with permanent sedentism. Groups such as the Northwest Coast Indian communities of the eighteenth and nineteenth century AD may be significant in studies of human behaviour, not because they were almost 'sedentary' in the conventional sense, but precisely because their material behaviour could not sustain permanent sedentism. Eyewitness reports in the eighteenth and nineteenth century AD clearly show that the Nootka and the Clayaquot used different residential locations during the year (Beaglehole 1967; Edwards 1989: 19; Jewitt 1967 edition; Mathes 1979: 112; Meares 1967 (1790): 146). They may therefore be key examples of the settlement patterns which result from a distinct growth trajectory below the 'mobile' I-limit. The differentiation of seasonal and permanent sedentism is consistent with the restrictive version of the I–C model. Though it allows many varieties of mobility and season sedentism below the 'mobile' I-limit, it also specifies that a profound change in behaviour was required for the initial development of permanent sedentism. We cannot assume that there is a simple continuum from season sedentism to permanent sedentism. Instead we should expect a range of variants, combined with shifts even from permanent sedentism to mobility. What I am seeking to argue is that both a continuum and a profound transformation are involved but relate to different ranges of residential density. I will first discuss the complex of mobile residence patterns and then consider the nature of permanent sedentism.

A 1–2 ha transition for mobile and seasonally sedentary communities

The 'restrictive' model predicts that a transition might occur across the 1–2 ha C-limit below the 'mobile' I-limit (Figure 7.1a). The eighteenth- to nineteenth- and early twentieth-century Inuit and Northwest Coast Indians provide examples of the kinds of settlements which would result from that trajectory. Numerous Northwest Coast Indian settlements cover up to 2–5 ha (Macdonald 1983). Inuit settlements with seasonal occupations reached sizes of 20 ha or more (Fletcher 1981a: 108;

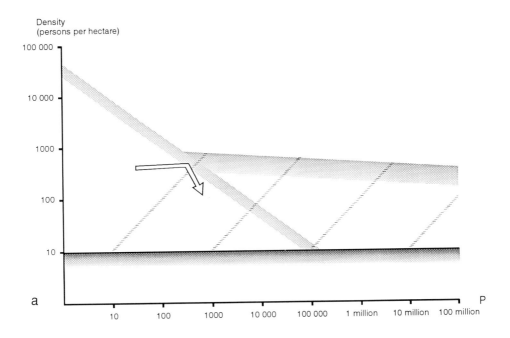

a

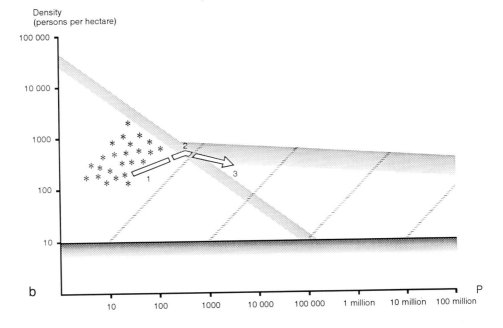

b

Figure 7.1 Different transitions across the 1–2 ha C-limit
(a) transition for 'mobile' communities across 1–2 ha C-limit
(b) transition to permanent sedentism
*source communities

Nelson 1896–7: 261–2). Archaeological sites such as Ipiutak at 3–4 ha (Larsen and Rainey 1948), or the 2 ha Dorset Palaeo-Eskimo site at Port-aux-Chois (Harp 1976) are potential examples, as are the Varangerfjord sites of the sixth to early first millennium BC in northern Scandinavia (Engelstad 1984; Renouf 1989). Site sizes and ethnohistoric reports for the Californian Indians indicate that some settlements were in excess of 10 ha in the seventeenth century AD (Brown 1967; Cook n.d.; Moratto 1984: 331–2). Extensive, lower density occupations are represented by the Calumet mound sites in Australia, some with overall areas of between 1 and 3 ha (Williams 1988). The problem is whether large sites are evidence of large occupation areas or are just agglomerations of numerous overlapping small sites. The latter scenario would create the paradox that all small sites were small settlements and all large sites also represent small settlements. This is *a priori* counter-intuitive, given the known occurrence of ethnographic cases of extensive settlements used by mobile communities and the likelihood that past settlements formed size hierarchies. If all settlements were small, that would be more remarkable in behavioural terms than the occurrence of large numbers of small settlements and a few very large ones. We should expect some large settlements. However, the assumptions about archaeo-logical sites like PPNA Jericho – once thought to represent 'sedentary' communities just because they are large (2–4 ha) for their period and contain substantial structures (Mellaart 1975: 50) – need to be reappraised. A 'village-like' appearance is not sufficient evidence of sustained sedentism since the settlements occupied by communities which are known to have relocated their place of residence during the annual cycle, such as the Inuit and the Northwest Coast Indians, also look like this. Mobile communities can build substantial structures.

The possibility of two transitions, one to large mobile and/or seasonally sedentary communities, and the other to permanent sedentism, is of interest because the former offers a further potential example of a major shift across a C-limit (see p. 172 and Figure 7.1b). We should expect different behavioural prerequisites for the two trajectories since the communities at lower densities, below the 'mobile' I-limit, would be less affected by interaction stresses, even though the communication stress levels would have been the same. The assemblage of prerequisites for the lower density transition ought to be more rudimentary than the initiating assemblage for permanent sedentism. We might expect that the required controls on interaction would be less stringent, and behavioural predictability would not be as important as in fully sedentary communities. The details of the prerequisite assemblage will probably have to be ascertained empirically. What we may find is that features such as substantial internal screening, which can effectively regulate interaction, are unnecessary for this kind of transition.

Given that the next C-limit is at 100 ha and that seasonally mobile communities are known to have occupied settlements larger than 1–2 ha, some communities should therefore have been able to produce settlements up to 100 ha in extent. Settlements of that size, as with all stasis settlements, should be relatively rare but spectacular. An example in the archaeological record would be of considerable significance. Identifying such a settlement, however, is complicated by the effects of palimpsest occupations. Even if there are no contemporary or recent cases of settlements of 70 ha or more used by non-pastoral nomadic or seasonally sedentary communities, this does not mean that there could not have been any in the past. Archaeologists are obliged to find out whether or not such communities existed either on a low-density trajectory or following a transition. Illustrations of what such sites might look like are provided by the moa-hunter sites at Rakaia Mouth(80 ha) and Waitaki Mouth (60–70 ha) in New Zealand (Anderson 1989: 129–35) (Figure 7.2).[2] The moa-hunter sites are presumed to be seasonal kill sites dating to the earlier part of the second millennium AD (Anderson 1989: 173–6). Rather than just assuming that the site is made up of adjacent or partially overlapping successive small occupations, we must consider the possibility that each occupation was extensive, with different functions scattered across the entire site, as it is in some Inuit settlements (Figure 7.3). To accept a minimal estimate because it will produce a 'safe' area estimate, i.e. less than the actual size of the settlement, is not a

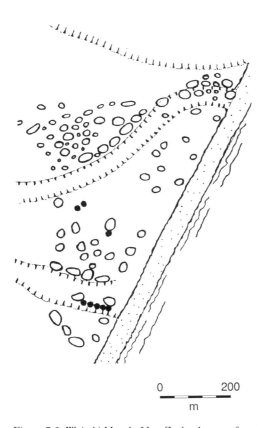

0 ____ 200

m

Figure 7.2 Waitaki Mouth, New Zealand: core of moa-hunter site, *c.* 110–150 AD (after Anderson 1983)

○ ovens   ● huts

beach   river terrace

reasonable research procedure. An underestimate is as patently inaccurate and inappropriate as an overestimate. At densities near the T-limit value (approx. 10 p/ha) Waitaki Mouth could have carried a community of about 600–700 people, well within the range of community sizes reported for large temporary residential aggregates of hunter-gatherers (Burch 1986: 260; Fletcher 1991a). An assessment of the food yields from a combination of moa kills and the collection of local vegetable resources, like fernroot, ought to indicate whether such group sizes were sustainable. If Waitaki Mouth is an example of a rare class of stasis settlement behind the 100 ha C-limit and below the 'mobile' I-limit, the damage caused to the site by border dyking is extremely regrettable. The I–C model may be of some use in arguing for the significance of sites and for justifying either their preservation or their prompt and detailed investigation.

Even larger mobile communities have existed in settlements with areas of 5–10 sq km, such as the Plains Indian camp on the Little Bighorn in AD 1856. The Ethiopian mobile state capitals of the medieval period and the nineteenth century AD covered 40–50 sq km (Fletcher 1991a) (Figure 4.7). These communities operated at relatively low densities. They, and the smaller communities of the Northwest Coast chiefdoms, indicate that social complexity does apparently serve to allow larger and larger group sizes under the 'mobile' I-limit but offer no indication that social action can take a mobile community through that I-limit (Fletcher 1991a 413–15).

The initial formation of permanent sedentary communities: the restrictive scenario

The formation of 'sedentary' communities is one of the most controversial and complicated issues of archaeological theorising. The different perspective of the I–C model may help to reveal the nature of that logical tangle. The discussion has to be

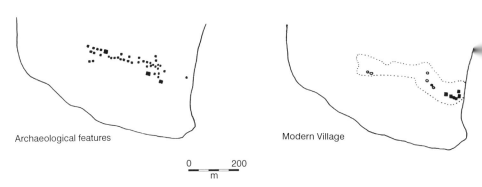

Archaeological features   Modern Village

0   200
m

Figure 7.3 Anvik Point, Alaska, USA, nineteenth–twentieth century AD (after de Laguna 1947)

archaeological features   ▪ ▪ hut pits

recent village   ▪ huts   ○ caches   ····· edge of midden

Note: Occupation at any one times makes use of the entire midden area even though the contemporaneous residential buildings are restricted to one part of the total settlement area.

phrased primarily in theoretical terms because the application and meaning of 'sedentism' is unstable, and its archaeological identification is currently uncertain (Edwards 1989; Kelly 1992). Furthermore, though there are several regions with archaeological sequences which straddle a proposed shift towards permanent sedentism, few provide substantial detail on the size and form of the occupation sites and their assemblages.

Within the terms of the stress matrix permanent sedentism can be defined as a class of behaviour which, whatever else it does, enables large groups of more than 200–300 people to function at higher residential densities than mobile or seasonally sedentary communities of the same size. The key behavioural implication of the 'mobile' I-limit is that, for mobile groups, dropping to lower densities is the simplest solution to increased stress as group size increases (Fletcher 1991a: 412–13). In addition, mobility keeps down interaction stress by making departure from a settlement relatively easy. Going across the 'mobile' I-limit would therefore require a very different way of controlling interaction. The key problem of permanent sedentism should be severe interaction stress (Cohen 1985: 99), especially at high densities. The presumption is that this kind of sedentism is difficult to manage. If a community were to persist with this way of life, the stresses would have to be alleviated in some way.

That interaction stress is handled differently by permanent sedentary communities is indicated by an elementary difference in their spatial patterning (e.g. Figure 4.5, cf. Figure 7.4). In any one region and cultural grouping the trend is towards a more restricted range of higher rather than lower residential densities as community size increases. Such communities can carry higher overall densities as their population size increases, e.g. in the UK (Figure 7.4).[3] Permanently sedentary groups are apparently able to manage the behaviour of more and more people at high residential densities, until the density impinges on the sedentary I-limit. Such a trend existed among the Pueblo Indians of the southwest of the USA in the first half of the twentieth century AD (Figure 7.4). At that time I would expect them to have been permanently sedentary. However, there is an opinion that previously they were, at least, more logistically mobile (Kelly 1992: 51; Preucel 1990). If so they will be a key case for studying the relationship between mobility and occupation density trends over time and defining the nature of permanent sedentism.

Permanently sedentary groups must also be able to trend towards low densities since they can form dispersed communities. By contrast, the obviously mobile and seasonally sedentary communities only appear to support general regional trends in which people gain more space per capita as community size increases. Since there is a trend towards declining density among seasonally sedentary groups, like other mobile communities, as is indicated by Whitelaw (1983: 55; 1989), a shift to permanent sedentism and the capacity to sustain high densities as community size increases, even if this occurred gradually, must involve a considerable behavioural inversion. By definition the time structure of daily life also alters during a shift to permanent sedentism. *A priori* it therefore seems that endogenously triggered shifts from mobility to permanent sedentism will be relatively rare because the entire time–space structure of the two kinds of residence may be very different as community size increases. An endogenous initial shift to permanent sedentism would, according to this version, require an unusual and specific material assemblage to manage the transition.

In the restrictive version an initial endogenous regional shift towards such a form of sedentism, in settlements larger than 1–2 ha, can only happen as part of a transition at relatively high residential densities across both the 'mobile' I-limit and the proposed 1–2 ha C-limit (Figure 7.1b). In the current version of the matrix the broadest specification of the sedentary I-limit zone coincides with the 'mobile' I-limit zone for group sizes of 100–500 people on settlement areas of between 0.1 ha (1,000 sq m) and 1 ha. The narrower description of the sedentary I-limit zone, i.e. its lower band, meets the 'mobile' limit at settlement sizes of about 0.4 ha (4,000 sq m) or more. If this junction is a sufficient description of the stresses inherent in a shift to permanent sedentism, then a community whose growth trajectory entered the band of the sedentary I-limit zone could begin a shift to permanent sedentism through this narrow 'window', without first having to make a transition across the 1–2 ha C-limit. As the known size distributions behind the 1–2 ha C-limit suggest that most settlements were less than 0.3 ha (3,000 sq m), it is likely that relatively few settlements would have taken this trajectory. It would have been a quite rare occurrence associated with compact settlements which would have had to become markedly larger than their immediate predecessors in order to move into the sedentary I-limit zone. To do so they must have derived the necessary material prerequisites (which could control interaction sufficiently for permanent sedentism to be feasible) from mobile communities in the smaller antecedent settlements. The assemblage preferentially selected by the stresses in the wedge between the I- and C-limits would then possess the potential to regulate long-term permanent residence in larger communities at relatively high residential densities.

A transition to high-density permanent sedentism (Figure 7.1b)
The development of permanent sedentism can be divided into phases associated with different settlement sizes, each of which required a different portion of the transition assemblage. In each phase the communities would have been workable and need not have developed any further. The logical trap inherent in a unitary view which requires that the changes occurred together can be avoided, providing a way out of the circularity of explanation. By dividing up both sedentism and the prerequisite assemblage into discrete operational components, we can escape the holistic quandary of having to decide whether 'sedentism' determines the assemblage or vice versa. The prerequisites could aggregate to varying degrees, but would only lead to breakthrough growth in a rare and random conjunction of all the required attributes. Outcomes are predictable but the associations are not.

The junction between the 1–2 ha C-limit and the 'mobile' I-limit provides the milieu for a multiphase development of high-density sedentism. The changes begin in small communities of around 10–100 people, below the 'mobile' I-limit, or settlement areas of between 0.01 ha and 0.3 ha (* on Figure 7.1b), where the pre adaptations for permanent sedentism should begin to develop in a piecemeal fashion (Stage 1). The components can each have come into the assemblage of a particular community for purposes independent of their eventual function in sustaining permanent sedentism. We should therefore find them mixed up with many other features which have no particular role in a transition to permanent sedentism. A great variety of residential forms and assemblages should occur in the rare, very large, compact settlements. We might be inclined to regard many or all of these settlements as cases of incipient sedentism. But appearances would be deceptive.

The model predicts three obvious trajectories (Figure 7.5). The first (S) will lead to stasis, when communities with the interaction controls of the transition assemblage hit the C-limit but do not have new communication aids. The second possible track (B) is towards low-density patterns and bypass trajectories. This would produce communities in settlements larger than 1–2 ha but of a rather dispersed form, unable to expand back up to higher density residence. No amount of economic change will assist the growth of these classes of settlement towards a larger high-density form, because they lack the essential material aids to communication.

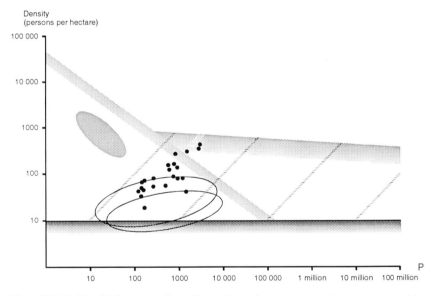

Figure 7.4 Residential density gradients for mobile and permanently sedentary communities

- Pueblos, southwest USA, 1940s (after Stubbs 1950). Some census figures include residents from elsewhere on the reservation; in these cases maximum population and density are therefore smaller

Kalahari Bushman camps, South Africa, 1970s–1980s
(after Draper 1973; Eibl-Eibesfeld 1972; Yellen 1977)

UK villages 1960s – two regional samples (after Best and Rodgers 1973)

Note: Whitelaw (1989: 159) plots a broadly similar trend of decreasing density with increasing community size for a larger sample of San camps from the Kalahari. The sample has a wider range of both densities and settlement areas. The Bushman cases provide a well-documented context in which to analyse the relationship between sedentising and prevalent density patterning.

The third and critical track is a special case of a transition trajectory (T) which includes a move across the 'mobile' I-limit. The initial phase of this trajectory (Figure 7.1b) has at least two stages, following the aggregation of a new interaction control suite in settlements which are below the 'mobile' I-limit. After crossing the 'mobile' I-limit the communities which go on at high residential densities will be further affected by intensely stressful interaction and communication. In Stage 2 communities which have crossed the 'mobile' I-limit might sustain some kind of permanent annual residence, even if only for brief periods of a year or two. They may have been fully sedentary or practising an intermediate form of sedentism which is now rare or has no contemporary equivalent. These intermediate sedentary communities, whatever their previous form of economy, do not require a change in their economic basis, since they are merely at the upper end of the operable size range behind the C-limit. Once the initial stresses are under control, those material features which increase communication range begin to have their effect, permitting further increases in settlement size (Stage 3) across the C-limit (Figure 7.1b). The resulting settlements are the carriers of the means to develop dense occupations in settlements larger than 1–2 ha. However, the hierarchy of explanation also rules that, once sedentary groups cross the 1–2 ha limit, the degree to which their growth can be maintained depends on the degree of change in resource supply, either before or at about the same time as the transition. Sustained growth of such permanent sedentary communities would require a profound economic change of the kind epitomised by a shift to agriculture.

The model predicts a variety of consequences but these are consistently dependent on prior combinations of material conditions which ought to be recognisable in the archaeological record. In Stage 3, communities with the prerequisite assemblage and a new economic system could cross the 1–2 ha limit and continue to grow while being permanently sedentary. The corollary is that agriculture can develop in settlements under the 'mobile' I-limit without producing a full sedentary system. This fits ethnographic examples such as the Pawnee (Hyde 1974) and the Osage (Bushnell 1922: 106), who planted maize and squash and then went on hunting trips covering hundreds of kilometres. The Marind Anim of Irian Jaya constructed elaborately drained gardens, planted their crops and went away to hunt, coming back several months later (Barrau 1958: 16–17; Bellwood 1978: 145). The Rararumi of northern Mexico are residentially mobile agriculturalists (Kelly 1992: 52). Commitment to a static resource on which effort has been expended does not predetermine that a community will become permanently sedentary. The subsistence economy need not mesh simply with social organisation, as Armit and Finlayson note (1992: 673–4) in concurrence with Bender. Hitchcock has contended that agriculture cannot be said to explain why people settle down (1980: 300–1; 1982). Economic rationalism will not suffice as an explanation of sedentism, nor can agriculture be considered a sufficient diagnostic marker of it (Kabo 1985; Kent 1989: 6). Conversely, there should be forms of sedentism without agriculture (Kelly 1992: 49). However, the stringent prediction remains – that permanent sedentary communities with relatively high residential densities, in settlements larger than 1–2 ha, cannot persist or expand without such a profound change in resource supply. While the change does not initiate permanent sedentism, it is nevertheless a parameter condition for the persistence of growth beyond the 1–2 ha C-limit. In that sense Rindos is correct that agro-ecology is inextricably associated with [permanent] sedentism (1984: 172–4).

According to the restrictive version a year-round supply of food resources in one place could not, either in itself or by some collateral social effect, generate permanent sedentism. On the Northwest Coast, for instance, fresh fish is available all year, a point which is underemphasised in the claims for seasonality (Kent 1989: 5; Huelsbeck 1983: 107). We should find year-round resources exploited by communities which visit their settlement in that location in every season of the year but do not permanently reside in it. This is feasible whether or not there are local resources. Yet it might produce seasonality data which imply permanent residence. From the late nineteenth century AD to the 1980s the inland Dena'ina around Lake Clark and the Stony river in Alaska visited their villages in every season and also departed to temporary camps in every season (Ellana 1989: 105–6). We must be wary of claims that year-round seasonal markers, as in the complex palimpsest site of Ozette on the north-west coast of America (Gleeson and Grosso 1976; Lieberman 1992; Wessen 1982), can suffice as secure evidence of permanent sedentary occupation. They may derive either from a palimpsest effect or from visits in every season of the year, or may even be due to successive seasonal use of the same site by different though related groups.

After the full transition assemblage has developed, each feature of the new suite of characteristics is then available to be exported to smaller settlements below the

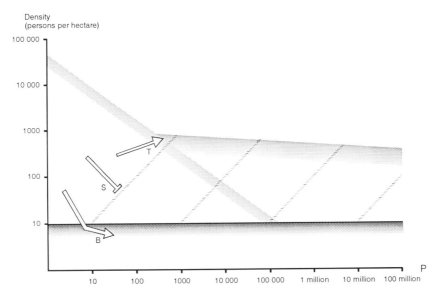

Fig. 7.5 Possible partial 'sedentary' trajectories
B = bypass   S = stasis   T = transition

'mobile' I-limit. This may promote a secondary, contingent development of varied kinds of sedentism. Numerous small sedentary communities would develop, e.g. by breaking away from their parent communities. But they might never take on the full assemblage of prerequisites. Instead they could sustain sedentism by using the strategies of social action which had begun to develop behind the shield of the material prerequisite assemblage in the preceding phase of growth. With the necessary 'social' features they could easily cross the 1–2 ha C-limit, since they would also have the economic means for sustaining such growth. These secondary communities, with a sustainable capacity for growth, would presumably overwhelm the descendants of the earlier Stage 2 communities. The latter could not attain the sizes of the secondary derivative groups, even if they had similar economic and time-scheduling strategies because they would lack the necessary communication aids. The Stage 2 descendants would break up into small communities as they approached the C-limit, unable to compete with the greater, more sustained growth of the sedentary secondaries. We might also expect that the Stage 2 communities would adopt the new I–C assemblage. Their earlier pattern of behaviour would then disappear.

Implications of the restrictive version of the I–C model
Settlement size, the prerequisite assemblage and mobility   The main prediction of the restrictive version of the I–C model is that an assemblage capable of controlling high interaction frequencies preceded the formation of the full assemblage essential for the transition to permanent sedentism. According to the 'restrictive' version the prerequisite assemblage builds up initially only in the larger settlements behind the 1–2 ha limit. The development of permanent sedentism will tend to produce a rather confusing pattern in the archaeological record. The partial assemblage of Stage 2, which controls interaction, will be 'fed back' into new, small settlements. But elements of the entire prerequisite assemblage would previously have begun to appear at random in small settlements. Simultaneously, however (at least in archaeological terms), the full prerequisite assemblage might also have come together and permitted considerable settlement size increases, leading to the growth of large communities across the C-limit. Fission of these communities would then distribute partial versions of the transition assemblage of Stage 3 into the next generation of new small settlements. This may lead to an impression that the class of small settlements was steadily developing a partial assemblage while the big settlements continuously produced an 'advanced' or total assemblage which was the basis for future growth. There is a risk of speciously perceiving two separate processes when what is going on is continual reflux between large settlements and their small descendants.

The full material assemblage has to precede the formation of permanent sedentism. Components of it must have arisen in communities which were, to varying degrees, mobile. The material behaviour approach specifies that we cannot logically ascribe prior probability to assumed connections between active behaviour and the material features. The prerequisites must therefore have been able to exist in association with non-sedentary residence and social actions other than the ones to which they would eventually connect. In addition, both assemblages (or some parts of them) might link with social complexity. If, however, the material features are viewed as products of sedentism, i.e. as diagnostic of its presence, rather than as prerequisites for its existence, an ambiguous and fictitious class of sedentism will be retrodicted substantially further into the past than is warranted. We will also be liable to believe that we are finding other cultural and economic markers of its origin when sedentism was not actually present.

The 'restrictive' model also emphasises that mobile and seasonally sedentary residence, in communities which occupy settlements larger than 1–2 ha, should be stable and unable to effect an endogenous change to a permanent sedentary form. Indeed, a shift to permanent sedentism could be precluded by the presence of large, seasonally sedentary communities because the initially smaller, permanent communities might not be able to compete for the same resources. Only if the seasonal strategy failed would a new shift towards high-density permanent sedentism be able to develop. The two different trajectories are alternative routes towards large residential aggregates sustained by different behavioural requirements. As has been apparent since the 1980s, the simple unilinear evolutionary ranking of sedentary agriculturalists and the late Glacial/Early Holocene 'mobile' communities is untenable (Edwards 1989; Renouf 1989; Rowley-Conwy 1983). The two modes of residential behaviour and their economies can be regarded as sets of divergent options with different growth trajectories.

Potential features of the 1–2 ha transition assemblage   The composition of the transition assemblage should be the same in all the regions where high-density sedentism first developed. However, it is not possible, as yet, to provide or predict a full list of the material prerequisites for that transition. An indication of the likely features is nevertheless feasible because some of them should be obvious simpler versions of the prerequisites for the 100 ha and 100 sq km C-limit transitions. We can expect that the prerequisites for the 1–2 ha C-limit either required lower energy input, had their effect over a more restricted areal extent, or were at least no more substantial in their effect than the prerequisites for the larger C-limits. As with the 100 ha C-limit, the categories of signal to be managed or assisted are the transmission of sight and sound, and the ordering of space and time. The assemblage which can be predicted by extension from the 100 ha and the 100 sq km prerequisites is somewhat surprising. Characteristics usually associated with 'sedentism' are combined with some unexpected features. Durable walling and the internal segregation of residence units would appear to be obvious enough as baffles and barriers to auditory and visual interaction. But a more surprising component is the inclusion of colour coding and motifs as a simpler version of the material information managers associated with the 100 ha transit. Decoration, whether by colour or pattern, serves to identify people at a distance – signalling their social ties without requiring verbal affirmation – and provides distinctive differentiation of buildings and movable items. The means of controlling time ought to require rudimentary versions both of calendrics and of the route access differentiation feature in the 100 ha suite. The latter could be provided by narrow route access between buildings.

Whether periodicity marking, as a simpler form of time management than calendrics, should also be included will be a matter of controversy given the disputes about time-marking in Upper Palaeolithic assemblages (d'Errico 1989; Holdaway and Johnston 1989; Marshack 1991). It should be noted, however, that much of this debate is at an excessively elaborate level. Claims for particular time sequences are not necessary, nor need the artefacts display the sequential addition of marks to qualify as time markers. The analytic problem is really the reverse. The form of a time marker could be exceptionally simple and static. A succession of lines or marks which divide up a linear distance into a hierarchy of units, e.g. groups of five small lines separated by longer lines, as on the Gontzi plaque, will suffice. Whether or not particular examples are 'merely' decoration, a representational device by which time could be ordered was available in the repertoire of European Upper Palaeolithic art. The problem will be to show that the markings were used for this purpose since decorative functions and time ordering are not mutually exclusive. In Europe during the sixteenth century AD, calendars of saints' days were inscribed on the blades of swords[4] and simpler equivalents are not hard to envisage.

The predictability of space might perhaps be provided by rectilinearity in a simpler form and by the arrangement of space into a serial order of some kind. In 1972 Flannery pointed out that rectilinearity was a distinct feature of the settlement plans of the villages occupied by early agrarian sedentary communities. He contended that it was related to particular changes in social organisation (1972: 29, 46–9). However, if it is a feature of the transitions across both the 1–2 ha and 100 ha C-limits, then the role of spatial repetition and predictability in managing interaction stress (see pp. 143 and 146) may be more effective as a high-level explanation for both, whatever the contextual particulars of each case. The claim is further reinforced by the contention that the prerequisites which provide high degrees of consistency and signal redundancy are required only in the transition settlements. Later settlements can dispense with some of the characteristics as active behaviour becomes better able to manage the stresses of social life (see p. 155).

Rectilinearity need not be a corollary of sedentism, but simply a necessity for the transition to permanent sedentism across the 1–2 ha C-limit. Settlements with only one way of dividing up space, that has little size differentiation, e.g. windbreaks, may simply lack a sufficiently varied spatial repertoire to carry a complex predictable spatial message. The behavioural analysis predicts that differentiated space will precede the development of permanent sedentism rather than be a derivative of it. This interpretation does not obviate an enquiry into the actions and verbal meanings which first generated such forms of space. What it does do is to provide an explanation for their long-term role without requiring a deterministic explanation of why each particular community began to make such spaces. The problem with a conventional social explanation is that the specific reasons offered for the initial occurrence of variegated space in different societies may be explanatory overdeterminations. The behavioural analysis avoids that problem because it is concerned with the longer term outcome of the behaviour and does not require that every community applied the same verbal meanings or action content of social significance to the buildings, or developed them for the same reasons.

What is not specified is that all permanent sedentary communities must have, at the present time, the same material characteristics. Some of the prerequisites may become redundant in later permanently sedentary communities, and secondary communities will have varied assemblages. Contemporary African sedentary agrarian communities occupy both round and rectilinear buildings (Denyer 1978; Duly 1979; Fraser 1968).[5] They can also shift from one to the other (see p. 146). The stringent conditions for initial growth should not be confused with the contextually unique possibilities which particular histories and secondary recombination may then produce.

The temporal occurrence of permanent sedentism   Because a transition can only take place when the entire prerequisite assemblage is present, permanent sedentism would have been impossible before the earliest occurrence of its components. Rectilinearity, colour coding and the ability to produce periodic marking have only been fully apparent as part of the behavioural repertoire of *Homo sapiens sapiens* in the past 20,000–30,000 years. On this view permanent sedentism, in the strict sense, was only possible for recent, modern humans. If our habitual sense of the distinctive nature of permanent sedentism is correct, and if that behaviour has made only a comparatively recent conspicuous appearance, then the restrictive version of the model is of some consequence. It not only has the capacity to predict the initial scarcity of such sedentism, but it may also be able to specify why it was only possible for *Homo sapiens sapiens*. The date of the earliest occurrence of permanent sedentism would then follow from the amount of time required for all the prerequisites to coincide at random. This would be conditional on the number of communities in a region and the rate at which they were producing variation and incorporating it into their assemblages.

Past positions of the I-limits   According to the restrictive version, a test is available for identifying the position of the I-limits in the past from the proposed relationship between the I-limits and the 1–2 ha C-limit. Only with the C-limit at 1–2 ha and the I-limits where they are now would the three-stage shift to permanent sedentism in high-density large settlements be possible. Examples of communities representing the brief phase of pseudo-permanent sedentism in Stage 2 should be rare. There is little latitude in the possible sizes of either their populations or their settlements. We may also find that they tend to die out and do not appear again in a region. They will not be common enough to form persistent settlement systems. However, if the C-limit was set lower (Figure 7.6a), then any shift to permanent sedentism had to be instantaneous and total – no intermediates could have existed. Conversely, if the C-limit was much larger, e.g. 10 ha (Figure 7.6b), then there could have been a very long intermediate phase of pseudo-permanent sedentism. This intermediate type of

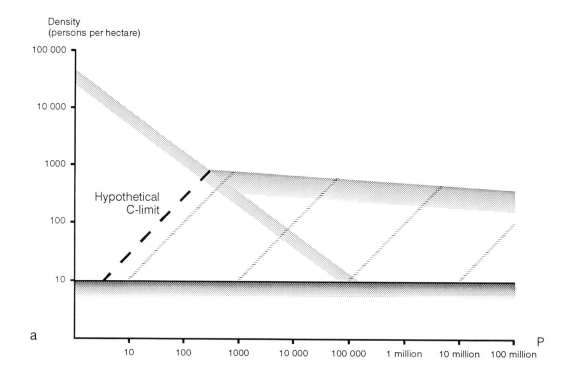

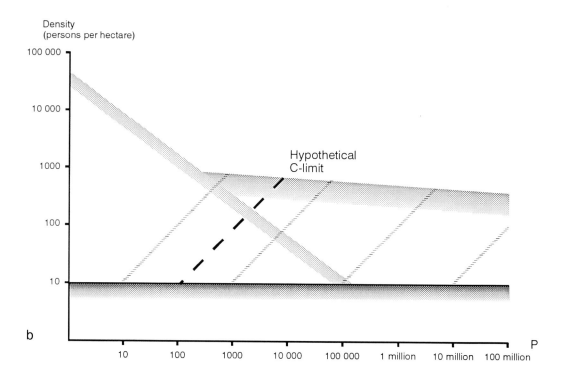

Density
(persons per hectare)

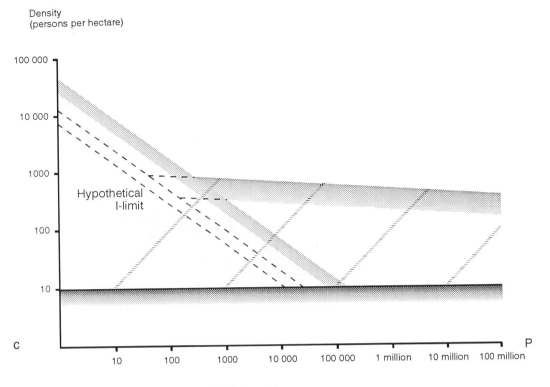

Figure 7.6 Different I- and C-limit positions
(a) smaller hypothetical C-limit
(b) larger hypothetical C-limit
(c) hypothetical shifts in I-limits

residential behaviour would have been very common and presumably well able to compete with other residence patterns. These possibilities also apply if either of the I-limits has moved and the C-limit has not (Figure 7.6c). A way of testing whether or not the interaction limits have been stable for 10,000–20,000 years is therefore available. The overall gross trajectories of settlement growth should be predictable, as should the sequence of material assemblages and the degree to which an intermediate form of permanent sedentism might prevail. If we can show that there is a 1–2 ha C-limit, the relationship between the two I-limits over the past 15,000–20,000 years or more may be identifiable from the overall development of cultural change in regions where permanent sedentism is considered to have first developed.

A material behaviour analysis and culture history A variety of possible events in settlements near the I- and C-limits can be predicted, depending on prior conditions set by differing material assemblages and varying degrees of economic change. Even within a single region there could be several simultaneous trajectories. Some communities will begin to be sedentary and stop growing. Others will carry partial assemblages of prerequisites but their communities will never be able to shift to permanent sedentism in larger settlements. We cannot assume a universal inevitable trend once sedentism became feasible. When we add repeated shifts in resource procurement – as Schrire (1980) has described for the San in the Early Colonial period; the recent evidence for a change from agriculture back to a hunting and gathering economy on Hokkaido in the ninth century AD (Crawford and Yoshizaki 1987); and the combinations of farming and hunting discussed by Kent (1989, 1992) – permanent sedentism might begin but not be sustainable because in the longer term no adequate economic change occurs.

An even more critical problem is that two obvious, long-term major growth trajectories are predicted, one towards high-density sedentary communities and the other towards large mobile or seasonally sedentary communities. A trajectory across the 1–2 ha limit below the 'mobile' I-limit can produce spectacular settlements. But these would appear as compact or partially compact settlements in the same size ranges as the settlements of expanding permanently sedentary communities. What should differentiate them archaeologically would be differences in the assemblages that preceded the growth and different biomechanical indices of mobility.[6] The serious complication is that instead of a single shift towards sedentism, which economic and social theory has previously emphasised, both overall tendencies and several secondary possibilities may be occurring concurrently in nearby regions. Versions of agriculture might have sustained growth along both of the predicted transition trajectories. The perspectives of current social theory, a combination of conventional ethnographic association analogy and the use of 'common-sense' prior probabilities (see Salmon 1982: 42–9) may obscure the potential complexity and significance of the varied behavioural possibilities.

According to the restrictive version there was only one class of trajectory which could allow the initial movement across an I-limit to permanent sedentism (Figure 7.1b). Secondary movements cannot be its operational equivalent and the original mechanism need no longer be applicable (see Price and Brown 1985: 203). For instance the growth of present-day sedentary communities across the position of the 'mobile' I-limit will not be informative about the initial transition to permanent sedentism, nor will recent shifts by mobile groups under external influence from sedentary communities. In both situations additional variables are involved. The 'mobile' I-limit is not an obstacle to the former, while for the latter the disruptive effects of outside influence prevent us from knowing what effects are particular to the shift across that I-limit. No recent or contemporary case can therefore be regarded as the equivalent of an initial transition to sedentism. However, the ethno-archaeological cases (e.g. Heppell 1979; Kent 1989; Yellen 1990) will be of critical value for gauging the impact of disease vectors and stress in settlements whose spatial arrangements and patterns of sensory screening may be inadequate to cope with a cumulatively more sedentary life style. We cannot assume that contemporary communities which are making substantial moves towards sedentism are doing so successfully. There is not sufficient time depth in present-day observations to allow direct equivalence to outcomes which may have taken many hundreds of years in the distant past or to operations which cannot be observed on a finer grain of temporal detail.

The operational uniformitarian basis is of consequence because it provides theoretical grounds for recognising that the past and the present may contain expressions of the same general operations or parameters but that these need not look substantively similar. It specifies the relevant processes on independent theoretical grounds, and does not rule that the absence of a particular effect in the present or in the ethnohistorical record excludes its possible occurrence in the more remote past. The archaeological record might inform us about modes of sedentism with no modern equivalent. Conversely, phenomena observed in the present need not have past equivalents, nor need they be typical or inevitable products of uniform operations.

The behavioural approach also allows predictions about a complex, historically particular past whose trajectories are comprehensible but whose beginnings are not. Instead of assuming simple shifts between different taxonomic classes, potential historical scenarios can be derived from the trajectories and outcomes indicated on the I–C matrix. For instance, both the proposed trajectories may have developed concurrently in one region, with consequent elaborate patterns of inter-association and exchange. Local culture histories may therefore be surprisingly complex and idiosyncratic, yet still be amenable to processual analysis. The implications should be of some value for our understanding of the detailed cultural sequences known from southwest Asia between 15,000 and 7000 BP, Peru, Ecuador and Colombia from 9000 to 3000 BP and Mesoamerica from 10,000 to 4000 BP. Inductive generalisations about the relationship between economic change, material assemblages, settlement size and the form of community life cannot be made on the basis of an assumption that we are observing a single process or a simple dichotomy between sedentism and mobility in these regions. Such an assumption would lead to specious generalisations if, in addition to several trajectories, oscillations between strategies were also involved.

This poses an empirical problem. The two kinds of transition settlement and their occupation densities are as yet hard to distinguish because the crude categories of compact and dispersed occupation will not suffice to differentiate them. Other more exact criteria for identifying the periodicity and degree of site use, such as biomechanical indices for the degree of residential permanence, will be needed (see note 6). Cultural markers are excluded because they can be prerequisites, not products, of the active behaviour with which they are eventually associated. Nor can economic change be a decisive marker because it is not deterministically coupled to particular degrees of residential permanence. Economic indicators, such as storage, should not be treated as sufficient either (Kent 1989: 135–6). To do so predefines the answer to a crucial question about the relationship between change in different components of the behaviour of human communities. An independent diagnostic index for sedentism is necessary if we are to sort out the value of differing theories as means of understanding the past.

Varieties of sedentism   The analysis suggests that the debate about sedentism and nomadism has erroneously conflated behavioural diversity into a simple, untenable continuum laid over a dichotomy. Among the different trajectories of growth and diverse kinds of sedentism, permanent sedentism has probably been the rarest type until well into the last 7,000 years. We might perhaps find degrees of sedentism which involve even less mobility than seasonal sedentism but still contain enough unpredictability in their interaction to keep communities below the 'mobile' I-limit. The incidence of mobility sufficient to keep a community below the 'mobile' I-limit needs further investigation. The hypothetical trajectories also suggest that even more variety might be introduced through the secondary derivatives of permanently sedentary communities which have reverted to more mobile schedules and divested themselves of parts of the prerequisite assemblage. Regional culture histories and parametric behavioural models provide complementary, not opposed, routes to explanation. Instead of a continuum and/or a dichotomy we may have diversity and a decisive threshold.

While permanent sedentism at high densities appears to have been critical to the future of sustained large-scale settlement growth, we should not presume that it has generally been the prevalent form. The matrix and the proposed 'mobile' I-limit help to explain why communities ranging from one or two individuals to several thousand could switch in and out of varying combinations of mobility and sedentism by remaining below the 'mobile' I-limit as their group size increases. In the Pacific, Australasia, southeast Asia and the forest regions of Amazonia a large proportion of substantially sedentary rural human groups have lived in small communities. We should find that they operate primarily at densities below the 'mobile' I-limit and without a full prerequisite assemblage. There should consequently have been behavioural limits on their capacity to grow which have to be taken into account when the constraints on regional settlement size differentiation, with all its attendant social implications, are being analysed.

An alternative, gradualistic scenario for the development of sedentism
The restrictive version of the I–C model predicts that the initial autonomous development of permanent sedentism cannot happen arbitrarily below the 'mobile' I-limit. Only the extreme stress levels near the junction of the I- and C-limits would suffice to whittle away other material features to leave only the material assemblage needed to make permanent sedentism operable. But an alternative can be envisaged which helps to highlight the essential features of the restrictive version. The identified 'mobile' I-limit specifies, as a minimum, that communities whose members predominantly relocate their place of residence for part of the year cannot operate above that limit. But this does not in itself disallow the initial formation of permanent sedentary communities at any density below the 'mobile' I-limit. We know that communities which we usually refer to as sedentary do now exist at such densities. The ethnographic record contains numerous examples, for instance in the Indian subcontinent (Figure 7.7). But we cannot gauge from ethnographic cases whether or not such communities are secondary to the appearance of permanent

sedentism at higher densities or were autonomously generated at the same densities as the mobile communities. In the alternative model the general class of sedentism is considered to be a readily sustainable form of behaviour which can develop at any density below the 'mobile' I-limit. This leads to the expectation that the controls on interaction, though necessary, are not difficult to produce and tend to be readily adopted because they confer some set of advantages other than the behavioural gains of mitigating stress. The spontaneous occurrence of sedentism at varied residential densities, without a consistent relationship to internal behavioural stresses which would select in its favour, requires a myriad local, contextual explanations, presumably without social or behavioural universality (Flannery 1987: 4–5).[7]

In principle, permanent sedentary communities might begin at varying occupation densities, whether in settlements which never exceed 1–2 ha or in settlements larger than 1–2 ha. The former would be constrained by the C-limit, while the latter lead to a distinctly different outcome from that of the 'restrictive' model (Figure 7.8). These sedentary communities should be able to effect a variety of growth trajectories producing a proliferation of settlements of diverse size and occupation density. There could then be a later shift to settlements of substantial size from a wide spectrum of settlement sizes and occupation densities. There should not be consistency in the initial features in the material assemblages because they will have developed to manage markedly different density conditions and community sizes,

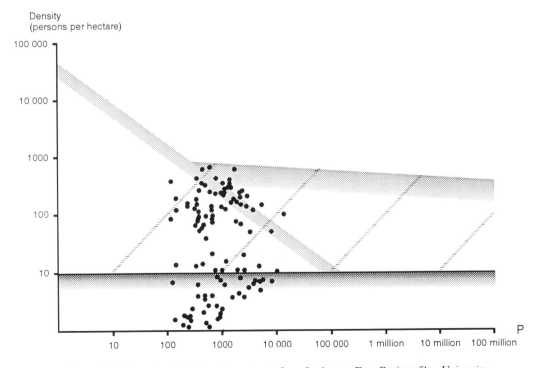

Figure 7.7 Villages in the Indian subcontinent (from Settlement Data Register files, University of Sydney)

nor will there be a difference between primary and secondary assemblages.

The 'restrictive' and the 'gradualist' versions differ in their logic. The former ascribes conditional necessity to a material assemblage and excludes a directive role for social action; the latter has to allocate directive cause to some other class of operator, whether social action or environmental resource supply. The restrictive model emphasises that the particular history of a trajectory alters the options open to a community and distinguishes primary from secondary development. The gradualist version, by contrast, emphasises local contextual uniqueness but does not ascribe much historical significance to temporal position.

The different versions also lead to divergent perspectives on movement across an I-limit. This is of consequence because the archaeological record is the only source of data on such a trajectory – the shift across the putative 'mobile' I-limit. Two different versions of the formation of permanently sedentary communities can be proposed, each predicated on a very different view of the nature of the 'mobile' I-limit. Depending on whether that limit is behaviourally very restrictive or merely represents part of a gradation between nomadic mobility and permanent sedentism, our predictions about future transformations in settlement behaviour will be very different (see p. 216). The former predicts a future of large-scale quantum changes while the latter predicts that the future will be very much a continuation of the

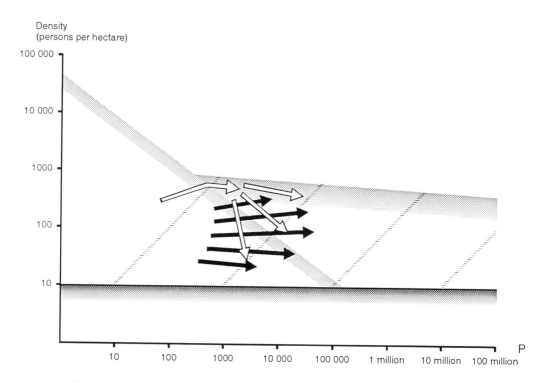

Figure 7.8 Differences in growth trajectories according to the gradualist and restrictive scenarios

➤ gradualist trajectories   ⇨ trajectories of the restrictive scenario specifics of the current range of residential behaviour contained by the current sedentary I-limit.

Conclusions

The stress matrix serves as a framework on which the evolution and development of human residential behaviour can be mapped. The nature of the successive major transformations in settlement growth which are incorporated in the labels of sedentism and urbanism should further help to clarify the nature of the limits. Two different scenarios for the development of permanent sedentism lead to different research issues and to radically different conclusions about the prospects for settlement growth. But this means that the way we perceive the spectrum of sedentism is of direct consequence for our views of the future. We should be wary of applying familiar expectations.

Further assessment of the nature of sedentism in archaeology will need a rigorous identification of site size, a biomechanical means of recognising degrees of sedentism and a way of obtaining estimates of 'community size', or the degree of site usage, without appealing to cultural markers. Proposed cultural markers or indices of population such as settlement area or house size are not valid because the use of space is locally culture-specific and we have to know first what degree of residential density was tolerated before making the estimates. Nor can specific classes of cultural type-marker be unique to the initial sedentary communities, since all the potential prerequisites for permanent sedentism must be able to form at random in the assemblages of more mobile groups which preceded them. We cannot assume that a particular kind of sedentary community will be characterised by one or two cultural diagnostics which do not appear in other residential patterns. That error will lead to identifications of sedentism which are so inclusive that they negate the significance of what is surely one of the fundamental transformations of human behaviour.

Recent or contemporary permanent sedentary communities may have jettisoned parts of the initial enabling assemblage and could possess secondary characteristics which played no role in the development of sedentism. We therefore cannot assume constancy of detail but will have to devise ways of gauging whether or not there is substantive equivalence between past and present. Envisaging what happened depends on large-scale theory derived from general principles about human residential behaviour. Predictions have to be assessed from the archaeological record of the initial transitions, without the expectation that contemporary or recent cases may help us to reconstruct those past events. Our use of the archaeological record has to bear a substantial theoretical burden.

8

The development of agrarian and industrial urbanism

The matrix specifies that the transitions which produced the initial, agrarian-based urban settlements and then the growth of industrially based cities are of a similar nature. Because they involved shifts only across C-limits, they were not of the same order as the shift to permanent sedentism which required a movement across an I-limit as well as a move across a C-limit. There has been a single class of major behavioural shift over the past 15,000 years – to permanent sedentism – and two subsidiary transitions.

A material behaviour analysis provides a basis for assessing and comparing the nature of the two urban transitions. Furthermore, because these two transitions are both known in rather more detail than any of the initial transitions to permanent sedentism, they can be more readily used to illustrate the methodological issues associated with the analytic procedure – particularly the problems and demands of refutation.

The development of agrarian urban settlements

Settlement form

A variety of different urban forms with differing growth dynamics can be identified on the matrix. The use of the term 'urban' has been vastly expanded during the past fifteen to twenty years and now includes agrarian settlements ranging from small compact towns of 20–30 ha up to immense dispersed giants of 100 sq km or more. Not only does it encompass the small settlements of the Aegean in the third and second millennia BC, such as Phylakopi or Mallia, few of which exceeded 30 ha (Haag and Konsola 1986; Renfrew 1972); the label now includes the oppida of Europe in the last quarter of the first millennium BC (Audouze and Büchsenschütz 1989; Alexander 1972; Wells 1984), some of which were as extensive as Uruk in the early third millennium BC; the great dispersed Maya settlements of Yucatan in the first millennium AD (Sabloff 1981); and African settlements such as Old Oyo in Nigeria which covered 60 sq km in the early nineteenth century AD (Connah 1987; Hull 1976; Soper and Darling 1980). Unlike the social designations of 'urbanism' and 'cities' (Redman 1978; Silverman 1988: 404), the I–C model predicts several quantifiably different potential growth trajectories and allows precise specifications within the broad, vague category 'urban'. That taxon in itself offers 'no set of precise well-understood additional characteristics for societies so described' (Adams 1981: 81). We need not deny the label to particular regional examples or become trapped in futile definitional conflict, nor do we end up with a vague all-encompassing category.

Social complexity

The significance of differing degrees of social complexity (Gledhill, Bender and Larsen 1988; Yoffee 1985) can be considered in the context of the stress matrix, since it specifies the behavioural limits with which social action contends. It is generally accepted that power elites and differentiated social rank were necessary for the formation of urban communities. Archaeologists have identified a broad range of actions and categories of verbal meaning which are considered necessary, if not sufficient. In the hierarchy of explanation these are basal active 'social' conditions for the functioning of a wide variety of urban settlements, whose different growth potential depends on differing material and economic characteristics further up the hierarchical scale of cultural operations. Social complexity may therefore have developed quite frequently but need not consistently correlate with markedly increased settlement size, which has been quite rare. We should not therefore expect specific socio-political forms of organisation, e.g. states, to be deterministically linked with the size or stability of settlements. Nor should material context, social action and ideology be consistently associated with profound changes in resource supply. The changes might be weak or, more perplexing, economic change could be strong but not channelled through the towns. What we should see are varying combinations of active and material behaviour, each combination having a con-sistent relationship to a differing kind of outcome in terms of the size and growth rate of the settlements and their residential communities.

Material prerequisites and economic factors

In Mesopotamia, northern China, Mesoamerica and the western montane littoral of South America expansion of rural resource management was either already in progress or began to develop substantially during the millennium following the expansion of compact settlements to areas of over 100 ha. This was achieved either by substantial canals and alterations to drainage patterns (Adams and Nissen 1972; Farrington 1977: 164–8; Greer 1979: 13, 24–6; Isbell 1977: 7, 9; McNeish *et al.* 1981: 181; Moseley 1982; Needham 1971: 237, 269–71, 282–3; Sanders *et al.* 1979: 266–73, 391–2, 394), or by extensive terracing and specialised field systems (Erickson 1988; Isbell 1984; Sanders *et al.* 1979: 250, 379, 382–4), or by expansion into underutilised agricultural land (Nicholas 1989). In Mesopotamia, and in the Mexico Basin and Oaxaca in Mesoamerica, the size not only of the largest settle-ments but also of the small and medium-sized ones increased (Adams 1981; Blanton *et al.* 1982; Parsons *et al.* 1983). Gradual and considerable changes in the basis, intensity and scale of the rural economy apparently accompanied the expansion of the larger urban centres. But there is not necessarily a simple determinative connection between the behavioural techniques which would allow the management of massive urban settlements and the economic means that might support such growth. This has previously been indicated in 'social' terms by the decoupling of state formation from irrigation in the criticisms of the Wittfogel thesis (Adams 1981; Butzer 1976; Farrington 1977).

The contentious issue of the absence of a necessary link between the behavioural capacity to manage larger communities and the capacity to expand and channel economic yield substantially and rapidly is apposite to the example of the Old Kingdom (late-fourth to late third millennium BC) in Egypt. Butzer has argued (1976: 46–8) that, though there was rudimentary artificial irrigation in the Old Kingdom, no substantial change in the Egyptian rural economy occurred until the Ptolomaic period.[1] Only in the Middle Kingdom (early twentieth to early eighteenth century BC) is the participation of the state in irrigation plans apparent in the Fayum, a separate basin into which the flow of water from the Nile could be controlled by sluices (Butzer 1976: 47; 1980: 521). The technology to lift water from canals, such as the *shaduf*, appeared in the Amarna period (1356–1334 BC) (Giles 1970: 91). Sophisticated canalisation and substantial use of water wheels in marginal areas only developed in the Ptolomaic period. Even in the eleventh century BC large parts of the floodplain were still underdeveloped (Butzer 1980: 519). Population growth does not appear to have been either rapid or strong (Wenke 1991: 301, 310–11).

Because the Nile flood fills a succession of basins on the way north and is not dispersed through a network of divergent channels, as happens in Mesopotamia, the alluvial plain receives whatever water and sediment is available. No enterprise other than local water management in each basin is required to ensure a crop from the total area that is flooded each year. Local basin irrigation did not yield an additional harvest of primary cereals, nor is there textual evidence for crops planted after the winter harvest (Butzer 1984: 105). Cropping was not extended to unproductive land except for some restricted development in the Delta to gain revenue or as stipends (Butzer 1976: 51). Dry-season crops were not grown on high ground or flood-free areas (Baer 1962, 1963). While Old Kingdom irrigation presumably increased productivity in the Delta, this was possible only in parts of the valley to the south. The large basins of Middle Egypt were not amenable to intensification. In addition the economy had to cope with a deteriorating water supply as the level of the Nile fell during the third millennium BC (1976: 28, 53–5). Eventually the state administration could not cope with the problem of the river's changing regime (Butzer 1984: 106–7, 109).

Excepting Hierakonpolis [Nekhen] (Hoffman 1979, 1982) and presumably Memphis, the maximum size of Predynastic and Old Kingdom sites did not extend much beyond 30 ha (Kemp 1977, 1989: 40; Trigger, Kemp, O'Connor and Lloyd 1983). Even Abydos, the major shrine settlement of Upper Egypt in the Old Kingdom, covered only about 10–20 ha and the walled settlement of Elephantine was 1–2 ha in extent (Bietak 1979: 108). Old Kingdom Memphis is problematic. The current research programme of the Egypt Exploration Society has indicated that the Old Kingdom settlement might not have been located beneath Mit Rahina (the southwest part of the Memphis ruin field) but may have been further north near the western edge of the floodplain. As yet, however, no evidence of intensive occupation has been reported (Jeffreys and Giddy 1992: 7). The actual size of Memphis in the third millennium BC becomes a critical test case. Old Kingdom Egypt was not a 'civilisation without cities', but it may have lacked the economic capacity to sustain large, compact urban settlements despite changes in the ideology of power and the formation of the state. Further analysis of community sizes, settlement hierarchies and the transport of resources is needed, as has been started by Hassan (1993: 560–2, 557–8). The economy may not have been sufficiently intensified to secure anything other than a gradually expanding rural population while peace and security lasted, or perhaps surpluses were diverted to the populace without passing through the urban milieu. If this were so, and Memphis was only about 100–150 ha in extent, the situation lasted until the end of the Second Intermediate Period when Tell el Da'aba in the Delta first exceeded 200 ha (O'Connor 1993: 581).

Another, rather convoluted test case is offered by the Harappan settlements of the third and second millennia BC in the Indus valley. Until recently reports of the areal extent of the largest, best known sites did not exceed 100 ha (Jansen 1979),[2] with Harappā at about 60–70 ha and Ganweriwala at 80–90 ha. Mohenjo-daro has been said to have an area between 50 and 90 ha (Figure 5.13). On these estimates Harappan urban settlements could have functioned without a reorganised economic basis in the form of water management or an extension of crop land. This would also be consonant with the lack of increase in the overall size range of the smaller settlements. Prior to 2600 BC most Indus valley sites were less than 30–40 ha in extent. In the Hakra phase (3200–2600 BC) in Bahawalpur, for instance, the largest site covered 23 ha (Mughal 1980), and the size distribution apparently did not change in the Mature or Late Harappan.

Although irrigation has generally been considered part of the Harappan economy, it is described primarily as backswamp water management (Allchin and Allchin 1982: 192), which did not involve any substantial change in agricultural practice. Good wheat and rice crops can be obtained without irrigation (Kenoyer 1991: 343, 346; Lambrick 1964: 72, 761; Vishnu-Mittre and Savithri 1982: 216). In addition, the Indus is an extremely powerful river which was only harnessed for extensive irrigation by the British administration in the nineteenth century AD and then only with difficulty (Lambrick 1973: 4; Raikes 1984: 457). When the irrigation network was expanded in the nineteenth and twentieth centuries, problems of salinity and waterlogging arose very quickly (Ahmad 1961: 1, 14–15). In his 1990 review Possehl makes no reference to substantial irrigation in the main valley. If it was not technically feasible there in the third millennium BC, the I–C model suggests that urban growth would not have gone much beyond the 100 ha C-limit. How far is the open question – though much beyond 150 ha would surely be stretching the model!

The interesting complication is new reports which indicate that Harappā covered 150 ha (Kenoyer 1991: 35) and Mohenjo-daro as much as 200 ha, extending down to the river (Jansen 1989).[3] On the plans of the proposed drainage system prepared for the conservation of the site it is represented schematically as an area of about 290 ha (Khan 1973, Fig. 2). If the settlement was as large as this then it should have been associated either with an intensification of the local crop economy or with some other substantial addition to the economic base. Alternatively, if contemporaneous occupation was not contiguous from the river to the 'citadel', then we need expect no substantial development of the local economy. One possibility is that the conspicuous site of Mohenjo-daro was part of a dual settlement, consisting of two adjacent, inter-functioning but separate communities. In Africa from the twelfth to the sixteenth century AD paired towns took several forms. The old capital of Ghana is said to have consisted of two towns, an Islamic settlement on the site of Koumbi Saleh and an as yet undiscovered Soninke royal town a few kilometres away (Connah 1987: 106; Shinnie 1965: 47–9). Fez in the time of the Marinides consisted of two immediately adjacent walled towns linked by suburbs into one settlement (Fletcher 1993b: 735, 741). Deciding where in the possible spectrum of association or separation the settlement at Mohenjo-daro should be located will require careful investigation. The I–C model directs specific attention to the details of settlement size and degree of compactness because the relationship between them and the supporting economic system becomes a critical issue. For instance, in the Ghaggar-Hakra valley, recent work has identified irrigation canals (Kenoyer 1991: 355). The task now is to assess whether this only represents an attempt to manage a deteriorating water supply in that river system, or whether it indicates a general capacity to manage water which could have been applied to the Indus river as well, where its existence would be consistent with the proposed larger settlement area estimates. We may yet end up with the reverse of the reasonable conclusion which could be derived from the evidence available in the mid-1980s!

Issues of refutation

This section reviews the way in which a material behaviour approach highlights potential anomalies and indicates the kind of enquiry needed to assess them. Just because refutation may be necessary (see Chapter 9, n. 1) does not make it easy, nor can a deliberate refutationist policy absolutely prevent the use of *ad hoc* hypotheses. However, it does direct attention to the problems and emphasises the research procedures which will enable us to assess the significance of an anomaly. Unlike Gould's approach to anomalies (1980: 29–36, 138–41) these examples are not a source of alternative explanation or a residual from other explanations. Instead they are problems for the I–C model which, if persistent, cause significant logical problems for the mode of explanation. The model is open to potential refutation. We must consider the procedures required to find out whether or not the anomalies are fundamentally damaging, or merely peripheral, or not what we supposed them to be at all.

There are two distinct kinds of refutation. Weak ones consist of cases in which a predicted feature has not been observed. The strong refutations are those in which a characteristic other than the predicted one is found. The former are weak because, no matter how many times we fail to find the expected feature in a regional assemblage, the next investigation can be decisively successful. In Mesoamerica the discovery of the 'Danzantes' slab in the site of San José Mogote (Figure 6.6b), dated to the seventh century BC prior to the growth of Monte Albán (Flannery and

Marcus 1983: 57), decisively introduced the evidence for the antecedents of the script system and the calendrics used in the Zapotec capital (Marcus 1980: 49). Before 1976 little or no evidence could be adduced for either of these prerequisites in Central Mexico.

Anomalies and the transition assemblage   Some of the proposed prerequisites for the 100 ha transit are not apparent in the currently available data from the antecedent settlements or even in all of the initial large urban settlements.

Large linear entities: A clear example of a problem with the proposed spatial prerequisites is provided by the curvilinear monuments of Cuicuilco (Figure 8.1) in Mesoamerica in the late first millennium BC. They are associated with an occupation area which is said to cover 400 ha (Sanders *et al.* 1979: 99, 106). The site is well in excess of the 100 ha limit and is plainly part of the initial development of large urban settlements in the region. According to the model, the site cannot be compact. The difficulty posed by the site is that the detail of its settlement layout is buried under several metres of lava flow, through which the large circular pyramid protrudes. Only a drilling programme could ascertain whether the site had a low-density occupation of adjacent 'villages' forming dispersed barrios, like the early phases of Teotihuacan (Millon *et al.* 1973: 50), or was densely occupied. If it was the latter, then the model will be in serious difficulties.

Figure 8.1 Cuicuilco, Mexico Basin, Mexico, early first millennium AD; schematic reconstruction from aerial photograph (after Sanders *et al.* 1979 with additions after Kubler 1962 and Marquina 1964)

Sign systems: The main issue concerning the sign system prerequisite is its apparent absence prior to the growth of the large compact Mochica centres (200 BC–AD 600) on the coast of Peru and the settlements of Marca Huamachuco (AD 300–800) (Topic and Topic 1987) and Huari (AD 500–900) in the Andes. At Moche signs have been found on the bricks of the Pyramids of the Sun and the Moon (Figure 8.2) (Hastings and Moseley 1975) but a claim that they were a fully integrated information storage system would need a substantial defence. The interpretation of their significance also depends upon the estimates of the size of Moche. Topic describes it as a 69 ha settlement centred around the main huacas (1982: 262–5) (Figure 8.3). At this size it would qualify as a carrier for a gradually developing suite of material features which would later facilitate the growth of Pampa Grande (4 sq km) (Figure 5.13) and Galindo (5 sq km). But the size referred to by Topic is the area of recognisable architecture. More ephemeral occupation may have extended further south, though probably not as far as the scatter of Mochica pottery, and westwards into the area now affected by fluvial erosion, covering about 1–1.5 sq km (Donnan and Mackay 1979: 57; Moseley 1992: 167).[4] If it was as large as that, then the prerequisites would have to be found in earlier settlements or in an earlier phase of occupation at Moche itself. Nor is there, as yet, secure evidence for an elaborated sign code in the Mochica IV–V settlements. Larco Hoyle's claim for the use of decorated beans (Figure 8.4) in the Mochica assemblage as an information system like the *quipu* (1939, 1943) has been controversial. In the

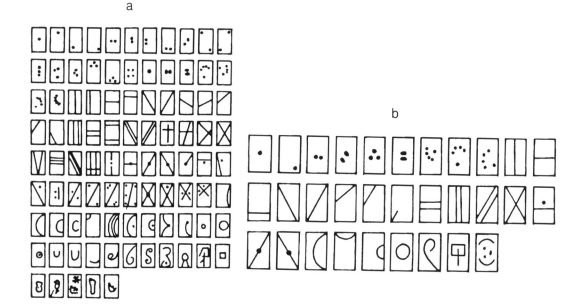

Figure 8.2 Signs on bricks, schematic and not to scale (after Hastings and Moseley 1975) Moche, Peru, early first millennium AD
(a) from Huaca del Sol
(b) from Huaca de la Luna

highlands, *quipu* (Figure 8.5) are associated with the Middle Horizon (Conklin 1982) but are not known prior to the growth of Huari and appear to be unknown on the coast until the Chimu period (AD 1000–1476). Huari, in the Ayacucho valley, was the first major compact settlement in its region to reach an area of 500 ha or more (Isbell 1984), well in excess of the proposed C-limit. It should therefore certainly have possessed a material system of information management.

Two approaches can be suggested. The first is to pursue the Mochica evidence to identify whether the proposed systems can be considered information storage and to identify whether they have antecedents in the preceding Gallinazo assemblage. The second track is to find out whether taphonomic factors have prevented the discovery of earlier *quipu* and other devices. Fortunately for the rigour of the enquiry, lack of preservation cannot be adduced as an easy but specious way out of the problem. The *quipu* from the Chimu and Inca periods survive because of the desiccating environment, especially on the coast (Ascher and Ascher 1981). If *quipu* are older than they currently appear to be, we should find that their production technology indicates a much earlier ancestry. For instance, the methods of preparing

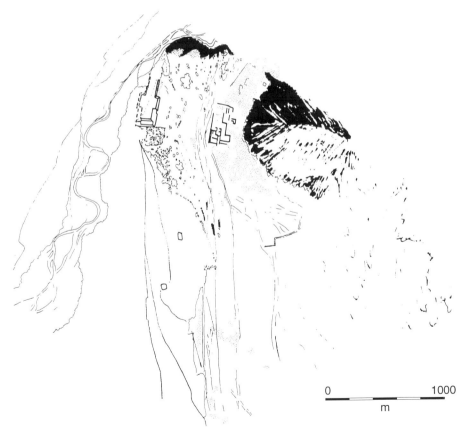

0   1000
m

Figure 8.3 Moche, Peru, early first millennium AD: sketch aerial view (derived from T. L. Topic 1982, with additions from advice courtesy of Ian Farrington)

a

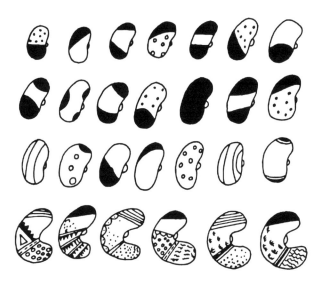

b

Figure 8.4 Mochica decorated beans, Peru, early first millennium AD (after Larco Hoyle 1939)
(a) illustration on ceramic vessel of schematised 'runners' decorated in the patterns which also occur on
the beans. Purported to be an illustration of *chasqui* runners who carried bags containing messages
marked on decorated beans
(b) decorated beans

thread and cord derive from the Chavin assemblages of the earlier half of the first millennium BC (Concklin 1982). The other possibility is that early *quipu* have not been observed because they were very simple. Knotted string is not uncommon in graves prior to the growth of Moche and the simplest *quipu* may be just an old piece of knotted string. The I–C model leads to a strong inference that *quipu* will be found prior to the Mochica period.

General: Apart from calendrics, which are generally hard to find as an antecedent to settlement growth beyond the 100 ha limit, the main problems are the dispute about the sign system of Teotihuacan (Caso 1958–9; Langley 1993; Millon 1973); the absence of any data on differential access in Oaxaca prior to the growth of Monte Albán (Flannery and Marcus 1983); and the same problem in the sites of the early second and third millennia BC in China before the growth of Cheng-chou. The site of Pucara (late first millennium BC) in the high Andes creates a general quandary both because it is very extensive but ill-defined (Mohr Chavez 1988; Mujica Barreda 1978: 280) and because no clear evidence for the transition assemblage has yet been adduced. The problems with calendrics and differential access may simply be due to limited sampling, small-area excavations and taphonomic effects on the preservation of small items. The role of scripts in Teotihuacan deserves a substantial re-examination, as does Pucara and its antecedents.

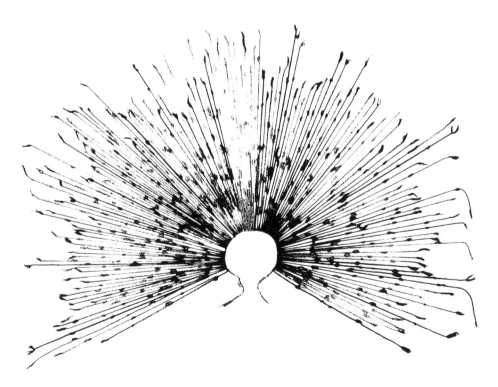

Figure 8.5 *Quipu* (Inca period), Peru, sixteenth century AD

Bypass trajectory cases and issues of refutation

The Late Tripolye-Cucuteni sites – an issue of occupation density:[5]   The Late Tripolye sites (3000–2920 bc) on the southern steppe of Ukraine and Moldova (Figure 8.6) are an example of the attention which the model focuses on a class of archaeological data. The largest sites cover 200–400 ha and are clearly larger than the predicted C-limit of 100 ha. They have a distinct settlement topography and a short occupation span. Nor can they be treated as palimpsests which might be readily broken down into component small sites of different periods. Their maximum extent cannot be conveniently obscured. The problem for the model is that several of the predicted prerequisites for the 100 ha transit are absent. No interior segregation of the settlement is apparent and the buildings do not carry rare, long, linear dimensions of the proposed magnitude. Nor do we have reports of an information system equivalent to the one known from the Vinča and Gumelnitsa sites of the fifth and fourth millennia BC in the Balkans (Winn 1981). If there was high-density, permanent occupation in these settlements then they are severe anomalies and are of major importance for our understanding of the dynamics of settlement growth. Their extent and environment suggest that our premises about urban growth may be quite inadequate. To refer to their societies as chiefdoms (Ellis 1984: 197–9) masks their significance, and neutralises the threatening nature of the past. Instead of homogenising the sites into present-day categories we should use the past as a source of potential refutations which may be able to reveal the restricted nature of contemporary experience.

Until we have further information the sites remain a fascinating enigma. Given that most of the previously well-known large compact 'non-urban' sites such as Poverty Point do not much exceed 100 ha and are the scale equivalent of T'ang Ch'ang-an at about 90–100 sq km, the discovery of these Late Tripolye sites is like finding several new, non-industrial, urban settlements which are perhaps compact and two to four times larger than Ch'ang-an! Plainly this would not be regarded as a trivial issue in the study of agrarian urban communities. The equivalent for the 100 ha limit should not be lightly dismissed. The conventional way of classifying societies according to developmental stages cannot adequately direct attention to the distinctiveness of the sites nor can they be plausibly incorporated in such a scheme. The brief mention in Taylor (1987: 4) notes that the sites might be either 'cities' or 'just overgrown villages'!

By contrast, the I–C model ascribes critical significance to them. They could either be serious refutations or, at the other extreme, possible examples of the rare hypothesised class of threshold trajectory settlements (p. 121). At residential densities near 10 p/ha, i.e. on the communication constraint threshold (T-limit), the largest settlement, Talljanky (400 ha), would have contained up to 4,000 people. However, we do not have sufficient information to make an assessment either way. That they operated at relatively low densities seems likely. Though there might have been as many as 3,000 buildings in Talljanky (an estimate extrapolated from the smaller sites: Ellis 1984: 185–9), the use and contemporaneity of the buildings is uncertain. Another site, Petereny (30 ha), contained 498 buildings. All the eight

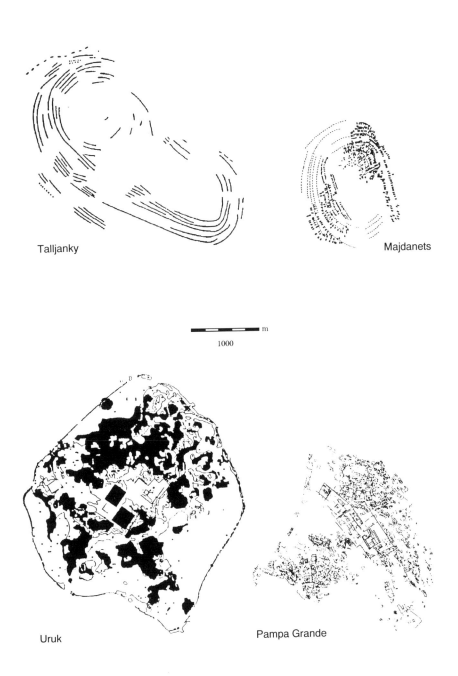

Figure 8.6 Late Tripolye-Cucuteni sites, Ukraine and Moldova, mid-fourth millennium BC (after Ellis 1984) in comparison to initial urban settlements represented by Uruk and Pampa Grande (see also Figure 5.13)

Note: Talljanky scale estimated from report of area of site.

excavated buildings were located on the margins of the site and are referred to as pottery workshops (Ellis 1984: 188). Others may have been storerooms. The number of buildings cannot directly be taken as an index of the number of house-holds in the settlement. Nor need all the buildings have been in use at the same time if the duration of the settlement exceeded the life span of each building. But we should beware of ascribing low densities to them on insufficient evidence. That would merely be a contrivance for avoiding an anomaly by allocating them to the general class of bypass settlement. For instance, all the sites are dated to within a brief period of 100–200 years. If the largest sites were successional rather than contemporaneous (i.e. each was only in use for a short time), this would have a significant effect on the estimate of the number of buildings in each that was in use at any one time.

The T-limit proposal is, however, potentially interesting because these sites are also odd in other ways. The site sizes for the Late Tripolye range up to areas of about 70 ha (Vladimirovka), with a jump to the next site, Majdanets, which is more than twice as large and may have extended over nearly 200 ha, while the largest of all, Talljanky, is more than twice as large again. Such an extreme skew of very rare cases is unusual. Furthermore, the very large sites are also much closer together within their region than is usual in the familiar, initial urban regions. The largest sites lie within 10 to 15 km of one another on an open grassland steppe and are surrounded by numerous smaller sites. Quite what was sustaining them is unclear, though hoe agriculture was presumably involved. By contrast, the transition towns of the southern Mesopotamian basin in the Early dynastic period were further apart, yet here the regional population was sustained by a developing irrigation network. It is unlikely that it was supported by lower, local food yields than hoe agriculture provided on the grassland steppe. The two largest early cities in Mesopotamia, Uruk and Larsa, are respectively 500 and 260 ha in extent and are more than 30 km apart. No other settlements of remotely similar magnitude lay within a hundred kilometres of them. The five large Late Tripolye sites were the terminal brief development of a cultural tradition. If each lasted 100 years, what were they all doing so close together? If they had only brief occupations, why was there such a rapid shifting of residence? A possible clue to the nature may be provided by the increased incidence of horse bones (Ellis 1984: 54) compared to earlier sites in the vicinity. We may be confronting settlements with no modern or recent equivalent. If they were seasonally occupied as part of an expanding horse pastoral economy, they have no ethno-graphic equivalent of that magnitude and form.

European Iron Age oppida – bypass trajectories and the role of outside economic influence in secondary urban growth: Another example of settlements larger than the 100 ha C-limit but lacking some of the prerequisites is provided by the numerous La Tène oppida of Europe (Collis 1975, 1984), some of which reach areas in excess of 200 ha. The oppida are also relevant as possible cases of secondary urban development under the impact of external economic influence (Wells 1984). Given the predictions, oppida larger than 100 ha should either have possessed the required prerequisites or else had low-density occupations. Oppida up to 30–40 ha in extent, such as Staré Hradisko (Collis 1975: 85–9), appear to have densely occupied residential areas, while most larger oppida, of which Kelheim at 600 ha and Berne Engelhalbinsel are excellent examples (Figure 8.7), do not. These larger oppida conform to the bypass trajectory, dropping to low occupation densities as settlement size increased beyond 100 ha. However, Manching is something of a problem because it covers 400 ha and there appears to have been substantial occupation in the central 100-200 ha of the site (Schubert 1972) (Figure 8.8a). Yet it lacked some of the proposed prerequisites for the 100 ha transition. Unless the palisade on the southern edge of the La Tène C2 area (Schubert 1972) (Figure 8.8b) enclosed the entire core, large-scale segregation was not complete. Nor did Manching have a material information management system. The few examples of signs scratched on pottery vessels are in scripts belonging to the Mediterranean region (Kraemer 1982). As yet we cannot precisely evaluate either the degree to which the timber and daub walls of the buildings could block the transmission of noise or the efficacy of the enclosure boundary walls as barriers to sight and sound. Whether Manching

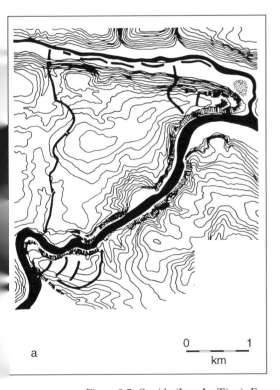

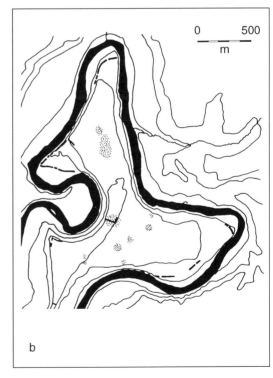

a

b

Figure 8.7 Oppida (Late La Tène), Europe, late first millennium BC

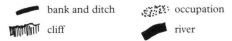 bank and ditch   occupation

cliff   river

(a) Kelheim, Germany (after Collis 1975; Burger and Geisler 1983; Wells 1987)
(b) Berne Engelhalbinsel, Switzerland (after Collis 1975, 1984)

could be said to have possessed conspicuous large linear features is also problematic. The 'barrack' buildings (Figure 8.8b) are potential claimants but because of their location and form would not have been conspicuous across the site. Nor could the enclosure walls be regarded as sufficient visual unifiers since they may have been simply low fences. Even if they were higher, each would only have been perceptually conspicuous along one street. By contrast, the enclosure walls of the early 'urban' transition settlements of Mesopotamia were very much longer and far more conspicuous. In some cases the rectilinear boundary walls were of considerable magnitude, as in the Harappan sites (Figure 6.11).

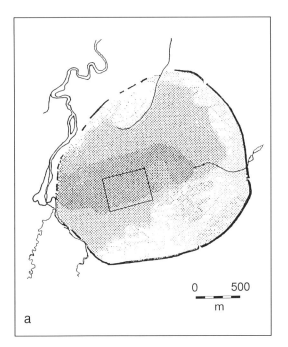

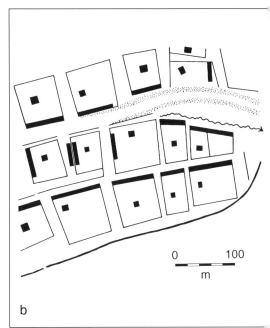

a

b

Figure 8.8 Manching oppidum (Late La Tène), Germany, late first millennium BC (after Collis 1975; Kraemer and Schubert 1970; Schubert 1972)
(a) form and development of settlement
The La Tène C occupation lay within the denser zone of occupation debris in the centre of the site. The bank and ditch boundary and the full extent of occupation only occurred in La Tène D which lasted for about 50–100 years (Collis 1984: 49).

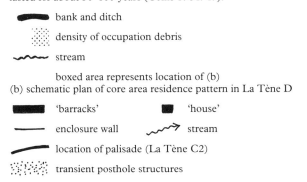

    bank and ditch

    density of occupation debris

    stream

    boxed area represents location of (b)
(b) schematic plan of core area residence pattern in La Tène D

    'barracks'   'house'

    enclosure wall   stream

    location of palisade (La Tène C2)

    transient posthole structures

There are two extreme alternative possibilities to be assessed. First, occupation may have been scant. If Manching was a periodic entrepôt market with only 2,000 people in occasional residence (Wells 1984: 168–9), then it would not be an anomaly but simply a case of a low-density bypass town. Were the long rectangular buildings residential and how many other residence units were present? The second possibility is that secondary growth may be different from initial transitions. Given that a prerequisite assemblage need not be retained in its entirety after a transition has taken place, an established urban region can exert influence on other societies while transferring only part of the suite of prerequisites to them. Varying combinations of a partial prerequisite assemblage and substantial economic influence might have a significant impact on settlement growth. In the case of the oppida the issue is whether or not local concentrations of wealth due to trading connections with the urbanised Mediterranean were a significant factor in triggering economic growth (Wells 1984), or whether the primary role of those connections was in aiding the initial stages of state formation (Haselgrove 1987). Can these kinds of economic input in themselves create concentrations of power sufficient to hold communities at relatively high densities in very large settlements by social regulation alone? Or will such influences only be able to produce low-density occupations or very unstable communities? If they are indeed limited in this way, this would suggest that social variables do not possess a substantial capacity to overrule the stress constraints on behaviour. Secondary urban developments are therefore critical for an assessment of the degree to which active behaviour can play a significant role in settlement growth. The issue is of general consequence for both our view of the past and our analysis of contemporary urbanism. Other instances of large settlements, such as the West African indigenous towns and cities of the sixteenth to the nineteenth centuries AD (Connah 1987; Posnansky 1980; Fletcher 1993b), which developed in the context of substantial external influence from Islamic and European urban societies, should be examined as comparative cases.

The development of industrial urban settlements
Duration of the stasis settlements behind the 100 sq km C-limit
We can gain an impression of the degree of behavioural stress which affects communities close to the sedentary I-limit and up against a C-limit by examining how long the largest compact pre-industrial cities were able to maintain their maximum size. By looking at a cross-cultural sample we can control for local historical effects and see whether there is an overall behavioural constraint on their longevity independent of the specific social crises which heralded their demise. The great imperial capitals of the preceding 2,000 years each maintained their maximum community size for a relatively short period of time. The growth and decline of a major city larger than 25–30 sq km usually occurred within a period of 300 to 500 years (Figure 8.9).[6] Such cities could sustain populations of over 750,000 for only 100 to 200 years and usually suffered a near-catastrophic population decline in the late centuries of their existence. Though population estimates are notoriously unreliable,[7] we can construct a diagram for a city, such as Hangchow (Cloud 1906;

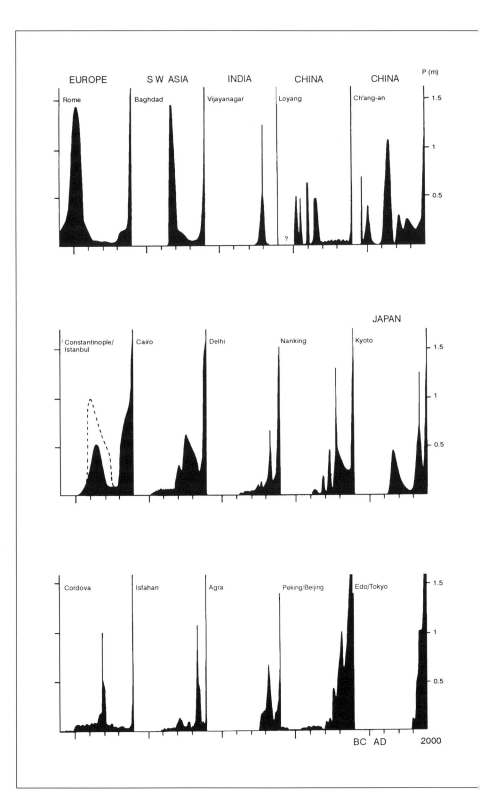

Gernet 1867; Moule 1957) (Figure 8.10),[8] which presents the cloud of purported values for its growth, maximum size and decline. The actual peak and fall should lie somewhere within that cloud of presumed overestimates and cautious commentaries. There are serious disputes about the likely maximum populations of pre-industrial cities (Lassner 1970: 107, 160, 282, 283; Russell 1985). As with estimates of settlement area, however, a careful underestimate is no more preferable or reliable than an overestimate. The sedentary I-limit indicates what the maximum possible viable community size ought to be for a given settlement area. For instance, a city of about 15–20 sq km could carry about 1 million people though it would be very crowded. Imperial Rome may therefore have carried such a population. But claims for 4 million, which were discussed by Lipsius (Hermansen 1978: 129), are either behaviourally fanciful or else profoundly significant. Interestingly, the maximum populations that might be possible for cities of 70–100 sq km such as Ch'ing Peking, Tokugawa Edo and T'ang Ch'ang-an lie, according to the matrix, at about 3–4 million but the maximum estimated or reported figures rarely exceed 1–1.5 million people.[9] These relatively low actual estimates make behavioural sense. What they would indicate is that, as communities reach high densities in very large settlements, there is a powerful brake on their growth, consistent with the model of extreme stress in the wedge between the I- and C-limits.

What can be done with the available data is to plot community size against time. This is done by superimposing the sequence of population estimates from each city (Figure 8.11)[10] to produce an aggregate, cross-cultural, probability cloud (Figure 8.12), from which we can roughly estimate the maximum duration that was possible at various community sizes. From sections across the probability distribution, at given population figures, we can read off the duration on the horizontal axis of the graph (Figure 8.13). Clearly the maximum population estimates at a given point in time could be exaggerations. In that case the outermost values of the distribution would be spurious. More restricted possible distributions may be estimated within

Figure 8.9 Growth and decline of population in agrarian-based imperial capitals (from Settlement Data Register files, University of Sydney)

Cities included in sample, schematically represented: Agra, India, AD 1400–1850; Baghdad, Iraq, AD 700–1850; Cairo, Egypt, AD 200–1850; Ch'ang-an/Hsien Yang, China, 250 BC–AD 1850; Constantinople/Istanbul, Turkey, AD 100–1850; Cordova, Spain, 100 BC–AD 1850; Delhi, India, AD 700–1850; Edo/Tokyo, Japan, AD 1400–1850; Isfahan, Iran, AD 600–1850; Kyoto, Japan, AD 800–1850; Loyang, China, 50 BC–AD 1850; Nanking, China, AD 1100–1850; Peking/Beijing, China, 500 BC–AD 1850; Rome, Italy, 50 BC–AD 1850; Vijayanagar, India, AD 1200–1600.

Sources: initial sources – Chandler and Fox 1974, *excluding the authors' estimates*; *Encyclopaedia of Islam*; *Imperial Gazetteer* 1853.

Additional source(s) for each settlement with historical overview and/or population estimates. The list below is only a brief indication of some major sources, not a comprehensive bibliography for every population estimate. Nor is it a list of definitive estimates because none exist.

Agra – Srivastava 1979. Baghdad – Lassner 1970. Cairo – Abu Lughoud 1971. Ch'ang-an/Hsien Yang – Schafer 1963; Rozman 1973. Constantinople/Istanbul – Celik 1986; Jacoby 1961. Cordova – Pidal 1957. Delhi – Frykenberg 1986. Edo – Yazaki 1968. Isfahan – Lockhart 1950. Kyoto – Ponsonby-Fane 1956; Yazaki 1968. Loyang – Bielenstein 1976; Jenner 1981; Rozman 1973. Nanking – Till 1984. Peking/Beijing – Bouillard 1929. Rome – Hermansen 1978; Russell 1985. Vijayanagar – see Fritz *et al.* 1984 for sources.

Note: Larger alternative estimates for population of Constantinople.

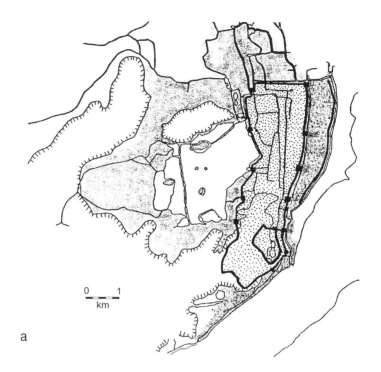

a

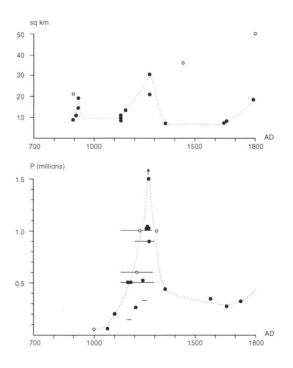

b

that probability envelope (Figure 8.13). From these we can also calculate durations. The result is a plot of the potential time spans over which a given community size might have persisted. From this we can gain an impression of the decline in the endurance of the cities as they approached the 100 sq km C-limit (Figure 8.14).

Longevity decreased markedly as compact settlements became very large – suggesting that the stresses of interaction and communication were substantially increasing. The chances of a large community generating the transition assemblage capable of extricating it from the trap were unlikely to improve as the population started to decline and adverse social and political situations became endemic. The picture is somewhat ominous. We should envisage a similar decay curve behind each C-limit including the next one – which presumably sets the limit on the maximum size of future compact settlements. By defining questions in terms of inter-comparable quantifiable characteristics such as settlement size and rates of growth, an issue raised by one settlement system becomes amenable to assessment using data from different kinds of communities of disparate size. If we could calculate even a rough version of the decay curve for each of the previous C-limits, we might find out whether the longevity of the largest settlements has been increasing or decreasing over the past 15,000 years, with some interesting implications for our future.

Growth trajectories, social process and hierarchies of explanation
The hierarchy of explanation, however, designates only the general outcome for each trajectory of settlement growth. The specific short-term, political and social, contextual phenomena in each local case cannot be predicted. Though my concern is the overall behavioural limits on tolerable interaction and communication within human communities, this emphasis does not presume that explanations in terms of social action and verbal meaning are erroneous or irrelevant. Without them the particulars of each city's history are incomprehensible. Both London and Paris reached very high overall and core area densities in the seventeenth and eighteenth centuries AD (Figure 5.11) up against the I-limit. While both followed a similar trajectory, which approached the upper density limit and then ricocheted away from it, their social expressions and historical experiences were very different because of

Figure 8.10 Hangchow, China, thirteenth–nineteenth century AD
(a) plan of Hangchow during the Southern Sung and the Yuan dynasties, thirteenth century AD; areal extent at maximum size (after Moule 1957)

hill slopes   lake and river

canal   walls and gates

urban core   suburban housing (schematic)

(b) growth, decline and stabilising of Hangchow (from Settlement Data Register, University of Sydney)
Note: Area estimates refer to the combined extent of the walled city and suburbs. The population figures are reported and estimated community sizes. The dotted line marks the 'envelope' within which the actual growth and decline is likely to lie. **O** represents figures referring to other than actual population figures, e.g. number of hearths, families(!), etc., or to ascriptions of maximum area to later periods.

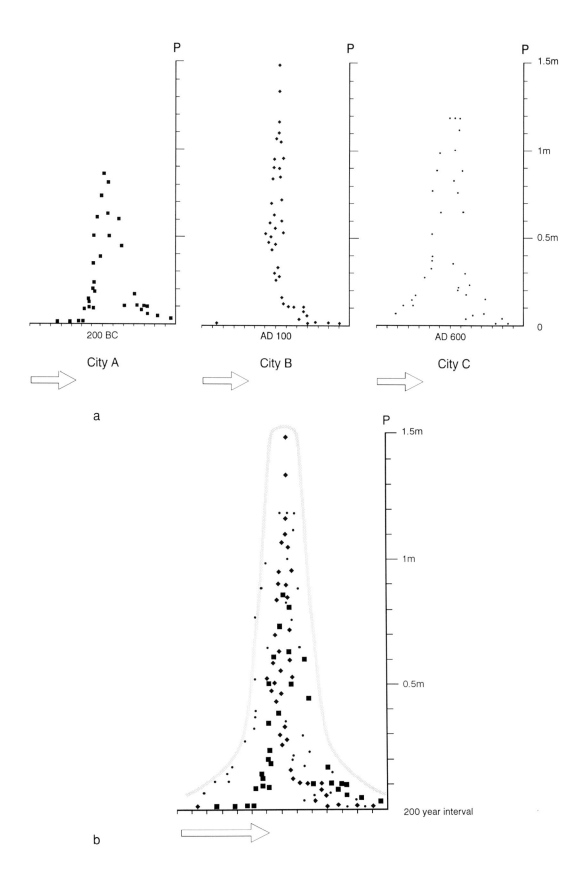

P   P   P
                                          1.5m

                                          1m

                                          0.5m

                                          0

200 BC   AD 100   AD 600

City A   City B   City C

a

                                         P
                                          1.5m

                                          1m

                                          0.5m

                                         200 year interval

b

their different cultural characteristics. A material behaviour approach cannot predict the occurrence, nature or course of the French Revolution from the high residential densities in Paris but, conversely, the similar trajectories displayed by London and Paris cannot be predicted from the details of their social and political change.

Though they are related, the behavioural scale of the growth trajectories and the social scale of human action cannot be reduced to each other. Instead of arguing for the priority of one over the other or claiming greater significance for one scale of observation over the other, we can more usefully recognise a hierarchy of processes in which each level of operation has to be analysed differently and is relevant to different issues. We can recognise parameters to viable behaviour and allow that each community will produce its own distinct, contextually unique social expressions within that context. This obviates the problem of determinism and retains the distinctiveness of the social life of each community. Since a community may either fail or persist when it approaches a limit to its viable existence, the parameters cannot be deterministic in their effect. To refer to communities responding to circumstances is unsatisfactory since it tacitly assumes that they somehow correctly perceive their situation! But the members of the community have their own agenda or agendas. What they do will presumably be an expression of the social style of their society and its inherent contradictions, combined with the human ability to exert creative social action – not a universally rational response.

What the parameters delimit is not what people can begin to do but the consequences or outcome of their actions. Faced with extreme behavioural stress, a community might either move to alternative ways of behaving which mitigate stress or continue obdurately with the same social activities that have produced the stress and be unable to maintain itself. Unless our models of social life encompass those extreme alternative possibilities, we risk becoming embroiled in theory structures which tacitly accept that problems inevitably lead to their own workable solutions – a Panglossian nonsense.

The 'Industrial Revolution' as an atypical conjuncture of behavioural and economic change

The settlement size transition which occurred in Europe in the nineteenth century AD is the only transition across the 100 sq km. No other independent examples can develop while the current mode of economic activity continues. The nature of the 'Industrial Revolution' will therefore have to be clarified by general comparisons to the nature of the more numerous earlier transitions, otherwise we are stuck with a unique case. The six initial urban transits and the potentially numerous different regional transitions to permanent sedentism must be regarded as a more representative sample of cases by which to gauge the nature of transitions and the degree to

Figure 8.11 Hypothetical, general 'envelope' of growth and decline of urban communities derived from *all* reports of community size
(a) schematic growth and decline graphs for three hypothetical cities

(b) combined plot to illustrate the 'envelope'

which they can vary. Though changes in resource movement and production technologies correlate with the early growth of the industrial city, equivalent changes need not have been typical of the initial stages of other earlier settlement size transitions. Resource supply and I–C behaviour, however elaborately described or integrated by social categories, cannot be viewed as inextricably or necessarily connected. Because their association cannot be presumed inevitable, the initial problem is to explain whatever happened in a particular case, not to generalise a supposedly inevitable association of the tangible and the intangible as an encompassing explanation. A generalised assumption that they will occur together and that economic change, however defined, has some directive role, is not tenable.

The identification of such cases in the archaeological record, whether for sedentism and agriculture, or for early urban growth, subjects the apparently close connection between material–'social' change and economic change during the 'Industrial Revolution' to renewed scrutiny in a cross-comparable analytical framework. If what happens along the different C-limits is comparable, then there is no

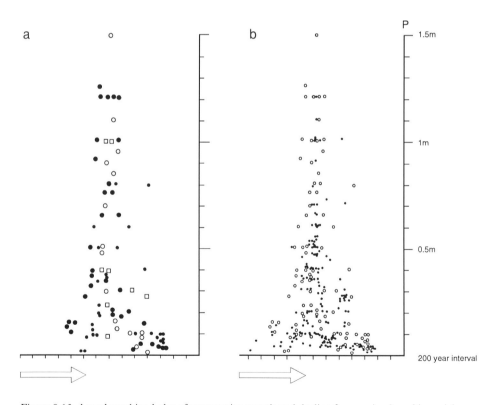

Figure 8.12 Actual combined plot of community growth and decline for agrarian-based imperial capitals (from Settlement Data Register files, University of Sydney)

(a) estimates for   ● Rome   ● Constantinople   □ Ch'ang-an   ○ Baghdad

Note: Han, Sui-T'ang, and Ch'ing Ch'ang-an overlaid.
(b) additional sample of estimates from other agrarian-based imperial capitals
cases represented in (a) ○

necessary connection between economic and behavioural change. This profoundly affects the kinds of questions we might ask about the early growth of the industrial cities and why the two kinds of change were apparently so intertwined in Europe from the eighteenth and nineteenth centuries AD onwards. The issue becomes predominantly a question of contextual history and ceases to be a paradigmatic instance of a universal process. Recognising that changes in resource supply and I–C behaviour are coincidental helps to shake loose a deterministic association for which there may be little logical need as an explanatory device.

Conclusions

If the recent history of Europe cannot be considered the definitive source of an exemplar of economic and social change, neither can any other ethnographic or historical case be an authoritative source of substantive analogy. Just because a recent or contemporary example is well documented at the level of individual action and the detail of local community changes, that does not make it the best source of

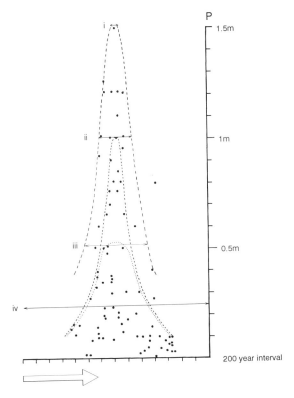

Figure 8.13 Hypothetical, maximum potential duration of community survival for given population sizes (schematic)

Community size	Duration
i 1.5 million	< 100 yrs
ii 1.0 million	approx. 500 yrs
iii 0.5 million	approx. 1000 yrs
iv 0.25 million	> 2500 yrs

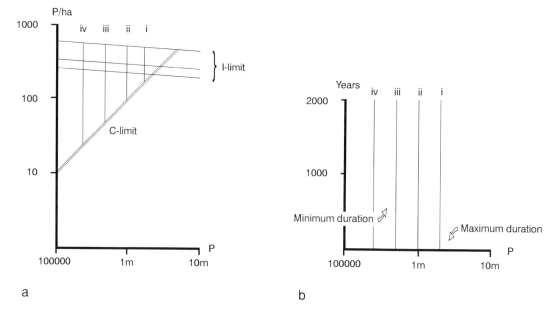

Figure 8.14 Proposed decay curve of community survival for agrarian-based imperial capitals
(a) community size values (from Figure 8.13)
(b) decline in possible duration relative to increasing community size (From Figure 8.13)

information on the large-scale patterns of settlement growth of which it is part. At present we allow the ethnographic present and the historically constructed past to exercise tyranny over our perception of past human behaviour (Wobst 1978) because we depend upon specific substantive association analogies from those contexts to inform our view of the more distant past. Once the information content of recent cases can no longer be considered paradigmatic and exemplary, the logical basis for seeking ratification from appeals to authority in contemporary or recent contexts loses its force (Murray 1987). We can instead make our understanding of recent or present-day examples subject to the conclusions we reach on the basis of high-level theories concerning much earlier equivalent examples. Assessment will depend upon the use of the archaeological record. Since we will need such theory to predict the constraints on future settlement growth, the archaeological study of the past is essential for checking potentially refutable predictions which are then referable to the future.

9

Future urban growth

The model of behavioural stress is of some relevance for our view of future settlement growth. We are confronted by major problems arising from huge population
increases, the rapid urbanisation of the planet over the past 200 years, and the
resultant debris, pollutants and material inertia. The predicted consequences of
different settlement trajectories might therefore be of some use in understanding
urban growth during the late twentieth century AD. To choose between alternative
views of settlement growth we will need to refer to evidence from the archaeological
record to judge which is more useful. Taking any particular position for granted may
lead to error in our assumptions about the future.[1]

Behavioural implications
The demographic significance of the material as behaviour
By treating the material as a class of behaviour we may be able to integrate the study
of ethology across the spectrum of its possible use, by removing a profound prior
classificatory distinction between what humans do and what other animals do. The
cross-comparability should then allow us to distinguish what is specifically human
in the use of the material as behaviour, without appeal to the differentiating label of
'culture'. Our community life has been mediated by the material for nearly 2 million
years and is now substantially affected by it. In human communities the active
expression of culture does not have to manage directly the physiological stresses of
aggregate interaction. The material has created a buffer between the logic of human
action and the demands of human biology. We are not Calhounian rats trapped by
the behavioural stress of overcrowding into pathological social action (Baron 1980;
Calhoun 1962, 1971; Freedman 1975: 25–40; Gifford 1987: 178–93; Gurkaynak
and LeCompte 1979). Instead of being just a recursive associate of action, the
material component of our behaviour has developed into a massive regulatory and
restrictive factor in community life. The magnitude of its effects has yet to be fully
perceived.

Permanently sedentary human communities lack the kinds of behavioural
controls which operate in other animal species to restrict sustainable maximum
group size relative to resource supply. In other animal populations spacing and
signalling controls play an essential role in regulating community sizes (Esser 1971;
Rubenstein and Wragham 1986; Tamarin 1978; Wynne-Edwards 1971), as is
illustrated by territory-fixing in grouse (Watson and Moss 1971),[2] or the effects of

stress on behaviour and reproduction in rats (Calhoun 1962, 1971) and Sitka deer (Christian 1960). But, as Freedman emphasises, no simple extrapolation to human communities is possible (1976: 41–54). We should be wary of analogies from other animals to ourselves. One of the proposed explanations of rapid and substantial population growth in permanently sedentary groups is that increased birthrates after settling down result from more frequent association between males and females (Harris 1978). But while this may be a factor, it will not suffice as a general explanation. The changes in frequency of association have been very different for different groups, such as the !Kung and the Nunamiut (Binford 1978), yet both have increased population growth rates after settling down. The connection is unclear (Kelly 1992: 58–9). If there were an active behavioural control on human group size, equivalent to the active behavioural controls in many other species, it would apply no matter what the breeding opportunities. But there is plainly no such control for permanently sedentary communities.

We need to find out in what ways humans differ from other animals in the mechanisms by which they cope with residential crowding and interaction stress. In short-term contexts, human action and verbal meaning can be applied to controlling the perception of crowding and our reactions to it (Baron 1980: 269). Rapoport has emphasised the role of these 'social' mechanisms in Japanese society (1975: 151), but, as Baron cautiously remarks, we cannot presume that such controls are as effective for humans as their counterparts are in the behaviour of other species (1980: 269–70; Davis 1972). The material has plainly come to play a critical and decisive role in the control of interaction stress among human beings. It is capable of overruling the constraints which active behaviour alone would set on human communal associations. Compared to other mammalian populations, humans have drastically changed their maximum group sizes during the Holocene. We now live in a wider range of persistent, habitual residential group sizes than is usual for mammalian species. According to the model, what has made this possible is the cumulative intervention of the material as a means of controlling interaction frequencies and aiding communication effectiveness. Selection has favoured spatial and temporal signalling mechanisms which make larger and larger aggregates possible.[3] The material may therefore be the critical factor which has removed the behavioural constraints on increasing group size in sedentary communities. The stress effects of increased group size, which might otherwise act as a brake on population growth, have been mitigated by our material strategies. If this is the case, then the few remaining nomadic mobile communities with low material loads should be intensively studied to identify the ways in which interaction stress operates in such groups (Draper 1973; Fletcher 1990, 1991a; Weissner 1974). Furthermore, those groups which have become increasingly sedentary under outside inducement or enforcement, but which do not possess a material assemblage appropriate to the size of their settlements, ought to display behavioural and population growth indicators significantly different from those of habitually mobile or established sedentary communities.

Future limits on interaction

All major settlement size increases, other than the presumed shift to permanent sedentism, have merely been changes in the possible maximum size, whereas the development of permanent sedentism opened up a profoundly new dimension of settlement growth. The matrix makes the magnitude of that change vividly clear. The shift to permanent sedentism in compact settlements required a move across a stress field of changing interaction tolerance, represented by the 'mobile' I-limit, whether abruptly (according to the restrictive model) or by increments (as in the gradualist variant). By contrast, the formation of urban communities and the later growth of industrial urban settlements were merely transitions across successive C-limits. An equivalent transformation of the same magnitude as the initial development of permanent sedentism requires a major jump in the tolerable maximum residential density to a much higher interaction limit. A critical issue for future settlement growth is whether such a jump is possible, since it would profoundly alter the number of people who might live in one place.

The restrictive and the gradualist models of the change towards permanently sedentary community life have radically different implications, which are presented below. The former predicts that a new upper density limit is attainable; the latter excludes that possibility. In the 'abrupt', restrictive version the current I-limit is merely a product of the relationship between our finite interaction capacity and the particular kinds of material entities that we have used over the past 10,000–15,000 years. By contrast, the gradualist view, which otherwise appears to favour a relatively plastic view of human behavioural potential, leads to a conclusion that the sedentary I-limit is an immovable universal.

Initially, at least, the option derived from the gradualist scenario (Figure 9.1) seems to be more obvious and straightforward. In this version the I-limit pivots up to the fully sedentary level for communities of more than about 200 people. A gradual process is involved, with larger communities able to live at higher and higher densities as they become more sedentary. The maximum densities for small communities going through the same process should decrease. The rotation implies that the more sedentary a small community becomes, the less it can cope with very high densities as interaction stress increases. An explanation of this phenomenon will depend upon demonstrating that persistent proximity adversely reinforces the signal burden of increased sedentariness, especially in groups which are too small for the number of people to provide a shield of social distance. According to the gradualist shift, maximum densities for sedentary communities of 100–200 persons or less should lie below the level of the back-extrapolated sedentary I-limit. They should not approach the high densities possible in small mobile communities.

According to the gradualist version the current 'mobile' and sedentary I-limits are just variants of the same constraint, dependent only on the degree of sedentism attained by a community. No other pattern is humanly possible because the rise in interaction stress which occurs as community size increases rules out the possibility of the sedentary I-limit rotating any further upwards towards higher densities for much larger communities. Larger communities cannot carry maximum interaction frequencies as high as those in smaller communities with the same general pattern of interaction (see p. 71).

The restrictive 'standard' version of the model leads to a quite different, radical outcome. According to this standard version the initial transition to permanent sedentism in each region was very restricted, occurring only within a small range of relatively high-density communities. If that shift to sedentism was abrupt, it consisted of a breakthrough which enabled the maximum tolerable densities to rise abruptly upwards from the threshold limit (T-limit). Both the sedentary I-limit and the T-limit either abut or intersect the 'mobile' I-limit (see Figures 4.13, 4.16) (Figure 9.2), but as yet we do not know which relationship actually applies. However, the potential growth of settlements is unconstrained below the T-limit compared to the range available under the 'mobile' I-limit. Likewise, below the sedentary I-limit communities can increase to sizes far beyond the range possible for communities under the 'mobile' I-limit. There seems to be some equivalence or correspondence between the sedentary I-limit and the T-limit. The overall shape of the angle between the 'mobile' I-limit and the T-limit appears the same as the angle between the 'mobile' I-limit and the sedentary I-limit, even though the exact slope of the T-limit is not known. On this view, the prerequisites which facilitated the shift to permanent sedentism had the effect of enabling communities at high residential densities to grow to the same potential community sizes as are available under the T-limit. This shift achieved a quantum jump in the operable density level which was possible for a wide range of larger human communities (Figure 9.2).

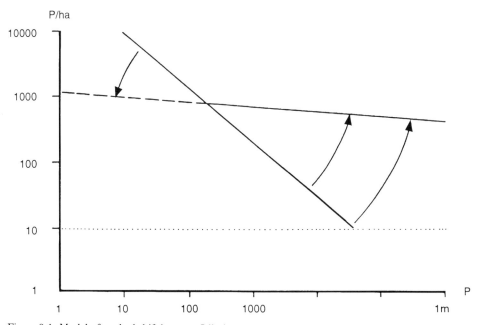

Figure 9.1 Model of gradual shift between I-limits

— — — — extrapolation of sedentary I-limit

shift in I-limit

The behaviour which could produce that effect deserves further investigation because, if the shift to permanent sedentism at high densities depends upon an assemblage of material prerequisites, the significance of the sedentary transition across the 1–2 ha C-limit is even greater than we have envisaged. If it produced a quantum jump in the maximum operable density level for human communities, then the current sedentary I-limit is not an immutable biologically defined limit, but is merely a function of the material assemblages which we have used over the past 10,000–15,000 years. We might therefore devise a new kind of material assemblage which will enable a further jump in the maximum operable residential density limit (Figure 9.3). If it is of the same magnitude as the sedentary jump, then maximum densities of at least 10,000 p/ha will eventually be tolerable for communities of several hundred people – with slightly lower maximum densities for settlements containing thousands or millions of people.

The jump should commence with the development of a new prerequisite assemblage able to overcome the interaction stresses at very high residential densities in small spaces no larger than single residence units or large rooms (e.g. up to 100 sq m) (Figure 9.3). The discussion can be conventionalised in terms of a C-limit at 100-200 sq m (100 times smaller than the 1–2 ha C-limit value). The initial development of the hypothetical prerequisite assemblage will presumably have a profound effect on the control of interaction and communication in very

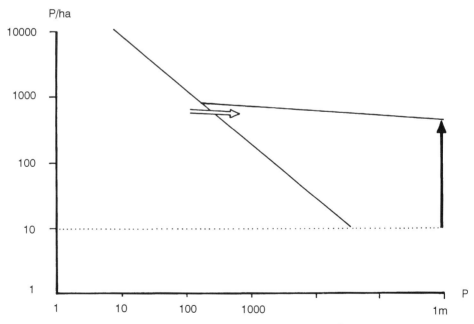

Figure 9.2 Model of abrupt shift between I-limits in the restrictive scenario

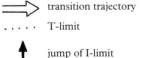

transition trajectory

. . . . . T-limit

jump of I-limit

small spaces, the size of rooms about 30–60 sq m in extent. In its second phase the complete prerequisite assemblage should allow the expansion of settlements to areas of up to 3,000 sq m at very high densities. That phase will require an economic change capable of sustaining the necessary energy demands. What happens afterwards will presumably depend on further changes in the material assemblage and the resource supply to allow transitions across the successive C-limits in the new high-density band (Figure 9.3). In this version the long-term future of settlement growth does not reside in our giant urban settlements or their descendants, any more than the future of settlement growth 10,000 years ago lay with large mobile and seasonally sedentary communities. The jump to a new maximum operable interaction limit would completely alter our inhabited world, as did the transition to permanent sedentism and its agrarian support economy. The alternative implications of the matrix lead to radically different arguments about the future condition of human community life. What we learn about the past should enable us to choose between these two possibilities. The comparison is of interest not only for culture history and explanations of the past but also for our views of the future. The content of the archaeological record and our interpretations of it may be of some consequence for the way we envisage our future.

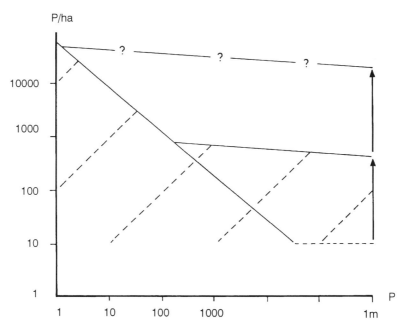

Figure 9.3 Hypothetical new I-limit

– – – – C-limits

– – – – – – T-limit

———— I-limits

— ? — postulated I-limit

Trajectories of the future

The more likely future of urban growth will be the continued growth of communities up to and across successively larger C-limits under the current sedentary I-limit. Predictions of future urban growth depend upon the relationship between the successive C-limits, the distribution of settlement sizes behind the C-limits, the prerequisites needed to cross each limit and the proportionate rates of growth after a transition has occurred.

Future prerequisites and a provisional 10,000 sq km C-limit

From the C-limits on the matrix we should be able to estimate the approximate size of the C-limit which will lie ahead of our industrial urban settlements, if we have not developed an appropriate prerequisite assemblage for getting across it. By convention each successive C-limit acts as a constraint upon settlements which are about 100 times larger than the previous C-limit. If there is a C-limit near 1 ha then the successive C-limits at 100 ha and 100 sq km should be followed by a C-limit with an approximate magnitude of 10,000 sq km. If the C-limit which lies within the 1–2 ha band is nearer 2 ha, then the successive C-limits may be progressively further apart rather than equidistant and the future C-limit would then be somewhat larger than 10,000 sq km. For the purposes of an initial presentation I will use the 10,000 sq km value as a convention.

Two implications follow. First, the maximum size of compact settlements which use the current I–C assemblage should be about 7,000 to 10,000 sq km. Secondly, a transition across the next C-limit will require a new prerequisite assemblage. Some components of that assemblage must begin to develop by the time settlements reach sizes of around 3,000 sq km if a future transition is to be feasible as soon as the C-limit size is reached. Previously, the prerequisites for crossing a C-limit have not been devised with that aim deliberately in mind and the entire assemblage cannot be expected to aggregate just because a collision with a C-limit is impending. Nor can we assume that the prerequisites cumulatively cause each other's development in an inevitable multiplier effect. They may be found in varied combinations with other kinds of material. Even the attributes which eventually combine to make up a single prerequisite can develop in disparate contexts. For instance, the parts of the steam-driven locomotives which were so necessary for the growth of industrial cities were derived from mine pumps and trackway carts (Lewis 1970; Smiles 1975: 23–6).

In principle we should be able to specify the nature of the prerequisites and the approximate magnitude of the effect they will need to produce to manage the stresses which they will encounter. This ought to be identifiable from a comparative analysis of the earlier prerequisite assemblages. For example, successive changes in time patterning appear to have required more and more precise subdivisions of time and a greater range of differentiation in the rates of movement along routes within settlements. Calendars divide up a year into formal seasons, months and days. Clocks split time into hours, minutes and seconds. Once we have properly identified the prerequisites for the shift to sedentism across the 1–2 ha C-limit, we will possess a third set of characteristics. These might be compared with the 100 ha and 100 sq km assemblages in an analysis of trends in the nature of transition assemblages.

The magnitude of the changes in mechanical printing, from the fourteenth century AD to the mid-nineteenth-century transition across the 100 sq km C-limit (Eisenstein 1983), give some idea of the proportionate magnitude of the behavioural changes required for the next transition. In Europe the mechanical printing press developed in small towns in central Germany. The Gutenberg press of AD 1342 (Painter 1984) was a rectangular frame of about 2 sq m. In the nineteenth century AD the printing presses which produced newspapers were many times larger than their manually operated predecessors. The press of the *Illustrated London News* in Fleet Street in London in 1843 was three to four times as high as its operators (Westmancott 1985: 28). By 1900 a newspaper printing press could fill an entire building several storeys high. As a comparison, electronic data processing began to develop during the 1940s in settlements in the lower third of the size range behind the 10,000 sq km C-limit. In proportion to their respective C-limits these industrial settlements were slightly larger than the size of European towns of the fifteenth to seventeenth century AD relative to the 100 sq km limit. Compared to the problems our communities will confront at the next C-limit, the current development of computing is probably the scale equivalent of the printing presses of the Renaissance. The equivalent, substantial increases in the development and elaboration of computing which will be needed for the next C-limit transition can be envisaged! Indices of complexity will be required to enable comparisons of material developments of differing scales from different regions to be made. By rating the efficacy of a communication assemblage against the scale of its context, we should be able to calculate consistently the proportionate magnitude of future change.

The general point to be derived from the I–C model and the transition across the 100 sq km limit is that there will be no single technological innovation which could facilitate the 10,000 sq km C-limit transition. A suite of features will be essential and must be available in the world-wide industrial complex before compact settlements reach the predicted C-limit. The timing and elaboration of the development of the new assemblage will be critical, especially if the rate of approach to the new C-limit at high densities is faster than it was prior to AD 1800 and if the demise of communities which hit the limit is swifter than the breakdown of the great pre-industrial capitals. Absolutely less time may be available for the happenstance conjunction of the assemblage. If, as appears to be the case, innovation rates are declining relative to cost (Tainter 1988), we might be caught in a trap of diminishing marginal returns unless we can predict what we need and assess it before the crisis arises.

The situation is rather delicate because an economic change is also required to sustain a transition. But if it occurs before the new assemblage comes together it will merely promote further, rapid urban population growth towards the next C-limit, propelling our communities into crisis conditions jammed against the I- and C-limits, or else, as currently appears to be happening, they will plunge below the

T-limit. The social and political mechanisms which affect behavioural innovation and the use of new energy sources are not quite the same. The former may seem a threat to established authority because they assist the transmission of the information on which people can act. They may therefore be suppressed. But there seems little likelihood that the use of a new energy source will be delayed by the authority of the state and no likelihood at all that it will be embargoed in deference to any hypothetical model of human behaviour! The options are rather narrow. The material changes must be developed first. Yet if a transition is to be sustained, substantial economic changes will also have to be phased in as compact settlements move towards the new C-limit. Predicting the new limit by extrapolation from past C-limits becomes a matter of some concern. A more precise assessment will be needed than the current rounded estimates. We will also need to find out what leeway might exist for the introduction of a new resource base which would significantly increase energy supplies. The lag times between C-limit transitions and substantial increases in economic yield, as in Mesopotamia in the third millennium BC, become potential indicators for future planning – as do the amounts of time which communities can spend as viable entities up against the C-limits.

Future costs of settlement growth

As well as assisting our perception of the scale of future material behaviour change, the I–C model also allows predictions about the derivatives of the preceding transition event (across the 100 sq km C-limit), and is directly relevant to assessments of the current growth of our settlements. Initially, a new prerequisite assemblage allows massive growth rates, especially in the largest settlements, as can be seen in Mesoamerica between 600 BC and AD 500 or in Europe after AD 1850 (Figure 4.11). At first a few settlements grow at phenomenal rates with little obstruction to their growth. But, as the settlement size distribution reaches its new potential probability form, population growth will create increasing numbers of small and medium-sized settlements. There may be a greater amount of growth in aggregate but it will be occurring in numerous smaller packages. Cost, wastage and inertia tend to increase because each of these development packages has its attendant commencement costs and administrative redundancy. The implications for 'economies of scale and scope' deserve attention. Such growth, because it requires more repetition of essential services and support, is relatively inefficient in economic terms.

The model also suggests that at the same time the largest compact cities will face cumulatively more extreme stress effects as they continue to grow into the high-stress zone closer to the proposed 10,000 sq km C-limit. At high densities our large cities will become cumulatively more costly to manage. Early industrial cities have been relatively inexpensive because the communication stress levels have not been high. Until the 1940s, when the growth of industrial cities was still confined to the lower third of their potential size range,[4] urban growth could occur at relatively low cost. Even so, the consumption of resources by such settlements was prodigious and has increased very substantially in the past forty years. As the biggest cities start to exceed 5,000–6,000 sq km at densities above the T-limit, the cost of sustaining their functions and growth should begin to increase exponentially as the level of behavioural stress within the settlements rapidly increases. The implication is that, while we are trying to reduce waste and consumption, attempts to mitigate the pressures of urban life in very large cities will exert ever greater demands on the preferred allocation and consumption of resources. If our resource supply becomes insufficient to sustain the material mechanisms and features which allow the cities to work, then presumably they will stagnate and perhaps even suffer a severe decline in their size.

The maturing of a settlement system appears to contain within it some inherent tendencies towards economic stagnation, increasing inertia in growth and escalating cost. The costs of sustaining growth and maintaining residential interaction patterns will increase markedly. In addition, the initial period of massive development has already led to a future in which communities are burdened with ever-increasing maintenance costs unless they drastically edit the older installations and constructions out of their cultural assemblage. If such problems of cumulative inefficiency and cost, however defined, are an integral part of major cultural change, then the debate about the rise and built-in collapse of cultural systems will become quite topical (Tainter 1988; Yoffee and Cowgill 1988). To manoeuvre our way through the problems of continued escalating costs, cumulative deterioration and loss of growth flexibility will demand precise strategies based on skilful prediction.

Future urban growth trajectories
Our settlements are currently filling up the lower third of the size range behind the provisional 10,000 sq km limit but we have no way of gauging when the largest settlements may reach that C-limit at high densities. For permanent, sedentary communities there have been only three previous transitions. Our particular moment in time therefore gives us access to a sample of only two inter-transition periods – an insufficient sample for predictive analysis. Though the two known periods between the transitions are very similar, that cannot be ascribed much significance. To pass from the 1–2 ha limit to the 100–200 ha limit in south-west Asia took about 3,000–5,000 years prior to the fourth millennium BC. Approximately the same amount of time elapsed between the earliest development of urban settlements over 100 ha in extent in Mesopotamia and the growth of settlements larger than 100 sq km in Europe during the nineteenth century AD. The time estimates cannot be more reliable because of the insecure definition of sedentism and the inevitable problem of defining exactly when the trends began. These durations offer no clue to the future until we devise an explanation for their similarity. Nor does the maximum rate of growth supply a guide, since a myriad local factors could stop it at any settlement size short of the C-limit, as it has done after the previous transitions. Among the biggest compact cities in the world at present are Tokyo, London, São Paulo, Mexico City and Buenos Aires, with areas at or moving towards 3,000–7,000 sq km. Most large urban settlements lie within the lower third of the size range behind the provisional 10,000 sq km C-limit and their

growth might therefore slow down in the near future as they run into cumulatively more communication stress. But we should note that the growth of individual settlements is precisely indeterminate. The time taken by the largest compact urban settlements to attain their current sizes is not a guide to the rate at which they are generally capable of attaining sizes of 10,000 sq km. For most, growth may slow down but those which happen to become large can still grow at the maximum possible rate.

However, several predictions can be made about future urban growth. The first is that the settlements which initially made the transit across the 100 sq km limit are unlikely to grow large enough to make another transition (Figure 9.4). The theoretical case is straightforward. To cross the 100 sq km C-limit, London and Paris were committed to very substantial investing in buildings and in mechanical systems such as railways. For the whole of the UK about 700–750 million bricks were used per annum in railway construction during the mid-1840s (Bagwell 1974: 118; Barker and Savage 1974: 79), approximately 33 per cent of the entire annual output of the brick industry. In London, Charing Cross station alone required 17 bridges, 190 brick arches, an iron viaduct and a hotel. Several neighbourhoods were demolished to make way for it (Konvitz 1985: 102). The initial industrial cities are now locked into a stock of old buildings and the constraints of the nineteenth-century transitional communication networks. Once across a C-limit, the entire prerequisite assemblage should no longer be needed. A community which still has the entire suite may then be burdened with a cumbersome and inflexible material

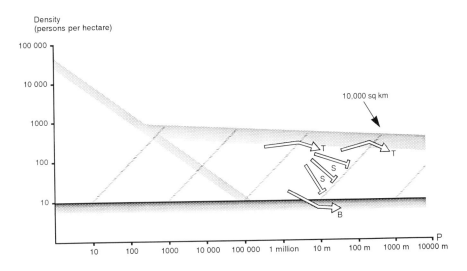

Figure 9.4 Settlement size trajectories and the proposed 10,000 sq km C-limit
T – transition trajectory
S – statis trajectories
B – bypass trajectory

carapace. The obsolete prerequisites could be removed but only at great cost. If they are not removed, their maintenance costs and massive obstructiveness can become a serious budgetary problem for municipal and central government. Unless a community disposes of the old framework, the inertia of that substantial material fabric will begin to act as a brake on further sustained growth. In the long term it could also exacerbate the interaction problems which result from the changing social patterns of daily life. No previous transition settlement has ever made a second transit across the next larger C-limit, and none of the initial urban settlements which substantially exceeded 100 ha endured for more than 500 to 1,000 years. Only Memphis, probably with an initial size near the 100 ha C-limit, persisted for longer. But it had a highly episodic occupation history and grew into an extensive, lower density settlement covering 20–25 sq km in the Ptolemaic period (Smith 1974).

Other predictions specify that our communities will eventually approach the next C-limit in several ways. These various trajectories offer predictions about future urban growth prospects. The future seems to lie not with the initial transit cases but with secondary developments towards high residential density, either in the region where the initial transit occurred or in adjacent regions to which some or all of the prerequisites were introduced. Another trajectory along which some contemporary cities are well advanced is towards low-density residence. The model allows that such settlements may attain areas in excess of 10,000 sq km, on a bypass trajectory, as the East Coast urban complex in North America has already done (Figure 9.5). But such settlements can never be the locus for the transformation to a sustained high-density settlement of equivalent size. They do not supply sufficient selective pressure to generate the use of the required new prerequisites. If we move towards a future of low-density, extensive urban residence (Doxiadis 1963: 376–80, 430–60), this will preclude further sustainable urban growth. We will be locked into a behavioural dead-end.

This analysis of the low-density settlements leads to a rather ominous outcome. They can only have a growth future if the required prerequisites are first elaborated elsewhere in high-density communities. Whether the low-density cases can persist in a static form is a moot question. No such case has ever transformed to a high-density equivalent or continued to grow at low density or produced a compact successor in the same location. Unfortunately, due to historical accident, we have not been able to observe an example of a very large (+ 100 sq km), literate, pre-industrial dispersed urban settlement adopting industrial communication technologies. None existed in the nineteenth century to be the recipients of such an experiment. Our understanding of the problems therefore depends on a comparative study of the equivalent archaeological cases and their circumstances. The ruins of Angkor, Tikal and Dzibilchaltun or Great Zimbabwe, Cahokia and Chaco Canyon may have more significance for the late twentieth century AD than we have supposed. Their duration and the degree to which they took up new classes of material features should be highly informative about the flexibility and endurance inherent in the behaviour of low-density settlements.

At the other extreme from the low-density cases are the potentially giant, high-density settlements which will halt behind the next C-limit to become stasis settlements covering 7,000 to 10,000 sq km – perhaps a future Tokyo covering the entire Kanto plain (Figure 9.6) and a Mexico City spilling out of the Basin of Mexico, reducing Teotihuacan, the great city of the first millennium AD, to the proportionate scale of a municipal park. If Sydney moves away from a quite low overall density and continues its rapid growth, it will merge with Wollongong and Newcastle to form a settlement extending for more than 200 km along the east coast of Australia. Once major cities reach that size and cease to grow in either population or area, they also will be unable to develop the prerequisites for the 10,000 sq km transition themselves. Pressures towards minimising variability and regulating communication rather than promoting communication changes will preclude that

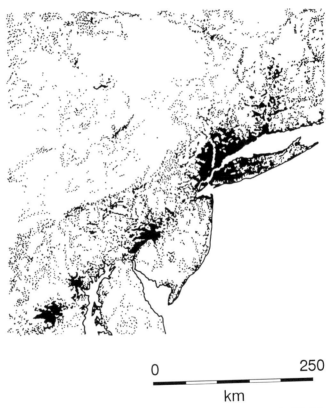

0   250

km

Figure 9.5 Greater New York and the East Coast urban complex, USA, 1960s AD (after Doxiadis 1968)
Note: New York developed from the town of New Amsterdam at the tip of Manhattan island and now extends across parts of New York State, New Jersey and Connecticut. It also can be seen as the core of the East Coast urban complex – the megalopolis of Gottman's definition (1961). The illustration was prepared for a paper presented at the PostModern Cities Conference, Department of Urban and Regional Planning, University of Sydney, NSW, Australia in April 1993. Because of the difficulty of precisely defining the extent of the urban area, several different estimates and associated community sizes now describe the urban complex. The overall density in the 22 counties of the Intermediate Ring (New York Regional Plan 1967) has levelled off at about 10 p/ha since the 1970s. The overall density in the 31 counties of the Outer Ring is below 10 p/ha in the 1990s and began to level off in the 1970s.

Table 9.1 Maximum rates of growth for compact settlements after C-limit transitions

Maximum Rates of Growth for Compact Settlements after C-limit transitions	
C - limit	**Max. Growth Rate after Transition**
1-2 ha	0.5 ha per century
100 ha	5 sq km per century
100 sq km	5000 sq km per century
10000 sq km (?)	5 million sq km per century (?)
1 million sq km (??)	(??)
Magnitude of C-limits increases by a multiple of 100.	Max. rate of growth increases by a multiple of 1000.

possibility. Their future persistence must depend on a stable economic and political milieu. Further growth will require outside influence and innovations from elsewhere, of the kind which enabled Edo to begin its growth into contemporary Tokyo in the nineteenth and twentieth centuries AD, using imported European communications technologies (Seidensticker 1983). The economic consequences of a process whereby the largest compact settlements in the world stabilise into a state of no-growth warrant attention. The history of the Chinese imperial capitals (Rozman 1973; Skinner 1977; Steinhardt 1990) may provide some insight into the process. Most importantly, however, no amount of economic change on its own will aid growth beyond a C-limit. A combination of new material behaviour and major economic transformation is required.

If there is a C-limit at 10,000 sq km, then the compact communities which come to lie just behind it, or initially make the transition across it, will contain 100–200 million people (Figure 9.4). If these settlements grow at a rate proportionate to previous growth rates (Table 9.1) (Figure 4.11), they will expand at a maximum rate of 5 million sq km per century, which would see much of New South Wales (Australia), or all of the UK, covered with buildings within twenty years. Doubts that this could happen will echo the belief of European scholars prior to the

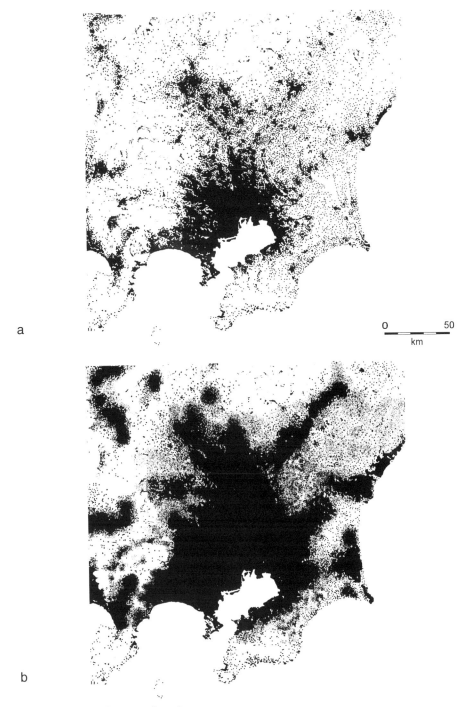

a

0 — 50
km

b

Figure 9.6 Tokyo, Japan – a future?
(a) Tokyo, Japan, 1980s (after *National Atlas of Japan* 1990)
(b) Tokyo, Japan – a future?
Representation (b) does not, of course, purport to read the exact future of Tokyo. There is a current
proposal, for instance, to fill in Tokyo Bay with a large artificial island for residence. I have not
included this on my diagram since its inclusion would allow latitude for adding further speculative
engineering! The hypothetical is derived primarily from assuming expansion across comparatively level
ground and along corridors of growth to other settlements. An alternative scenario to this compact
future, is that Tokyo will become part of a low-density megalopolis extending as far as Osaka to the
south. We must also note that Tokyo might never attain the indicated size (in b) due to local factors
such as military action or socio-economic collapse.

nineteenth century AD that the largest cities of Europe, such as London, were reaching the limits of their maximum operable size (Clark 1958; Petty 1888: 113; Say 1880: 385–6) and could not possibly grow further except to the severe detriment of their inhabitants. The predicted growth rates will require new material pre-requisites, new sources of energy and the development of new construction technologies. We may already be developing both the prerequisites and the technologies for other purposes, without envisaging or imagining their potential. What we need to consider is whether we want growth rates of this magnitude or would prefer to lock ourselves into great static cities, the future equivalents of T'ang Ch'ang-an and Tokugawa Edo. A transition across a C-limit is unpleasant, as is apparent in the health of the people who inhabited the initial permanent sedentary communities and the early agrarian-based urban settlements (Cohen 1989). The social stresses of the early industrial metropolis (Mayhew 1858; see Canning 1986), our images of London during the eighteenth century AD (Rudé 1971), and our knowledge of its mortality rates (Landers 1987) and living conditions (Gauldie 1974) also tell us that. We might not want the prospect of future generations living through an equivalent experience on an even vaster scale. But are rigidly controlled, economically unstable, stasis settlements a preferable future for humanity?

Conclusions
The combination of the proposed model of interaction and communication stress with a material behaviour approach assists cross-comparability, manages large amounts of data and directs attention to potentially interesting anomalies and research issues. The material component of human behaviour apparently plays a substantial and essential role in the large-scale transformation of human community life. The material becomes recognisable as an actor without intent, whose operations are played out on a vast scale beyond the limited perceptions of daily life. The approach has a role in culture history because it can predict the characteristics of settlements and cultural trends which have no direct contemporary analogue. Conversely, it also facilitates intercomparability. We can make use of the available data to point out significant equivalence between settlement growth patterns in different regions, despite differences of temporal scale and settlement size.

The analysis of interaction and communication stress affects the way we understand the present and the future of our own settlement systems. The past allows us to put the present in perspective and to offer predictions for the future. The archaeological record of the past is an essential context because no other cultural milieu provides the time perspective and the range of comparative cases necessary for the recognition of the immense, slow consequences of community behaviour. The past provides a context in which theories of large-scale cultural change can be assessed. If the model of interaction and communication is tenable, it has some relevance for our understanding of the present and the future. For the parametric model to be of more specific predictive value we need to find out how to quantify interaction and communication stress, cross-culturally. We also need to identify how the degree of stress relates to the material and active practices which human communities use to try and control interaction. The operational uniformitarian basis of the interaction and communication model requires that ideas derived from it cannot be safely treated as topics of entertaining curiosity. They bind together the past and present, demand our responsibility and care, and oblige us to pay attention to the social impact of our knowledge.

1 *ARCHAEOLOGY, SETTLEMENT GROWTH AND THE MATERIAL COMPONENT OF HUMAN BEHAVIOUR*

1 Gould and Vrba (1982) have argued that the label 'pre-adaptation' is liable to produce a mis-statement of neo-Darwinian theory. Their summary of what is involved and the argument for the term 'exaptation' are preferable to the old label but regrettably are almost unknown in archaeology. For my occasional references to the issue I have retained the more familiar label even though I prefer the Gould and Vrba terminology.

2 Gould (1965) defines two kinds of uniformitarianism – the methodological and the substantive. He reiterated this classification in 1987 in a review of the logical flaws inherent in Lyell's original case for a uniformitarian approach. The concept of uniformitarianism may be a general propensity of human thought (Hookyas 1963; Ricketts 1988) but it has been plagued both by theoretical errors and by common-sense fallacies (Rymer 1978; Shea 1982). Though there are several different ways in which uniformitarianism can be envisaged, as is apparent in Gould's assessment (1987: 117–26) and in the elaborate paper by Simpson (1970), the dichotomy will suffice for an initial approach to the topic. Methodological uniformitarianism derives from the basic premiss that order and consistency exist in the universe. Substantive uniformitarianism by contrast refers to the extrapolation of some specific aspect of the present into the past. Gould emphasises that such extrapolations, whether of constant rates of process, or the co-occurrence of phenomena, are not in themselves logically valid. What is required is an explanation or specification for why a process, or an operation which subsumes those phenomena, must be constant over space and time – not just a declaration that it is. Methodological uniformitarian principles define the logical form of operational uniformitarian, high-level theories. What is critical is that specifics or associations observed in the present need not have remained constant even if the process or operation which subsumes them has remained the same. The two proposed taxa each lead to varied interpretations, as is apparent in the views of Bailey (1983) and R. A. Gould (Gould and Watson 1982).

My concern is the logical structure of the high-level theories which are actually used in the biological and the hard sciences – not because studies of human behaviour ought to be based on the same theories but because we might use the same kind of logical structure to make sense of the human past. It is not my aim to create a proxy scientific air for studies of culture but instead to apply a consistent logic which allows us to make sense of the past without imposing a logically invalid, substantive equivalence to the present. What cannot be done validly is to treat substantive cases as a basis for a uniformitarian claim and then extrapolate from particulars of the present to particulars of the past. The exercise of human imagination is needed to devise appropriate, particular, operational uniformitarian propositions about the processes and conditions of being human which will help us to understand the terms within which human communities can sustain themselves.

An understanding of the behavioural parameters which are applicable over long spans of time requires a methodological uniformitarian frame of reference which defines what constitutes constancy, specifies the sense in which a process or constraint can be considered constant over time and space, and may also help us to understand why that is so. If the analysis of past residential behaviour is to be consistently linked to the present and to the future, uniformitarianism has to be rigorously defined. As Gould has pointed out (1965), the vague claim 'that the present is the key to the past' is logically insufficient, since it allows the use of unwarranted substantive associations between the details of the present and the past.

From an operational uniformitarian statement about a constant condition or process, such as natural selection, we can specify varied and differing substantive effects over time, encompassing the appearance of differing specific products or effects at different times and in different places. The process or condition defines the parameters within which particular phenomena can persist. But it does not predefine their particular form. Nor does it specify that all particular products of the process will be adequate or successful, or appear in appropriate contexts and associations. What is required in the explanation of human behaviour is an operational uniformitarian proposition which conforms to the logical structure of methodological uniformitarianism and avoids the fallacy of substantivism.

Statements about an operational proposition are conspicuously open to refutation. Their power resides in the degree to which they have not been contradicted by observational statements despite the odds against them (Hendy and Penny 1986; Simpson 1970: 64). For instance, the claim for natural selection as a universal process holds good because, without it, the universe would look exceptionally weird. Without biological selection there could be no constraint on the growth of biomass. At the most extreme, as Stewart points out (1989: 267), unconstrained exponential breeding by rabbits (i.e. in the absence of any selective mechanism) would fill the universe in 114 generations! If extraterrestrial life exists, as seems likely, then natural selection also applies to it, otherwise the universe would be full of something resembling processed meat. The irony is that we have difficulty envisaging the very strange but potential realities in which uniformitarian operational propositions might, in principle, be inapplicable. We either tend to regard operational uniformitarian propositions as self-evidently true, even though they are not, or else we mistakenly incline to presume them untestable (Rymer 1978: 248–9). Either way we are at risk of deceiving ourselves. We can ill afford this when using high-level theories which have potentially serious implications for our understanding of contemporary issues.

2 THE MATERIAL AS BEHAVIOUR

1 Termite nests are a frequent problem in archaeological sites in West Africa. The remains of the nests are often quite hard and substantial. They can severely disrupt site stratigraphies. From observing their bulk I suspect that an archaeology of the evolution of termite nests would be possible.

2 The members of different societies show significant differences in their response to visual illusions, as is illustrated by responses to the Müller-Lyer and Horizontal–Vertical tests (Worrall and Firth 1974). The difficulty with analyses of this kind is that the categories of shape used may affect the conclusions. Jahoda (1966), for instance, found that the relationship of the Müller-Lyer illusion with shape was not simple. People in both round and rectangular buildings could recognise the illusion which depends upon a juxtaposition between a vertical corner and the wall lines which diverge from it. However, Gregory's discussion of the illusion (1966: 161) concerned the absence of this effect

among people who live in curvilinear structures, not merely those with round floor-plans. The implication is that the response to the illusion will be highly particular to specific spatial associations, which is precisely what would be necessary for material space to act as a behavioural training referent.

3 I studied the Vagala village reported here, during several periods of fieldwork between 1970 and 1972, both as a pilot project and while I was working at the University of Ghana, Legon. I observed the eating groups on several occasions. Some of my colleagues, among them Professor Jack Goody, were surprised at my report because they had concluded that the Vagala eating groups had become a notional social convention and did not actually meet. That was not my experience, having eaten with them on more than one occasion.

4 Note that consistency is a feature of location on the ground not of social relations. Casimir (1979) could find no consistent relationship between social status and the spacing between nests. The distances between the nests of gorillas of equivalent social rank produced random-frequency occurrence distributions. Specific social relationships cannot be considered the direct cause of the spatial patterning.

5 At this stage of the analysis I confine the discussion to permanently sedentary agriculturalists because we cannot assume that particular kinds of spatial order are universal. Different spatial message forms may occur in different sizes of settlement and these differences may play a role in the ways space, time and interaction are managed in communities with different degrees of mobility.

6 I studied Munyimba in 1971–2 when I was a member of staff in the Department of Archaeology, University of Ghana. Details of the field procedure are in Fletcher 1976 (unpublished Ph.D., Department of Archaeology and Anthropology, University of Cambridge).

7 The development of the buildings and the measurement of features at the Top site were carried out during fieldwork at Deir el Medina in 1974. The sequence of building additions was identified from wall abutments and route analysis. See Fletcher 1976.

8 Actual spatial messages can be expected to be more complex than the simple hypothetical model, as is indicated by the methodology, results and logical issues discussed in Fletcher 1977, 1981b and 1984. Even this crude level of analysis suggested that there are disjunctions within the spatial format of a settlement. Analysis must therefore proceed from a simple model to identify the gross consequences of spatial patterning which will be readily and clearly observable. We may then have good reason to expend effort on sophisticated methods of periodicity analysis to identify complex formal logic structures in settlement space.

Recognising spatial patterns depends upon the class interval which we use. Differing degrees of bunching in signals will be apparent at different grades of observational detail (Fletcher 1984). In addition, human perceptual accuracy decreases with increased distance (see p. 149) and a calibrated change in class interval may be necessary to observe comparable degrees of similarity for small and large distances. What this suggests is that the serial signature of a settlement will more properly be described by a diagram resembling an orchestral score of interlinked equations rather than by a single simple equation. The old methodology which I used in Fletcher 1977, 1981b and 1985a to identify whether or not a serial pattern can be recognised was very cumbersome and required prior choices by the researcher about the categories of distance to be recognised. This procedure generates polymodal distributions which another classification might divide by prior categorisation. The crude distribution splitting procedure then allocates more significance to individual distance values than is desirable in a robust methodology. A procedure will also be needed which can solve the problem of dealing with the inherently small samples which define spatial patterning in many small-scale settlements. A statistical method for handling the role of small total populations of values is required which does not regard the existing features as a sample of some hypothetical population. A form of message analysis will be needed which treats the available signals as the total representation of the message available to the communicators. Without this facility much of the patterning of spatial message analyses will simply fall below sample recognition levels of standard statistical procedure.

9 Sample from Ghanaian settlements between 1970 and 1972 (see Fletcher 1976 and 1977 for details of settlements). The central tendency and variation values are derived from unimodal distributions only.

10 There are numerous sources of variation. Change will take place in a material message because human replication of material entities is neither perfect nor constant. Individuals can always produce anomalous material signals which will endure in the perceptual field of the community simply because social authority does not continually extend to preventing such an occurrence. Because variation, however slight, is introduced by copying, there is always a process going on which generates change. Alterations in the degree to which members of the community want to increase or reduce their domestic interaction frequencies will also lead to intentional or tacit preferences for more or less screening than is usual in the community. Walls might be made thicker or thinner or positioned differently relative to each other. Some change may follow from external pressures such as scarcity. Consequent reuse of materials will generate slightly different material signals. For instance, some builders may have to be more parsimonious about the structure they wish to build than they would prefer. Whatever the cause, the builders' offspring will regard the space and its interaction effects as a habitual feature of daily life and should tend to replicate the form they learned in their childhood.

3 A HIERARCHY OF SOCIAL EXPLANATION: LOCATING THE MATERIAL

1 The hierarchy does not allow deterministic control on the internal workings of the genetic system, either by the substantive particulars of the larger scale milieu of the external environment or by energy input–output parameters of a viable ecological system. The genetic output is indeterminate relative to external circumstances. A variety of products can result from a given genetic code. What external circumstances do is to produce an outcome by selecting against some of that variation, whether arbitrarily, because one particular variant collides with a lethal environmental feature, or more generally because a variant fails to sustain the necessary balance between its energy needs and its energy expenditure. External circumstances do not predetermine what can be produced, only the long-term enduring product of the smaller scale level of operations.

2 Refutation does not hold between levels of a hierarchy because the explanations relevant to each level are about different classes of operation and concern the effects of different parameters. Economic data cannot therefore logically provide a refutation for a claim about processes within the scale of individual behaviour. What does apply between levels is the demonstration that an argument from one level has been overextended into a fallacious deterministic or reductionist proposition. Propositions which do this just produce futile contrived conflict which does little to further enquiry. The disputes consist primarily of holding intractably to inclusive claims which reject the prior validity of other explanatory devices at different levels of analysis.

3 To define an explanatory level concerned with the parameters of resource supply requires the deconstruction of the synchronous term 'economic' by detaching the scale of human action from the means of production and also disengaging the environmental parameters which constrain the viability of production. A sense of the term 'economy' is required

which more nearly resembles the restricted meaning prevalent in archaeology as the supply of food, materials and energy.

4 A material message cannot be a reflection of 'ideal' concepts or a normative set in the minds of its makers. Though the human beings who make the material entities may carry a transient electrochemical version of the message in their brains, and some equivalence should exist between the two versions of the message, that is not what we are looking at nor is it what we need to study when we are analysing material behaviour.

5 Presumably the same will apply to the material messages, whatever they are, which carry signals about time patterning.

6 My analysis of Mug House was carried out in 1981 with a follow-up study in 1982. The purpose of the survey was to study the development sequence in more detail than was available in the published report and to measure the sizes of features in the settlement in order to identify the serial pattern of its spatial message.

4 THE BEHAVIOURAL PARAMETERS OF INTERACTION AND COMMUNICATION

1 Even a census figure in an industrialised state is only a statement about the overnight resident population on a given day. The better historical reports are extrapolations from numbers of households multiplied by some constant for the average size of a household. But many reports are comparative estimates by observers judging the number of people in a place from their knowledge of other settlements. There are also inherent problems in defining the edge of a settlement (Best and Rodgers 1973; Gould and Yellen 1987; Grytzell 1963; Linge 1965). Either we accept rough approximations or we are committed to cumbersome conventions for the sake of consistency. Linge's rules for defining the edge of Australian urban settlements covered 26 foolscap pages (Carter 1972). Gould and Yellen's elaborate routine for consistently describing the area of hunter-gatherer camps (1987: 82) would not coincide with the edge of the cleared space around a forest camp.

2 A wide range of density descriptions is possible for any settlement (see Figure 4.2 in Fletcher 1981a). None is definitive, though each may be appropriate to different research purposes. For instance, in his analysis of residential space and kin relationships, Whitelaw (1989) uses a more delimiting area definition than mine, predicated on the position of the residential structures. Such a definition will produce higher densities, as will a definition which confines the estimate of area and community size to the denser, more clearly defined central portions of a large settlement. The proposed limit is not therefore the only possible description of a density limit. We should find different, but successively higher, density limits for increasingly narrow definitions of the relevant sample area. For instance, built area will yield higher estimates than total occupation settlement space, which includes built area and adjacent, open occupation space. Roofed living space alone will produce a limit even higher than the area of built space. A major future topic of research will be concerned with the relationship between changes in core densities as community size increases and changes in overall density for the maximal areal extent of the settlements. We cannot assume that one description of density will suffice as the sole referent. For instance, densities in the built area may remain almost constant as community size increases but the density for the maximum area may drop markedly as proportionately more open ground is incorporated into the peripheral occupation space. The behavioural implications are of some significance because the two trends may indicate that interaction stress is being alleviated by adding more activity space adjacent to a settlement as its community size increases, not by distributing the additional space per person evenly across the settlement.

Throughout this study, settlement area estimates refer to approximations of an overall settlement area which includes occupation space and built space and immediately adjacent utilised land, e.g. for dumps, and the density figures relate to the overall population resident in that area (Fletcher 1981a, 1986) – except when other kinds of density and area definitions are specifically referred to.

3 The term 'permanent sedentism' is applied to those communities which conform to our familiar conception of sedentism, as in European or North American villages and urban settlements (Kent 1989: 2).

The relationship between Community size (population) and Density (population/area) is not a statistical artefact of self-correlation (see Pearson 1897 and Atchley *et al.* 1976, for a discussion of this issue). The identified trend towards an inverse correlation, in which X increases as maximum values for X/Y decline, is the reverse of the correlation found in random number associations where X increases as X/Y increases.

Furthermore, divergent trends in maximum density as community size increases are found in permanently sedentary and 'mobile' communities (see Figures 4.5, 4.7 and 7.8). I am grateful to Professor R. V. S. Wright (Department of Anthropology, University of Sydney) for the statistical procedure used to check this.

4 Comprehensive sources have been used to check on the position of the 'sedentary' I-limit in order to minimise the possibility of selective bias by the data collectors. The pueblo data come from a review of the pueblos of the Southwest based on aerial survey. The Indian data come from the 1961 census of towns and cities.

5 Record of settlements on file in Settlement Data Register, Department of Prehistoric and Historical Archaeology, University of Sydney.

6 The examples are a grab sample of cases from different continents. The data were collected primarily in the Fisher Library at the University of Sydney, and in the University Library and the Haddon Library in Cambridge. Tod Whitelaw kindly provided the data on some of the pygmy camps and directed my attention to the large Bushman camps. Dick Gould generously provided examples from central Australia.

Data: Africa (twentieth century AD) – Elmolo, Hadza, Kalahari Bushman (!Kung and Gwi San), Pygmies (Efe and Mbuti, and camps of Patinepunga and Djembe I). Ainu (Japan nineteenth century AD) – Nitmap. Asia (twentieth century AD) – Birhor, Bersiak, Mrabi. Australia (twentieth century AD) – Tikatika, Pulykara, Mulyangiri Well, Wanampi Well, Konapandi, Bendaijerun Ridge and Bendaijerun Flat, Ngarulurutja, Partjar, Mangabal, Matata-miripa, Gurlanda A, B and C, Aulaterra and Angungera (see Fletcher 1990 for discussion). Californian Indians (Chumash) (seventeenth century AD) – Kasil, Mishopshnow, Shuku (Rincon), Dos Pueblos, Miquiqui, Guyamu, Carpintaria, Tajigus Creek, Mescalitan, La Quemada. Californian Indians (late nineteenth century to earlier twentieth century AD) – Tolowot (Site 67), Rekwoi, Woxtek, Pekwan, Meta, Arcata, Tsurai. Canadian Indians (twentieth century AD) – Donnelly River, Ole Jacobsen camp, Kurt George's camp, Norbert Bell camp 1, Martin Burstad camp, Cree River, Durocher-McCallum, Cree Lake 17, Lake Indicator, Stony Narrow, Red Sucker River, Sandy Lake I, Patuanak, Chalkyitsik, Teslin, Round Lake. Ethiopian wandering capitals – medieval 'ketema', Addis Ababa 1890s. Inuit (nineteenth and twentieth century AD) – Old Fish camp, Gambell, Tikchik, Tigara, Wales, Hotham Inlet, Anvik, Old Bonasila, Chogiung, Grant's village, Hopedale village, Kananakpok, Nunachuak, Nunamiut, Old Stuyahok, Utkiavwin, Vuktuli. North American Plains Indians (nineteenth century AD) – Osage, Cheyenne, Little Bighorn 1876. Northwest Coast Indians (late seventeenth century to early twentieth century AD) – Cheslakee, Gilford, Carcross, Actis, Hagwilgate, Angoon, Daxatkanada, Echatchet, Yuquot, Kasaan, Neltushkin, Ninstins, Qalahaituk, Sitka, Skedans, Uttewas, Yakutat, Cumshewa, Tanu, Skidegate.

Records filed under settlement name or society as indicated. Files held in the

Settlement Data Register, Prehistoric and Historical Archaeology, School of Archaeology, Classics and Ancient History, University of Sydney. Some of the examples used on this diagram are on Figure 4.1 in Fletcher 1981a. The Tasaday data have been deleted because they cannot now be regarded as a secure instance of a mobile community. The Mrabi figures have been recalculated as a total for the entire occupation area instead of for each part of the settlement. The density figures for the Mbuti have to be derived from estimated scales. I discussed this problem with Tod Whitelaw and very much appreciated his advice on an appropriate scaling convention.

Presentation: To control for the problem of consistent area definition in the overall sample I have adopted the policy of including settlements whose limits are recognised according to differing criteria. These are: verbal reports which merely state an area; approximate areas as mentioned above; careful specification of Absolute Limit of Scatter (ALS); and cases where the boundary of the settlement is clearly defined by natural features such as shorelines, steep slopes, and the edges of cleared ground and areas derived from archaeological reports of the extent of occupation debris. We cannot presume that any one class of limit is definitive. But if all the varied specifications of settlement area produce a consistent aggregate pattern, that pattern cannot be an artefact of any specific areal definition. A major task of settlement analysis will be the designation of standard criteria for identifying the limits of settlements and archaeological sites (Fletcher 1986).

Some of the settlements are represented by several estimates, e.g. the encampment on the Little Bighorn in AD 1876, to allow for differences of opinion about community size and to include maximum and minimum estimates of the total area of the settlement.

The diagram is not restricted to hunter-gatherer communities but includes groups with seasonal patterns of aggregation. It also includes groups, such as the Alyawara at Bendaijerum Ridge in Australia (O'Connell 1977, 1987), which periodically relocate their residence units within one extensive settlement area. The Birhor and Addis Ababa in the 1890s are included as examples of longer-term transient residence. The degree to which even transient communities of this kind conform to the 'mobile' upper density limit will be an important clue to the inflexibility of that proposed I-limit.

Comment: The additional sample suggests that the gradient for the limit on 'mobile' communities is more gradual than I had envisaged on the basis of the 1981a estimate (Figure 4.7).

7 One implication of this analysis is that other animals should also have distinct I-limits. Whether these would be distinct at the species level or for some higher order of biological taxon requires empirical research, e.g. comparing the densities in gorilla camps with the modern 'mobile' I-limit for humans.

8 In this figure the I-limit is as presented in Figure 4.2. The angled alignment of the communication limits is due to constant area values being the diagonals of a graph with community size (P) on one axis and density (D, i.e. P/ha) on the other. Communities of very different sizes can occupy settlements of the same areal extent. Communities with high or low levels of interaction can therefore be found on settlement areas of identical sizes.

9 Presenting these settlements at standard scales poses some problems. In some cases we cannot entirely rely on the reported scales. For example, the Baghdad plan is derived from Le Strange but, as Lassner points out (1970: 282), he overestimated the conversion for the size of the Islamic units to imperial units of scale. The city should appear a bit smaller than it does in Figure 4.10 but it will suffice as an indication of size in the absence of a precise plan of the Abbasid city that includes its suburbs. The perimeters of Delhi and Vijayanagar are hard to estimate. In Delhi urban settlements developed for short periods of time at various points in the region between AD 1050 and the nineteenth century

creating a complex distribution of urban remnants. In Vijayanagar the nature of the suburbs on the plain to the south-west of the walled settlement is as yet unclear.

10 The broad estimate for the smallest of the currently identified X-limits is a function of two problems. First there is more uncertainty in the identification of the size of the relatively tenuous sites which lie behind that C-limit. Secondly, I have not as yet had the opportunity to study a large enough number of regional sequences to identify securely where in the range up to 1-2 ha the maximum site sizes usually occur.

11 The C-limits are not an artefact of data presentation. They were first recognised in a diagram of imperial units where the limits are approximately 250 acres (100 ha) and 30–40 sq miles (100 sq km). Nor do they coincide with every multiple of 10 and therefore cannot be an artefact of rounded metric figures. However, I doubt that the C-limits actually do coincide with the 100 multiples. The indications for the better known C-limits lie between 70 and about 150 ha, and between 70 and 100 sq km. There may therefore be a drift away from the round 100 multiple concealed within the range of the current estimates.

12 In principle, any surface-dwelling, intelligent species which lives in communities and forms residential groups ought to display a pattern of I- and C-limits, with attendant implications for the trajectories of settlement growth, the role of the material and the large-scale pattern of sustained cultural change.

5 SETTLEMENT GROWTH TRAJECTORIES

1 Such distributions are also found in the large-scale structure of biological populations, e.g. the frequency of occurrence of species per genus or the incidence of body size in a regional ecology (Williams 1964; van Valen 1973; Bonner 1965; Calder 1984; Cousins 1985), and are related to the dynamics of evolutionary selection. The biological size distributions can be understood in terms of the energy available to sustain animals higher in the food chain, explaining *Why Big, Fierce Animals Are Rare* (Colinvaux 1980: 15–27).

2 The use of site and settlement size distributions is a different way of expressing the pattern which geographers have studied using the rank-size rule. The rank-size rule and preparation of a rank-size diagram from settlement size or community size data are succinctly summarised in Johnson (1981: 146), and by Smith (1982). The difference between the size distribution curve and the rank-size plot is that the shape of the rank-size gradient is used to make comparisons between different regions independent of the size of the settlements, while the critical feature of the size distribution is the comparison of the absolute magnitude of the settlements. The distribution curves plot comparative absolute size and the rank-size plots represent relative magnitude. In a rank-size plot the primary settlements of two regions appear equivalent but may be of very different absolute size.

3 At this gross level of generality I have considered the distributions of site size as an envelope for the description of the settlement size distribution which produced the sites (Fletcher 1986). The relationship between settlements and sites, and the role of sites in archaeology, are contentious topics, as for instance Dunnell cf. Binford in Rossignol and Wandsnider 1992. The specific issue for this study, well illustrated by a careful review of the alternative models of the extent of Selevac (Tringham and Krstić 1990: 584–8), is the degree of contemporaneity within the total areal extent of a single stratigraphic phase (see p. 239). In addition, the definition of settlement area needs to include dumps and reused abandoned residential areas (see n. 9 below). What is now required, especially for the sites produced by mobile communities, is a large-scale, cross-regional assessment of the way

in which the original site size distribution, the selective effects of observer preference and the impact of taphonomic factors interact to product the reported site size distributions.

Taphonomic effects may perhaps place the proposed 1–2 ha C-limit close to a horizon of invisibility caused by the massive impact of successive depositional and erosive events. For the Palaeolithic the additional factor of geomorphic redeposition becomes particularly significant. Prior to the Upper Palaeolithic there is a very obvious tendency for sites to be larger the further back we go in time. Hassan identified this taphonomic effect in Egypt (1979: 444–5). It severely complicates the study of the settlements created by earlier hominids.

4 These cases exclude the low-density and dispersed settlements of the fifth to the first millennium BC. In the Late La Tène, during the last few centuries of the first millennium BC, when the oppida began to develop, there was an immense increase in site size. However, most of the very large sites in excess of 100–200 ha had low occupation densities with small areas of occupation and extensive areas of open land enclosed by bank and ditch boundaries. These sites have to be considered within the category of bypass settlement discussed below (this chapter). The case of the oppida is discussed in detail on p. 203.

5 The problem with the identification of the C-limits is that the likely frequency of occurrence of examples has dropped almost to zero well before the putative C-limit value. By extrapolation an odd very rare case might grow to a size far beyond a predicted C-limit. But the likelihood would be extremely low and such a hypothetical instance should be almost solitary and quite spectacular. That such a case is unlikely is, however, suggested by the model of the stress gradient, which specifies that the stress level will be rising very steeply near the C-limit. Viewed in those terms, an instance beyond the C-limit value indicated by several regional distributions is improbable.

6 The operational uniformitarian basis of the model does not exclude the possibility of aberrant distributions, e.g. with more medium-sized settlements. But it does specify that such a distribution should involve stressful consequences – presumably involving drastic distortions of group behaviour and regional energy consumption. Such a situation ought to be highly visible in the growth trajectories and energy usage of the communities, in their behaviour and in the limited duration of the settlements.

7 These figures are prepared by taking a range of community sizes, e.g. from 10 million down to 300,000 for Japan, and plotting the frequency of occurrence of residential densities for those communities. This produces a transect across the range of densities, with the highest densities closest to the proposed I-limit. Sources detailed in Fletcher 1981a.

8 Issues:

Memphis – the size of the Old Kingdom capital is problematic as it does not appear to be located where it was expected under the ruin field of Mit Rahina (see pp. 190–1).

Cheng-chou is represented by its walled area. There is an extensive region of small settlements around Cheng-chou forming a settlement complex but the walled settlement does not appear to have extensive continuous suburbs (Chang 1980: 272–3; Fletcher 1986: 76).

Mohenjo-daro – there are indications that it may have covered a larger area extending down to the river as noted by Jansen (1989) and see also Harappā (p. 191).

Moche itself might not have much exceeded 100–200 ha (1–2 sq km) (p. 194). It was abandoned in the late sixth century AD due to flood erosion and dune movement (Moseley and Richardson 1992; Shimada *et al.* 1991: 251), and was succeeded by Pampa Grande and Galindo, which continued the transition trajectory to sizes over 3 sq km (Bawden 1982; Shimada 1978).

9 The problem of palimpsests is discussed in Chapter 7 in the context of extensive, seasonally occupied sites (see Figure 7.2). With apparently sedentary sites we must beware assuming that the extent of a settlement is defined by the area covered by the diagnostic pottery or implements of a given period. The use of adjacent derelict occupation areas for functions which do not have a distinct period marker has to be envisaged (Fletcher 1986: 73–4). The extent of a settlement will also be marked by non-diagnostic pottery, especially plain wares, which can form a significant proportion of the cultural assemblage at any one time.

   The proposed C-limit at 100 ha would allow Tringham and Krstić's Model 2 of an extensive occupation in Selevac (i.e. about 50 ha) over much of the site in Stratigraphic-Architectural phases III–IV (1990: 586), though they prefer a minimalist size estimate and hypothesise that the whole area was not simultaneously occupied (1990: 584–5). As they note, however, the limited extent of the excavations prevents a decisive conclusion.

10 The issue of contemporaneity in archaeological sites requires far more attention (see Wandsnider 1992: 257–82). The difficulties involved in studying contemporaneity are illustrated by a careful study of the issue and problems associated with the radiocarbon dates for buildings of the Grossbakken sites (Varanger) in northern Scandinavia (Helskog and Sweder 1989). There appear to be unresolved ambiguities inherent in our notions of contemporaneity which lead to alternative but internally inconsistent interpretations of sequence, numbers of contemporaneous households and the use-life of the buildings within a settlement.

6 SETTLEMENT GROWTH TRANSITIONS AND THE ROLE OF THE MATERIAL

1 The growth of London and Paris in the nineteenth century shows clearly the scattered periphery of small settlements adjacent to the urban area. See Figure 4.10 for sources on pre-industrial capitals.

2 Though the development of sedentary communities is a fundamental issue of archaeological enquiry, it cannot at the present time be used as a critical case study of a C-limit transition because even the definition and use of the term 'sedentary' is in flux, and the identification of such communities is highly uncertain (Edwards 1989; Hitchcock 1982; Rafferty 1985). Detailed data on the settlement forms associated with the purported shifts to sedentism are also relatively difficult to obtain at present, except in a few regions such as south-west Asia and Peru. As yet the material behaviour requirements of sustained sedentism are neither obvious nor readily observable, though we can envisage without difficulty that features such as durable walling, which block sound transmission, might be of some consequence in controlling the effects of interaction, whatever the initial reasons for building in such materials. Claims about the development of sedentism cannot therefore be used, at the present time, to clarify the prerequisites argument. Instead the stress model and a behavioural analysis should be applied to the debate about sedentism to see whether they have led to unexpected implications which we might assess in the archaeological record (see p. 179).

   If a suite of features, some of them expected and familiar but unexpected as behavioural operators, can be recognised, then a comparison of the 100 ha and the 100 sq km cases may later be useful for predicting at least part of the assemblage which should be associated with the 1–2 ha C-limit and whatever connection it had with the issue of the initial development of sedentism.

3 If there is some equivalence between the patterning of space and the patterning of time, we should expect there to be a material corollary of the known active patterning of

time. There should be a linkage because space can be described in terms of time based on constant speeds per unit distance. As yet, however, we do not know how we might describe the tacit time messages carried by material behaviour in the same way as spatial messages are carried by buildings. In general, the ordering of time requires far more attention. Social anthropologists have offered a valuable start in the study of ceremonies and dance as time markers (Leach 1976; Levine 1960). What is now needed is for a new generation of archaeologists interested in contemporary communities to study the periodics of time budgeting in human communities, as Carlstein (1982), Watanabe (1977) and Neville White (1985) have begun to do, and to study the material patterning of time.

4 An issue which remains open to debate is whether the arrangement of routes within residence units can also be said to order time. The scale of the effect may be too small to be of behavioural consequence in large urban communities. In due course, however, we might pursue the study of storage and garbage dump locations as markers of time patterning. Storage within each residence unit and bulk storage on the periphery of a settlement will have different time-scheduling consequences for domestic activity. Dispersed garbage scattered around the residence units and a single major dump at the edge of the settlement affect the time patterning of the journeys required to dispose of domestic trash.

5 The regularity usually derives from looking at one category of space, such as rooms, rather than all the rectilinear spaces in the settlement. If this is done then several ratio rules might appear for each settlement. Though a ratio rule is to be expected if a series is in use (because successive associations along the series will lead to proportionate increases in the sides of rooms), the overall effect of a series on length–width ratios will be more complex. Ratio rules are usually identified within a single category of space, e.g. rooms, but a series pattern should be able to produce this effect in other classes of space as well, such as built-in bed platforms or benches. Given that each value in a series could constitute the wall length normal to any other distance value, what we should find is that a given class of space, such as rooms, is being patterned by a restricted set of relationships within the range of options which the series alone would permit. As well as the series, there should therefore be an additional set of algorithms defining which parts of the series go together.

6 The Vinča sites are a critically interesting case study because their occupation densities may have been comparatively low. Chapman suggests a population for Selevac of 600–1200 (1990: 38), i.e. just about the 10 p/ha T-limit, if spread across about 50 ha. Tringham (in Tringham and Krstić) prefers no more than ten families (600 people) in much less space (1990: 585). Tringham's thesis about the organisational limits of a social formation (p. 164) restricting settlement growth would, according to the I–C model, be better served by a larger area estimate with a somewhat higher population, as Chapman (1990) suggests.

7 THE DEVELOPMENT OF SEDENTISM

1 My concern is residential, not logistical mobility *per se*. There is substantial logistic mobility in industrialised society yet we are in no doubt that the communities which occupy the towns and cities are what we normally refer to as sedentary and constitute permanent communities.

Note, however, that the simple duration of a community cannot be a sufficient factor in the recognition of permanent sedentism even if it is a frequent corollary of it. Many communities whose members come from other, permanently sedentary communities, who also intend to be sedentary, may fail to sustain themselves. The same applies to individual households. The rate at which they depart may be indicative of the failure of a permanently sedentary community but will not demonstrate that the community was not habitually and fully sedentary. Declining numbers of people would not disqualify a community from being called permanently sedentary; only an alteration in the time scheduling of its occupants would do so. We might ultimately remark that when the community finally disappeared it had failed to sustain a permanently sedentary lifestyle, but could not sensibly claim that it was actually mobile, since that would equate the failure of permanent sedentism with the presence of mobility. The converse would be considered nonsensical. Lack of taxonomic parity should be avoided unless we intend to make an overt progressionist claim for the superiority of permanent sedentism.

2 Anderson also mentions an opinion that Rakaia Mouth was once much larger. The argument is that the site was once symmetrical and has been cut away by the river and the sea. While possible, the claim should be treated with caution. The same form of argument might have been made for Poverty Point, claiming that it was once a polygon that is now half eroded. But what is apparent from other Poverty Point sites is that the middens were located in a semi-circle facing towards the river.

3 Note: The Eibl Eibesfeld plans have no Absolute Limit of Scatter (ALS) perimeter and an approximation boundary close to the huts has been used to estimate the area. As a result the density estimates for these larger camps are rather higher than they would be if the full extent of the ALS area were known. The decrease in density for total settlement area as community size increases is therefore probably steeper than indicated.

   Issues: The regression for population against density in permanently sedentary communities is interesting because, unlike the trends noted for some mobile groups, it corresponds quite closely to the regression produced by self-correlation (see Chapter 4, n. 3). Random number associations will produce regressions in which X/Y is positively correlated with X (i.e. equivalent to P/Ha compared to P) with a coefficient of about 0.5. The behavioural implications are quite considerable since this suggests both that the factors which generate density relations in mobile and seasonally sedentary communities compared to permanently sedentary groups can be very different, and also that these factors may be more nearly random in the way they operate in permanently sedentary groups! Only if the coefficient exceeded 0.7 for the positive correlation of X/Y with X could non-random operations be considered significant in permanently sedentary groups. Yet we must also regard the positive correlation as behaviourally significant because we know that it is not an inevitable product of human residential life. It may perhaps be a function of some forms of sedentism. Why that should be so required further enquiry to see what correlation coefficients usually occur.

4 The Fitzwilliam Museum in Cambridge possesses an example of a calendar sword probably made in Germany in the sixteenth century AD (Catalogue number: M-9-1947). The calendar is engraved along the length of the blade. My thanks to R. A. Crighton, Keeper of Applied Arts, for this information.

5 Contemporary towns in northern Nigeria (Schwerdfeger 1971) and in north Ghana (e.g. Bologatanga) contain residence units with round and rectilinear buildings. They were also present in medieval Timbuktu (see Hull 1976).

6 The degree to which a community is sedentary will have to be diagnosed from bio-mechanical characteristics of human behaviour using the methodological uniformitarian basis of biology and the physical sciences, not from substantive cultural correlations (Edwards 1989: Wyncoll and Tangri 1991). Secure indices of sedentism are not yet available (Kelly 1992). Biomechanical indices such as physical effects on skeletal and dental structure will have to be identified – perhaps more varied trace element or isotope signatures in mobile groups, or, if we could recognise them, major seasonal differences within the annual layers of dentine or enamel in teeth.

7 If I–C stresses are not critical in controlling the development of permanent sedentism but changes in action or verbal meaning content are required, these must necessarily be particular to the meaning content and the unique historical circumstances of each community. Since, on this view, permanent sedentism could commence in settlements of similar size but with a wide variety of community sizes, the organisation of the communities cannot in itself be a critical factor. Only by shifting emphasis towards the larger scale components of the hierarchy of explanation could explanatory generality be obtained. Apart from local factors of meaning content, the main interregionally consistent restriction on year-round residence in one place must then be the relationship to the supply of resources (Kelly 1992: 51–4). If the sustained supply of food throughout the year is the determining factor (Niederberger 1979; Renouf 1989; Rowley-Conwy 1983), leading to or allowing the occurrence of sedentism, succinct explanation of the behaviourally unrestricted development of sedentism primarily requires economic and resource opportunism. On this view the capacity of the economy of a group to sustain year-round supplies of food in one place ought to be the visible causal factor.

In contrast to the restrictive version, the social action and economic models of sedentism impose no material preconditions on the development of sedentism and suggest instead that it has always been a feasible option for human communities, restricted only by social rules about the use of surpluses and the number of localities in which year-round resources are available. Accordingly, these associated viewpoints must also contend that no substantial change in human residential behaviour, other than an increase in community size, has occurred in the last 15,000 years, compared to the preceding existence of modern humans. The implications are considerable. The resource versions would allow forms of sedentism, equivalent to those of the contemporary agrarian communities which we usually call sedentary, back to either 40,000–50,000 BP, or even to 90,000–100,000 BP (depending on the early dates allocated to *Homo sapiens sapiens*).

For the debate to be sustained as a meaningful discourse we will need to state more precisely the way in which 'sedentism' is to be applied, otherwise the arguments are futile. The risk in such arguments is that the categories will subsume the logic of the debate. Calling the Northwest Coast Indians seasonally sedentary and thereby placing them in a general class of sedentary groups will lead to very different forms of contention from those arising from a taxonomy which reserves sedentism as the label for what Kent calls permanent sedentism. In the latter taxonomic scheme, seasonally sedentary communities would be renamed and placed in a general class of communities practising varying degrees of consistent annual mobility. No matter what labels we use, the critical behavioural difference may actually lie between Kent's seasonally sedentary communities and permanently sedentary groups, even if this division lies within the general class of sedentism as currently defined. Where the critical behaviour difference (if any) lies is what matters – not the cachet associated with a label in the obsolete evolutionary stage taxonomy.

8   THE DEVELOPMENT OF AGRARIAN AND INDUSTRIAL URBANISM

1 No administrators for water management are named among the senior officers of the state in the Old Kingdom (Strudwick 1985). But the absence of administrators concerned with irrigation is not in itself a critical feature since there is also no record of such officials in the early states of China or Mesopotamia, as Wheatley (1971) and R. McC. Adams (1981) have shown, even though those regions did have expanding and eventually very extensive irrigation and water management systems.

2 Brief reports also state that several other Indus sites, including Rangpur, Kotadi and Pathani Damb, may have reached sizes of between 75 and 100 ha (Chakrabati 1979: 206) but on inspection they all appear to be either much smaller or somewhat tenuously reported. The site of Kerasi is said to have an area of 3.75 sq km (Jansen 1979: 304). Were it indeed that size, roughly equivalent to the size of Uruk in the early third millennium BC or the Shang settlement of Cheng-chou, it would be a profoundly significant addition to the Harappan settlement system. Possehl (1990: 271) refers only to an 80–85 ha range for the largest sites.

3 On the Unesco management plan for Mohenjo-daro (Khan 1973) there is also a patch of occupation debris indicated to the south-west of the known settlement.

4 The site of Moche has probably been seriously damaged on the western side by the movement of the river channel. Considerable loss of sites due to erosion and redeposition has occurred in the Moche valley (Moseley 1983). More than half of the Huaca del Sol has been destroyed by the river. On the aerial photographs patches of bare ground are visible within the adjacent agricultural area. These resemble the surface of the site. To the south of the huacas there is also a linear feature running from the hill slopes towards the river. Its alignment is very unclear but near the hill it makes a short return in line with the track of the canal which passes just to the west of the Huaca de la Luna. If it is a feature associated with the Mochica period canal, then it may mark the southern edge of the settlement. We also need to ascertain whether an ephemeral occupation (like the SIAR structures at Chan Chan – see J. R. Topic 1982) extended up the slopes of the hill to the east of the Huaca de la Luna.

5 Though Petereny was identified at the beginning of the century and Vladimirovka was published in 1949, most of the large Tripolye-Cucuteni sites were only surveyed in the 1970s (Ellis 1984: 183, 186). The site plans of the largest settlements such as Dobrovody, Majdanets and Talljanky are known from aerial surveys, especially by Siskin, combined with excavation. Majdanets is the most extensively excavated large site.

6 Issues: There is serious dispute about the size of the population of Imperial Rome (e.g. see Hermansen 1978) and of Constantinople (see Mango 1985).

7 Population estimates are by common agreement notoriously unreliable. They can only be used as a cloud of estimates within which probable values tend to lie. The advantage of the overall comparative approach is that estimates from markedly divergent sources - such as self-interested entrepreneurs, military calculations, census reports and off-hand remarks can be compared in order to identify the limits on our confidence in claims for the validity of particular estimates. The varying estimates suggest that as yet we must either reject attempts to estimate population or we must accept that overall only gross estimates are worth proposing and even then we must allow possible maximum and meaningful minimum community size estimates.

8 Hangchow sources: primarily Cloud 1906, Gernet 1967 and Moule 1957 for the Sung period; and sources for Marco Polo's description of the city under Mongol control in the early fourteenth century AD.

9 Population estimates for Ch'ing Peking (Rozman 1972; Skinner 1977), T'ang Ch'ang-an (Schafer 1963) and Tokugawa Edo (Yazaki 1968).

10 To produce the diagram the peak estimates are superimposed along a median line with the lower estimates which are earlier and later lying on either side.

9 FUTURE URBAN GROWTH

1 The uniformitarian basis of the study necessitates the use of a refutationist procedure. Though the concept of refutation was introduced by Popper as a conceptual device to

demarcate science from non-science, a view which has engendered serious dispute (Lakatos and Musgrave 1970; Kelley and Hanen 1988), that is not my concern. Nor is the emphasis of this study directed at how to do refutation, or the way it relates to politics and the intellectual traditions which define plausibility in archaeology (Bell 1982; Murray 1990; Murray and Walker 1987; Tangri 1989). My concern is the moral imperatives inextricably associated with the use of operational uniformitarian propositions, if we accept responsibility for the consequences of the views which we espouse (Fletcher 1991b). The discussion is about why refutation is required. It is not a ruling about exactly how refutation ought to be done – only a contention that, however difficult, it needs to be done.

What is at issue is that our theories may lead to expectations or policies which have profound and deleterious consequences. If, as is argued, the material can both facilitate and obstruct active, social behaviour, then it has the potential seriously to affect our societies. Its obstructive capacity could adversely affect the quality of life, prejudice the maintenance of community life, or cause massive expense with unpredictable consequences. We can devise morally undesirable policies even from theoretically valid propositions. The proposals may seem quite mundane at the time but we might incline to disregard hints of adverse consequences for the sake of temporary advantage. In addition, erroneous assessments of the role of the material could have serious consequences. We may fail to recognise the risk inherent in a particular combination of active and material behaviour, or claim such a risk when none is present, or else mistakenly identify a material feature as a solution to a social problem. Behavioural analyses have to be carried out on the prior assumption that significant potential risk can result from our interpretations.

An operational uniformitarian proposition establishes a fundamental equivalence between the parameters of behaviour in the past and the present, independent of differences in spatial or temporal location. It refers to fundamental conditions and processes which can have powerful derivative effects. Conclusions derived from such a proposition may therefore have considerable relevance for the management of the contemporary relationship between people and material entities. Because the past may contain particular substantive examples with no contemporary equivalent, we could identify in the past the nature and consequences of phenomena of which we might otherwise have no knowledge. An operational uniformitarian model makes these comprehensible and accessible to imitation for good or ill.

The necessary epistemology follows from the logical consequences of the operational uniformitarian basis of the approach. A refutationist procedure is needed to mitigate the risks which would otherwise follow from self-deception. The risk can be managed by trying to check rigorously the statements which we make. What puts us most at risk is a tendency to believe what we would prefer to believe (Fletcher 1991b). Proposals about the role of the material as behaviour must therefore be stated in a form that is deliberately open to refutation. The circumstances and logical derivatives of the model which complicate that exercise should be identified and clearly reported. As is apparent from Popper's own view (1976: 42; 1980), Wisdom's appraisal of Popper's thesis (1987) and the reassessment by Lakatos (1978), refutation is far from straightforward (Harding 1976; Harré 1985: 51–2; Kelley and Hanen 1988: 79–89; Lakatos and Musgrave 1970), but that does not remove the obligation to try (Miller [David] 1982). We ought to apply an epistemology which promotes systematic critical doubt about our conclusions and expectations.

Refutations can define the limits within which a theory is useful and warn us where to take care with our assumptions. This applies even to high-level operational uniformitarian propositions. Newton's theory of dynamics suffered from anomalies, such as the non-correspondence of the perihelion of Mercury with prediction, well before it was superseded by Einsteinian relativity and quantum mechanics (Bernstein 1973: 125–8; Berry 1987). Yet within its limits Newtonian mechanics sufficed for the development of nineteenth–early twentieth-century industrial technologies and still does for many mechanical purposes. Error does not exclude usefulness and an apparent refutation does not oblige us to reject an otherwise useful theoretical tool. All we need to do is deliberately recognise the contexts in which the tool does not work. We need not suppose that we are pursuing truth to do this. Nor should we imagine that our opinions are somehow tested directly against reality. They are tested against the observational statements we should be able to obtain from standard measuring instruments if the propositions are efficacious. Their usefulness is to be assessed in terms of the amount of information they organise, the simplicity of their structure and the predictions which they generate in competition with other commensurable theories.

A behavioural analysis with an operational uniformitarian basis needs to follow a refutationist policy because of its potentially serious consequences. The argument for the use of refutation for this purpose does not purport to set a standard for others or a rule for all representations of the past (Fletcher 1991b). Refutation is not universally appropriate or necessary, nor is the aim to obtain external validation for archaeology as a science. The epistemology is required for this particular approach because of an obligation to other people that we should carefully assess the implications of what we learn and what we seek to know.

2 The territorial control in grouse and many other species appears to be managed by the effect of stress on the hormonal triggers of conflict, defence and flight behaviour.

3 This discussion approaches an issue which was raised in the debate about group selection. The proposed model is not a claim for selection in favour of a mechanism whose competence is displayed in larger aggregate populations – that would land us back in the fallacies of the group selection thesis. Rather it is selection in favour of a mechanism which permits larger aggregates but does not directively cause them. The hierarchy of operations and the indeterminacy inherent in it rule out directive cause. Selection in favour of a material mechanism is not simply a variant of biological selection whose fitness index is the numbers of people who survive (see decoupling of biological and material behaviour survival, pp. 52–3).

4 Sizes according to criteria specified in Chapter 4 n. 2, and discussed in more detail in Fletcher 1981a and 1986.

REFERENCES

Note: The references for the plans in the text and the numerical data referred to in the notes to each chapter can be obtained from the Settlement Data Register, School of Archaeology, Classics and Ancient History, University of Sydney, NSW 2006, Australia, c/o A/Prof. Roland Fletcher. The references file is labelled SOURCE.DOC. It can also be obtained by E-mail enquiry from ROLAND.FLETCHER @ ANTIQUITY.SU.EDU.AU.

Adams, B. and Conway, J. 1975. *The Social Effects of Living off the Ground*. Occasional Paper 1/75, Housing Development Directorate, Department of Environment: London.

Adams, R. McC. 1981. *Heartland of Cities*. University of Chicago Press: Chicago.

Adams, R. McC. and Nissen, H. J. 1972. *The Uruk Countryside*. University of Chicago Press: Chicago.

Agorsah, E. K. 1985. Archaeological interpretation of traditional house construction among the Nchumuru of northern Ghana. *Current Anthropology* 26 (1): 103–15.

Ahmad, K. S. 1961. Reclamation of waterlogged and saline lands in west Pakistan. *Pakistan Geographical Review* 16 (1): 1–15.

Aiello, J. R. and Aiello, T. de C. 1974. The development of personal space: proxemic behaviour of children 6 through 16. *Human Ecology* 2: 177–89.

Alexander, C. 1964. *Notes on the Synthesis of Form*. Harvard College Press: Cambridge, Mass.

Alexander, J. 1972. The beginnings of urban life in Europe. In P. J. Ucko, R. Tringham and G. W. Dimblely (eds.), *Man, Settlement and Urbanism*, pp. 843–50. Duckworth: London.

Alland, A. 1967. *Evolution and Human Behaviour*. Tavistock Press: London.

Allchin, B. and Allchin, R. 1982. *The Rise of Civilisation in India and Pakistan*. Cambridge University Press: Cambridge.

Altman, I. 1975. *The Environment and Social Behaviour: privacy, personal space, territory, crowding*. Brooks-Cole: Monterey.

Altman, K., Wohlwill, J. F. and Rapoport, A. (eds.) 1980. *Environment and Culture*. Plenum: New York.

Anderson, A. 1989. *Prodigious Birds: moas and moa-hunting in prehistoric New Zealand*. Cambridge University Press: Cambridge.

Anderson, E. N. 1972. Some Chinese methods of dealing with overcrowding. *Urban Anthropology* 1: 141–50.

Ankerl, G. 1981. *Experimental Sociology of Architecture – a guide to theory, research and literature*. Mouton: The Hague.

Annis, R. C. and Frost, B. 1973. Human visual ecology and orientation anisotropies in acuity. *Science* 182 (4113): 729–31.

Anquandah, J. 1993. Urbanization and state formation in Ghana during the Iron Age. In T. Shaw, P. Sinclair, B. Andah and A. Okpoko (eds.), *The Archaeology of Africa: foods, metals and towns*, pp. 642–51. One World Archaeology 20 (Series editor P. J. Ucko). Routledge: London.

Appadurai, A. (ed.) 1986. *The Social Life of Things: commodities in cultural perspective.* Cambridge University Press: Cambridge.

Archer, I. 1971. Nabdan compounds, northern Ghana. In P. Oliver (ed.), *Shelter in Africa*, pp. 6-57. Barrie and Jenkins: London.

Ardener, E. (ed.) 1976. *Social Anthropology and Language.* Tavistock Press: London.

Ardener, S. 1981. *Women and Space: ground rules and social maps.* Croom Helm: London.

Argyle, M. 1975. *Bodily Communication.* Methuen: London.

Armit, I. and Finlayson, B. 1992. Hunter-gatherers transformed: the transition to agriculture in northern and western Europe. *Antiquity* 66: 664–76.

Ashby, W. R. 1960. *Design for a Brain.* Chapman and Hall: London.

Ascher, M. and Ascher, R. 1981. *Code of the Quipu: a study in media, maths and culture.* University of Michigan Press: Ann Arbor.

Atchley, W. R., Gaskin, C. T. and Anderson, D. 1976. Statistical properties of ratios. I: Empirical results. *The Society for Systematic Zoology* 25 (2): 137–48.

Audouze, F. and Büchsenschütz, O. 1989. *Villes, villages et campagnes de l'Europe Celtique:du début du IIe millénaire à la fin du Ie siècle avant J.-C.* Hachette: Paris.

Aveni, A. F. 1983. *Calendars in Mesoamerica and Peru: native American computations of time.* BAR International Series 174, British Archaeological Reports: Oxford.

Ayres, W. S., Haun, A. E. and Mauricio, R. 1983. *Nan Madol Archaeology: 1981 Survey and Excavations.* The Pacific Studies Institute, Guam, for the Historic Preservation Committee, Ponape State, Federated States of Micronesia and Historic Preservation Program, Saipan, Trust Territory of the Pacific Islands.

Baer, K. 1962. The low price of land in ancient Egypt. *Journal of the American Research Center in Egypt* 1: 25–42

1963. An 11th Dynasty farmer's letters to his family. *Journal of the American Oriental Society* 83: 1–19.

Bagwell, P. S. 1974. *The Transport Revolution from 1770.* Batsford: London.

Bailey, G. N. 1983. Concepts of time in Quaternary prehistory. *Annual Review of Anthropology* 12: 165–92.

1987. Breaking the time barrier. *Archaeological Review from Cambridge* 6 (1): 5–20.

Bak, P. and Chen, K. 1991. Self-organised criticality. *Scientific American* (Jan.): 26–33.

Bamforth, D. B. and Spaulding, A. C. 1982. Human behaviour, explanation, archaeology, history and science. *Journal of Anthropological Archaeology* 1: 179–95.

Barker, T. C. and Robbins, M. 1975. *A History of London Transport.* Allen and Unwin: London.

Barker, T. C. and Savage, C. I. 1974. *An Economic History of Transport in Britain* (3rd edition). Hutchinson Universal Library: London.

Barlow, G. W. and Silverberg, J. (eds.) 1980. *Sociobiology: beyond nature/nurture?* Westview Press: Boulder, Colo.

Baron, R. M. 1980. The case for differences in the responses of humans and other animals to high density. In M. N. Cohen, R. S. Malpass and H. G. Klein (eds.), *Biosocial Mechanisms of Population Regulation*, pp. 247–73. Yale University Press: New Haven.

Barrau, J. 1958. Subsistence agriculture in Melanesia. *Bernice P. Bishop Museum Bulletin* 219 (IX).

Bateson, P. P. G. 1972. *Steps to an Ecology of Mind: collected essays in anthropology, psychiatry, evolution and epistemology.* Paladin: St Albans.

Beaglehole, J. C. (ed.) 1967. *The Journals of Captain James Cook on his Voyage of Discovery. The Voyage of the* Resolution *and the* Discovery, *1776–1870. Part II.* Cambridge University Press: Cambridge.

Beg, M. A. J. 1986. *Historic Cities of Asia: an introduction to Asian Cities.* Percetakan Ban Huat Seng: Kuala Lumpur.

Bell, J. A. 1982. Archaeological explanation – progress through criticism. In C. Renfrew, M. J. Rowlands and B. A. Seagraves (eds.), *Theory and Explanation in Archaeology: the Southampton conference,* pp. 65–72. Academic Press: New York.

Bellwood, P. 1978. *Man's Conquest of the Pacific: the prehistory of Southeast Asia and Oceania.* Oxford University Press: New York.

Berger, P. L. and Luckmann, T. 1967. *The Social Construction of Reality.* Penguin: Harmondsworth.

Bernstein, J. 1973. *Einstein.* Fontana/Collins: London.

Berry, B. and Silverman, L. (ed.) 1980. *Population Redistribution in the United States in the 1970s.* National Academy of Sciences: Washington, D.C.

Berry, J. W. 1971. Ecological and cultural factors in spatial perceptual development. *Canadian Journal of Behavioural Science* 3 (4): 324–36.

Berry, M. 1987. Quantum physics on the edge of chaos. *New Scientist* 19 (Nov.): 44–7.

Best, B. H. and Rogers, W. A. 1973. *The Urban Country-side.* Faber and Faber: London.

Betzig, L. L. and Turke, P. W. 1985. Measuring time allocation. *Current Anthropology* 26 (5): 647–50.

Bhaskar, R. 1981. The consequences of socio-evolutionary concepts for naturalism in sociology: commentaries on Harré and Toulmin. In U. J. Jensen and R. Harré (eds.), *The Philosophy of Evolution,* pp. 96–109. Harvester Press: Brighton.

Bietak, M. 1979. Urban archaeology and the 'town problem' in ancient Egypt. In K. R. Weeks (ed.), *Egyptology and the Social Sciences,* pp. 97–144. The American University in Cairo Press: Cairo.

Binford, L. R. 1962. Archaeology as anthropology. *American Antiquity* 28 (2): 17–25.

1965. Archaeological systematics and the study of culture process. *American Antiquity* 31 (2): 203–10.

1967. CA* Comment on 'Major aspects of the interrelationship of archaeology and ethnology' by K. C. Chang. *Current Anthropology* 8: 234–5.

1977. General Introduction. In L. R. Binford (ed.), *For Theory Building in Archaeology,* pp. 1–10. Academic Press: New York.

1978. *Nunamiut Archaeology.* Academic Press. New York.

1981. Behavioural archaeology and the Pompeii Premise. *Journal of Anthropological Research* 37 (3): 195–208.

1987. Data, relativism and archaeological science. *Man* (NS) 22 (3): 391–404.

Bintliff, J. L. (ed.) 1991. *The* Annales *School and Archaeology.* Leicester University Press: Leicester.

Bintliff, J. L. and Gaffney, C. F. (eds.) 1986. *Archaeology at the Interface: studies in archaeology's relationship with history, geography, biology and physical sciences.* BAR International Series 300, British Archaeological Reports: Oxford.

Birdwhistell, R. L. 1970. *Kinesics and Communication.* University of Pennsylvania Press: Philadelphia.

Blier, S. P. 1987. *The Anatomy of Architecture: ontology and metaphor in Batammaliba architectural expression.* Cambridge University Press: Cambridge.

Blanton, R. E. 1978. *Monte Albán: settlement patterns at the Zapotec capital.* Academic Press: New York.

Blanton, R. E., Kowaleski, S., Feinman, G. and Appel, J. 1982. Monte Albán's hinterland, Part I: the prehistoric settlement patterns of the central and southern parts of the Valley of Oaxaca, Mexico. In K. V. Flannery and R. E. Blanton (gen. eds.), *Prehistory and Human Ecology of the Valley of Oaxaca 7.* Museum of Anthropology, University of Michigan, Memoirs 15.

Blute, M. 1979. Sociocultural evolutionism: an untried theory. *Behavioural Science* 24: 46–59.

Boehmer, R. M. 1991. Uruk 1980–90: a progress report. *Antiquity* 65 (248): 465–78.

Bonner, J. T. 1965. *Size and Cycle*. Princeton University Press: Princeton.

1980. *The Evolution of Culture in Animals*. Princeton University Press: Princeton.

Bonner, J. T., Wilson, E. O. and Lumsden, C. J. 1981. *Genes, Mind and Culture: the coevolutionary process*. Harvard University Press: Cambridge, Mass.

Böök, A. 1991. Spatial cognition as events. In T. Gärling and G. W. Evans (eds.), *Environment, Cognition and Action: an integrated approach*. Oxford University Press: New York.

Bourdieu, P. 1977. *Outline of a Theory of Practice* (trans. R. Nice). Cambridge University Press: Cambridge.

1984. *Distinction: a social critique of the judgement of taste*. Routledge and Kegan Paul: London.

Boyd, R. and Richerson, P. J. 1985. *Culture and the Evolutionary Process*. University of Chicago Press: Chicago.

Braudel, F. 1981. *On History*. Weidenfeld and Nicolson: London.

1985. *The Structures of Everyday Life* (trans. S. Reynolds). Vol. 1 of *Civilization and Capitalism 15th–18th Century*. Fontana Press: London.

Bronowski, J. 1973. *Ascent of Man*. British Broadcasting Corporation: London.

Bronowski, J. and Mazlich, B. 1963. *The Western Intellectual Tradition*. Pelican: Harmondsworth.

Brown, A. K. 1967. *The Aboriginal Population of the Santa Barbara Channel*. University of California Survey Reports 69: 1–99.

Brush, S. G. 1976. Irreversibility and indeterminism: Fourier to Heisenberg. *Journal of the History of Ideas* 38 (4): 603–30.

Burch, E. S. 1986. Eskimo kinsmen: changing family relationships in northwest Alaska. *The American Ethnological Society Monograph 59*. West Publishing Co.: St Paul.

Burnham, B. C. and Kingsbury, J. (eds.) 1979. *Space, Hierarchy and Society: interdisciplinary studies in social area analysis*. BAR International Series (Supp.) 59. British Archaeological Reports: Oxford.

Bushnell, D. I. 1922. Villages of the Algonquian, Siouan and Caddoan tribes west of the Mississippi. *Bureau of American Ethnology Bulletin 77*, Smithsonian Institution.

Butzer, K. W. 1976. *Early Hydraulic Civilisation in Egypt: a study in cultural ecology*. University of Chicago Press: Chicago.

1980. Civilizations: organisms or systems? *American Scientist* 68: 517–23.

1982. *Archaeology as Human Ecology*. Cambridge University Press: Cambridge.

1984. Long-term Nile flood variation and political discontinuities in Pharaonic Egypt. In J. D. Clark and S. A. Brandt (eds.), *From Hunters to Farmers: the causes and consequences of food production in Africa*, pp. 102–20. University of California Press: Berkeley.

Calder, W. B. 1984. *Size, Function and Life History*. Harvard University Press: Cambridge, Mass.

Calhoun, J. B. 1962. Population density and social pathology. *Scientific American* 206 (2): 139–48.

1971. Space and the strategy of life. In A. H. Esser (ed.), *Behaviour and Environment: the use of space by animals and men*, pp. 329–87. Plenum Press: New York.

Cameron, C. M. 1992. An analysis of residential patterns and the Oraibi split. *Journal of Anthropological Archaeology* 11 (2): 173–86.

Campbell, J. 1989. *Winston Churchill's Afternoon Nap*. Paladin: London.

Canning, J. (ed.) 1986. *The Illustrated Mayhew's London. The classic account of London street life and characters in the time of Charles Dickens and Queen Victoria.* Weidenfeld and Nicolson: London.

Canter, D., Stringer, P., Griffiths, I., Boyce, P. and Kenny, C. 1975. *Environmental Interaction: psychological approaches to our physical environment.* Surrey University Press: London.

Carlstein, T. 1982. *Time Resources, Society and Ecology: on the capacity for human interaction in space and time.* Allen and Unwin: London.

Carlstein, T., Parkes, D. and Thrift, N. (eds.) 1978. *Timing Space and Spacing Time.* Edward Arnold: London.

Carter, H. 1972. *The Study of Urban Geography.* Edward Arnold: London.

Casimir, M. J. 1979. An analysis of gorilla nesting sites in the Mt Kahuzi region (Zaire). *Folia Primatologica* 32: 290–308.

Caso, A. 1958–9. Glifos Teotihuacanos. *Revista Mexicana de Estudios Antropologicos* 15: 51–70.

Casselbury, S. E. 1974. Further refinement of formulae for determining population from floor area. *World Archaeology* 6: 117–22.

Casteel, R. W. 1979. Relationships between surface area and population size: a cautionary note. *American Antiquity* 44 (4): 803–7.

Cavalli Sforza, L. L. and Feldman, M. W. 1981. *Cultural Transmission and Evolution: a qualitative approach.* Princeton University Press: Princeton.

Cěrný, J. 1973. *A Community of Workmen at Thebes in the Ramesside Period.* Institut Français d'Archéologie Orientale de Caire, Bibliothèque d'Etude: Cairo.

Chaffer, N. 1984. *In Quest of Bowerbirds.* Rigby: Adelaide.

Chaitin, G. 1990. A random walk in arithmetic. *New Scientist* 125 (no. 1709): 30–2.

Chakrabati, D. K. 1979. Size of Harappan sites. In D. P. Agrawal and D. K. Chakrabati (eds.), *Essays in Indian Protohistory,* pp. 205–15. B.R. Publ. Corp.: New Delhi.

Chalmers, A. 1983. *What is this Thing Called Science?* 2nd edn, University of Queensland Press: St Lucia.

Chang, K.-C. 1967. Major aspects of the interrelationship of archaeology and ethnology. *Current Anthropology* 8: 227–43.

1980. *Shang Civilisation.* Yale University Press: New Haven.

Chapman, J. 1981. *The Vinča Culture of Southeast Europe* (vol. 1). BAR International Series 117 (i), British Archaeological Reports: Oxford.

1990. The Neolithic in the Morava–Danube confluence area: a regional assessment of settlement pattern. In R. Tringham and D. Krstić (eds.), *Selevac: a Neolithic village in Yugoslavia.* Monumenta Archaeologica 15, pp. 13–43. Institute of Archaeology Publications, University of California: Los Angeles.

Chapman, S. D. 1971. *The History of Working-Class Housing.* David and Charles: Newton Abbot.

Cherry, C. 1966. *On Human Communication: a review, a survey, a criticism,* 2nd edn. Massachusetts Institute of Technology: Cambridge, Mass.

Cheung, K.-Y. 1983. Recent archaeological evidence relating to the origin of Chinese characters. In D. N. Keightley (ed.), *The Origins of Chinese Civilisation,* pp. 323–91. University of California Press: Berkeley.

Childe, V. G. 1946. Archaeology and anthropology. *Southwestern Journal of Anthropology* 2 (3): 243–51.

Chisholm, M. 1979. *Rural Settlement and Land Use: an essay on location.* Hutchinson: London.

Chomsky, N. 1957. *Syntactic Structures.* Mouton: The Hague.

Christian, J. J. 1960. Factors of mass mortality in a herd of Sika deer. *Chesapeake Science* 1: 79–95.

Cipolla, C. 1967. *Clocks and Culture*. Collins: London.

Clark, C. 1958. Transport – maker and breaker of cities. *Town Planning Review* 28: 237–50.

Clark, W. C. 1989. Managing Planet Earth. *Scientific American* 261 (3): 19-26.

Clarke, D. L. 1968. *Analytical Archaeology*. Methuen: London.

Cloak, F. T. 1975. Is a cultural ethology possible? *Human Ecology* 3: 161–82.

Cloud, F. D. 1906. *Hangchow: the 'City of Heaven' with a brief historical sketch of Soochow*. Presbyterian Mission Press: Shanghai.

Cohen, M. N. 1985. Prehistoric hunter-gatherers: the meaning of social complexity. In B. J. Price and J. A. Brown (eds.), *Prehistoric Hunter-Gatherers: the emergence of cultural complexity*, pp. 99–122. Academic Press: Orlando.

    1989. *Health and the Rise of Civilisation*. New Haven: Yale University Press.

Cohen, M. N. and Armelagos, G. J. (eds.) 1984. *Paleopathology at the Origins of Agriculture*. Academic Press: New York.

Colinvaux, P. 1980. *Why Big Fierce Animals are Rare*. Penguin Books: Harmondsworth.

Collis, J. 1975. *Defended Sites of the Late La Tène in Central and Western Europe*. BAR Supplementary Series 2, British Archaeological Reports: Oxford.

    1984. *Oppida. Earliest Towns North of the Alps*. Department of Prehistory and Archaeology, Sheffield University, Sheffield.

Conklin, W. J. 1982. The information system of the Middle Horizon quipus. In A. F. Aveni and G. Urton (eds.), *Ethnoastronomy and Archaeo-astronomy in the American Tropics*, pp. 261–82. Annals of the New York Academy of Sciences 385.

Connah, G. 1987. *African Civilisation*. Cambridge University Press: Cambridge.

Cook, S. F. n.d. *Papers held in Bancroft Library*. University of California: Berkeley.

Cordell, L. S. 1984. *Prehistory of the Southwest*. Academic Press: Orlando.

Courbin, P. 1988. *What is Archaeology?: an essay on the nature of archaeological research* (trans. P. Bahn). University of Chicago Press: Chicago.

Cousins, S. 1985. Ecologists build pyramids again. *New Scientist* 4 July: 50–4.

Crawford, G. W. and Yoshizaki, M. 1987. Ainu ancestors and prehistoric Asian agriculture. *Journal of Archaeological Science* 14 (2): 201–14.

Crawford, H. 1982. Analogies, anomalies and research strategies. *Paléorient* 8: 5–9.

Cromar, P. 1979. Spatial change and economic organisation: the Tyneside coal industry (1751–1770). *Geoforum* 10 (1): 45–57.

Cruickshank, D. 1985. *A Guide to the Georgian Buildings of Britain and Ireland*. Weidenfeld and Nicolson: London.

Cullen, B. 1990. Darwinian views of history: Betzig's virile psychopath versus the cultural virus. *Crosscurrents* 4 (Autumn): 61–8.

    1993. The Darwinian resurgence and the cultural virus critique. *Cambridge Archaeological Journal* 3 (2): 179–202.

Czanyi, V. 1989. *Evolutionary Systems and Society: a general theory of life, mind and culture*. Duke University Press: Durham.

Daniel, G. E. (ed.) 1981. *Towards a History of Archaeology: being the papers read at the first conference on the History of Archaeology in Aarhus, 29 Aug.–2 Sept. 1978*. Thames and Hudson: London.

Davies, P. 1987. The creative cosmos. *New Scientist* (Dec.): 41–4.

Davis, D. E. 1972. The regulation of human population. In J. A. Behnke (ed.), *Challenging Biological Problems: directions towards their solution*. Oxford University Press: New York.

Deane, P. 1979. *The First Industrial Revolution*. Cambridge University Press: Cambridge.

Deetz, J. 1970. Archaeology as social science: current directions in anthropology. *Bulletin of the American Anthropological Association* 3 (32): 115–25.
  1977. *In Small Things Forgotten*. Anchor Books: New York.
Denyer, S. 1978. *African Traditional Architecture: an historical and geographical perspective*. Heinemann: London.
d'Errico, F. 1989. Paleolithic lunar calendars: a case of wishful thinking. *Current Anthropology* 30 (1): 117–18.
De Greene, K. B. 1981. Limits to societal systems adaptability. *Behavioural Science* 26: 103–13.
Dewall, M. V. 1964. *Pferd und Wagen im Frühen China* vol. I. Saarbrücker Beiträge zur Altertums-kunde. Rudolf Habelt Verlag: Bonn.
De Walt, B. and Pelto, P. 1985. *Micro and Macro Levels of Analysis in Anthropology: issues of theory and research*. Westfield Press: London.
Dixon, N. F. 1981. *Preconscious Processing*. Wiley: Chichester.
Donley, L. W. 1982. House Power: Swahili space and symbolic markers. In I. Hodder (ed.), *Symbolic and Structural Archaeology*, pp. 63–72. Cambridge University Press: Cambridge.
Donnan, C. B. and Mackay, C. J. 1979. *Ancient Burial Patterns of the Moche Valley, Peru*. University of Texas Press: Austin.
Doxiadis, C. A. 1968. *Ekistics: an introduction to the science of human settlements*. Hutchinson: London.
Draper, P. 1973. Crowding among hunter-gatherers: the !Kung Bushmen. *Science* 182: 301–3.
Driscoll, J. M. and Corpolango, M. J. 1980. Uncertainty estimation and the uncertainty-probability shift under information load. *Behavioural Science* 25: 205–18.
Duly, C. 1979. *The Houses of Mankind*. Thames and Hudson: London.
Dunnell, R. C. 1978. Archaeological potential of anthropological and scientific models of function. In R. C. Dunnell and E. S. Hall Jr (eds.), *Archaeological Essays in Honor of Irving Rousse*, pp. 41–73. Mouton: The Hague.
  1980. Evolutionary theory and archaeology. *Advances in Archaeological Method and Theory* 3: 35–99.
  1982. Science, social science and common sense: the agonising dilemma of modern archaeology. *Journal of Anthropological Research* 38: 1–25.
Durham, W. H. 1982. Interactions of genetic and cultural evolution: models and examples. *Human Ecology* 10: 289–323.
  1990. Advances in evolutionary culture theory. *Annual Review of Anthropology* 19: 187–200.
Earle, T. K. and Preucel, R. W. 1987. Processual archaeology and the radical critique. *Current Anthropology* 28 (4): 501–38.
Earle, T., D'Altroy, T., Hastorf, C., Scott, C., Costin, C., Russell, G. and Sandefur, E. 1987. *Archaeological Field Research in the Upper Mantaro, Peru: investigations of Inka expansion and exchange*. Monograph XXVIII. Institute of Archaeology, University of California: Los Angeles.
Eco, U. 1973. Function and sign: semiotics of architecture. In J. Bryan and R. Sauer (eds.), *Structures, Implicit and Explicit*. VIA Publications of the Graduate School of Fine Arts 2, University of Philadelphia Press: Philadelphia.
  1979. *Theory of Semiotics*. Advances in Semiotics (gen ed. T. A. Sebeok), Indiana University Press: Bloomington.
Edwards, P. C. 1989. Problems of recognising earliest sedentism: the Natufian example. *Journal of Mediterranean Archaeology* 2 (1): 5–48.
Eibl-Eibesfeld, I. 1975. *Ethology: the biology of behaviour*. Holt, Rinehart and Winston: New York.
  1989. *Human Ethology*. Aldine de Gruyter: New York.

Eisenstein, E. 1983. *Printing Revolution in Early Modern Europe*. Cambridge University Press: Cambridge.

Eldredge, N. 1985. *Unfinished Synthesis: biological hierarchies and modern evolutionary thought*. Oxford University Press: New York.

Eldredge, N. and Gould, S. J. 1972. Punctuated equilibrium: an alternative to phyletic gradualism. In T. J. M. Schopf (ed.), *Models in Paleobiology*, pp. 82–115. Freeman, Cooper and Co.: San Francisco.

Ellana, L. J. 1990. Demographic change, sedentism, and western contact: an inland Dena'ina Athabaskan case study. In B. Meehan and N. White (eds.), *Hunter-gatherer Demography: past and present*, pp. 101–16. Publication of papers presented at CHAGS 1988, Darwin. Oceania Monographs.

Elliot, R. C. 1976. Observations on a small group of mountain gorillas (*Gorilla gorilla beringei*). *Folia Primatologica* 25: 12–24.

Ellis, L. 1984. *The Cucuteni-Tripolye Culture: a study in technology and the origins of complex society*. BAR International Series 217, British Archaeological Reports: Oxford.

Engelstad, E. 1984. Diversity in Arctic maritime adaptations; an example from the Late Stone Age of Arctic Norway. *Acta Borealis* 1 (2): 21–35.

Erasmus, C. 1965. Monument building: some field experiments. *Southwestern Journal of Anthropology* 21: 277–301.

Erickson, C. L. Raised fields in the Lake Titicaca basin. *Expedition* 30 (3): 8–16.

Esser, A. H. (ed.) 1971. *Behaviour and Environment: the use of space by animals and men*. Plenum Press: New York.

Farrington, I. S. 1977. Land use, irrigation and society on the north coast of Peru in the Prehispanic era. *Zeitschrift für Bewässerungswirtschaft* 12 (2): 151–86.

Fetzer, J. H. 1983. Probability and objectivity in deterministic and indeterministic situations. *Synthese* 57: 367–86.

Flannery, K. V. 1972. The origin of the village as a settlement type in Mesoamerica and the Near East: a comparative study. In P. J. Ucko, R. Tringham and G. W. Dimbleby (eds.), *Man, Settlement and Urbanism*, pp. 25–53. Duckworth: London.

1973. Archaeology with a capital S. In C. L. Redman (ed.), *Research and Theory in Current Archaeology*, pp. 47–53. Wiley: New York.

(ed.) 1987. *Guila Naquitz: archaic foraging and early agriculture in Oaxaca, Mexico*. Academic Press: Orlando.

Flannery, K. V. and Marcus, J. (eds.) 1983. *The Cloud People: divergent evolution of the Zapotec and Mixtec civilisations*. Academic Press: New York.

Fletcher, R. J. 1977. Settlement studies (micro and semi-micro). In D. L. Clarke (ed.), *Spatial Archaeology*, pp. 47–162. Academic Press: London.

1981a. People and space: a case study on material behaviour. In I. Hodder, G. L. Isaac and N. Hammond (eds.), *Pattern of the Past: studies in honour of David Clarke*, pp. 97–128. Cambridge University Press: Cambridge.

1981b. Space and community behaviour. In B. Lloyd and J. Gay (eds.), *Universals of Human Thought: the African evidence*, pp. 71–110. Cambridge University Press: Cambridge.

1984. Identifying spatial disorder: a case study of a Mongol fort. In H. J. Hietala (ed.), *Intrasite Spatial Analysis*, pp. 196–223. Cambridge University Press: Cambridge.

1985. Intensification and interaction: a material behaviour analysis of Mug House. In I. S. Farrington (ed.), *Prehistoric Intensive Agriculture in the Tropics*, BAR International Series 232, pp. 653–82, British Archaeological Reports: Oxford.

1986. Settlement archaeology: world-wide comparisons. *World Archaeology* 18 (1): 59–83.

1988. The messages of material behaviour: an analysis of non-verbal meaning. In I. Hodder (ed.), *The Meaning of Things: material culture and symbolic expression*, pp. 33–40. One World Archaeology 6, Unwin Hyman: London.

1989. Social theory and archaeology: diversity, paradox and potential. In J. R. Rhoads (ed.), *Australian Reviews of Anthropology. Mankind* 19 (1): 65–75.

1990. Residential densities, group size and social stress in Australian Aboriginal settlements. In B. Meehan and N. White (eds.), *Hunter-gatherer Demography: past and present*, pp. 81–95. Publication of papers presented at CHAGS 1988, Darwin. Oceania Monographs.

1991a. Very large mobile communities: interaction stress and residential dispersal. In C. Gamble and B. Boismer (eds.), *Ethnoarchaeological Approaches to Mobile Campsites: hunter-gatherer and pastoralist case studies*, pp. 395–420. International Monographs in Prehistory: Ann Arbor.

1991b. Refutation and tradition: an uneasy relationship. *Australian Archaeology* 33: 59–62.

1992. Time perspectivism, *Annales* and the potential of archaeology. In A. B. Knapp (ed.), *Archaeology,* Annales *and Ethnohistory*, pp. 35–49. Cambridge University Press: Cambridge.

1993a. The evolution of human behaviour. In G. Burenhult (gen. ed.), *The Illustrated Encyclopedia of Humankind*, vol. 1, pp. 3–15. University of Queensland Press: St Lucia.

1993b. Settlement area and communication in African towns and cities. In T. Shaw, P. Sinclair, B. Andah and A. Okpoko (eds.), *The Archaeology of Africa: foods, metals and towns*, pp. 732–49. One World Archaeology 20 (Series editor P. J. Ucko), Routledge: London.

In press. Organised dissonance in cultural message systems. In H. Maschner (ed.), *Darwinian Archaeology*. Plenum Press: New York.

Fortes, M. 1959. Primitive kinship. *Scientific American* 200 (6): 146–58.

Frankel, H. 1988. From continental drift to plate tectonics. *Nature* (8 Sept.) 335: 127–30.

Fraser, D. 1968. *Village Planning in the Primitive World*. Studio Vista: London.

Fréderic, L. 1972. *Daily Life in Japan at the Time of the Samurai*. Macmillan: New York.

Freedman, J. L. 1975. *Crowding and Behaviour*. Freeman and Company: San Francisco.

1979. Reconciling apparent differences between responses of humans and other animals to crowding. *Psychological Review* 86: 80–5.

Fritz, J. M. 1978. Palaeopsychology today: ideational systems and human adaptation in prehistory. In C. L. Redman *et al.* (eds.), *Social Archaeology: beyond subsistence and dating*, pp. 37–60. Academic Press: New York.

Fung Pineda, R. 1988. The Late Preceramic and Initial periods. In R. W. Keatinge (ed.), *Peruvian Prehistory: an overview of pre-Inca and Inca society*, pp. 67–96. Cambridge University Press: Cambridge.

Furet, F. 1983. Beyond *Annales. The Journal of Modern History* 55: 389–410.

Galle, O. R., Grove, W. R. and McPherson, J. M. 1972. Population density and pathology: what are the relations for man? *Science* 176: 23–30.

Gamble, C. 1987. Archaeology, geography and time. *Progress in Human Geography* 11 (2): 227–46.

Gauldie, E. 1974. *Cruel Habitations: a history of working-class housing 1780–1918*. Allen and Unwin: London.

Gernet, J. 1976. *Daily Life in China on the Eve of the Mongol Invasion*. Macmillan: New York.

Gibbon, G. 1989. *Explanation in Archaeology*. Basil Blackwell: Oxford.

Giddens, A. 1979. *Central Problems in Social Theory: actions, structures and contradiction in social analysis*. Macmillan: London.

Gifford, R. 1987. *Environmental Psychology: principles and practice*. Allyn and Bacon: Boston.

Giles, F. J. 1970. *Ikhnaton: legend and history*. Hutchinson: London.

Glass, D. C. and Singer, J. E. 1972. *Urban Stress: experiments on noise and social stressors*. Academic Press: New York.

Glassie, H. 1975. *Folk Housing of Middle Virginia: a structural analysis of historical artifacts*. University of Tennessee Press: Knoxville.

Gledhill, J., Bender, B. and Larsen, M. T. (eds.) 1988. *State and Society: the emergence and development of social hierarchy and political centralization*. Unwin Hyman: London.

Gleeson, P. and Grosso, G. 1976. Ozette site. In D. R. Croes (ed.), *The Excavation of Water-Saturated Archaeological Sites (Wet Sites) on the Northwest Coast of North America*, pp. 13–34. National Museum of Man, Mercury Series, Archaeological Surveys of Canada Papers 50.

Glymour, C. 1983. Social science and social physics. *Behavioural Science* 28: 126–34.

Goodstadt, L. 1969. Urban housing in Hong Kong 1945–63. In I. C. Jarvie (ed.), *Hong Kong: a society in transition*, pp. 257–98. Routledge and Kegan Paul: London.

Goody, J. R. 1956. *The Social Organisation of the Lowilli*. HMSO: London.

Gould, R. A. 1980. *Living Archaeology*. Cambridge University Press: Cambridge.

Gould, R. A. and Watson, P. J. 1982. A dialogue on the meaning and use of analogy in ethnoarchaeological reasoning. *Journal of Anthropological Archaeology* 1: 355–81.

Gould, R. A. and Yellen, J. E. 1987. Man the hunted: determinants of household spacing in desert and tropical foraging societies. *Journal of Anthropological Archaeology* 6: 77–103.

Gould, S. J. 1965. Is Uniformitarianism necessary? *American Journal of Science* 263: 223–8.

1980. *The Panda's Thumb: more reflections in natural history*. Penguin: Harmondsworth.

1982. The meaning of punctuated equilibrium and its role in validating a hierarchical approach to macroevolution. In R. Milkman (ed.), *Perspectives on Evolution*, pp. 83–104. Sinauer Associates: Sunderland, Mass.

1986. Evolution and the triumph of homology, or why history matters. *American Scientist* 74: 60–9.

1987. *Time's Arrow and Time's Cycle: myth and metaphor in the discovery of geological time*. Harvard University Press: Cambridge, Mass.

1991. *Bully for Brontosaurus: reflections on natural history*. Hutchinson Radius: London.

Gould, S. J. and Vrba, E. S. 1982. Exaptation– a missing term in the science of form. *Paleobiology* 8 (1): 4–15.

Green, D., Haselgrove, C. and Spriggs, M. (eds.) 1978. *Social Organisation and Settlement*. BAR International Series (Supp. 47), British Archaeological Reports: Oxford.

Green, M. W. 1981. The construction and implementation of the cuneiform writing system. *Visible Language* 15 (4): 345–72.

Greer, C. 1979. *Water Management in the Yellow River Basin of China*. University of Texas Press: Austin.

Gregory, R. L. 1966. *Eye and Brain*. World University Library, Weidenfeld and Nicolson: London.

Grene, M. 1987. Hierarchies in biology. *American Scientist* 75 (5): 504–10.

Gribbin, J. 1989. Quantum rules, OK! *New Scientist* 1682: Inside Science no. 25.

Grøn, O. 1988. General spatial behaviour in small dwellings: a preliminary study in ethnoarchaeology and social psychology. In C. Bonsall (ed.), *The Mesolithic in Europe*. Papers presented at the Third International Symposium, Edinburgh, pp. 99–105. John Donald: Edinburgh.

Gross, D. R. 1984. Time allocation: a tool for the study of cultural behaviour. *Annual Review of Anthropology* 13: 519–58.

Grove, D. C. 1985. *Chalcatzingo: excavations on the Olmec frontier*. Thames and Hudson: London.

Groves, C. P. and Sabater Pi, J. 1985. From ape's nest to human fix-point. *Man* 20 (1): 22–47.

Grytzell, K. G. 1963. *The Demarcation of Comparable City Areas, by Means of Population Density*. Lund Studies in Geography, Ser. B, Human Geography no. 25, Gleerup: Lund.

Gurkaynak, M. R. and LeCompte, W. A. (eds.) 1979. *Human Consequences of Crowding*. Plenum Press: London.

Haag, R. and Konsola, D. (eds.) 1986. *Early Helladic Architecture and Urbanisation*. Proceedings of a seminar held at the Swedish Institute in Athens, 8 June 1985. Studies in Mediterranean Archaeology LXXVI. Paul Astroms Forlag: Goteborg.

Halford, G. S., Maybury, M. T. and Bain, J. D. 1988. Set-size effects in primary memory: an age related capacity limitation? *Memory and Cognition* 16 (5): 480–7.

Hall, E. T. 1966. *The Hidden Dimension*. Doubleday: Garden City: N.Y.
1968. Proxemics. *Current Anthropology* 9 (2/3): 83–108.
1974. *Handbook for Proxemic Research*. Society for the Anthropology of Visual Communication: Washington.
1977. *Beyond Culture*. Anchor Books: Garden City, N.Y.
1983. *The Dance of Life: the other dimension of time*. Anchor Books, Doubleday: New York.

Hallam, A. 1973. *Revolution in the Earth Sciences: from continental drift to plate tectonics*. Oxford University Press: Oxford.
1983. *Great Geological Controversies*. Oxford University Press: Oxford.

Hansell, A. H. 1984. *Animal Architecture and Building Behaviour*. Longman: London.

Hantzschel, W. 1975. Trace fossils and problematica. In C. Teichert (dir. and ed.), *Treatise on Invertebrate Paleontology. Part W. Miscellanea, Supplement 1*. The Geological Society of America Inc. and the University of Kansas: Boulder, Co.

Harding, S. G. (ed.) 1976. *Can Theories Be Refuted?: essays on the Duhem-Quine thesis*. Reidel: Dordrecht.

Harp, E. 1976. Dorset settlement patterns in Newfoundland and southeastern Hudson Bay. In E. Maxwell (ed.), *Eastern Arctic Prehistory: palaeoeskimo problems*, pp. 119–29. Memoirs of the Society of American Archaeology 31.

Harré, R. 1985. *The Philosophies of Science: an introductory survey* (2nd edn). Oxford University Press: Oxford.

Harris, D. 1978. Settling down: an evolutionary model for the transformation of mobile bands into sedentary communities. In J. Friedman and M. Rowlands (eds.), *The Evolution of Social Systems*, pp. 401–17. University of Pittsburgh Press: Pittsburgh.

Haselgrove, C. 1987. Culture process on the periphery: Belgic Gaul and Rome during the Late Republic and the Early Empire. In M. Rowlands, M. Larsen and K. Kristiansen (eds.), *Centre and Periphery in the Ancient World*, pp. 104–24. Cambridge University Press: Cambridge.

Hastings, C. M. and Moseley, M. E. 1975. Adobes of Huaca del Sol and Huaca de la Luna. *American Antiquity* 40 (2): 196–203.

Hastings, M. H., Waner, S. and Wu, Y. 1989. Evolutionary learning and hierarchical systems. *Biosystems* 23: 161–70.

Hassan, F. A. 1979. Prehistoric settlements along the main Nile. In M. A. J. Williams and H. Faure (eds.), *The Sahara and the Nile*, pp. 421–50. Balkema: Rotterdam.
1982. *Demographic Archaeology*. Academic Press: New York.
1993. Town and village in ancient Egypt: ecology, society and urbanization. In T. Shaw, P. Sinclair, B. Andah and A. Okpoko (eds.), *The Archaeology of Africa: foods, metals and towns*, pp. 551–69. One World Archaeology 20 (Series editor P. J. Ucko), Routledge: London.

Hastorf, C. A. 1993. *Agriculture and the Onset of Political Inequality before the Inka.* Cambridge University Press: Cambridge.

Hawking, S. 1988. *Brief History of Time.* Bantam: London.

Heisenberg, W. 1959. *Physics and Philosophy: the revolution in modern science.* Allen and Unwin: London.

Helskog, K. and Sweder, T. 1989. Estimating numbers of contemporaneous houses from 14C dates. *Antiquity* 63 (238): 168–72.

Hendy, M. D. and Penny, D. 1986. How the Theory of Evolution could be disproved but isn't. In J. B. Brook, G. C. Arnold, T. H. Hassard and R. M. Pringle (eds.), *The Fascination of Statistics*, pp. 173–82. Marcel Dekker: New York.

Heppell, M. (ed.) 1979. *A Black Reality: Aboriginal camps and housing in remote Australia.* Australian Institute of Aboriginal Studies: Canberra.

Hermansen, G. 1978. The population of Imperial Rome: the Regionares. *Historia* 27: 129–69.

Herrnstein, R. J. and Mazur, J. E. 1987. Making up our minds. *The Sciences* Nov./Dec.: 41–7.

Higgs, E. S. 1968. Archaeology – where now? *Mankind* 6: 617–20.

  1972. *Papers in Economic Prehistory.* Cambridge University Press: Cambridge.

Higgs, E. S. and Jarman, M. R. 1975. Palaeoeconomy. In E. S. Higgs and M. R. Jarman (eds.), *Palaeoeconomy*, pp. 1–7. Cambridge University Press: Cambridge.

Higham, C. 1989. *The Archaeology of Mainland Southeast Asia: from 10,000 BC to the fall of Angkor.* Cambridge University Press: Cambridge.

Hill, J. N. 1968. Broken K Pueblo: patterns of form and function. In S. R. Binford and L. R. Binford (eds.), *New Perspectives in Archaeology*, pp. 103–42. Aldine: Chicago.

Hillier, B. and Hanson, J. 1984. *The Social Logic of Space.* Cambridge University Press: Cambridge.

Hinde, R. A. 1974. *Biological Bases of Human Social Behaviour.* McGraw-Hill: New York.

Hitchcock, R. K. 1980. The ethnoarchaeology of sedentism: a Kalahari case. In *Proceedings of the 8th Pan African Congress of Prehistory and Quaternary Studies*, pp. 300–3 (Nairobi, Sept. 1977). International L. Leakey Memorial Institute: Nairobi.

Hitchcock, R. K. 1982. Patterns of sedentism among the Basarwa of Botswana. In E. Leacock and R. B. Lee (eds.), *Politics and History in Band Societies*, pp. 223–67. Cambridge University Press: New York.

Hobsbawm, E. 1979. An historian's comments. In B. C. Burnham and J. Kingsbury (eds.), *Space, Hierarchy and Society: interdisciplinary studies in social area analysis.* BAR International Series 59: 247–52, British Archaeological Reports: Oxford.

Hodder, I. R. (ed.) 1982. *Symbolic and Structural Archaeology.* Cambridge University Press: Cambridge.

  1984a. Burials, houses, women and men in the European Neolithic. In D. Miller and C. Tilley (eds.), *Ideology, Power and Prehistory*, pp. 51–68. Cambridge University Press: Cambridge.

  1984b. Archaeology in 1984. *Antiquity* 58: 25–32.

  1985. Post-processual archaeology. In M. B. Schiffer (ed.), *Advances in Archaeological Method and Theory* 8: 1–26.

  1986. *Reading the Past.* Cambridge University Press: Cambridge.

  1987. The contribution of the long term. In I. R. Hodder (ed.), *Archaeology as Long Term History*, pp. 1–8. Cambridge University Press: Cambridge.

Hoffman, M. A. 1972. Process and tradition in Cypriot culture history: time theory in anthropology. *Quarterly Review of Anthropology* 5 (1): 15–34.

  1979. *Egypt Before the Pharoahs: the prehistoric foundations of Egyptian civilisation.* Alfred Knopf: New York.

1982. Settlement patterns and settlement systems. In M. A. Hoffman (ed.), *The Predynastic of Hierakonpolis: an interim report*, pp. 122–38. Faculty of Science, Department of Sociology and Anthropology, W. Illinois University: Macomb, and Cairo University Herbarium: Giza.

Holdaway, S. and Johnston, S. A. 1989. Upper Paleolithic notation systems in prehistoric Europe. *Expedition* 31 (1): 3–11.

Hookyas, R. 1963. *Natural Law and Divine Miracle: the principle of uniformity in geology, biology and theology*. Brill: Leiden.

Huelsbeck, D. 1983. Mammals and fish in the subsistence economy of Ozette. Ph.D. dissertation, University Microfilms: Ann Arbor.

Hull, R. W. 1976. *African Cities and Towns before the European Conquest*. Norton: New York.

Hyde, G. E. 1974. *The Pawnee Indians*. Oklahoma University Press: Norman.

Ingold, T. 1986. *Evolution and Social Life*. Cambridge University Press: Cambridge.

Institute of Archaeology, Academia Sinica and the Pan P'o Museum (eds.) 1962. *The Neolithic Village at Pan-p'o*. Wen Wu Press: Peking.

Isaac, G. Ll. 1972. Chronology and tempo of cultural change during the Pleistocene. In W. W. Bishop and J. A. Miller (eds.), *Calibration of Hominoid Evolution*, pp. 281–430. Scottish Academic Press: Edinburgh.

Isbell, W. H. 1977. *The Rural Foundations for Urbanism: economic and stylistic interaction between rural and urban communities in eighth-century Peru*. Illinois Studies in Anthropology no. 10, University of Illinois Press: Urbana.

1984. Huari urban prehistory. In A. Kendall (ed.), *Current Archaeological Projects in the Central Andes: some approaches and results*, pp. 95–131. BAR International Series 210, British Archaeological Reports: Oxford.

Jahoda, G. 1966. Geometric illusions and environment: a study in Ghana. *British Journal of Psychology* 57: 193–9.

Jansen, M. 1979. *Architektur in der Harappakultur: eine kritische Betrachtung zum umbauten Raum im Industal des 3–2 Jahrtausends*. Veröffenlichungen des Seminars für Orientalische Kunstgeschichte an der Universität Bonn, series B. Antiquitates Orientales vol. 2. Rudolf Habelt Verlag GmbH.

1989. Water supply and sewage disposal at Mohenjo-daro. *World Archaeology* 21 (2): 177–92.

Jantsch, E. 1979. *The Self Organising Universe: scientific and human implications of the emerging paradigm of evolution*. Pergamon Press: Oxford.

Jeffreys, D. G. and Giddy, L. 1992. Towards Archaic Memphis. *Egyptian Archaeology* 2: 6–8.

Jewitt, J. R. (1967 edition). *Narrative of the Adventures and Sufferings of John R. Jewitt: only survivor of the crew of the ship Boston, during a captivity of nearly three years among the savages of Nootka Sound*. Ye Galleon Press: Fairfield.

Jochim, M. A. 1991. Archaeology as long-term ethnography. *American Anthropologist* 93 (2): 295–308.

Johnson, G. A. 1981. Monitoring complex system integration and boundary phenomena with settlement size data. In S. E. van de Leeuw (ed.), *Archaeological Approaches to the Study of Complexity*, pp. 143–88. University of Amsterdam Press: Amsterdam.

1982. Organizational structure and scalar stress. In C. R. Renfrew, M. Rowlands and B. A. Seagraves (eds.), *Theory and Explanation in Archaeology: the Southampton conference*, pp. 389–421. Academic Press: London.

Kabo, V. 1985. The origins of the food producing economy. *Current Anthropology* 26 (5): 601–16.

Kaplan, D. 1963. Men, monuments and political systems. *Southwestern Journal of Anthropology* 19: 397–410.

Kauffman, S. A. 1993. *The Origins of Order: self-organization and selection in evolution.* Oxford University Press: New York.

Kaye, B. 1960. *Upper Nankin Street Singapore: a sociological study of Chinese households living in a densely populated area.* University of Malaya Press: Singapore.

Keegan, J. 1976. *The Face of Battle.* Cape: London.

Kelley, J. and Hanen, M. 1988. *Archaeology and the Methodology of Science.* University of New Mexico Press: Albuquerque.

Kelly, R. L. 1992. Mobility/sedentism: concepts, archaeological measures and effects. *Annual Review of Anthropology* 21: 43–66.

Kemp, B. J. 1977. The early development of towns in Egypt. *Antiquity* 51: 185–200.
   1989. *Ancient Egypt: anatomy of a civilisation.* Routledge: London.

Kendon, A. and Ferber, A. 1973. A description of some human greetings. In J. H. Crook and R. P. Michael (eds.), *Comparative Ecology and Behaviour of Primates*, pp. 591–668. Academic Press: London.

Kenoyer, J. M. 1991. The Indus valley tradition of Pakistan and western India. *Journal of World Prehistory* 5 (4): 331–85.

Kent, S. 1986. The influence of sedentism and aggregation on porotic hyperostosis and anemia in the North American Southwest. *Man* 21 (4): 605–36.
   (ed.) 1989. *Farmers as Hunters: the implications of sedentism.* Cambridge University Press: Cambridge.
   (ed.) 1990. *Domestic Architecture and the Use of Space: an interdisciplinary cross-cultural study.* Cambridge University Press: Cambridge.
   1992. The current forager controversy: real versus ideal views of hunter-gatherers. *Man* (NS) 27: 45–70.

Khan, A. N. (ed.) 1973. *Proceedings of International Symposium on Moenjodaro.* National Book Foundation: Karachi.

Kinser, S. 1981. Annaliste paradigm? The geohistorical structuralism of Fernand Braudel. *The American Historical Review* 86 (1): 63–105.

Knapp, A. B. 1992. Archaeology and *Annales*: time, space and change. In A. B. Knapp (ed.), *Archaeology,* Annales *and Ethnohistory*, pp. 1–21. Cambridge University Press: Cambridge.

Kobylinski, Z. 1986. *Ethnoarchaeological cognition and cognitive archaeology.* In *Archaeological 'Objectivity' in Interpretation, vol. 1, section A,* Conference Proceedings, World Archaeological Congress, pp. 1–10. Allen and Unwin: London.

Kobylinski, Z., Lenata, J. L. and Yacabaccio, H. D. 1987. On processual archaeology and the radical critique. *Current Anthropology* 28 (5): 680–2.

Koestler, A. and Smythies, J. R. (eds.) 1969. *Beyond Reductionism: new perspectives in the life sciences.* Hutchinson: London.

Kohl, P. 1985. Symbolic cognitive archaeology: a new loss of innocence. *Dialectical Anthropology* 9: 105–17.

Kolb, C. C. 1985. Demographic estimates in archaeology. See CA* Comment by R. J. Fletcher. *Current Anthropology* 26 (5): 581–99.

Konvitz, J. W. 1985. *The Urban Millennium: the city building process from the early Middle Ages to the present.* Southern Illinois University Press: Carbondale and Edwardville.

Kraemer, W. 1982. Graffiti auf Spätlatènekeramik aus Manching. *Germania* 60: 489–99.

Krishna, K. and Weesner, F. M. (eds.) 1970. *Biology of Termites II*, pp. 73–125. Academic Press: New York.

Krupat, E. 1985. *People in Cities: the urban environment and its effects.* Cambridge University Press: Cambridge.

Kudoh, T. and Matsumoto, D. 1985. Cross-cultural examination of the semantic dimension of body postures. *Journal of Personality and Social Psychology* 48 (1): 54–62.

Lakatos, I. 1978. *The Methodology of Scientific Research Programmes*. Cambridge University Press: Cambridge.

Lakatos, I. and Musgrave, A. (eds.) 1970. *Criticism and the Growth of Knowledge*. Cambridge University Press: Cambridge.

Lambrick, H. T. 1964. *Sind: a general introduction*. Sindhi Adabi Board: Hyderabad.

1973. *Sind Before the Muslim Conquest*. Oxford University Press: Karachi.

Landers, J. 1987. Mortality and metropolis: the case of London 1675–1825. *Population Studies* 41 (1): 59–76.

Landes, D. S. 1983. *Revolution in Time: clocks and the making of the modern world*. Belknap Press of Harvard University Press: Cambridge, Mass.

Langer, S. K. 1971. The great shift: instinct to intuition. In J. F. Eisenberg and W. S. Dillon (eds.), *Man and Beast: comparative social behaviour*. Smithsonian Institution Press: Washington, D.C.

Langley, J. C. 1993. Symbols, signs and writing systems. In K. Benin and E. Pasztory (eds.), *Teotihuacan: art from the city of the gods*, pp. 128–39. Thames and Hudson: New York.

Langton, J. and Morris, R. J. (eds.) 1986. *Atlas of Industrialising Britain, 1780–1914*. Methuen: London.

Larco Hoyle, R. 1939. *Los Mochicas I–II*. Casa Editora: Rimac, Lima.

1943. La escritura Peruana sobre pallares. *Revista Geográphica Americana* Año XI.

Larsen, H. and Rainey, F. 1948. *Ipiutak and the Arctic Whale Hunting Culture*. American Museum of Natural History, Anthropological Papers 42, American Museum of Natural History: New York.

Lassner, J. 1970. *Topography of Baghdad in the Early Middle Ages: texts and studies*. Wayne State University Press: Detroit.

Lawrence, R. J. 1982. Domestic space and society: a cross-cultural study. *Comparative Studies in Society and History* 24 (1): 104–31.

Leach, E. R. 1973. Concluding remarks. In C. Renfrew (ed.), *The Explanation of Culture Change*, pp. 761–71. Duckworth: London.

1976. *Culture and Communication: the logic by which symbols are connected*. Cambridge University Press: Cambridge.

1979. Discussion. In B. C. Burnham and J. Kingsbury (eds.), *Space, Hierarchy and Society: interdisciplinary studies in social area analysis*. BAR International Series 59: 119–24, British Archaeological Reports: Oxford.

LeBlanc, S. 1971. An addition to Naroll's suggested floor area and settlement population relationship. *American Antiquity* 36 (2): 210–11.

Lenntorp, B. 1976. *Paths in Space–Time Environments: a time geographic study of movement possibilities of individuals*. Meddelanden, Fran Lunds Universitets, Geografiska Institution.

Lenzen, H. J. (with H. J. Nissen) 1968. *Uruk-Warka XXIV*. Deutsches Archäologisches Institut. Abteilung Baghdad. Mann Verlag: Berlin.

Leonard, R. D. and Jones, G. T. 1987. Elements of an inclusive evolutionary model for archaeology. *Journal of Anthropological Archaeology* 6: 199–219.

Leone, M. P. 1982a. Childe's offspring. In I. Hodder (ed.), *Symbolic and Structural Archaeology*, pp. 179–84. Cambridge University Press: Cambridge.

1982b. Some opinions about recovering Mind. *American Antiquity* 47 (4): 742–60.

Leone, M. P., Potter, P. B. and Shackel, P. A. 1987. Toward a critical archaeology. *Current Anthropology* 28 (3): 283–302.

Levine, D. N. 1960. On the conceptions of time and space in the Amhara world view. *Studi Etiopici* 48: 22–32.

Lewin, J. 1980. Available and appropriate timescales in geomorphology. In R. A. Cullingford, D. A. Davidson and J. Lewin (eds.), *Timescales in Geomorphology*, pp. 3–10. Wiley and Sons: Chichester.

Lewis, M. J. T. 1970. *Early Wooden Railways*. Routledge and Kegan Paul: London.

Lewontin, R. C. 1974. *The Genetic Basis of Evolutionary Change*. Columbia University Press: New York.

Lieberman, D. E. 1992. Seasonality and gazelle hunting at Hayonim cave: new evidence for 'sedentism' during the Natufian. *Paléorient* 17 (1): 47–57.

Linge, G. J. R. 1965. *The Delimitation of Urban Boundaries for Statistical Purposes: with special reference to Australia. A report for the Commonwealth statistician*. Department of Geography, Research School of Pacific Studies, Publication G/2. Australian National University Press: Canberra.

Littauer, M. A. 1977. Rock carvings of chariots in Transcaucasia, Central Asia and Outer Mongolia. *Proceedings of the Prehistoric Society* 43: 243–62.

Lloyd, C. 1988. *Explanation in Social History*. Blackwell: Oxford.

Longacre, W. 1970. *Archaeology as Anthropology: a case study*. University of Arizona Press: Tucson.

Lucas, C. 1985. Introduction. In J. LeGoff and P. Nora (eds.), *Constructing the Past: essays in historical methodology*, pp. 1–11. Cambridge University Press: Cambridge, and Editions de la Maison de Sciences de l'Homme: Paris.

Lumsden, C. J. and Wilson, E. O. 1981. *Genes, Mind and Culture*. Harvard University Press: Cambridge, Mass.

Lym, O. R. 1980. *A Psychology of Building* (The Patterns of Social Behaviour Series). Prentice-Hall: New Jersey.

McBreaty, S. 1990. Consider the humble termite: termites as agents of post-depositional disturbance at African archaeological sites. *Journal of Archaeological Science* 17: 111–43.

Macdonald, G. F. 1983. *Haida Monumental Art: villages of the Queen Charlotte Islands*. University of British Columbia Press: Vancouver.

McNeish, R. S., Garcia Cook, A., Lumbreras, L. G., Vierra, R. K. and Nelken-Turner, A. 1981. *Prehistory of the Ayacucho Basin, Peru, Vol. II. Excavations and Chronology*. The University of Michigan Press: Ann Arbor.

Mango, C. 1985. *Le Développement urbain de Constantinople (IVe–VIIe siècles)*. Travaux et Mémoires du Centre de Recherches d'Histoire et Civilisation de Byzance. Monographies 2. Collège de France.

Marcus, J. 1980. Zapotec writing. *Scientific American* (Feb.): 46–60.

Marshack, A. 1991. The Tai plaque and calendrical notation in the Upper Palaeolithic. *Cambridge Archaeological Journal* 1 (1): 25–61.

Mathes, V. S. 1979. Wickaninnish: a Clayoquot chief as recorded by early travellers. *Pacific Quarterly* (July): 110–20.

Matrix, 1984. *Making Space: women and the man-made environment*. Pluto Press: London.

Mayhew, A. 1858. *Paved with Gold, or, The Romance and Reality of the Streets of London: an unfashionable novel*. Chapman and Hall: London.

Meares, J. 1790. [1967 edition]. *Voyages made in the Years 1788 and 1789 from China to the North-West Coast of America*. Bibliotheca Australiana 22. N. Israel: Amsterdam, and Da Capo Press: New York.

Mehrabian, A. 1976. *Public Places and Private Spaces: the psychology of work, play and living environments*. Basic Books: New York.

Meier, R. L. 1962. *A Communications Theory of Urban Growth*. MIT Press: Cambridge, Mass.

Mellaart, J. 1975. *The Neolithic of the Near East*. Charles Scribner's Sons: New York.

Meltzer, D. 1979. Paradigms and the nature of change in archaeology. *American Antiquity* 46 (4): 644–57.

Miller, D. 1982. Explanation and social theory in archaeological practice. In C. R. Renfrew, M. Rowlands and B. A. Seagraves (eds.), *Theory and Explanation in Archaeology: the Southampton conference*, pp. 83–95. Academic Press: London.

  1985. *Artifacts as Categories*. Cambridge University Press: Cambridge.

  1987. *Material Culture and Mass Communication*. Blackwell: Oxford, New York.

Miller, D. and Tilley, C. (eds.) 1984. *Ideology, Power and Prehistory*. Cambridge University Press: Cambridge.

Miller, D(avid). 1982. Conjectural knowledge: Popper's solution of the problem of induction. In P. Levinson (ed.), *In Pursuit of Truth: essays in honour of Karl Popper's 80th birthday*, pp. 17–49. Humanities Press and Harvester Press: London.

Miller, G. A. 1956. The magical number seven, plus or minus two. Some limits on our capacity to process information. *Psychological Review* 63: 81–97.

Millon, C. 1973. Painting, writing and polity in Teotihuacan, Mexico. *American Antiquity* 38 (3): 294–314.

Millon, R., Drewitt, B. and Cowgill, G. 1973. *Urbanization at Teotihuacan, Mexico, Vol. I: The Teotihuacan Map. Part I: text*. University of Texas Press: Austin.

Mitchell, R. E. 1971. Some social implications of high-density housing. *American Sociological Review* 36: 18–29.

Mithen, S. J. 1989. Evolutionary theory and post-processual archaeology. *Antiquity* 63: 483–94.

Mohr Chavez, K. L. 1988. The significance of Chiripa in Lake Titicaca basin developments. *Expedition* 30 (3): 17–26.

Monter, E. W. 1975. *Calvin's Geneva*. Kreiger: Huntingdon, N.Y.

Montgomery, R. G., Smith, W. and Brew, J. O. 1949. *Franciscan Awatovi*. Papers of the Peabody Museum 36.

Moore, H. 1986. *Space, Text and Gender: an anthropological study of the Marakwet of Kenya*. Cambridge University Press: Cambridge.

Moratto, M. J. 1984. *California Archaeology*. Academic Press: Orlando.

Moseley, M. E. 1982. The land in front of Chan-Chan. In M. E. Moseley and K. C. Day (eds.), *Chan-Chan: Andean desert city*, pp. 25–53. University of New Mexico Press: Albuquerque.

  1983. Patterns of settlement and preservation in the Viru and Moche valleys. In E. T. Vogt and R. Leventhal (eds.), *Prehistoric Settlement Patterns: essays in honour of Gordon Willey*, pp. 423–42. University of New Mexico Press: Albuquerque.

  1992. *The Incas and their Ancestors: the archaeology of Peru*. Thames and Hudson: London.

Moseley, M. E. and Richardson, J.B. III. 1992. Doomed by natural disaster. *Archaeology* 45 (6): 44–5.

Moule, A. C. 1957. *Quinsai with Other Notes on Marco Polo*. Cambridge University Press: Cambridge.

Mughal, M. R. 1972. Present state of research on the Indus valley civilisation. In A. N. Khan (ed.), *Proceedings of International Symposium on Moenjodaro*, pp. 1–28. National Book Foundation: Karachi.

  1980. Archaeological surveys in Bahawalpur (189 pages). Cyclostyled: Karachi.

Mujica Barreda, E. 1978. Nueva hipotesis sobre el desarrollo temprano del antiplano, del Titicaca y de sus areas de interaccion. *Arte y Arquelogia* 5–6: 285–308.

Munn, N. 1992. The cultural anthropology of Time. *Annual Review of Anthropology* 21: 93–123.

Murray, T. A. 1987. Remembrance of things present. Ph.D. thesis, Dept of Anthropology, University of Sydney.

1988. Ethnoarchaeology or palaeoethnology? In B. Meehan and R. Jones (eds.), *Archaeology with Ethnography: an Australian perspective*, pp. 1–16. Department of Prehistory, Research School of Pacific Studies, Australian National University: Canberra.

1990. Why plausibility matters. *Australian Archaeology* 31: 98–102.

Murray, T. and Walker, M. 1987. Like WHAT? A practical question of archaeological inference and archaeological meaningfulness. *Journal of Anthropological Archaeology* 7: 248–87.

Naroll, R. 1962. Floor area and settlement population. *American Antiquity* 27 (4): 587–9.

Nash, S. (ed.) 1985. *Science and Uncertainty*. Science Reviews: Northwood.

Needham, J. 1965. *Time and Eastern Man*. Royal Anthropological Institute of Great Britain and Ireland: London.

1971. *Science and Civilisation in China. Vol. 2, Physics and Physical Technology, Part III – Civil Engineering and Nautics*. Cambridge University Press: Cambridge.

Needham, J., Wang Ling and De Solla Price, D. J. 1960. *Heavenly Clockwork: the great astronomical clocks of medieval China*. Cambridge University Press: Cambridge.

Nelson, E. W. 1896–7. *The Eskimo about Bering Strait*. Bureau of American Ethnology, 18th Annual Report: 3–518.

Netting, R. McC. 1965. Household organisation and intensive agriculture: the Kofyar case. *Africa* 35: 422–9.

Newman, O. 1973. *Defensible Space*. Architectural Press: London.

Nicholas, L. M. 1989. Land use in prehispanic Oaxaca. In S. A. Kowalewki, G. M. Finsten, R. E. Blanton and L. M. Nicholas (eds.), *Monte Albán's Hinterland, Part II: Prehispanic settlement in Tlacolula, Etla, and Ocotlan, the valley of Oaxaca, Mexico*. Memoirs of the Museum of Anthropology, University of Michigan 23.

Niederberger, C. 1979. Early sedentary economy in the Basin of Mexico. *Science* 203 (4376): 131–42.

O'Connell, J. F. 1977. Room to move: contemporary Alyawara settlement patterns and their implications for Aboriginal housing policy. *Mankind* 11: 119–30.

1987. Alyawara site structure and its archaeological implications. *American Antiquity* 52 (1): 74–108.

O'Connor, D. 1993. Urbanism in bronze age Egypt and northeast Africa. In T. Shaw, P. Sinclair, B. Andah and A. Okpoko (eds.), *The Archaeology of Africa: foods, metals and towns*, pp. 570–86. One World Archaeology 20 (Series editor P. J. Ucko). Routledge: London.

Oliveira, D. L. 1986. Monuments and social complexity: a new line of enquiry. *Oxford Journal of Archaeology* 5 (1): 103–10.

Oreskes, N. 1988. The rejection of continental drift. *Historical Studies in the Physical Sciences* 18 (2): 311–48.

Orme, B. 1981. *Anthropology for Archaeologists: an introduction*. Duckworth: London.

Painter, G. D. 1984. *Studies in Fifteenth Century Printing*. Pindar Press: London.

Parkes, D. and Thrift, N. 1980. *Times, Spaces and Places: a chronogeographic perspective*. Wiley: Chichester.

Parsons, E. C. 1929. *The Social Organisation of the Tewa of New Mexico*. Memoirs of the American Anthropological Association 36: 7–309.

Parsons, J. R., Kintigh, K. W. and Gregg, S. A. 1983. *Archaeological Settlement Pattern Data from the Chalco, Xochimilco, Ixtapalapa, Texcoco and Zumpango Regions*. Research Report in Anthropology, Contribution 9. Technical Reports 14. Museum of Anthropology, University of Michigan.

Pasher, H. 1993. Doing two things at the same time. *American Scientist* 81 (1): 48–55.

Paynter, R. 1982. *Models of Spatial Inequality*. Academic Press: New York.

Pearce, D. 1976. *Social Cost of Noise.* Organisation of Economic Cooperation and Development Environment Directorate: Paris.

Pearson, K. 1897. On a form of spurious correlation which may arise when indices are used in the measurement of organs. *Proceedings of the Royal Society of London* 60: 489–502.

Pettit, P. 1975. *The Concept of Structuralism: a critical analysis.* Gill and Macmillan: Dublin.

Petty, W. 1888. *Essays on Man and Political Arithmetic.* Cassell and Co.: London.

Ponsonby-Fane, R. A. B. 1956. *Kyoto: the old capital of Japan (794–1869).* The Ponsonby Memorial Society: Kamikamo, Kyoto.

Popper, K. R. 1976. *Unended Quest: an intellectual autobiography.* Fontana: London.
  1980. *The Logic of Scientific Discovery,* 10th edn. Hutchinson: London.

Posnansky, M. 1980. Trade and the development of the state and town in Iron Age West Africa. In R. E. Leakey and B. A. Ogot (eds.), *Proceedings of the 8th Pan-African Congress of Prehistory and Quaternary Studies* (Nairobi, 1977), pp. 373–5. International Louis Leakey Memorial Institute for African Prehistory: Nairobi.

Possehl, G. L. 1990. Revolution in the Urban Revolution: the emergence of Indus urbanization. *Annual Review of Anthropology* 19: 261–82.

Pottinger, G. 1983. Explanation, rationality and micro-economic theory. *Behavioural Science* 28: 109–25.

Poyatos, F. 1988. Introduction. Non-verbal communication studies: their development as an interdisciplinary field and the term 'non-verbal'. In F. Poyatos (ed.), *Cross-Cultural Perspectives in Nonverbal Communication,* pp. 1–32. Hogrefe: Toronto.

Pozorski, S. and Pozorski, T. 1991. Early civilisation in the Casma valley. *Antiquity* 66 (253): 845–70.

Preucel, R. 1990. *Seasonal Circulation and Dual Residence in the Pueblo Southwest: a prehistoric example from the Pajarito Plateau, New Mexico.* Garland: Hamden, Conn.
  (ed.) 1991. *Processual and Postprocessual Archaeologies: multiple ways of knowing the past.* Center for Archaeological Investigations, Southern Illinois University: Carbondale.

Preziosi, D. 1979. *Semiotics of the Built Environment: an introduction to architectonic analysis.* Indiana University Press: Bloomington.

Price, B. J. 1982. Cultural materialism: a theoretical review. *American Antiquity* 47 (4): 709–41.

Price, T. D. and Brown, J. A. 1985. *Prehistoric Hunter-Gatherers: the emergence of cultural complexity.* Academic Press: Orlando.

Price-Williams, R. 1885. The population of London 1801–1881. *Journal of the Royal Statistical Society* 48: 349–440.

Prigogine, I. 1978. Time, structure and fluctuations. *Science* 201: 777–85.

Prigogine, I. and Stengers, I. 1984. *Order out of Chaos: man's new dialogue with nature.* Bantam Books: Toronto.

Pryor, E. G. 1983. *Housing in Hong Kong,* 2nd edn. Oxford University Press: Hong Kong.

Raab, L. M. and Goodyear, A. C. 1984. Middle-range theory in archaeology: a critical review of origins and applications. *American Antiquity* 49 (2): 255–68.

Rafferty, J. E. 1985. The archaeological record of sedentariness: recognition, development and implications. *Advances in Archaeological Method and Theory* 8: 113–56.

Raikes, R. L. 1984. Mohenjo-daro environment. In B. B. Lal, S. P. Gupta and S. Asthana (eds.), *Frontiers of the Indus Civilisation,* pp. 455–60. Books and Books: New Delhi.

Rainwater, L. 1974. *Social Problems and Public Policy.* Aldine: Chicago.

Ramsey, S. C. and Harvey, J. D. M. 1972. *Small Georgian Houses and their Details 1750–1820.* Architectural Press: London.

Rapoport, A. 1969. *House Form and Culture.* Prentice Hall: Englewood Cliffs.

1975. Towards a redefinition of density. *Environmental Behaviour* 7: 133–58.

1982. *The Meaning of the Built Environment (a Non-verbal Communication Approach)*. Sage Publications: Beverly Hills.

1988. Levels of meaning in the built environment. In F. Poyatos (ed.), *Cross-Cultural Perspectives in Nonverbal Communication*, pp. 317–36. Hogrefe: Toronto.

1990. Systems of activities and systems of settings. In S. Kent (ed.), *Domestic Architecture and the Use of Space: an interdisciplinary cross-cultural study*, pp. 9–20. Cambridge University Press: Cambridge.

Rathje, W. L. 1974. The Garbage project: a new way to look at the problems of archaeology. *Archaeology* 27 (4): 236–41.

1978. Archaeological ethnography. In R. A. Gould (ed.), *Explorations in Ethnoarchaeology*, pp. 49–76. University of New Mexico Press: Albuquerque.

1979. Modern material culture studies. In M. B. Schiffer (ed.), *Advances in Archaeological Method and Theory* 2: 1–37.

Redman, C. L. 1978. *The Rise of Civilisation: from early farmers to urban society in the Ancient Near East*. Freeman and Co.: San Francisco.

1991. In defense of the seventies – the adolescence of New Archaeology. *American Anthropologist* 93 (2): 295–307.

Redman, C. L., Berman, M. J., Curtin, E. V., Langhorne, W. T. Jr, Vesaggi, N. M. and Wanser, J. C. (eds.) 1978. *Social Archaeology: beyond subsistence and dating*. Academic Press: New York.

Renfrew, C. 1972. *The Emergence of Civilisation: the Cyclades and the Aegean in the third millennium B.C.* Methuen: London.

1979. Dialogues of the deaf. In B. C. Burnham and J. Kingsbury (eds.), *Space, Hierarchy and Society: interdisciplinary studies in social area analysis*, pp. 253–9. BAR International Series 59, British Archaeological Reports: Oxford.

1982. Explanation revisited. In C. Renfrew, M. J. Rowlands and B. A. Seagraves (eds.), *Theory and Explanation in Archaeology: the Southampton conference*, pp. 1–23. Academic Press: New York.

Renouf, M. A. P. 1989. Sedentary coastal hunter-fishers: an example from the Younger Stone Age of northern Norway. In G. N. Bailey and J. Parkington (eds.), *The Archaeology of Prehistoric Coastlines*, pp. 102–15. Cambridge University Press: Cambridge.

Reynolds, V. 1972. Ethology of urban life. In P. J. Ucko, R. Tringham and G. W. Dimbleby (eds.), *Man, Settlement and Urbanism*, pp. 401–8. Duckworth: London.

Ricketts, B. D. 1988. Uniformitarianism – a metaphor of human experience. *Modern Geology* 13: 69–82.

Rindos, D. 1984. *The Origins of Agriculture: an evolutionary perspective*. Academic Press: Orlando.

1988. Diversity, variation and selection. In R. B. Leonard and G. T. Jones (eds.), *The Concept and Measure of Archaeological Diversity*, pp. 13–23. Cambridge University Press: Cambridge.

1989. Undirected variation and the Darwinian explanation of cultural change. In M. B. Schiffer (ed.), *Archaeological Method and Theory* 1, pp. 1–45. University of Arizona Press: Tucson.

Robben, A. C. G. M. 1989. Habits of the home: spatial hegemony and the structuration of house and society in Brazil. *American Anthropologist* 91 (3): 570–88.

Rohn, A. 1971. *Mug House, Mesa Verde National Park Colorado: Wetherill Mesa excavations*. National Parks Service, US Department of the Interior: Washington.

Rossignol, J. and Wandsnider, L. (eds.) 1992. *Space, Time and Archaeological Landscapes*. Plenum Press: New York.

Rowley-Conwy, P. 1983. Sedentary hunters: the Ertebølle example. In G. N. Bailey (ed.), *Hunter-gatherer Economy in Prehistory*, pp. 111–26. Cambridge University Press: Cambridge.

Rozman, G. 1973. *Urban Networks of Ch'ing China and Tokugawa Japan*. Princeton University Press: Princeton, N.J.

Rubenstein, D. I. and Wragham, R. W. (eds.) 1986. *Ecological Aspects of Social Evolution*. Princeton University Press: Princeton.

Rudé, G. 1971. *Hanoverian London. 1714–1808*. Secker and Warburg: London.

Russell, J. C. 1985. *Late Ancient and Medieval Population Control*. The American Philosophical Society: Philadelphia.

Rymer, L. 1978. The use of uniformitarianism and analogy in paleoecology, particularly in pollen analysis. In D. Walker and J. Guppy (eds.), *Biology and Quaternary Environments*, pp. 245–57. Australian Academy of Sciences: Canberra.

Sabloff, J. A. (ed.) 1981. *Handbook of Middle American Indians. Supplement 1. Archaeology* (gen. ed. V. R. Bricker). University of Texas Press: Austin.

Sahlins, M. 1977. *The Use and Abuse of Biology: an anthropological critique of sociobiology*. Michigan University Press: Ann Arbor.

Salmon, M. H. 1982. *Philosophy and Archaeology*. Academic Press: New York.

Salthe, S. N. 1985. *Evolving Hierarchical Systems: their structure and representation*. New York: Columbia University Press.

Samuel, G. 1990. *Mind, Body and Culture: anthropology and the biological interface*. Cambridge University Press: Cambridge.

Sanders, D. H. 1985. Ancient behaviour and the built environment: applying environmental psychological methods and theories to archaeological contexts. In S. Klein and R. Wener (eds.), *Environmental Change/Social Change*. (EDRA 16), pp. 296–305. EDRA: Washington, D.C.

 1990. Behavioural contentions and archaeology: methods for the analysis of ancient architecture. In S. Kent (ed.), *Domestic Architecture and the Use of Space: an interdisciplinary cross-cultural study*, pp. 43–72. Cambridge University Press: Cambridge.

Sanders, W. T., Parsons, R. J. and Santley, R. W. 1979. *The Basin of Mexico: ecological processes in the evolution of a civilisation*. Academic Press: New York.

Sangalli, A. 1987. The incompleteness of arithmetic. *New Scientist* 1585: 42–5.

Say, J. B. 1880. *A Treatise on Political Economy or the Production, Distribution and Consumption of Wealth* (1964 reprint edn). Kelley: New York.

Schaller, G. B. 1963. *The Mountain Gorilla: ecology and behaviour*. University of Chicago Press: Chicago.

Schiffer, M. B. 1981. Some issues in the philosophy of archaeology. *American Antiquity* 46: 899–908.

 1985. Is there a Pompeii premise in archaeology? *Journal of Anthropological Research* 41: 18–41.

Schmandt-Besserat, D. 1986. The origins of writing: an archaeologist's perspective. *Written Communication* 3 (1): 31–45.

 1992. *Before Writing: from counting to cuneiform*. University of Texas Press: Austin.

Schmid, M. and Wuketits, F. M. (eds.) 1987. *Evolutionary Theory in Social Science*. Reidel: Dordrecht.

Schrire, C. 1980. An inquiry into the evolutionary status and apparent identity of San hunter-gatherers. *Human Ecology* 8 (1): 9–30.

Schubert, F. 1972. Manching IV. Vorbericht über die ausgrabungen in den jahren 1965 bis 1967. *Germania* 50: 110–21.

Schumm, S. A. and Lichty, R. W. 1965. Time, space and causality in geomorphology. *American Journal of Science* 263: 110–19.

Schwerdfeger, F. 1971. Housing in Zaria. In P. Oliver (ed.), *Shelter in Africa*, pp. 58–79. Barrie and Jenkins: London.

Seidensticker, E. 1983. *Low City, High City: Tokyo from Edo to the earthquake, 1867–1923*. Penguin: Harmondsworth.

Seilacher, A. 1977. Evolution of trace fossil communities. In A. Hallam (ed.), *Patterns of Evolution as Illustrated in the Fossil Record*, pp. 359–76. Developments in Palaeontology and Stratigraphy 5. Elsevier Scientific Publishing: Amsterdam.

Shanks, M. and Tilley, C. 1987a. *Re-constructing Archaeology*. Cambridge University Press: Cambridge.

1987b. *Social Theory and Archaeology*. Polity Press: Cambridge.

Shannon, C. E. and Weaver, W. 1949. *The Mathematical Theory of Communication*. University of Illinois Press: Urbana.

Shea, J. H. 1982. Twelve fallacies of uniformitarianism. *Geology* 10: 455–60.

Shennan, S. 1989. Cultural transmission and cultural change. In S. E. van der Leeuw and R. Torrence (eds.), *What's New? A closer look at the process of innovation*, pp. 331–46. Unwin Hyman: London.

Shimada, I., Schaat, C. B., Thompson, L. G. and Mosley-Thompson, E. 1991. Cultural impacts of severe droughts in the prehistoric Andes: application of a 1,500 year ice core precipitation record. *World Archaeology* 22 (3): 247–70.

Shinnie, M. 1965. *Ancient African Kingdoms*. Edward Arnold: London.

Siegman, A. W. and Feldstein, S. (eds.) 1979. *Of Speech and Time: temporal speech patterns in interpersonal contexts*. Erlbaum: Hillsdale.

Silverman, H. 1988. Cahuasi: non-urban cultural complexity on the south coast of Peru. *Journal of Field Archaeology* 15 (4): 403–30.

Simpson, G. G. 1970. Uniformitarianism, an inquiry into principle, theory and method in geohistory and biohistory. In M. K. Hecht and W. C. Stiere (eds.), *Essays in Evolution and Genetics in Honour of Theodosius Dobzhansky*, pp. 43–96. Appleton: New York.

Skinner, G. W. (ed.) 1977. *The City in Late Imperial China*. Stanford University Press: Stanford.

Small, D. B. 1987. Towards a competent structuralist archaeology: a contribution from historical studies. *Journal of Anthropological Archaeology* 6: 105–21.

SMH 1990. *Sydney Morning Herald*. Wednesday 24 January.

Smiles, S. 1874. *The Lives of George and Robert Stephenson* (1975 edn). Folio Society: London.

Smith, B. D. 1977. Archaeological inference and inductive confirmation. *American Anthropologist* 79: 598–617.

Smith, C. A. 1982. Placing formal geographical models into cultural contexts: the anthropological study of urban systems. *Comparative Urban Research* 9 (1): 50–9.

Smith, H. S. 1974. *A Visit to Ancient Egypt: life at Memphis and Saqqara (c. 500–30 BC)*. Aris and Phillips: Warminster.

Smith, M. E. 1992. Braudel's temporal rhythms and chronology theory in archaeology. In A. B. Knapp (ed.), *Archaeology,* Annales *and Ethnohistory*, pp. 23–34. Cambridge University Press: Cambridge.

Sober, E. 1984. *The Nature of Selection: evolutionary theory in philosophical focus*. MIT Press: Cambridge, Mass.

Soffer, O. 1985. *The Upper Paleolithic of the Central Russian Plain*. Academic Press: London.

Sommer, R. 1974. *Tight Spaces: hard architecture and how to humanise it*. Prentice-Hall: Englewood Cliffs, N.J.

Soper, R. and Darling, P. 1980. The walls of Old Oyo. *West African Journal of Archaeology* 10: 61–81.

South, S. 1977. *Method and Theory in Historical Archaeology*. Academic Press: New York.

Spate, O. H. K. 1963. The growth of London 1660–1800. In H. C. Darby (ed.), *Historical Geography of England, before AD 1800*, pp. 529–48. Cambridge University Press: Cambridge.

Spaulding, A. C. 1988. Archaeology and anthropology. *American Anthropologist* 90: 263–71.

Spector, J. D. 1993. *What This Awl Means: feminist archaeology at a Wahpeton Dakota village*. Minnesota Historical Society Press: St Paul.

Spriggs, M. (ed.) 1977. *Archaeology and Anthropology: areas of mutual interest*. BAR Supplementary Series 19, British Archaeological Reports: Oxford.

1988. The Hawaiian transformation of ancestral Polynesian society: conceptualizing chiefly states. In J. Gledhill, B. Bender and M. T. Larsen (eds.), *State and Society: the emergence and development of social hierarchy and political centralization*, pp. 57–73. Unwin Hyman: London.

Stanislawski, M. B. 1976. The relationship of ethno-archaeology, traditional and systems archaeology. *Current Research Reports Publication* 3: 1–5. Department of Anthropology, Simon Fraser University: Vancouver.

Steinhardt, N. S. 1990. *Chinese Imperial City Planning*. University of Hawaii Press: Honolulu.

Stewart, I. 1989. *Does God Play at Dice? The mathematics in chaos*. Basil Blackwell: Oxford.

Stone, E. C. 1987. *Nippur Neighbourhoods*. Studies in Ancient Oriental Civilisation 44, Oriental Institute of the University of Chicago: Chicago.

Strong, W. D. and Evans, C. 1952. *Cultural Stratigraphy in the Viru Valley, North Peru*. Columbia University Studies in Archaeology and Ethnology 4.

Strudwick, N. 1985. *The Administration of Egypt in the Old Kingdom: the highest titles and their holders*. Routledge and Kegan Paul: London.

Sumner, W. M. 1989. Population and settlement area: an example from Iran. *American Anthropologist* 91 (3): 631–41.

Tainter, J. A. 1988. *The Collapse of Complex Societies*. Cambridge University Press: Cambridge.

Tamarin, R. 1978. Dispersal, population regulation, and K-selection in field mice. *American Naturalist* 112: 545–55.

Tangri, D. 1989. Early physical anthropology, confirmation, and Australian Aboriginal brains. *Australian Archaeology* 28: 26–34.

Tangri, D. and Wyncoll, G. 1989. Of Mice and Men: is the presence of commensal animals in archaeological sites a positive correlate of sedentism? *Paléorient* 15 (2): 85–94.

Taylor, T. 1987. Aspects of settlement diversity and its classification in south-east Europe before the Roman period. *World Archaeology* 19 (1): 1–22.

Tempest, W. 1985. *Noise Handbook*. London: Academic Press.

Thorpe, W. H. 1979. *The Origins and Rise of Ethology: the science of the natural behaviour of animals*. Heinemann: London.

Tilley, C. 1982. Social formation, social structure and social change. In I. Hodder (ed.), *Symbolic and Structural Archaeology*, pp. 26–38. Cambridge University Press: Cambridge.

Tinbergen, N. 1951. *The Study of Instinct*. Oxford University Press: Oxford.

Todorova, H. 1978. *The Eneolithic Period in Bulgaria in the Fifth Millennium B.C.* BAR International Series 49, British Archaeological Reports: Oxford.

Topic, J. R. 1982. Lower-class social and economic organisation at Chan-Chan. In M. E. Moseley and K. C. Day (eds.), *Chan-Chan: Andean desert city*, pp. 145–75. A School of American Research Book, University of New Mexico Press: Austin.

Topic, J. R. and Topic, C. L. 1987. *Huamachuco Archaeological Project: preliminary report on the 1986 field season*. Trent University Occasional Papers in Anthropology 4: 1–40. Peterborough: Ontario.

Topic, T. L. 1982. The Early Intermediate period and its legacy. In M. E. Moseley and K. C. Day (eds.), *Chan-Chan: Andean desert city*, pp. 255–84. University of New Mexico Press: Albuquerque.

Trewartha, G. T. 1952. Chinese cities: origins and functions. *Annals of the Association of American Geographers* 424: 69–93.

Trigger, B. 1967. Settlement pattern archaeology. *American Antiquity* 32 (2): 149–60.

1978. *Time and Traditions: essays in archaeological interpretation.* Edinburgh University Press: Edinburgh.

1981. Archaeology and the ethnographic present. *Anthropologica* 23: 3–17.

1984. Archaeology at the cross-roads: What's new? *Annual Review of Anthropology* 13: 275–300.

1991. Post-processual developments in Anglo-American archaeology. *Norwegian Archaeological Review* 24 (2): 65–76.

Trigger, B. G., Kemp, B. J., O'Connor, D. and Lloyd, A. B. 1983. *Ancient Egypt: a social history.* Cambridge University Press: New York.

Tringham, R. 1973. *Territoriality and Proxemics: archaeological and ethnographic evidence for the use and organisation of space.* Warner Module Publications: Andover, Mass.

Tringham, R. and Krstić, D. (eds.) 1990. *Selevac: a Neolithic village in Yugoslavia.* Monumenta Archaeologica 15, Institute of Archaeology Publications, University of California: Los Angeles.

van Andel, T. H. 1985. *New Views on an Old Planet.* Cambridge University Press: Cambridge.

van Dorn, A. J., van de Grind, W. A. and Koenderink, J. J. (eds.) 1984. *Limits of Perception: essays in honour of Maarten A. Bouman.* VNU Science: Utrecht.

van der Leeuw, S. E. 1981. Information flows, flow structures and the explanation of change in human institutions. In S. E. van der Leeuw (ed.), *Archaeological Approaches to the Study of Complexity*, pp. 229–329. University of Amsterdam Press: Amsterdam.

1989. Risk, perception, innovation. In S. E. van der Leeuw and R. Torrence (eds.), *What's New? A closer look at the process of innovation*, pp. 300–29. Unwin Hyman: London.

van Valen, L. 1973. Body size and numbers of plants and animals. *Evolution* 27: 27–35.

Vernon, M. D. 1962. *The Psychology of Perception.* Penguin: Harmondsworth.

von Frisch, K. 1974. *Animal Architecture.* Harcourt Brace Jovanovich: New York.

Vishnu-Mittre and Savithri, R. 1982. Food economy of the Harappans. In G. Possehl (ed.), *Harappan Civilisation: a contemporary perspective*, pp. 205–21. Aris and Phillips: Warminster.

Voorhies, M. R. 1975. Vertebrate burrows. In R. W. Frey (ed.), *The Study of Trace Fossils: a synthesis of principles, problems and procedures in ichnology*, pp. 325–50. Springer-Verlag: Berlin.

Vrba, E. S. and Gould. S. J. 1986. The hierarchical expansion of sorting and selection: sorting and selection cannot be equated. *Paleobiology* 12 (2): 217–28.

Wandsnider, L. 1993. The spatial dimension of time. In J. Rossignol and L. Wandsnider (eds.), *Space, Time and Archaeological Landscapes*, pp. 257–82. Plenum Press: New York.

Washburn, W. E. 1987. A critical view of critical archaeology. *Current Anthropology* 28 (4): 544–55.

Watanabe, H. (ed.) 1977. *Human Activity System: its spatiotemporal structure.* Tokyo University Press: Tokyo.

Watson, A. and Moss, R. 1971. Spacing as affected by territorial behaviour, habit and nutrition in red grouse (*Lagopus i. scoticus*). In A. H. Esser (ed.), *Behaviour and Environment: the use of space by animals and men*, pp. 92–111. Plenum Press: New York.

Watson, O. M. 1970. *Proxemic Behaviour: a cross-cultural study.* Mouton: The Hague.

Watson, P. J., Redman C. and LeBlanc, S. 1971. *Explanation in Archaeology: an explicitly scientific approach.* Columbia University Press: New York.

  1984. *Archaeological Explanation: the scientific method in archaeology.* Columbia University Press: New York.

Watt, R. J. 1988. *Visual Processing: computational, psychological and cognitive research.* Lawrence Erlbaum Assocs.: London.

Webb, M. C. 1988. Broader perspectives on Andean state origins. In J. Haas, S. Pozorski and T. Pozorski (eds.), *The Origin and Development of the Andean State*, pp. 161–7. Cambridge University Press: Cambridge.

Weissner, P. 1974. A functional estimator of population from floor area. *American Antiquity* 39 (2): 343–50.

Weitz, S. 1984. *Nonverbal Communication.* Oxford University Press: New York.

Wells, G. 1985. *Language Development in the Pre-school Years.* Cambridge University Press: Cambridge.

Wells, P. S. 1984. *Farms, Villages and Cities: commerce and urban origins in late prehistoric Europe.* Cornell University Press: Ithaca.

Wenke, R. J. 1991. The evolution of early Egyptian civilisation: issues and evidence. *Journal of World Prehistory* 5 (3): 279–329.

Wessen, G. C. 1982. Shell middens as cultural deposits: a case study from Ozette. Ph.D. thesis, Washington State University 1982. University Microfilms International: Ann Arbor.

Westmancoat, J. 1985. *Newspapers.* The British Library: London.

Wetzel, F. 1967. *Die Stadmauern von Babylon.* Deutsche orient-Gesellschaft Ausgrabungen in Babylon 4. Zeller: Oznabruck.

Wheatley, P. 1971. *Pivot of the Four Quarters.* Edinburgh University Press: Edinburgh.

Wheatley, P. and See, T. 1978. *From Court to Capital: a tentative interpretation of the origins of the Japanese urban tradition.* University of Chicago Press: Chicago.

White, J. P. 1979. *The Past is Human.* Angus and Robertson: London.

White, N. 1985. Sex differences in Australian Aboriginal subsistence: possible implications for the biology of hunter-gatherers. In J. Ghesquiere, R. D. Martin and F. Newcombe (eds.), *Human Sexual Dimorphism*, pp. 323–61. Taylor and Francis: London.

Whitelaw, T. 1983. People and space in hunter-gatherer camps: a generalising approach in ethnoarchaeology. *Archaeological Review from Cambridge* 2 (2): 48–66.

  1989. The social organisation of space in hunter-gatherer communities: some implications for social inference in archaeology. Ph.D. thesis, University of Cambridge.

Whittle, A. 1985. *Neolithic Europe: a survey.* Cambridge University Press: Cambridge.

Wilcox, D. R., McGuire, T. R. and Sternberg, C. 1981. *Snaketown Revisited.* Cultural Resource Management Division, Archaeological Series 55, Arizona State Museum, University of Arizona.

Willey, G. R. and Phillips, P. 1958. *Method and Theory in American Archaeology.* University of Chicago Press: Chicago.

Willey, G. R. and Sabloff, J. A. 1980. *A History of American Archaeology.* Freeman: San Francisco.

Williams, C. B. 1964. *Patterns in the Balance of Nature and Related Problems of Quantitative Ecology.* Academic Press: London.

Williams, E. 1988. *Complex Hunter-Gatherers: a late Holocene example from temperate Australia.* BAR International Series 423, British Archaeological Reports: Oxford.

Wilson, E. O. 1971. *Sociobiology.* Harvard University Press: Cambridge, Mass.

  1972. *The Insect Societies.* Harvard University Press: Cambridge, Mass.

  1978. *On Human Nature.* Harvard University Press: Cambridge, Mass.

Wimsatt, W. C. 1976. Reductionism, levels of organization, and the mind–body problem. In G. C. Globus, G. Maxwell and I. Savodnik (eds.), *Consciousness and the Brain: a scientific and philosophical inquiry*, pp. 205–67. Plenum Press: New York.

Wing, E. S. 1980. Faunal remains. In T. F. Lynch (ed.), *Guittarrero Cave: early man in the Andes*, pp. 149–72. Academic Press: New York.

Winn, S. M. M. 1981. *Pre-writing in Southeastern Europe: the sign system of the Vinča culture ca. 4000 BC*. Western Publishers: Calgary.

Wisdom, J. O. 1987. *Challengeability in Modern Science*. Avebury: Aldershot.

Wobst, H. M. 1978. The archaeo-ethnology of hunter-gatherers or the tyranny of the ethnographic record in archaeology. *American Antiquity* 43 (2): 303–9.

Woodforde, J. 1976. *Bricks to Build a House*. Routledge and Kegan Paul: London.

Worrall, N. and Firth, D. 1974. The components of the standard and reverse Müller-Lyer illusions. *Quarterly Journal of Experimental Psychology* 26: 342–54.

Wylie, M. A. 1982a. Positivism and the New Archaeology. Ph.D. thesis, SUNY, Binghampton.

1982b. Epistemological issues raised by a structuralist archaeology. In I. Hodder (ed.), *Structural and Symbolic Archaeology*, pp. 39–45. Cambridge University Press: Cambridge.

1985a. Between philosophy and archaeology. *American Antiquity* 50: 478–90.

1985b. The reaction against analogy. In M. B. Schiffer (ed.), *Advances in Archaeological Method and Theory* 8: 63–111.

1989. Matters of fact and matters of interest. In S. Shennan (ed.), *Archaeological Approaches to Cultural Identity*, pp. 94–122. Unwin Hyman: London.

Wylie, M. A. and Pinsky, V. (eds.) 1990. *Critical Traditions in Contemporary Archaeology*. Cambridge University Press: Cambridge.

Wyncoll, G. and Tangri, D. 1991. The origins of commensalism and human sedentism. *Paléorient* 17 (2): 157–9.

Wynne-Edwards, V. C. 1971. Space use and community in animals and men. In A. H. Esser (ed.), *Behaviour and Environment: the use of space by animals and men*, pp. 267–80. Plenum Press: New York.

Yang, H-h. 1975. A preliminary study of the house development in the Yangshao culture. *Kaogu Xuebao (Acta Archaeologia Sinica)* 1: 39–72.

Yazaki, T. 1968. *Social Change and the City in Japan: from earliest times through to the Industrial Revolution*. Japan Publications Inc.: Tokyo.

Yellen, J. E. 1990. The transformation of the Kalahari !Kung. *Scientific American* 262(4): 72–9.

Yengoyan, A. 1985. Digging for symbols: the archaeology of every day material life. *Proceedings of the Prehistoric Society* 51: 329–34.

Yoffee, N. 1977. *The Economic Role of the Crown in the Old Babylonian Period*. Undena: Malibu, Calif.

1985. Perspectives on 'trends towards social complexity', in prehistoric Australia and Papua New Guinea. *Archaeology in Oceania* 20: 41–8.

Yoffee, N. and Cowgill, G. L. (eds.) 1988. *The Collapse of States and Civilizations*. University of Arizona Press: Tucson.

Yoffee, N. and Sherratt, A. (eds) 1993. *Archaeological Theory: who sets the agenda?* Cambridge University Press: Cambridge.

Zechmeister, E. B. and Nyberg, S. E. 1982. *Human Memory*. Brooks/Cole: Monterey.

NEW STUDIES IN ARCHAEOLOGY

Series editors
Clive Gamble, *University of Southampton*
Colin Renfrew, *University of Cambridge*
Jeremy Sabloff, *University of Pittsburgh*

Other titles in the series